Palgrave Studies in Risk, Crime and Society

Series Editors
Kieran McCartan
Department of Criminology
University of the West of England
Bristol, UK

Beth Weaver
School of Social Work and Social Policy
University of Strathclyde
Glasgow, Lanarkshire, UK

Risk is a major contemporary issue which has widespread implications for theory, policy, governance, public protection, professional practice and societal understandings of crime and criminal justice. The potential harm associated with risk can lead to uncertainty, fear and conflict as well as disproportionate, ineffective and ill-judged state responses to perceived risk and risky groups. Risk, Crime and Society is a series featuring monographs and edited collections which examine the notion of risk, the risky behaviour of individuals and groups, as well as state responses to risk and its consequences in contemporary society. The series will include critical examinations of the notion of risk and the problematic nature of state responses to perceived risk. While Risk, Crime and Society will consider the problems associated with 'mainstream' risky groups including sex offenders, terrorists and white collar criminals, it welcomes scholarly analysis which broadens our understanding of how risk is defined, interpreted and managed. Risk, Crime and Society examines risk in contemporary society through the multi-disciplinary perspectives of law, criminology and socio-legal studies and will feature work that is theoretical as well as empirical in nature.

More information about this series at
http://www.palgrave.com/gp/series/14593

John Pratt • Jordan Anderson
Editors

Criminal Justice, Risk and the Revolt against Uncertainty

palgrave
macmillan

Editors
John Pratt
Institute of Criminology
Victoria University of Wellington
Wellington, New Zealand

Jordan Anderson
Institute of Criminology
Victoria University of Wellington
Wellington, New Zealand

Palgrave Studies in Risk, Crime and Society
ISBN 978-3-030-37947-6   ISBN 978-3-030-37948-3   (eBook)
https://doi.org/10.1007/978-3-030-37948-3

This Palgrave Macmillan imprint is published by the registered company Springer Nature Switzerland AG.
The registered company address is: Gewerbestrasse 11, 6330 Cham, Switzerland

Contents

Notes on Contributors

Jordan Anderson is completing her PhD in Criminology at the Institute of Criminology at Victoria University of Wellington. Her research focuses on risk and dangerousness in modern society, with particular attention to post-sentence regulation of sex offenders in New Zealand. Anderson's research interests include risk, post-sentence regulation, sentencing, and youth justice.

Harry Annison is Associate Professor of Criminal Law and Criminology at Southampton Law School. His work focuses primarily on the intersections between penal politics and penal theory through the examination of specific case studies including developments in indeterminate sentencing. His first monograph *Dangerous Politics: Risk, Political Vulnerability and Penal Policy* was published by Oxford University Press in 2015.

David Brown Law Faculty, UNSW, is a co-author of the innovative *Criminal Laws* (7th Edition 2020). He has widely authored across the broad areas of criminal law, criminal justice, criminology, and penology, both in Australia and internationally, and has served as a part-time NSW Law Reform Commissioner. His most recent co-authored books include *Penal Culture and Hyperincarceration: The Revival of the Prison* (2013) and *Justice Reinvestment: Winding Back Imprisonment* (2015).

Henrique Carvalho is an associate professor and co-director of the Criminal Justice Centre at the School of Law, the University of Warwick. His research explores the links between criminal law and justice, punishment, and identity, subjectivity, and belonging. He is working on a project on "The Dangerous Essence of Criminal Law", funded by the Independent Social Research Foundation. Carvalho is the author of The Preventive Turn in Criminal Law (2017), and is writing a co-authored book on the problem of punishment today.

Elliott Currie is Professor of Criminology, Law and Society at the University of California, Irvine, USA, and Adjunct Professor in the Faculty of Law, School of Justice, Queensland University of Technology, Australia. He is the author of number of books such as *Confronting Crime: An American Challenge, Dope and Trouble: Portraits of Delinquent Youth, Reckoning: Drugs, the Cities, and the American Future, The Road to Whatever: Middle Class Culture and the Crisis of Adolescence,* and *The Roots of Danger: Violent Crime in Global Perspective.* His book *Crime and Punishment in America,* revised and expanded in 2013, was a finalist for the Pulitzer Prize in General Nonfiction in 1999. He is a co-author of *Whitewashing Race: The Myth of a Colorblind Society,* winner of the 2004 Book Award from the Benjamin L. Hooks Institute for Social Change and a finalist for the C. Wright Mills Award of the Society for the Study of Social Problems. Most recently, he is the co-editor, with Walter S. DeKeseredy, of *Progressive Justice in an Age of Repression: Strategies for Challenging the Rise of the Right.* He is a graduate from Roosevelt University in Chicago, and holds a PhD in Sociology from the University of California, Berkeley.

Netanel Dagan is a lecturer at the Institute of Criminology, Faculty of Law, Hebrew University of Jerusalem. His research is focused on penal theory, sentencing, parole, and prisons.

Hadar Dancig-Rosenberg is an associate professor at Bar-Ilan University, Faculty of Law and was a visiting professor (2017–2018) and a visiting scholar (2016–2018, summer 2019) at UC Berkeley School of Law. Her fields of interest include the philosophy of criminal law, socio-legal analysis of the criminal justice system, and non-adversarial criminal justice. She serves as a member of the Advisory Committee for the Minister of Justice on Criminal Procedure and Evidence Law in Israel.

Murray Lee is Professor of Criminology at the University of Sydney Law School. His research focuses on representations, perceptions, and public responses to crime. He has researched extensively on fear of crime in NSW and Victoria. Lee is author of *Inventing Fear of Crime: Criminology and the Politics of Anxiety*, co-author of *Sexting and Young People*, *Policing and Media: Public Relations, Simulations and Communications*, co-editor of *Fear of Crime: Critical Voices in an Age of Anxiety*, and *The Routledge International Handbook on Fear of Crime*.

Bernadette McSherry is the Foundation Director of the Melbourne Social Equity Institute and Professor of Law, Melbourne Law School, the University of Melbourne, Australia. She holds BA(Hons), LLB(Hons), and LLM degrees from the University of Melbourne; a PhD from York University in Canada, and a Graduate Diploma in Psychology from Monash University. She has written widely on mental health law and criminal law and is a Fellow of the Academy of the Social Sciences in Australia and the Australian Academy of Law.

Gabe Mythen is Professor of Criminology at the University of Liverpool, United Kingdom. His research is oriented toward engaging in critical analyses of the construction, mobilization, and management of risk across different areas of state regulation. Mythen has written over 100 peer-reviewed papers and 6 books. His most recent work focuses on the impacts of UK government's counter-terrorism policy, most notably in relation to strategies designed to prevent radicalization. He is the Director of the pan-institutional Economic and Social Research Council North-West Doctoral Training Partnership.

Rebecca Powell is the Managing-Director of the Border Crossing Observatory and the Research and Centre Manager of the Monash Migration and Inclusion Centre at Monash University. She is completing a PhD with Monash Criminology titled "I Still Call Australia Home: Balancing Risk and Human Rights in the Deportation of Convicted Non-Citizens from Australia to New Zealand".

John Pratt is Professor of Criminology at the Institute of Criminology, Victoria University of Wellington, New Zealand. His fields of research are comparative penology and the history and sociology of punishment. He has published in 11 languages and has been invited to lecture at universities in South America, North America, Europe, Asia, and Australia. His books include *Punishment and Civilization* (2002), *Penal Populism* (2007), and *Contrasts in Punishment* (2013). In 2009, he was awarded the Sir Leon Radzinowicz Prize by the Editorial Board of the *British Journal of Criminology*. In 2012, he was elected to a Fellowship of the Royal Society of New Zealand and was awarded the Society's Mason Durie Medal, given "to the nation's pre-eminent social scientist".

Jonathan Simon is the Lance Robbins Professor of Criminal Justice Law at UC Berkeley. His recent scholarship has dealt with the aftermath of mass incarceration in the United States and the challenge of deep reform in punitive culture shaped by slavery, eugenics, and predatory capitalism.

Elizabeth Stanley is Professor of Criminology at the Institute of Criminology, Victoria University of Wellington, Aotearoa New Zealand. Her research focuses on state crimes, human rights, incarceration and social justice. Her publications include *Torture, Truth and Justice* (Routledge), *State Crime and Resistance* (edited with Jude McCulloch, Routledge), *The Road to Hell: State Violence against Children in Post War NZ* (Auckland University Press) and *Human Rights and Incarceration* (edited, Palgrave).

Stephen Tomsen is Professor of Criminology at Western Sydney University. He has researched violence including hate crimes, homicides, assaults related to night leisure, and urban drinking and drug use, in studies that began with a pioneering 1989 ethnographic analysis of life in Sydney's "bloodhouse" venues. He has authored or co-authored and edited or co-edited eight books and research monographs. These include *Homophobic Violence, Lawyers in Conflict: Australian Lawyers and Legal Aid, Violence Prejudice and Sexuality*, and *Australian Violence: Crime, Criminal Justice and Beyond*.

Phillip Wadds is Senior Lecturer in Criminology at UNSW Sydney. He has spent the last decade undertaking ethnographic and field-based research examining various features of nightlife in Sydney with an enduring focus on its policing and regulation. More recently, he has been appointed to a number of local government advisory panels tasked with developing new nightlife policy. Each of these experiences has provided unique and first-hand insight into the dramatic and ongoing recent changes in Sydney's night-time economy. His forthcoming monograph *Policing Nightlife: Security, Transgression and Urban Order* is due for publication with Routledge in 2020 alongside an edited collection with Palgrave Macmillan entitled *Navigating the Field: Stories of Danger, Risk and Reward.*

Leanne Weber is Associate Professor of Criminology, co-Director of the Border Crossing Observatory, and Australian Research Council Future Fellow in the School of Social Sciences at Monash University, Melbourne, Australia. She researches border control and migration policing using criminological and human rights frameworks.

List of Figures

List of Tables

Crime, Pre-crime and Sub-crime: Deportation of 'Risky Non-citizens' as 'Enemy Crimmigration'

Introduction

John Pratt and Jordan Anderson

This book is the outcome of papers presented by scholars from the United Kingdom, United States, Australia, New Zealand, and Israel at a symposium held at Victoria University of Wellington, November 2018. The purpose of the symposium, and now this book, was to examine the impact and implications of the relationship between risk and criminal justice in the context of what we have referred to as 'the revolt against uncertainty' that can be discerned, to varying degrees and extents, across advanced liberal democracies. The global nature of this subject area and attendant themes is demonstrated by the international representation at the symposium.

But what is it that we mean by this term 'the revolt against uncertainty'? There is a duality to it. First, it refers to growing demands and pressures from governments, usually in turn responding to demands from sections of the media, law and order activists, some victims' groups, and

J. Pratt (✉) • J. Anderson
Institute of Criminology, Victoria University of Wellington,
Wellington, New Zealand
e-mail: john.pratt@vuw.ac.nz; jordan.anderson@vuw.ac.nz

© The Author(s) 2020
J. Pratt, J. Anderson (eds.), *Criminal Justice, Risk and the Revolt against Uncertainty*,
Palgrave Studies in Risk, Crime and Society,
https://doi.org/10.1007/978-3-030-37948-3_1

the like, for more certainty, and thereby more security, in the processing of crime and the punishment of offenders. These demands themselves are often driven by dreadful, atypical one-off incidents that are then addressed as if they are typical, and are met with vows to safeguard the general public from any repetition. The nature of these safeguards, though, frequently traverses new territory in the criminal justice systems of Western democracies. Responses might now take the form, for example, of an insistence that some (non-capital) offenders pose such a high risk that they should never be let out of prison: if they have come to the end of their sentence, then simply detain them indefinitely, rather than take the risk of setting them free. For those who are released on parole, ensure that they are subject to rigorous scrutiny, supervision, and control, in a bid to eliminate any further risks they might pose to the public—and return them to prison for any normative breach of their order, do not just sit and wait for them to commit more crimes.

Indeed, it is this same revolt against uncertainty, and the sense of anxiety and insecurity that comes with it, that has propelled risk control out of the somewhat remote location of parole adjudication where Feeley and Simon (1992) came across the shift to actuarialism taking place, to better predict any such future propensities. Thus, in addition to informing parole adjudications at the prison's exit door, the need to control risk has also come to determine much bail decision-making at the entrance to it. Furthermore (and demonstrating the widespread impact of Wilson and Kelling's (1982) 'broken windows' hypothesis), the threat of crime to come if anti-social behavior and other forms of objectionable street life are tolerated, informs ordinances and an assortment of similar para-penal measures against beggars, vagrants, and other unwanted street people.

Overall, these preventive measures can range from post-prison 'civil detention' to public space protection orders, and are of a kind that were previously thought to have only a very limited place, if any place at all, in the democratic world. At the same time, in a bid to provide these more extensive guarantees of certainty, risk assessment has also become much more central to the administration of justice: whether this takes the form of increasingly sophisticated prediction tools in some parts of its orbit, or commonsensical counts of previous convictions, which are then thought to indicate the likelihood of future conduct, or assumptions that this can be done on the basis of identifying characteristics such as gang member, beggar, and so on. Meanwhile, previous safeguards, conventions, and norms of criminal justice in advanced democratic societies, intended to protect the rights of individuals from excessive use of the state's power have been overturned or pushed aside. Protecting the community from those individuals who would otherwise put them at risk has become paramount. Devices and strategies, including hybrid and retrospective legislation, and changes to rules of evidence have been used to enable these initiatives and to bring about the desired result: risk control rather than crime control. In these respects, the utilitarian nature of risk control and its emphasis on effectiveness and efficiency demands a rebalancing of the way in which 'rights' are understood. Issues such as due process and individual rights get in the way of its central preventive purposes (Ericson 2007).

However, these expansions of risk control in criminal justice have not brought an end to the increasingly invasive way in which risk impinges on, directs, and even controls the way in which everyday life is lived and experienced. Controlling risk in the criminal justice system has not been sufficient to allow us to live risk free beyond this arena. Indeed, risk itself does not exist in some sort of constant, steady state phase. Characteristic of the uncertainty of these times, new permutations constantly transform our understanding and comprehension of it. Indeed, it is as though risk has become an unstoppable force, irrespective of the protections against it that have been built into the criminal justice system. It is regularly able to frighten us with newly uncovered areas of danger, or to suddenly bring into sharper focus longstanding but dormant concerns that then keep on growing in magnitude: risks of becoming a victim of seemingly random terrorist attack amidst anxieties about the radicalization of local Muslim youth (white nationalist terrorism rarely comes to the forefront of the way in which such risks feature in public discourse); risks to the well-being of both individual citizens and the nation state itself from the vast flow of unwanted immigrants, who leave behind unsustainable lives and push against the barriers that advanced societies put in their way to prevent them starting again; risks to personal safety in regenerated inner-city areas, offering excitement and pleasure to attract consumers only for this to lead to new dangers from alcohol-related violence. Some of these risks are intensely localized, as with mass shootings in the US. Others are global in their consequences. Climate change—or what is increasingly referred to as 'the climate crisis', as its proximity and effects become ever more alarming and obvious—is in this latter category.

Even though many of these immediate risks in this short catalogue (in reality it could probably be of infinite length) lie outside the criminal justice system, the heightened fears and anxieties they produce are in themselves likely to generate further demands for preventive action, putting a greater onus on the criminal justice process to provide still more certainty in risk protection and the control of any risk subsets: how many potential terrorists are the immigrants hiding amongst them?; how many 'murderers and rapists' do they conceal? Technological advances further inflame and disseminate such alarms. The 24/7 news media cycle has ensured that risk concerns are transportable. This allows citizens at one end of the globe to watch and experience risk events at the other and then make their own adaptations in response, however remote they are from the original source. Not only this, but the arrival of social media has also meant that risk, and those who pose risks are unhindered by national boundaries and can distribute their threat around the globe. In New Zealand, the Christchurch terrorist, who murdered fifty-one Muslim worshippers in two mosques in March 2019, live streamed his actions online. It was not only watched on social media, but cable news networks also screened some of the video. He has since become a social media 'inspiration' to other white nationalist terrorists and would-be terrorists in Europe and the US.

These acts of terrorism and the role of social media in communicating risks and anxieties—as well as conspiracy theories and hate speech—lead into the second aspect of our concept of 'the revolt against uncertainty'. This also refers to the way in which alarm about risk has contributed to the ascendancy of populist politics across these societies (again, to varying degrees and extents). This populism presents itself as the antidote to all the accruing tensions and anxieties generated in the course of the era of neo-liberal governance, strongly correlated, at least, with the increasing prominence of risk-based criminal justice. Why should there have been this correlation? We need to address this before we can understand what the relationship between populism and preventive criminal justice might then be.

From the 1980s, the course of Beck's (1992) risk society was driven by something more than the unanticipated outcome of modern technology. It also became the *intended outcome* of political decisions taken by governments to set risk free from its previous economic restraints (O'Malley 2004). They engineered a dramatic restructuring across these societies that gave shape to neo-liberalism's aspirations for deregulated economies, in which enterprising individuals would be able to flourish, thrive, and become involved in extensive wealth creation—for themselves rather than the state. In the course of this restructuring, risk thus became more than something to be avoided at all costs because of its innate dangers, notwithstanding the mass of risk-awareness programs and the like that we are likely to encounter on an infinite number of levels in the course of everyday life. Instead, risk also became a highly sought after commodity that many have been willing to pay large sums of money to experience. 'Adventure tourism' in New Zealand, for example, is just one small outlet in a vast sea of such opportunities. The Tourism New Zealand website thus advertises 'helicopter tours, jet boating, glacier walks, bungee jumping and the luge'. There were half a million such tourists in this country in 2013, with 367,000 of them being designated as 'extreme adventure tourists'. The greater the risks on offer, the more attractive they seem to those pursuing such excitement.

In this modified neo-liberal version of risk society, opportunities became available for its winners—great or small in the casino-like economies it created (Reiner et al. 2001). They were able to experience rewards for their successes and all the attendant excitement and pleasures that came with this: overseas holidays, for example, that may range from uncomfortable, even highly stressful travel on a budget airline, to a grossly overcrowded resort, to private jets whisking the world's wealthiest entrepreneurs off to islands in the sun that they actually own. We cannot all be Richard Branson, of course, and the gulf in costs and the actual experiences at both ends of this spectrum of the way in which life in these societies can now be lived is not the point here. Instead, the point is that the provision of such dreams and the possibilities of such indulgences all became a means of legitimating the neo-liberal mode of governance.

Tailored to suit individual aspirations, they became symbols of the way in which it was possible to become wealthy and also possible as well to enjoy being wealthy on a greater level than ever known before. Economic liberalism did not simply provide more opportunities for careful wealth accumulation, or for some utilitarian economic revitalization of the nation state. Indeed, it tantalizingly made prizes available that celebrated extravagance and pleasure rather than austerity and thrift: prizes that were no longer the automatic prerogative of an elite few by virtue of blue blood or inherited wealth, but which were projected as being within the grasp of all if they were sufficiently skilled, entrepreneurial and hard working.

At the same time, the neo-liberal mode of governance brought no guarantees of security. It was presaged instead on the uncertainties of the market. And so long as this did indeed produce winners on a large scale, or even potential winners—those who believed that eventually their enterprise would be rewarded with their own jackpot—neo-liberalism and its commitment to market forces became politically sustainable. This also meant that in the course of the restructuring it generated, governments would no longer offer guarantees of security, certainty, and well-being to all their citizens. The strong and the successful would thrive. As for the rest...

It was its role in the management of such divisions that brought about the correlation between risk-driven criminal justice and neo-liberal governance. While risk, risk taking, and risk calculations have come to inform so much of everyday life (consciously or unconsciously), so the relationship between risk and criminal justice has become much stronger. Growing uncertainty in the broader social fabric was matched by demands for much greater certainty in the criminal justice arena: at least this could be deployed to keep us safe.

However, in the early twenty-first century, there have been continually growing numbers of people who have lost faith in the dreams and enticements that neo-liberalism proffered. That 'rest' cohort has dramatically expanded and is no longer so easily containable and controllable. It has been swollen by people who have been left behind, with no prospects of advancement, no likelihood of ever experiencing the everyday luxuries and indulgences that seem to have been dispersed so liberally amongst those who continue to thrive. These sharp tears in the social fabric represented, as it were, the dark side of risk that has been unleashed, adding to the already existing sense of insecurity and uncertainty that was the price to be paid as a matter of course for neo-liberal governance. While these tears have opened up longstanding fissures based around race and class, and reawoken old ones based around religion, new ones have emerged as well—age, for example. While the Baby Boomers have most enjoyed the fruits of restructuring, the Millennial generation are at the forefront of many of its dangers—above all else, the climate crisis.

It has been from these social divisions and all their attendant fears, suspicions, and lack of trust that populism has emerged and has radically shifted the terms of political debate. It presents itself as being fundamentally opposed to the risk-driven economic program of the neo-liberal era and the uncertainty and insecurity this has created. It proclaims that it can bring into existence a new era of certainty, safety, and security, if we are just prepared to put our trust in the 'strong men' at its helm and the authoritarianism they espouse. As such, the rise of populism threatens to undermine the central elements of the neo-liberal shaping of risk society.

We thus wanted to use the opportunity that the symposium gave us to investigate and analyze both the dynamics and dilemmas of the existing operation of risk-driven criminal justice, with the demands for greater certainty that it has to meet in its own right; and the political and social forces of populism, also responding to demands for an end to uncertainty. If risk is so strongly related to the era of neo-liberal governance, where does this then leave the concept of risk society and risk-driven criminal justice? If populism foregoes the paths of globalization and deregulation, what impact will its demands for certainty and security, and the insistence that national identity be reasserted against a variety of insidious threats to this, have on criminal law and penal policy? Will this also bring an end to the growing emphasis on preventive justice that had been thought necessary to control risky behavior prior to criminality? Or will populism's insatiable search for new enemies and dangerous populations, necessary to sustain its own existence, lead to still more extensions of risk-based criminal justice to achieve these ends?

Given this changing political context, it is timely to ask, as Carol Steiker (1998) did some time ago, what limits there might then be to prevention? What does this drive to protect the public from risk mean in terms of human rights issues? And in relation to the operation of this mode of justice administration, are there other models of intervention, reflected in the rise of resilience and therapeutic jurisprudence, for example, that stand in the way and act as barriers to its progression? Has this 'new penology', with the growing sophistication and complexity of risk management procedures, become merely a form of computerized social control, or does it in reality provide for new opportunities for constructive engagement between corrections agencies as enforcement officials and those subject to its controls (Hannah-Moffat 2005)? If risk itself is a dynamic rather than a static object, to what extent do risk-control mechanisms have this dynamic potential?

In pursuing these and related questions, the book addresses the issue of risk, criminal justice, and prevention in the context of this dramatically changing political context that has begun to question much of the direction of economic and social change of recent times. In addition, it updates scholarship on risk and criminal justice in this changing context and the pertinent issues that this raises in its own right. It is divided into the following four sections.

The Dynamics of Risk Assessment and Preventive Justice

Here, Bernadette McSherry examines the re-emergence and new parameters of 'preventive justice', particularly its most recent adaptation—preventive algorithms that are used to inform sentencing practices. As this has occurred, new ethical and human rights issues have come to the fore in relation to risk-prevention: in particular, as here, the fates of individuals can be determined by machines. She makes the case for a return to 'structured professional judgement' in relation to predicting future crime. David Brown's chapter, based on empirical research in New South Wales, Australia, opens up the dynamics of risk control regimes imposed on parolees. For him, while it may be that the risk/needs/responsivity framework has opened up spaces for transformative rehabilitative work in the interaction between the parolees and community corrections officers, the structural realities of actually being an ex-prisoner and the limits on levels of assistance available to the Corrections agencies undermine this. While this highlights the problems of risk assessment and control in actually addressing risk itself, it also shows how such mechanisms have a professional and political utility all the same: they become evidence of the way in which corrections management and governments can show the public they are responding to demands for more certain and protective criminal justice. Meanwhile Hadar Dancig-Rosenberg and Netanel Dagan put the case for a form of 'just deserts' retribution against utilitarian risk assessment in parole decision-making. In these respects, what they refer to as 'character retribution' may function as a brake on excessive punishment as a product of the over-prediction of risk. In so doing, they place individualistic assessment in parole within a retributive framework.

Risk and Penal Policy

This section examines the broader implications of risk on the development of penal policy. Harry Annison examines controversies arising from a resurgence of indeterminate sentencing in the UK in the first decade of this century. The proposed release on parole of one particular notorious prisoner—multiple rapist John Worboys—after successfully complying with his risk assessment requirements, was over-ruled by the relevant government minister, compelling the head of the Parole Board to resign. News of Worboys' release had prompted womens' groups to organize in vociferous opposition to this. The prominence of these new voices challenging the 'establishment' decision making processes, even with the safeguards of their risk assessment tools, seems to have been instrumental in bringing about the strong reaction from the government and their subsequent (almost unprecedented) intervention in overturning the release decision. If populism unleashed these new voices of opposition to the criminal justice establishment from the public that undermine the utility (and apparent neutrality) of risk assessment, it demonstrates the potential for both convergence and clash between risk and populism around demands for greater certainty and security in the administration of justice.

Jordan Anderson uses community notification to examine the ways in which risk control drives a distinct strand of penal policy development. Using the example of New Zealand, the chapter explores the way that communities are often informed about the presence of sex offenders in ad hoc and unpredictable ways, triggering a range of fear based responses. It considers whether the nuances of the community reaction, in particular the depth of insecurity and range of proposed 'sensible' solutions, are typical of lived experiences of risk control and regulation in these societies, and the way that they are becoming increasingly intolerant of particular 'risky individuals.'

Henrique Carvalho investigates the way in which the expanding category of risk control has brought about changes in 'joint enterprise' (that is, the common law doctrine that allows a person to be found guilty of a crime committed by someone else) aspects of criminal law in England and Wales to meet demands for greater security and certainty. It argues that the discriminatory and exclusionary character of this area of law exposes how risk-based logics are a pervasive aspect of criminalization and are not easily dispelled by legal reform to the contrary (as with the decision of the Supreme Court in *R v Jogee* 2016) and may well, as here, find ways round barriers intended to block them.

New Dimensions of Risk

As mentioned, risk is a dynamic, not a static phenomenon. It constantly changes its shape and dimensions and, as it does so, envelops us with fresh or renewed anxieties and insecurities that in turn lead to renewed demands to bring risk under control. However, Gabe Mythen's chapter probes some of the ambiguities and contradictions that then emerge in the application of pre-emptive, risk-based techniques of crime regulation. He scrutinizes measures designed to prevent radicalization in the UK, in particular the impact of *Prevent*, a nationwide strategy to combat terrorism. The chapter demonstrates that reactive and hastily implemented security may produce iatrogenic effects on specific minority groups who are the targeted populations of these interventions, in addition to their consequences for understandings of human rights and civil liberties.

Murray Lee, Stephen Tomsen, and Phillip Wadds examine the dilemmas stemming from large Western metropolitan centers attempting to establish themselves as 'global' cities. Using Sydney as their example, they argue that this entails a certain branding and refashioning to make it attractive to international visitors as well as locals. This branding involves projecting the city as exciting, connected, culturally diverse and welcoming, and 'open for business'. One way to demonstrate this has been the cultivation of a vibrant and dynamic nightlife. However, as has happened in Sydney, one of the unintended attendant consequences of this has been the consumption of alcohol and illicit drugs and the both real and imaginary risks associated with these behaviors. Risks, which this chapter will argue, became cast as too great in the context of competing symbolic, economic, and demographic views of what the city should be. This has prompted a new level of state intervention in the form of 'lockout' laws and draconian legal deterrents. However, for many, this attempt to regulate uncertainty has also meant the end of fun and excitement. The ongoing conflict over the regulation of Sydney's nightlife explored in the chapter offers a snapshot of attempts to manage uncertainty through risk narratives and the implications of this regulation.

Elizabeth Stanley's chapter is focused on the most ominous risk of all—climate change. It illustrates the way in which this is already bringing about manifest insecurities through the loss of nation states and mass population displacement in its wake. The chapter critically examines the most obvious response of democratic societies in the West to this phenomenon: the erection of increasingly difficult to penetrate border controls. In this way, risk prevention targets and penalizes those least responsible for this crisis. Yet the emergence of a new social movement, spreading rapidly internationally and led primarily by young people (in a revolt against the *certainty* of climate change), is aimed at changing public awareness and consciousness. Perhaps this represents the best hope for the future—not just for individuals, or societies, or even nations—but for the planet itself. Meanwhile, as Leanne Weber & Rebecca Powell show, the way in which the nation state is seen as under threat from risks posed by non-citizens within or at its borders have ensured that risk-based criminal justice paradigms are continuing to evolve and extend its presence and influence. As this occurs, established legal norms and procedures are further nullified.

Living with Risk

Despite all the emphasis on risk awareness, risk prevention, risk avoidance, and so on, risk still permeates so much of everyday life. What have been and are the consequences, then, of living with risk? John Pratt argues that the message of the neo-liberal version of risk society was that risk was something to be celebrated and enjoyed rather than feared and hidden away. This was because of all the new opportunities for enterprise, wealth, and success. The growing number of casualties that were by-products of the economic and social restructuring it necessitated were able to be swept up by risk control initiatives. Prioritizing public safety over individual rights—one of the usual justifications for this—was a means of governments demonstrating that they were still steering the ship of state: even though they had long since let market forces chart its uncertain route. Indeed, growing anxieties over the course it was taking have led to the emergence of populism, demanding an end to risk and that life should be made knowable and predictable again. What happens, then, when risk and populism collide? The inherent contradictions and fantasies on which this populism is based is likely to lead to chaos rather than certainty, while further extending risk control measures to secure its own foundations.

Taking as his motif mass shootings and climate change consequences in the US, Elliott Currie is critical of government crackdowns on easy risk targets (illegal immigrants, drug dealers and so on)—which reflects as well the failure of many liberal social scientists to confront the deep anxieties that an essentially rudderless and predatory global social order has generated in countries around the world, particularly among working people whose lives have been rendered precarious in new ways and to an unprecedented degree. There is, then, a reality to risk, a reality to fears of getting caught up in yet another mass shooting—these cannot be simplistically dismissed as just another moral panic. To counter this, he calls for the strengthening of a political and social perspective that acknowledges the depth and pervasiveness of dislocation and dispossession in contemporary global society; one that offers credible and politically compelling alternatives to both the authoritarian commitment to stamping out perceived threats from risky 'others' and the complacent liberal withdrawal from confronting everyday dislocation and disintegration.

For Jonathan Simon, changing demographics are likely to bring an end to the highly punitive penal climate of the 1990s and first decade or so of this century. In fact, this emphasis on punitiveness limited the moderating effects that the risk paradigm, based on science and evidence, might otherwise have brought into effect. However, the Millenial generation, largely decoupled from Black communities and decentered urban landscapes—hitherto the main *loci* of crime fears—are likely to be more receptive to rational risk logics about crime. They are not immune to crime fears but are much more exposed to sources of anxiety or dread like climate change and economic inequality. Against this backcloth, crime is perceived as merely one more problem to manage rather than the most significant one.

References

Beck, Ulrich. 1992. *Risk Society: Towards a New Modernity*. London: Sage.

Ericson, Richard. 2007. *Crime in an Insecure World*. Cambridge: Polity.

Feeley, Malcolm, and Jonathan Simon. 1992. "The New Penology: Notes on the Emerging Strategy of Corrections and its Implications." *Criminology* 30 (4): 449–474.

Hannah-Moffat, Kelly. 2005. "Criminogenic Needs and the Transformative Risk Subject: Hybridizations of Risk/Need in Penality." *Punishment and Society* 7 (1): 29–51.

O'Malley, Pat. 2004. *Risk, Uncertainty, and Government*. London: GlassHouse.

Reiner, Robert, Sonia Livingstone, and Jessica Allen. 2001. "Casino Culture: Crime and Media in a Winner-Loser Society." In *Crime, Risk and Justice: The Politics of Crime Control in Liberal Democracies*, edited by Kevin Stenson and Richard Sullivan, 174–194. Cullompton: Willan Publishing.

R v Jogee (2016) UKSC 8.

Steiker, Carol. 1998. "The Limits of the Preventive State." *Journal of Criminal Law and Criminology* 88 (3): 771–808.

Wilson, James Q., and George L. Kelling. 1982. "Broken Windows: The Police and Neighborhood Safety." *Atlantic Monthly* 243 (3): 29–38.

Part I

The Dynamics of Risk Assessment and Preventive Justice

Risk Assessment, Predictive Algorithms and Preventive Justice

Bernadette McSherry

Introduction

In 1753, Sir William Blackstone used the term "preventive justice" to refer to laws that aimed to prevent future crime by enabling the state to intervene where there exists a "probable suspicion, that some crime is intended or likely to happen" (Blackstone, Book IV, 2001 edition: p. 251). Andrew Ashworth and Lucia Zedner (2014: p. 11) make the point that "governmental concern about the prevention of harm is certainly not a new phenomenon; on the contrary, prevention motivated the very founding of the modern criminal justice system".

However, while laws of preventive justice have long existed in English-speaking jurisdictions, their use and indeed, lack of use, have reflected dominant views about the role of the state in preventively detaining its citizens. John Stuart Mill (1859: p. 165) pointed out that "the preventive

B. McSherry (✉)
Melbourne Law School, University of Melbourne, Melbourne, VIC, Australia
e-mail: bernadette.mcsherry@unimelb.edu.au

© The Author(s) 2020
J. Pratt, J. Anderson (eds.), *Criminal Justice, Risk and the Revolt against Uncertainty*,
Palgrave Studies in Risk, Crime and Society,
https://doi.org/10.1007/978-3-030-37948-3_2

function of government ... is far more liable to be abused to the prejudice of liberty, than the punitory [sic] function".

During a large part of the twentieth century, proposed laws of preventive justice met with concerted opposition (Bottoms 2009) and existing laws, such as those dealing with "sexually violent predators", fell into disuse (Petrila 2011). Judges have also displayed "their suspicion and distrust" of such laws (Pratt 1997: p. 190), particularly post-sentence indefinite detention, because such laws offend against the principle of proportionality in sentencing (McSherry and Keyzer 2009: p. 42) and the right to liberty (e.g. *Fardon v Attorney-General (Qld)* (2004) 223 CLR 575: p. 623 per Kirby J).

During the twentieth century, up until around the 1980s, indefinite sentence laws were rarely used (McSherry and Keyzer 2009: p. 4), but sometimes, a single offender, or single crime subject to extensive media coverage, prompted calls for preventive justice schemes to be reinvigorated (McSherry and Keyzer 2009, chap. 1). The next section provides an overview of modern laws of preventive justice and how risk assessment techniques have driven their use over the past four decades.

Laws of Preventive Justice and the Involvement of Mental Health Practitioners

The concept of preventive justice is now used to justify schemes across many English-speaking jurisdictions which are weighted in favor of the detention of certain individuals through a variety of means, from control orders to post-sentence detention and supervision.

One of the central justifications for preventive detention (and supervision) schemes is that removing those considered to be at high risk of serious offending from the community, or at the very least intensively monitoring them, is the best way to stop them from harming others. These schemes may be viewed as being on a continuum from pre-crime to post-sentence detention. They encompass not only detention of suspected terrorists without charge and accused persons held on remand, but also indefinite detention of high-risk recidivist offenders and post-sentence detention of sex offenders (McSherry 2014: pp. 77–88).

During the 1980s, mental health practitioners began to be called upon to assess the risk of future harmful behavior. Prior to that time, during the mid-twentieth century, there was skepticism about mental health practitioners' ability to identify just who was dangerous. The case of Johnnie K Baxstrom exemplifies this concern. Baxstrom was convicted of up to three years' imprisonment for assault, but during his incarceration, he was determined to be "insane" and transferred to a correctional hospital, which housed convicted offenders diagnosed with mental illness. Baxstrom was kept there after his sentence expired and he subsequently brought a writ of habeas corpus to be transferred to the civil system with a view to release. The United States Supreme Court held in *Baxstrom* v *Herold* (383 US 107 (1966)) that Baxstrom had been denied equal protection of the law by not being allowed the right of a jury trial as permitted under New York's then civil mental health law and by being detained in a Department of Corrections facility without proper review as to whether he was "dangerously mentally ill" at the close of his prison term. A subsequent jury trial found that Baxstrom did not satisfy the criteria for involuntary hospitalization under the civil law and he was released. Unfortunately, he died shortly after release due to epileptic seizures.

Following the decision in *Baxstrom's* case, the New York State Department of Mental Hygiene transferred 967 individuals from two correctional hospitals to 18 civil facilities with few adverse consequences. Henry Steadman (1973: p. 190) concluded that these individuals "caused much less trouble than most people expected". Steadman argued (2000: p. 266) that clinical assessments of dangerousness leading to more individuals than necessary being incarcerated in correctional hospitals involved "issues of legal judgment and definition, as well as issues of social policy".

The concerns about assessing dangerousness led to a search for other, more certain, ways of assessing future harm. The next section examines the revolt against uncertainty that clinical prediction methods then represented in identifying dangerous people. The chapter then turns to the role of mental health practitioners in assessing risk for current regimes of preventive detention and supervision. It outlines the rise of actuarial risk assessment tools for both management and predictive purposes. It argues that while there are serious ethical, legal and human rights concerns with the movement toward algorithms alone to predict the risk of future harmful behavior, risk assessment tools have become a part of preventive justice schemes because of an increasing political emphasis on public protection rather than on safeguarding the rights of individuals.

Identifying "Dangerous" People: From (Potential) Offender Characteristics to Actuarial Justice

The quest to identify just who will commit crimes has provided fodder for psychiatrists, psychologists and criminologists for centuries. The French psychiatrist, Félix Voisin, posited that phrenology could assist in diagnosing criminal tendencies. An offender could be diagnosed as "insane", "an idiot" or "a brute", and once labeled, an appropriate course of action could be taken (Staum 2003: p. 76). Similarly, the Italian criminologist and physician, Cesare Lombroso, in his 1876 work *L'Uomo Delinquente* (Criminal Man), attempted to classify individuals according to their physical "defects" (p. 152). For him, offenders were throwbacks to primitive "savages" (Staum 2003: p. 166).

As outlined above, during the twentieth century, there was skepticism expressed as to whether clinical assessments of dangerousness were little more than guesswork. John Monahan (1981), for example, concluded that predictions of future violence were only accurate in about one third of cases.

Using data to classify potential offenders and recidivists can be viewed as an extension of this quest for certainty. "Actuarial justice" is the term used by Malcolm Feeley and Jonathan Simon (1994: p. 173) to explain a growing reliance by governments on "techniques for identifying, classifying and managing groups assorted by levels of dangerousness". Their thesis is that the prevalence of concerns about risk and the impact of actuarialism on the construction and delivery of criminal justice amount to a "new penality". This is seen as a key shift not just in terms of crime management, but also in terms of how the individual is viewed within the system.

According to Feeley and Simon (1992: p. 455, 1994: p. 197), there has been a shift away from a focus on individual offenders and the prospect of rehabilitating them. Now, the focus is on large groups of offenders, who are sought to be managed by reference to actuarial inferences from statistical data sets. As a result, risk assessment is now based on classifying the individual within a large group, the profile of which is derived from large scale data sets rather than direct clinical knowledge of the individual.

The use of data sets parallels the rise of what has been termed the "precautionary principle" in public policy. This principle stems from environmental science and posits that, where the risk of harm is unpredictable and uncertain, and where the damage wrought will be irreversible, any lack of scientific certainty in relation to the nature of the harm or its consequences should not prevent action being taken (Ericson 2007). Thus, in 2007, the then Australian Prime Minister, John Howard, was quoted as saying "it's better safe than sorry", in justifying preventive detention measures for suspected terrorists (Smiles and Marriner 2007). Zedner (2009: p. 84) points out that although the precautionary principle might have originally been permitted on "grave and irreversible harms", it has broadened "to provide a warrant for decision making in situations of uncertainty even where the anticipated harms are of a lesser gravity". Therefore, Zedner concludes (2009: p. 85), incarceration becomes "increasingly central to the security complex" and it becomes the norm for those who pose potential threats to public safety.

Having statistical data sets available to classify who is likely to commit crimes in the future gives an air of legitimacy to an emphasis on precaution outweighing individual rights. While there has been debate about the extent to which actuarial justice has in fact displaced traditional penal practice (Pratt 2000: p. 50; Garland 2003: pp. 140–141), when it comes to preventive detention regimes, the reliance on actuarial methods of risk assessment is clearly manifest.

In Australia and New Zealand, for example, risk assessment tools are widely used for risk management purposes in correctional settings. They are also used for predictive purposes in relation to post-sentence detention and supervision schemes. It is in relation to such schemes that the use of risk assessment tools is the most problematic.

Forensic psychologists and psychiatrists are often called upon to provide predictive risk assessment for the purposes of preventive detention schemes. Forensic psychologists in particular have developed a role in providing evidence of risk based on actuarial tools that combine previously empirically identified risk factors into a numerical risk score using an algorithmic approach.

The next section outlines how evidence of risk has developed through the court system and the section following this summarizes the criticisms that have been made of risk assessment tools.

The Rise of Actuarial Risk Assessment Tools and Structured Professional Judgment

During the 1970s and early 1980s, there was a focus on making clinical assessments of "dangerousness" which did not merely provide a medical diagnosis, but involved "issues of legal judgment and definition, as well as issues of social policy" (Steadman 2000: p. 266). The terminology of "dangerousness" still pervades legal discourse. In Australia, for example, titles of statutes refer to "dangerous" or "high-risk" people, such as the *Dangerous Prisoners (Sexual Offenders) Act 2003* (Qld), the *Dangerous Sexual Offenders Act 2006* (WA) and the *Terrorism (High Risk Offenders) Act 2017* (NSW).

From the mid-1980s, the focus shifted from assessing dangerousness to a focus on assessment scales based on statistical or actuarial risk prediction. Such assessment tools assign numerical values to risk and (in more recent versions) protective factors and then weigh and combine the item ratings to produce risk scores. The methods through which item ratings are weighted and combined differ, but generally reflect the degree to which the items are related to future offending and the statistical association between the items in the development sample(s). Much of the research on risk prediction has been developed in relation to violence and there are more than 200 violence risk assessment tools available (Douglas et al. 2017: p. 134; Singh et al. 2014: p. 197).

There is now a growing emphasis on using clinical methods alongside statistical or actuarial risk prediction. This is generally referred to as "structured professional judgment" and it has become an accepted way to identify those who are at low, moderate or high risk of harming others. The structured professional judgment approach uses risk assessment tools which are designed to act as guidelines for clinical assessment. Davis and Ogloff (2008: p. 146) describe the process for evaluation as follows:

> These instruments include a number of risk factors, both static and dynamic, that are derived rationally from consideration of the literature. The evaluator must carefully score each of these risk factors from an administration manual. While a total "score" can be calculated, it has no substantive meaning in terms of a probability estimate, other than the fact that a higher score means that more risk factors are present. Thus, assessing clinicians are advised not to sum the items in an actuarial fashion. Rather, after carefully coding each risk factor they make what is considered to be a structured clinical opinion of low, moderate or high risk.

The structured professional judgment approach has been reinforced by most preventive detention schemes in Canada, Australia and New Zealand relying on risk assessments from mental health practitioners. The development of actuarial risk assessment instruments has in many ways been a boon for the growth of forensic psychology as a profession. Cynthia Mercado and James Ogloff (2007: p. 58), two forensic psychologists, have pointed out that most research published on risk assessment has been conducted by psychologists. This has entrenched the role of forensic psychologists in assessing risk for the purpose of preventive justice. However, as will be explored later in this chapter, this role may be tested by the courts accepting risk assessment tools without the need for clinical expertise.

Main Criticisms of Actuarial Risk Assessment Tools

Structured professional judgment is only as good as the tools upon which such judgment is based. There have been several criticisms of risk assessment tools. The following is a selection of the main ones.

The Specific Variables Used and the Variable-Based Approach Itself

The empirical research on the prediction of risk is "variable-oriented" (Lussier and Davies 2011: p. 534). Researchers have focused on identifying the main risk variables or factors associated with the risk of reoffending.

Some risk assessment scales focus exclusively on variables that are historical in nature (Sullivan et al. 2005: p. 319). The focus is on "static" risk factors that cannot change over time and that cannot be changed through treatment and intervention, such as the age of first offending and the offender's prior criminal history. Many risk assessment scales do not consider current clinical variables (such as response to treatment or motivation), protective factors (such as stable employment) or variables that reduce the risk of reoffending (such as physical illness or frailty).

There has also been criticism of the actual variables chosen as predictors of violence. The category of personality constructs is perhaps the most controversial of violence predictor variables. Robert Hare (2002: p. 27) states that psychopathy is "a personality disorder defined by a cluster of interpersonal, affective, and lifestyle characteristics that results in serious, negative consequences for society. Among the most devastating features of the disorder are a callous disregard for the rights of others and a propensity for predatory behaviour and violence".

Hare's Psychopathy Checklist-Revised (PCL-R) has been found to be a good predictor of violence and general recidivism amongst Anglo-American groups (Salekin et al. 1996: p. 203). However, its use as a predictive tool has been questioned by Skeem and Cooke (2010a: p. 433, 2010b: p. 455) and the terms "psychopath" and "antisocial personality disorder" have been criticized as being social constructs (Cavadino 1998: p. 6; McCallum 2001: p. 13).

As well as criticism of the variables used in different scales, other authors have noted that "there are different types of offenders and risk profiles which may not be accounted for by a single instrument based on a variable-oriented approach" (Lussier and Davies 2011: p. 535). There have thus been attempts by developmental psychologists to shift the focus away from variables to individuals through a "person-orientated" approach (Bergman and Magnussuon 1997). Developmental criminologists have also begun focusing on longitudinal studies examining individual-level trajectories of offending (Thornberry and Krohn 2003; Farrington 2005). Such trajectories are characterized by certain phases such as an activation phase, a plateau and a desistance phase, which vary at different levels (Lussier and Davies 2011: p. 536).

It is unlikely that the debates about which variables should be used and possible alternatives to variable-based risk assessment tools will end anytime soon.

Applying Group Data to the Individual

Actuarial scales are based on determining whether an individual offender has the same characteristics or risk factors as a "typical" kind of offender (Campbell 2000: p. 120). Risk assessments can classify an individual within a group—as "high risk", "medium risk" or "low risk"—but they cannot say where, in this group, a given person lies and, therefore, cannot identify the precise risk an individual poses. As Kris Gledhill (2011: p. 86) explains:

> [A] conclusion that a defendant presents a 30 per cent risk of committing a further offence within the next 10 years means that 30 per cent of people sharing the defendant's characteristics will commit a further offence if they act in the same way as the group on whom the study was based. The tool cannot say whether an individual will be one of the group who will [offend] or one of the group who will not.

There are also problems with the populations upon which these tools are tested. In *Ewart v Canada* ([2018] SCC 30), the Supreme Court of Canada held that Correctional Services Canada breached its obligation under section 24(1) of the federal *Corrections and Conditional Release Act 1992* to take all reasonable steps to ensure that any information about an offender that it uses is as accurate as possible. This was on the basis that in assessing the risk of Indigenous offenders, it used actuarial risk assessment tools that were developed and tested on predominantly non-Indigenous populations. Expert witnesses in Australian cases have also questioned whether instruments that have not been validated through studies involving Australian Indigenous offenders should be relied on in Australian courts (*Attorney-General (Qld) v McLean* [2006] QSC 137: para. 26; *Attorney-General (Qld) v George* [2009] QSC 2: para. 33).

Christopher Slobogin (2012: p. 207) has pointed out, "the population on which the actuarial device is validated may be quite different from the population to which it is applied". For example, Australian Indigenous offenders as a group have higher rates of childhood abuse victimization and early substance abuse, both of which are included as factors associated with high-risk status in many risk assessment instruments. Indigenous offenders are therefore more likely to be classified as high risk than are non-Indigenous offenders (Sullivan et al. 2005: p. 319).

Some judges are aware of this problem. In *Director of Public Prosecutions (WA) v Moolarvie* ([2008] WASC 37: para. 44), Justice Blaxell remarked in relation to the Static 99 risk assessment tool:

> Yet another problem with the "Static 99" is that it was developed for use with Canadian and English offenders of European origin. The literature suggests that risk factors for indigenous violence may well differ from those for non-indigenous Australians and people of other cultures.

Rather than abandoning the use of these risk assessment tools on diverse populations, researchers have instead viewed these judicial pronouncements as providing an opportunity for further research. For example, Mark Olver et al. (2018) have argued that their research indicates the Hare Psychopathy Checklist-Revised (PCL-R) is an appropriate risk assessment tool for men of Indigenous ancestry. Meanwhile Stephen

Hart (2016: p. 91) has called for developers of risk assessment tools to "take into account the relevant scientific and professional literature dealing with diverse groups ... and caution[s] users about the intended target groups of their tools". It is, therefore, unlikely that the use of risk assessment tools will cease, but that they will continue to be refined.

Management Versus Prediction

Predictive machine learning algorithms have been used to inform judicial decision-making, including for sentencing and post-sentence preventive detention schemes, as well as for management purposes. Kelly Hannah-Moffat (2013: p. 272) argues that "actuarial risk logic offers managerial and organizational benefits". However, when it comes to the use of risk assessment tools in the courtroom, Hannah-Moffat (2013: p. 278) points out that there can be slippage between correlation and causation:

> Instead of understanding that an individual with a high risk score shares characteristics with an aggregate group of high-risk offenders, practitioners are likely to perceive the individual *as* a high-risk offender.

Giving evidence on risk for the purpose of taking away a person's liberty has given rise to ethical concerns in the psychiatric literature. Danny Sullivan, Paul Mullen and Michele Pathé (2005: p. 320) have questioned the ethics of requiring clinicians to assess risk for the purposes of continued detention or coercive supervision after sentence. They have pointed out that being required to give evidence for preventive detention and supervision schemes raises the specter of mental health practitioners being "agents of supervision, social control and monitoring" rather than "independent clinicians". Similarly, Eric Janus (2004: p. 50) is of the view that mental health practitioners should not engage in giving testimony for sexually violent predator laws in the United States because such testimony involves what he terms "political judgments that determine the balance between public safety and individual liberty".

The Royal College of Psychiatrists for the United Kingdom and the Republic of Ireland held a seminar on the ethics of giving evidence for extended sentencing purposes in 2002. It published an overview of the discussion in its Psychiatric Bulletin (2005: p. 75) and stated that one view aired was that "it is not ethically part of medicine to assist the courts in increasing punishment and public protection by applying medical skills to such a purpose".

Nevertheless, from a practical perspective, there will always be some mental health practitioners willing to engage with legislative requirements to provide assessments of risk. Even where the evidence of risk provided is substandard, the courts continue to rely on risk assessment tools. For example, in *R v Peta* ([2007] 2 NZLR 627), Justice Glazebrook provided a scathing critique of the evidence that had been provided in support of a continuing supervision order, but accepted the need for evidence of risk. She set out (paras. 51–53) several requirements for "best practice" in providing an "individualised assessment" in the courtroom, including:

- the proper administration and scoring of risk assessment instruments;
- the integration of the results from such instruments with "other relevant information known to relate to the risk of reoffending" (para. 51);
- the explicit identification of factors other than those in the actuarial instruments that have been used to formulate the individual assessment;
- the identification of any "recognisable contingencies that will influence the degree of risk present" (para. 51);
- reference to "the likely victims and the likely severity of harm of subsequent offences" (para. 51);
- adequate training in the effective communication of properly conducted risk assessment; and
- the use of categories of risk such as "high, moderate or low risk should be qualified by probability statements that give corresponding reoffence rates for groups of similar offenders and the numbers of offenders in each category should be specified" (para. 53).

Justice Glazebrook (2010: p. 101) expanded on these requirements in a subsequent article which accepted the need for risk assessment evidence, but stressed that the "limitations of the risk assessment instruments and the health professional's expertise must be conveyed to the court".

Back to the Future: Predictive Algorithms

Hannah-Moffat (2013: p. 279) points out that "actuarial instruments continue to be appealing because of their purported ability to classify offenders based on a set of "defensible" statistically relevant factors, without the need to rely on clinical discretion, and because they offer the prospect of greater certainty". In some jurisdictions, there may be challenges to the status quo of evidence of risk based on structured professional judgment by the rise of privately designed risk assessment tools.

In *State v Loomis* (881 N.W.2d 749 (Wis. 2016)), the Wisconsin Supreme Court considered whether the use of a risk assessment tool entitled COMPAS (Correctional Offender Management Profiling for Alternative Sanctions), which was developed by a private company, violated due process rights. COMPAS had originally been intended for use as a case management tool for corrections agencies, but had come to be used in presentence reports. The tool was used in a pre-sentence hearing for Mr. Loomis, who was subsequently sentenced to six years' imprisonment for involvement in a drive-by shooting. He argued on appeal that the use of this tool violated his due process rights (p. 757).

A complicating factor was that the company which developed COMPAS relied upon a proprietary algorithm that was not available to the defendant or the court. The Wisconsin Supreme Court acknowledged there were concerns with racially biased outcomes associated with COMPAS (p. 763), but nevertheless found that Mr. Loomis' due process rights were not violated because the tool was not the *sole* basis for sentencing decisions. A petition for a writ of certiorari (a process for seeking judicial review) to the Supreme Court of the United States was denied in 2017 (*Loomis v Wisconsin* 137 S.Ct. 2290 (2017)). An amicus curiae brief for the US federal government in relation to that petition noted that the use of actuarial risk assessments in sentencing "raises novel constitutional questions" that may merit the Supreme Court's attention in the future, but that a review of the use of COMPAS did not warrant review on the facts of Mr. Loomis' case (Brief for the United States as Amicus Curiae, 2017: p. 12).

Preventive Justice Schemes and Human Rights Concerns

The use of predictive algorithms in predicting the risk of harm appears to mark a return to the presumption that bypassing clinical judgment will provide more certainty in decisions about preventive justice. The lack of transparency in the development of such risk assessment tools is troubling because any limitations in the operation of such tools can have deleterious consequences for a person's human rights as set out in international treaties such as the *International Covenant on Civil and Political Rights*. However, the consequences of such schemes breaching human rights may vary according to whether there is strong or weak domestic human rights protection. This section compares the validity of preventive justice schemes in Australia and New Zealand, which have relatively weak rights protection, to that of Germany, where human rights are enshrined in the German Constitution (the "Basic Law").

In Australia, which does not have a federal Bill or Charter of Human Rights, Robert John Fardon was the first person to be subjected to post-sentence preventive detention in prison. Fardon challenged the constitutional validity of the *Dangerous Prisoners (Sexual Offenders) Act 2003* (Qld) under which he was detained. He argued that the legislation authorized the Supreme Court of Queensland to order the civil commitment of a person to prison without a fresh crime, or a trial or conviction for that crime, meaning that the law authorized double punishment. He argued that for these reasons, the law was inconsistent with the essential character of a court and, consequently, the separation of judicial power under the Australian Constitution (*Attorney-General (Qld) v Fardon* [2003b] QSC 200; *Attorney-General (Qld) v Fardon* [2003a] QCA 416).

The High Court of Australia held, by a majority of six judges to one in *Fardon v Attorney-General (Qld)* ((2004) 223 CLR 575), that the Queensland Act was valid. Chief Justice Gleeson (p. 586), however, was careful to point out that the High Court had no jurisdiction to consider policy issues concerning the legislation:

There are important issues that could be raised about the legislative policy of continuing detention of offenders who have served their terms of imprisonment, and who are regarded as a danger to the community when released. Substantial questions of civil liberty arise. This case, however, is not concerned with those wider issues. The outcome turns upon a relatively narrow point, concerning the nature of the function which the Act confers upon the Supreme Court.

Justice Kirby, the sole dissentient in Fardon's case, held that continued detention in prison did amount to double punishment (pp. 634–644) and he was also concerned with the "free hand given to the psychiatric witnesses upon whose evidence the Act requires the State court to perform its function" (p. 639). He stated (p. 647):

> punishment is reserved to courts in respect of the crimes that prisoners are proved to have committed. It is not available for crimes that are feared, anticipated or predicted to occur in the future on evidence that is notoriously unreliable and otherwise would be inadmissible and by people who do not have the gift of prophesy.

In 2006, Fardon instructed the Prisoners' Legal Service of Queensland to initiate a communication to the United Nations Human Rights Committee on the basis that his continued detention breached international human rights law (Keyzer and Blay 2006: p. 408). A separate communication was also filed in relation to Kenneth Davidson Tillman, who was the first person to be preventively detained in prison in New South Wales under the *Crimes (Serious Sex Offenders) Act 2006* (NSW). Both communications were filed in 2007 and the Human Rights Committee delivered its views on both in March 2010.

The main arguments raised in the Fardon and Tillman communications dealt with the right to liberty under Article 9(1) and the right not to be punished again for an offence under Article 14(7) of the *International Covenant on Civil and Political Rights* (ICCPR). The Human Rights Committee made several observations in both decisions concerning Article 9(1) and did not consider it necessary to examine the matter separately under Article 14(7).

Eleven of the 13 members of the Human Rights Committee agreed that both the preventive detention legislative schemes in Queensland and New South Wales were in violation of Article 9(1). They pointed to four significant factors leading to their conclusion (*Re Fardon v Australia* 2010, Communication No. 1629/2007; *Re Tillman v Australia* 2010, Communication No. 1635/2007):

1. The continued detention in prison "amounted to a fresh term of imprisonment which ... is not permissible in the absence of a conviction" (para. 7.4(1)).
2. Because imprisonment is penal in nature, both Fardon's and Tillman's continued detention in prison amounted to a "new sentence" which meant they suffered a heavier penalty than that applicable at the time the offences were committed. This is prohibited under Article 15(1) of the ICCPR (para. 7.4(2)).
3. The procedures under the Acts, being civil in nature, did not meet the due process guarantees under Article 14 of the ICCPR "for a fair trial in which a penal sentence is imposed" (para. 7.4(3)).
4. Because of the problematic nature of the concept of feared or predicted dangerousness, "the Courts must make a finding of fact on the suspected future behaviour of a past offender which may or may not materialise." Accordingly, the onus was on the Commonwealth of Australia as a State Party to the ICCPR to demonstrate that rehabilitation could not have been achieved by "means less intrusive than continued imprisonment or even detention" (para. 7.4(4)).

In both decisions, the Human Rights Committee requested that Australia provide it with information within 180 days as to the remedy taken to give effect to its views. The Australian government did not respond within this time limit. On 6 September 2011, the Australian government filed a five-page document, setting out the reasons why both Fardon and Tillman remained in prison and stating that it rejected the Human Rights Committee's finding that there were less restrictive means available to achieve the purposes of the New South Wales and Queensland legislation other than preventive detention in prison. The statement pointed out that both men had failed to attend rehabilitation programs while incarcerated and that there were no intensive treatment and rehabilitation options available in the community for either Tillman or Fardon. The response (Australian Government 2011: para. 18) stated:

> Australia stresses that the community has a legitimate expectation to be protected from these offenders, and at the same time, that authorities owe these offenders a duty to try and [sic] rehabilitate them. The purpose of these schemes is not to indefinitely detain serious sex offenders, but rather to ensure as far as possible that their release into the community occurs in a way that is safe and respectful of the needs of both the community, and the offenders themselves.

The statement concluded with the observation that both the New South Wales and Queensland state governments did not consider any further action needed to be taken. Thus, despite the Human Rights Committee's finding that Fardon and Tillman's continued imprisonment breached their right to liberty under international human rights law, the Australian government has clearly signaled that there will be no changes made to current preventive detention schemes.

Human rights discourse in Australia is still nascent largely because of its lack of a federal Bill or Charter of Rights. Yet, even where there is some legislative protection for human rights, such as in New Zealand through its *Human Rights Act 1993*, rights arguments can be trumped by community protection considerations.

In New Zealand, section 87(1) of the *Sentencing Act 2002* enables a sentence of preventive (indeterminate) detention where an offender poses "a significant and ongoing risk to the safety" of members of the community. Allan Brian Miller and Michael John Carroll were respectively convicted of rape in 1991 and 1988 and were sentenced to preventive detention. Despite being eligible for parole after 10 years of imprisonment, both remained incarcerated. In 2014, individual communications to the Human Rights Committee about their continued detention were filed. It was argued that New Zealand did not afford them access to adequate rehabilitative programs in prison, and that as a result, their continued detention was arbitrary and violated their right to liberty.

The United Nations Human Rights Committee found (*Re Miller and Carroll v New Zealand*, 2014, Communication No. 2502/2014: para. 8.5) that New Zealand had violated its obligations under Article 9 of the ICCPR:

> The Committee considers that as the length of preventive detention increases, the State party bears an increasingly heavy burden to justify continued detention and to show that the threat posed by the individual cannot be addressed by alternative measures. As a result, a level of risk which might reasonably justify a short-term preventive detention, may not necessarily justify a longer period of preventive detention.

The Human Rights Committee referred to New Zealand's obligation to provide an effective remedy to the two men and for it to take steps to facilitate their release (para. 10). As with the *Fardon* and *Tillman* communications, there was a requirement imposed for a response to the decision within 180 days. New Zealand responded on 27 November 2018, arguing that there was no lesser form of restriction than continued detention that could be placed upon either of the men. At the time of writing, both men are still detained.

In the broader international context, it is those countries with enforceable human rights protection through Constitutions or Bills or Charters of Rights that are more likely to have limitations placed on laws of preventive justice. Much of the European jurisprudence in this area concerns the system of indefinite and preventive detention in Germany, which has a constitutional rights protection. Hans-Jörg Albrecht (2012: pp. 44–45) describes the German criminal justice system as "two-track" in that it has punishment in the form of fines or imprisonment on conviction for offences as well as "measures of rehabilitation and protection of public security which can be added to a prison sentence (preventive detention) or replace prison sentences (committal to a psychiatric hospital)".

The European Court of Human Rights has held that post-sentence preventive detention breaches the right to liberty under Article 5 of the European Convention on Human Rights. In *M v Germany* (2010) and *Grosskopf v Germany* (2010), the European Court of Human Rights did not consider that preventive detention that had been ordered at the time of sentence was in itself a breach of the right to liberty. Rather, in order to find a breach, the Court found it necessary to consider issues in relation to the causal connections between the respective offenders' convictions and deprivations of liberty, as well as the relevant law that applied at the time they were sentenced (see Drenkhahn et al. 2012; Slobogin 2012 for a full analysis of M's case).

However, in *Haidn v Germany* (2011), the European Court of Human Rights held that the applicant's post-sentence preventive detention did breach his right to liberty. The main reason for this was that the detention in prison had been ordered retrospectively and so was not foreseeable. The Court stated (2011: para. [96]) that "in order to be 'lawful', the detention must conform to the substantive and procedural rules of national law, which must, moreover, be of a certain quality and, in particular, must be foreseeable in its application, in order to avoid all risk of arbitrariness".

Following these rulings by the European Court of Human Rights, Germany's Federal Constitutional Court, the Bundesverfassungsgericht (BVerfG) subsequently reconsidered the system of preventive detention in the decisions known as Preventive Detention Cases I and II (BVerfG 2011a), which were handed down on 4 May 2011.

The two cases, known as Preventive Detention I, concerned two men who were subject to preventive detention orders at the time of their sentences, but these orders had been made before the 1998 laws. At that time, there was a ten-year cap upon such orders. Both men had been preventively detained for longer than ten years and the question was whether the original orders could be prolonged.

The two cases, known as Preventive Detention II, concerned two men who were subject to retrospective detention orders under the 2004 amendments. All four applicants relied upon the European Court of Human Rights decisions, arguing that the provisions of the Basic Law should be interpreted in the light of this jurisprudence. They argued that the orders for preventive detention contravened the fundamental right to liberty protected under Article 2(2) in conjunction with Article 104(1) of the Basic Law.

The BVerfG allowed all four complaints, concluding that the orders had breached the applicants' right to liberty. It clarified that the Basic

Law should be interpreted in a manner compatible with international law. The European Convention and the judgments of the European Court of Human Rights were viewed as providing interpretative guidance in relation to the Basic Law.

The BVerfG ordered that the provisions that were declared unconstitutional could remain until the entry into force of new legislation to be enacted prior to 31 May 2013. It did not go so far as to declare all forms of preventive detention unconstitutional, but held that the serious encroachment upon the right to liberty, which preventive detention constitutes, could be justified only if it is subject to a strict review of proportionality and if strict requirements were satisfied. As Hans-Jörg Albrecht (2012: 52) points out, the decision means that preventive detention "can be tolerated only under the condition that preventive detention is implemented in a way differing significantly from the implementation of prison sentences".

The BVerfG stressed that the underlying rationale for preventive detention was the minimization of danger through a therapeutic regime aimed at reducing the deprivation of liberty to that which was absolutely necessary. It, therefore, called upon the legislature to develop a "liberty-oriented overall concept of preventive detention aimed at therapy" (Michaelsen 2012: p. 163). This decision was confirmed by the BVerfG in a subsequent decision handed down on 8 June 2011 (BVerfG 2011b).

Overall, it is clear from an international human rights law perspective that post-sentence preventive detention laws violate the right to liberty. For those countries with strong, enforceable human rights protections such as Germany, such schemes may be limited because of the deleterious consequences of them on human rights. However, governments with weak human rights protections can dismiss the Human Rights Committee's findings because they are not legally binding on them and they are simply interpretations of the ICCPR. As exemplified by the Tillman, Fardon, Miller and Carroll communications, governments may simply stress that community protection outweighs individual rights.

In summary, risk assessments remain integral to the operation of preventive justice schemes, and while structured professional judgment, with all its challenges, is currently the preferred mode of assessment in many English-speaking countries, the development of risk assessment tools by private companies, which guard the data upon which they are based, provide extra cause for concern. The results generated and the methodology underlying risk assessment tools must be interpretable in order for appropriate judicial decisions to be made.

Conclusion

Laws enabling preventive justice schemes have long existed. However, the use of such schemes has reflected different policy perspectives on the scope of state power. Since the 1980s, there has been a rise in the use of preventive detention and supervision laws in conjunction with the language of risk to detain those perceived as some form of threat to members of the community.

Currently, English-speaking countries with weak human rights protection are prepared to override individual human rights in favor of preventive justice schemes aimed at protecting the community from possible harm. The use of risk assessment tools in decisions to deprive people of their liberty for fear of future harmful behavior may be viewed as part of the "revolt against uncertainty" as to who will commit crimes. Bill Hebenton and Toby Seddon (2009: p. 358) have pointed out that "many lay people are in fact not much interested in assessing or controlling 'risk' in a probabilistic sense. They actually want certainty". Actuarial risk assessment provides such an illusion of certainty that it may become embedded as a normative feature of preventive justice schemes.

It should be acknowledged, however, that the use of such tools remains highly contentious. Structured professional judgment, which combines actuarial and clinical approaches, is now well established in many courtrooms, where judges must consider community safety in sentencing and post-sentence preventive detention. However, structured professional judgment not only entrenches the power of forensic mental health practitioners, it raises serious ethical and human rights issues because of the consequences for the individuals concerned.

There remains a perception that predictive machine learning algorithms make more accurate predictions of future crimes than clinical judgments. The acceptance of a privately developed risk assessment tool in the United States' *Loomis* case is concerning because the unavailability of the data on which it is based means that it cannot be tested. The use of predictive algorithms may be viewed as both a return to the past in focusing on preventive justice as well as a logical extension of the "risk society's" impact on the quest for security in criminal justice policy and practice. Preventive justice schemes in countries such as Australia and New Zealand still mandate expert evidence on risk, but perhaps the allure of scientific reliability will eventually bypass the need for human experts altogether. Because of the potential for violations to human rights and the lack of any practical alternatives, the existing emphasis on structured professional judgment remains the "least worst" option for preventive justice schemes.

References

Albrecht, H-J 2012, 'The Incapacitation of the Dangerous Offender: Criminal Policy and Legislation in the Federal Republic of Germany', in M Malsch & M Duker (eds), *Incapacitation: Trends and New Perspectives,* Farnham, Ashgate Publishing Ltd, pp. 39–61.

Ashworth, A & Zedner, L 2014, *Preventive Justice,* Oxford University Press, Oxford.

Attorney-General (Qld) v Fardon [2003a] QCA 416.

Attorney-General (Qld) v Fardon [2003b] QSC 200.

Attorney-General (Qld) v George [2009] QSC 2.

Attorney-General (Qld) v McLean [2006] QSC 137.

Australian Government 2011, *Response of the Australian Government to the Views of the Committee in Communication No. 1635/2007 Tillman v Australia and Communication No. 1629/2007 Fardon v Australia,* Attorney-General's Department, Canberra.

Baxstrom v Herold 383 US 107 (1966).

Bergman, LR & Magnussuon, D 1997, 'A Person-Oriented Approach in Research on Developmental Psychopathology', *Development and Psychopathology,* vol. 9, no. 2, pp. 291–319.

Blackstone, W (1753/2001), *Commentaries on the Laws of England in Four Books* Routledge, London.

Bottoms, AE 2009, 'Reflections on the Renaissance of Dangerousness', *Howard Journal of Penology and Crime Prevention*, vol. 16, no. 2, pp. 70–96.

BVerfG (2011a) 2 BvR 2365/09 of 4.5.2011.

BVerfG (2011b) 2 BvR 2846/09 of 8.6.2011.

Campbell, TW 2000, 'Sexual Predator Evaluations and Phrenology: Considering Issues of Evidentiary Reliability', *Behavioral Sciences and the Law*, vol. 18, no. 1, pp. 111–130.

Cavadino, M 1998, 'Death to the Psychopath', *Journal of Forensic Psychiatry* vol. 9, no. 1, pp. 5–8.

Davis, MR & Ogloff, JRP 2008, 'Risk Assessment', in K Fritzon & P Wilson (eds), *Forensic Psychology and Criminology: An Australian Perspective*, McGraw-Hill Australia, North Ryde, New South Wales, pp. 141–150.

Director of Public Prosecutions (WA) v Moolarvie [2008] WASC 37.

Douglas, T, Purgh, J, Singh, I, Savulescu, J & Fazek, S 2017, 'Risk Assessment Tools in Criminal Justice and Forensic Psychiatry: The Need For Better Data,' *European Psychiatry*, vol 42, pp. 134–137.

Drenkhahn, K, Morgenstern, C & van Zyl Smit, D 2012, 'What is in a Name? Preventive Detention in Germany in the Shadow of European Human Rights Law', *Criminal Law Review*, issue 3, pp. 167–187.

Ericson, RV 2007, *Crime in an Insecure World*, Polity Press, Cambridge.

Ewart v Canada [2018] SCC 30.

Fardon v Attorney-General (Qld) (2004) 223 CLR 575.

Farrington, DP (ed) 2005, *Integrated Development and Life Course Theories of Offending*, Transaction, London: Transaction.

Feeley, M & Simon, J 1992, 'The New Penology: Notes on the Emerging Strategy of Corrections and its Implications', *Criminology*, vol 30, no. 4, pp. 449–474.

Feeley, M & Simon, J 1994, 'Actuarial Justice: The Emerging New Criminal Law', in D Nelken (ed), *The Futures of Criminology*, Sage, London, pp. 173–201.

Garland, D 2003, 'Penal Modernism and Postmodernism', in T Blomberg & S Cohen (eds), *Punishment and Social Control: Essays in Honor of Sheldon Messinger*, 2nd edn, Aldine de Gruyter, New York, pp. 45–73.

Glazebrook, S 2010, 'Risky Business: Predicting Recidivism,' *Psychiatry, Psychology and Law*, vol. 17, no. 1, pp. 88–120.

Gledhill, K 2011, 'Preventive Sentences and Orders: The Challenges of Due Process', *Journal of Commonwealth Criminal Law*, vol. 1, pp. 78–104.

Grosskopf v Germany [2010] 53 EHRR 7.

Haidn v Germany [2011] ECHR 39.

Hannah-Moffat, K 2013, 'Actuarial Sentencing: An 'Unsettled' Proposition', *Justice Quarterly*, vol. 30, no. 2, pp. 270–296.

Hare, RD 2002, 'Psychopathy and Risk for Recidivism and Violence', in N Gray, J Laing & L Noaks (eds), *Criminal Justice, Mental Health and the Politics of Risk*, Cavendish, London, pp. 27–47.

Hart, SD 2016, 'Culture and Violence Risk Assessment: The Case of Ewert v. Canada', *Journal of Threat Assessment and Management*, vol. 3, no. 2, pp. 76–96.

Hebenton, B & Seddon T 2009, 'From Dangerousness to Precaution: Managing Sexual and Violent Offenders in an Insecure and Uncertain Age', *British Journal of Criminology*, vol. 49, no. 3, pp. 343–362.

Janus, ES 2004, 'Sexually Violent Predator Laws: Psychiatry in Service to a Morally Dubious Enterprise', *Lancet*, vol. 364, pp. 50–51.

Keyzer, P & Blay, S 2006, 'Double Punishment? Preventive Detention Schemes Under Australian Legislation and their Consistency with International Law: The Fardon Communication,' *Melbourne Journal of International Law*, vol. 7, no. 2, pp. 407–424.

Lombroso, C (1876/2006). *Criminal Man [L'uomo delinquent]*, trans. M Gibson & NH Rafter, Duke University Press, Durham, North Carolina.

Loomis v Wisconsin 137 S.Ct. 2290 (2017).

Lussier, P & Davies, G 2011, 'A Person-Oriented Perspective on Sexual Offenders, Offending Trajectories, and Risk of Recidivism: A New Challenge for Policymakers, Risk Assessors and Actuarial Prediction?', *Psychology, Public Policy and Law*, vol. 17, no. 4, pp. 530–561.

M v Germany [2010] 51 EHRR 41.

McCallum, D 2001, *Personality and Dangerousness: Genealogies of Antisocial Personality Disorder*, Cambridge University Press, Cambridge.

McSherry, B 2014, *Managing Fear: The Law and Ethics of Preventive Detention and Risk* Assessmen, Routledge, New York.

McSherry, B & Keyzer, P 2009, *Sex Offenders and Preventive Detention: Politics, Policy and Practice*, The Federation Press, Sydney.

Mercado, CC & Ogloff, JRP 2007, 'Risk and the Preventive Detention of Sex Offenders in Australia and the United States', *International Journal of Law and Psychiatry*, vol. 30, no. 1, pp. 49–59.

Michaelsen, C 2012, '"From Strasbourg with Love": Preventive Detention Before the German Federal Constitutional Court and the European Court of Human Rights' *Human Rights Law Review*, vol. 12, no. 1, pp. 148–167.

Mill, JS 1859 [1991], *On Liberty and Other Essays*, Oxford World Classics edn, Oxford University Press, Oxford.

Monahan, J 1981, *The Clinical Prediction of Violent Behavior*, National Institute of Mental Health, Rockville, Maryland.

Olver, ME, Neumann, CS, Sewall, L, Lewis, K, Hare, RD & Wong, SCP 2018, 'A Comprehensive Examination of the Psychometric Properties of the Hare Psychopathy Checklist-Revised in a Canadian Multisite Sample of Indigenous and Non-Indigenous Offender,' *Psychological Assessment*, vol. 30, no. 6, pp. 779–792.

Petrila, J 2011, 'Sexually Violent Predator Laws: Going Back to a Time Better Forgotten', in B McSherry & P Keyzer (eds), *Dangerous People: Policy, Prediction and Practice,* Routledge, New York, pp. 63–72.

Pratt, J 1997, Governing the Dangerous, Sydney: Federation Press.

Pratt, J 2000, 'The Return of the Wheelbarrow Men: Or, The Arrival of Postmodern Penality?', *British Journal of Criminology*, vol. 40, no. 1, pp. 127–145.

Royal College of Psychiatrists 2005, 'The Psychiatrist, Court and Sentencing: The Impact of Extended Sentencing on the Ethical Framework of Forensic Psychiatry', *Psychiatric Bulletin*, vol. 29, no. 2, pp. 73–77.

Salekin, RT, Rogers, R & Sewell, KW 1996, 'A Review and Meta-Analysis of the Psychopathy Checklist and Psychopathy Checklist-Revised: Predictive Validity of Dangerousness', *Clinical Psychology: Science and Practice*, vol. 3, no. 3, pp. 203–215.

Singh, JP, Desmarais, SL, Hurducas, C, Arbach-Lucioni, K, Condemarin, C, Dean, K, Doyle, M, Folino, JO, Godoy-Cervera, V, Grann, M, Ho, RMY, Large, MM, Nielsen, LH, Pham, TH, Rebocho, MF, Reeves, KA, Rettenberger, M, de Ruiter, C, Seewald, K & Otto, RK 2014, 'International Perspectives on the Practical Application of Violence Risk Assessment: A Global Survey of 44 Countries,' *International Journal of Forensic Mental Health*, vol. 13, no. 3, pp. 193–206.

Re Fardon v Australia, Human Rights Committee, Communication No. 1629/2007, UN Doc. CCPR/C/98/D/1629/2007 (12 April 2010).

Re Miller and Carroll v New Zealand, Human Rights Committee, Communication No. 2502/2014, UN Doc. CCPR/C/121/D/2502/2014 (21 November 2014).

Re Tillman v Australia, Human Rights Committee, Communication No. 1635/2007, UN Doc. CCPR/C/98/D/1635/2007 (12 April 2010).

R v Peta [2007] 2 NZLR 627.

Skeem, JL & Cooke, DJ 2010a, 'Is Criminal Behavior a Central Component of Psychopathy? Conceptual Directions for Resolving the Debate,' *Psychological Assessments*, vol. 22, no. 2, pp. 433–445.

Skeem, JL & Cooke, DJ 2010b, 'One Measure Does Not a Construct Make: Directions Toward Reinvigorating Psychopathy Research – Reply to Hare and Neuman (2010)', *Psychological Assessment*, vol. 22, no. 2, pp. 455–459.

Slobogin, C 2012, 'Risk Assessment', in J Petersilia & KR Reitz (eds), *Oxford Handbook of Sentencing and Corrections*, Oxford University Press, Oxford, pp. 196–214.

Smiles S & Marriner C 2007, 'PM Defiant: No Visa and No Apology', *The Age,* 31 July.

State v Loomis 881 N.W.2d 749 (Wis. 2016).

Staum, M 2003, *Labelling People: French Scholars on Society, Race and Empire, 1815–1848*, McGill-Queen's University Press, Montreal.

Steadman, HJ 1973, 'Implications from the Baxstrom Experience', *Journal of the American Academy of Psychiatry and the Law*, vol. 1, no. 3, pp. 189–196.

Steadman, HJ 2000, 'From Dangerousness to Risk Assessment of Community Violence: Taking Stock at the Turn of the Century,' *Journal of the American Academy of Psychiatry and* Law, vol. 28, no. 3, pp. 265–271.

Sullivan, DH, Mullen PE & Pathé MT 2005, 'Legislation in Victoria on Sexual Offenders: Issues for Health Professionals', *Medical Journal of Australia*, vol. 183, no. 6, pp. 318–320.

Thornberry, T P & Krohn, MD (eds) 2003, *Taking Stock of Delinquency: An Overview of Findings from Contemporary Longitudinal Studies*, Kluwer Academic, New York.

United States Government 2017, 'Brief for the United States as Amicus Curiae', *Loomis v Wisconsin*, No. 16-6387.

Zedner, L 2009, *Security*, Routledge, London.

Reflections on Risk Assessment in Community Corrections

David Brown

Introduction

Risk mentalities, technologies and practices have permeated prison regimes and community sanctions in many modern societies under the banner of discourses of "what works" and "evidence-based policy" (Maurutto and Hannah-Moffat 2006; Robinson 2016). In practice, the use of risk instruments such as the LSI-R and the "risk-needs-responsivity" (RNR) framework have been harnessed to the political imperative of reducing recidivism rates. Recidivism rates, which previously had gone largely unremarked upon, deterrence theory's guilty secret, became a political issue in the 1990s as part of the critique of mass incarceration. Across the political spectrum, the demand for efficiency from the criminal justice system started to be applied to corrections agencies, previously immune from the cost-benefit calculus applied under neoliberal managerialism to other sectors such as health, welfare and education. Why, it was asked, were so

D. Brown (✉)
Law Faculty, University of New South Wales, Sydney, NSW, Australia
e-mail: d.brown@unsw.edu.au

© The Author(s) 2020
J. Pratt, J. Anderson (eds.), *Criminal Justice, Risk and the Revolt against Uncertainty*,
Palgrave Studies in Risk, Crime and Society,
https://doi.org/10.1007/978-3-030-37948-3_3

many tax dollars being expended on incarcerating increasing numbers of (mainly black and poor) people, to such little effect given that half of those released were back behind bars within two years and crime rates continued to climb? "What works", "evidence-based policy" and the rapid adoption of risk instruments in corrections were thus a response to the popular and political demand for better community protection from, and greater efficiency in, criminal justice agencies and processes, and a way, it seemed, of providing more certain protection from future crime.

In a sustained series of theoretically sophisticated publications over two decades, Kelly Hannah-Moffat (1999, 2005, 2009) has challenged reductive readings of risk in the penal and criminal justice sphere and crafted an argument around the creation of what she calls a "transformative risk subject", who unlike the risk subject of fixed or static conceptions of risk, exemplified in actuarial practices, "is amenable to targeted therapeutic interventions" (2005: 29). Her argument is that this shift in constructions of the RNR formula from static to dynamic has opened up the space for a "new politics of punishment" (ibid.), more specifically the revival of notions of rehabilitation, a repudiation of "nothing works", and a revitalization of community corrections agencies as helping agents rather than compliance managers. In other words, predictive technologies may not simply be another toll of repression and control (cf Feeley and Simon 1992).

This chapter, based on an ongoing collective project investigating community sanctions in three Australian states,[1] will explore some of the tensions arising from the claims that the use of risk technologies could both meet the political imperative of reducing recidivism rates and deliver the promised efficiency and certainty, by way of examining some of the effects of risk assessment in the practice of community corrections as experienced and recounted by frontline community service workers in one of the jurisdictions under study. Interviews and an extended workshop conducted with the managers of five leading Sydney-based organizations providing post-release accommodation and support services for people leaving prison threw up a set of issues and problems faced in the daily practice of these agencies.[2]

The aim of the chapter is to draw on the interview material from these frontline post-release services in New South Wales (NSW) to sketch out the background context within which struggles over attempts to utilize risk to reduce recidivism and promote rehabilitation and desistance are waged. Such an examination is of additional salience in NSW as the NSW government and Corrective Services NSW (CSNSW) have recently launched a $330 million expansion of community corrections programs, structured mainly around the RNR and "what works" frameworks. It is hoped that this examination might shed some light on the extent to which the potential promised in Hannah-Moffat's "transformative risk subject" is or is not being realized in the practice of this one small sector, and if not, to identify some of the obstacles.

After a brief overview of the dominant development in the community sanctions field in Australia, the take-up of risk instruments, a series of issues that emerged in the interview and workshop research will be outlined. These issues demonstrate that the project of producing a "transformative risk subject" tends to be undercut in practice by the failure of particular conceptions of risk practice to address structural problems faced in the provision of post-release services. Finally, some general comments will be offered on tendencies in risk assessment practices in community sanctions.

The Rise and Rise of Risk Instruments

In an illustration of the explosion of risk assessment instruments of various kinds in penal practice the NSW *Compendium of Offender Assessments* (CSNSW 2006) sets out some 102 different instruments, scales and interview schedules which can be administered by a range of different agents including Community Corrections Officers and psychologists. In NSW, the two most widely used instruments are the Level of Service Inventory-Revised (LSI-R) (Andrews and Bonta 1995, 2010) and the Community Impact Assessment (CIA) (CSNSW 2013). The LSI-R, ubiquitous internationally, an actuarial tool used to identify an individual's risk and needs with regard to recidivism, has 54 questions in 10 subscales that assess criminogenic needs (such as criminal history, education, employment, relationships, alcohol and drug use) and contain both static and dynamic factors. It is used on all people under community supervision and on all people in prison with an aggregate sentence of more than six months, including newly sentenced inmates. The Community Impact Assessment, devised by CSNSW using NSW data in 2013, complements the LSI-R by introducing a standardized method by which to assess the consequence of reoffending both to the community and to the organization. In combination with the LSI-R, it is used to focus attention and resources on more serious offenders and is administered by Community Corrections Officers.

The adoption of the RNR framework by CSNSW is all encompassing.

> Across both community and custody the risk, need and responsivity principles of correctional practice (Andrews & Bonta, 2010) are the foundation of all offender assessments, services, and programs. Offender assessments, services, and programs are standardized and accredited to achieve evidence. (Grant et al. 2017: 168)

Greater certainty and efficiency in outcomes through use of these assessments will flow from "improving the intervention potential of Community Corrections officers" (ibid.: 174) and redirecting the focus from non-criminogenic needs and compliance to "specifically addressing attitudes and behavior underpinning their offending" (ibid.: 175). Andrews and Bonta (2010: 58–59) identify the "Big Four" criminogenic needs which predict recidivism as a history of anti-social behavior, anti-social personality, anti-social attitudes or thinking, and anti-social associates, and this finding has driven the CSNSW approach.

> Some criminogenic needs are more common and have a stronger association with reoffending than others. The strongest predictors of criminal behaviour are pro-criminal attitudes and pro-criminal associates (Andrews and Bonta, 2010). These have stronger associations with offending than factors such as substance abuse, dysfunctional families and accommodation, which tend to be viewed as more 'obvious' causes of crime. This is especially relevant for Community Corrections, because most external services focus on addressing these other factors by providing social support, and do not target the underlying attitudes which contribute most to offending. (Grant et al. 2017: 175)

This approach received a major political and funding boost in NSW in 2018, illustrated in the following press release (NSW Government 2018).

> Corrective Services NSW is undertaking the biggest expansion of therapeutic program delivery in the state's history, reinforcing its place among the best correctional systems in the world in its efforts to reduce domestic violence and other reoffending. ... Corrective Services NSW Commissioner Peter Severin said the funding was being used to increase the availability of therapeutic programs to ensure more inmates received treatment and longer doses of it. 'This investment aims to ensure that the right offenders receive the right interventions at the right dosage, in order to achieve maximum reductions in reoffending among the highest risk offenders in the state,' Mr Severin said.

There are a number of features of interest in this enthusiastic proclamation of future directions and of being among world's best practice. One is the political injection of $330 million into prison therapeutic programs, although it should be noted that this is dwarfed by the 2016 allocation of $3.8 billion over four years to add 7000 prison beds by expanding existing prison sites and building new prisons (NSW Government 2016). Another is that the justification for such expenditure is tied to crime reduction aimed at "reoffending among the highest risk offenders in the state". A third is the adoption of the scientistic tone of the medical model, evident in the repetition of the word "dosage". Thus therapeutic programs are compared with drug treatment, the aim being "to ensure that the right offenders receive the right treatment at the right dosage".

Issues Arising from Interviews

Having set the general context, the following section will raise some of the issues which emerged in the project interviews with five NSW post-release accommodation and drug and alcohol/rehabilitation service providers partly funded by CSNSW under the Transitional Support Accommodation program to provide support to people on parole and partly funded by other government agencies.

Problems with the Focus on Recidivism

Various problems with emphasis on recidivism reduction emerged in the interviews with the managers of these agencies which tender for grants and are dependent on CSNSW but are not departmental employees. Direct quotation will be cited simply as AOD (Alcohol and Other Drugs) focus group interviews, and individual organizations and participants will not be identified. The providers were under no illusions that CSNSW's expectation was that "our role is to stabilize them [offenders] so that they don't commit crime. That's what they want us to do" (AOD focus groups interview, 2018). "This is not about the health and well-being of our clients, even though it's a by-product. … This is about stopping reoffending" (ibid.).

The adequacy of recidivism as the key measure of success conflicts with the service providers' concerns around housing, drugs and alcohol, employment, trauma, family and community connection, and so on. "What we actually do is look after the health, safety, welfare, hopes and aspirations of our clients to move back into society in some form" (ibid.). Thus agencies are given a list, "this is what we want you to do", which is at odds with "what we actually do", namely, "find a house, address drug and alcohol issues etc." (ibid.)

An allied problem is the 12-week program focus which derives from risk-based research showing that most reoffending occurs within a 12-week period after release from prison. Where this understanding is institutionalized in rigid program funding cutoffs, allowing only 12 weeks for program services to be delivered, there are clear clashes with service agencies' outreach work and the longer term support needed.

> On paper our stats look good. What does success mean? That's a key question. If we write a success because he has lasted for eight weeks and then gone to accommodation, … that's not necessarily a success. They can still be unstable, undiagnosed, suffering in a whole range of ways. We're being pressured to answer in the paradigm that suits the minister's wishes in terms of recidivism'. (Ibid.)

> That's a problem … their belief that it's the first 12 weeks that counts … the literature from which that was taken also included quite a substantial

argument about the merits of long term support ... and they conveniently ignored that part ... all we're saying, it actually is about a much more longer term process of ... holding the persons' hand. (Ibid.)

The 12-week funding model meant that the considerable outreach, mentoring and other long-term provision by service providers are not funded or not adequately funded. At one agency, for example, there was a peer support program where previous house members returned to engage with current members to tell their stories.

Every Tuesday night we run a peer support group here. The most we've ever had is 34, and these guys can all come back for the spaghetti, ... the guys sitting here in their first three or four weeks in the program, they'll see people coming back to celebrate the seven years of sobriety and hear them say they've got their own house now, they're working, they're doing this, they're doing that. There's nothing I can say that's as powerful as that sort of role modeling and example. We're not actually funded specifically for any of that outreach work. FACS acknowledges we do it and Health acknowledges that we do it. Corrective Services have told me that we got the contract because we provide an awful lot more with no additional funding. (Ibid.)

The various concerns expressed in the interviews about the dominance of recidivism as a measure of effectiveness were consistent with Butts and Schiraldi's (2018: 1) argument that reliance on recidivism is confusing "a complex, bureaucratic indicator of system decision-making with a simple measure of behavior and rehabilitation" and is too simple a measure for the complex process of desistance.

The Effects of the Portal System

It is the LSI-R score which determines who is eligible to undergo the agencies' programs and applications for access to these post-release services are made through a 'portal' system, which attracted criticism on a number of grounds.

First, it meant the agencies lost control over who could be accepted into their programs, which in some cases led to a failure to fill the small number of beds available. Previously, the agencies interviewed people to see how they would fit in with the program, a process which facilitated a more grounded assessment of suitability and fitness in terms of the ethos of the different services. However with that control removed and replaced with the portal system based on the LSI-R, "the criminogenic needs assessment is almost like a formula. It's a formula that Corrective Services apply and if someone hits that criteria, they end up on the portal" (ibid.).

Secondly, the agencies see the emphasis on medium high/high risk offenders as creating distortions, as people who would be suited to the programs move up and down these categories and lose eligibility to enter.

> With the LSI-R there are people I've taken that have been medium who have done 15 to 20 years in gaol, who were hugely institutionalized, but because they've been good during their prison history, their LSI-R, which once was higher, has been reduced. They're now penalized because they're told, "You can't come". (Ibid.)

> Once upon a time we used to be able to do intake directly with inmates, but now we need to go through a portal system. … That portal system is based on their LSI-R rating. So we also take medium high to medium offenders … and they do a risk needs response and then they give us a list of tasks based on that, 'this is what we want you to do', but when they come to us, what we actually do … is … find a house, address drug and alcohol issues. It's all neatly there, but it doesn't encompass all the other things that we do, and one of the big components of that is trauma, particularly for women. (Ibid.)

> It's a dysfunctional competition … we have clients … who have trauma saturated lives, and just because someone is a high it doesn't mean that he will be harder to manage than a medium high. They're real people with real lives and real difficulties'. (Ibid.)

Agencies felt that the LSI-R and RNR formula did not take sufficient account of the centrality of trauma in various forms in the lives of offenders. "Some of the stats that we've been collecting, so far 100% of them have experienced trauma. So when I say that I mean sexual assault, violence, domestic violence or family violence" (ibid.).

The objections of loss of control over admissions, the artificiality of rigid adherence to the risk score rating and the failure to factor in the pervasive effects of trauma are all challenges to the assumption that predictive tools offer more accuracy, reliability and objectivity than personal interaction, engagement and interpretation.

The Lack of Pre-release Support Services

A considerable source of frustration among post-release service providers was the failure to initiate support services in prison prior to release, such as providing ID, access to Centrelink (for social security benefits and assistance), Medicare (state funded health care), a bank account and the like, so that this has to be done post release by the agencies, tasks which take up much of their time and resources better devoted to more intensive supervision. Another complaint was that prisoners were released on "half a cheque, so you only get enough for one week, but its got to last you two weeks" (ibid.).

> Sorting things like their Centrelink and sorting out all these other things ... a lot of this stuff isn't done while people are in custody ... people come out with a half a cheque... They come out with half a cheque. Seriously? And you don't want them to go and rob you? (Ibid.)

Agencies were similarly exasperated that they had to do their own advertising by way of information leaflets and get them into prisons so that prisoners and parole officers could become aware of their programs.

> One of our problems is finding quality referrals, whereas I know that there were 7,000 on the portal to get in to [our service]. We sometimes are struggling to have people actually referred to us and part of the problem is that the parole staff within the gaol system are so overrun, overworked, they don't have time to identify suitable inmates for us. ... We've recently put together a flyer that goes into the gaols ... but ... the majority of parole officers don't know anything about [our service]. (Ibid.)

Such objections highlight the more general problem that while correctional resources can be devoted to conducting risk assessments in prison, the provision of actual services such as accessing psychologists, psychiatrists, counselors and basic pre-release assistance is minimal and non-existent for many.

Tokenism and Imaginary Penalities

The interviews revealed an awareness on the part of the agencies that their services and programs are a drop in the bucket and enable CSNSW to claim they are engaged in intensive support services. The agencies' managers felt that this was a form of tokenism and that they were being used as cover.

> With our three services, Corrective Services are paying lip service to the idea of putting money into post release boards and working with NGOs and providing that but because we are so tiny in terms of the number of people who are being exited from custody every day—its almost as if they keep us around so they can go: 'look, see, that's what we do'. (Ibid.)

> There's only maybe 60/70 beds in the State like us and there's hundreds and thousands of people coming out that need the services. (Ibid.)

Such an awareness of tokenism evokes Pat Carlen's notion of "imaginary penalities" in her influential discussion of "risk crazed governance". Carlen (2008: 1) defined imaginary penalities as:

> Penal policies and practices where agents charged with the authorization, development and/or implementation of systems of punishment address themselves to its principles and persist in manufacturing an elaborate system of costly institutional practices acting 'as if' all objectives are realizable.

Here, at a system-wide level, post-release accommodation-based drug and alcohol rehabilitation services are a form of "imaginary penality" in that they simply do not exist for the vast majority of released offenders, roughly 18,000 per year in NSW (Russell and Sotiri 2018). At the same time on the ground, the small group of agencies who are providing those services to the few lucky enough to gain entry, along with the Extended Reintegration Service program which links released offenders with housing and support services, are attempting, heroically in terms of the limited funding, staffing and resources available to them, to show that rehabilitation beyond criminogenic need is not a complete fiction.

Responsibility, Trust and Accountability

A theme highlighted by the agency managers was the difficulties faced by released offenders in taking responsibility for a range of daily tasks, a responsibility not fostered in the prison where they had been largely infantilized.

> People come to me usually between seven and ten days of having been released from gaol … and say 'Look, I just want to go back to gaol.' And I go 'Why?' and they're 'I can't cope with this, it's just too much responsibility. I'm having to take on too much, I'm full of anxiety, I can't do crowds, I can't do government departments, I can't do Coles [a supermarket]. It's just all too much. I'm overwhelmed'. (Ibid.)

> It's about holding these clients until that extreme anxiety, which is based on a lot of institutionalization, everything's on a plate and they say: 'it was just so much easier in gaol. I didn't have to think about anything. I know the rules. I can just shut myself down almost completely, emotionally, put up my big barriers and I know exactly what's going on. Now I want a much, much richer, fuller, better life than I've ever had, but I'm so fucking scared of how I start getting that right now that I'd rather be back in gaol.' Usually two to three weeks in those guys will have been with us for long enough that they'll start to be able to engage and those kind of big feelings go out the window, but that is the reality for a lot of people that have done a lot of gaol time, given the sort of people they are and the issues they have. (Ibid.)

> Some of the men have been so affected with their mental health/drugs, etc. that prison becomes a reboot. So they go back to prison, they will dry out, they will clean out, they will do whatever to try and get out again. (Ibid.)

Another key task of the agencies was seen as building trust and relationships. This was evident in much of what was said and in what the agencies do in their programs and conduct: "the key thing we do is build relationships with the clients. … Generally in prison it's not about building relationships, it's about containment" (ibid.).

What the agencies are grappling with here is that the mentality and demeanor required to survive in prison (maintain a closed hard front, do not reveal self) is the opposite of that required in a post release support setting (openness, reflexivity, revealing self) and that the transition between the two is difficult and ongoing.

Accountability Cuts Both Ways

Managers also placed a heavy emphasis on accountability, both system and individual. They saw their task as being to assist offenders to take responsibility for the harm they have caused, but also argued that the system take some responsibility to assist them to do this and acknowledge past failures to protect them from harm. In several cases this involved helping house residents prepare submissions to the Royal Commission into Institutional Responses to Child Sexual Abuse (2017).

> Incarceration is not about accountability. It is a very poor model of accountability. We believe as a service in the importance of accountability, meaning where you've caused harm to somebody else or to an organization or property associated with it, you have a responsibility to address that harm to make things better. Locking people up is not an accountability process. (Ibid.)

> Accountability for us is deep accountability, not superficial, they're locked up, they're now paying for their sentence. It is far more than that … the paradigm is safety, respect, responsibility and accountability, and accountability is really about serving the people who have been harmed, not serving a system. (Ibid.)

Reference to system accountability evokes Duff's communicative theory (Duff 2001, 2003) where he argues that community corrections staff can be "moral mediators" (McNeil and Farrall 2015: 159). For, "if personal virtue is partly about the development of good citizenship, then collective virtue is about the character of the polity to which we all belong, for better or worse" (ibid.: 159). Duff argues that the existence of social injustice, and, in consequence, the denial of citizenship to some, creates profound moral problems for the punishing polity. The response must be a "genuine and visible attempt to remedy the injustices and exclusion that they [i.e. some offenders] have suffered" (Duff 2003: 194)

"Systemic Responsivity"

The interviews with the agencies revealed a set of mundane issues and problems, what Taxman (2014: 38) calls "stabilizers and destabilizers". Ideally this chapter would proceed by drawing on interviews with both senior departmental managers and community corrections officers by way of response, but after considering the ethics clearance proposal from the researchers in a process which took nearly one year, CSNSW unexpectedly denied permission to interview any departmental employees. Presumably what they might have said was: there is a huge gap between available resources and what would be necessary to meet recidivism reduction targets, which are unsustainable; only approximately one quarter of all people under CSNSW control receive some kind of intervention; there is a lack of available programs; we target high risk offenders as the most efficient use of limited resources; simply providing social support will not produce fundamental change in offender thinking compared to Cognitive Behavior Therapy (CBT) which does lead to fundamental change.

But in the absence of responses from departmental employees, the chapter will conclude with a brief treatment of five thematic issues arising from the interviews: "systemic responsivity"; the tendency for risk assessment practices to be highly individualizing, bracketing out structural and systemic issues; the need to link risk discourses with the desistance literature; the applicability of risk assessment practices to vulnerable populations; and the extent to which risk assessment practices bolster professional authority and control, precluding a more democratic approach which would empower people to take greater control over their own lives.

While the issues and problems thrown up in the interviews discussed above do not all derive from specific risk practices, they do tend to show that particular risk practices, or at least their inflexible deployment, have distorting and regressive effects on the ability of community service agencies to provide broadly rehabilitative support services and programs in the way they think would be most constructive. The concerns highlight a lack of what Taxman (2014: 38; cited in Brown et al. 2016: 180) calls "systemic responsivity": that programs and services should be provided, be available and be accessible to individuals to participate in.

Risk instruments and the therapeutic programs designed around them are not free floating and self-enforcing; they only take shape and make sense in some wider context of operation. There is a belief apparent in the "dosage" metaphor that risk assessments and their associated therapeutic programs can be "administered", like medicine, and that, assuming the correct dosage, they will produce personal transformations in and of themselves. The ability of those under community supervision such as probation and parole to respond (responsivity) to programs designed to address the precipitating factors of their offending (criminogenic need) in the context of their assessed risk profile (risk) will depend among other factors on whether they are in stable accommodation or are homeless or couch surfing; whether they have family and community support; whether they have access to employment or social service support; whether they are severely traumatized by histories of domestic violence, sexual assault in families and in institutions, alcohol and drug abuse; whether they are in debt; and so on. While some of these factors are addressed in dynamic versions of risk instruments, the momentum in CSNSW risk assessment practice is clearly to focus on individual behavior and attitudinal change to criminogenic needs factors, and, in particular, "pro-criminal attitudes" and "pro-criminal associates". But all the cognitive behavioral change in the world by way of insight into antisocial, addictive and damaging attitudes and behavior will only go so far if someone is released from prison with "half a cheque" and a green garbage bag containing their belongings to join the ranks of homeless living rough in a park (Baldry et al. 2006; Russell and Sotiri 2018).

The Individualizing Tendency of Risk Assessment

There is a fundamental ethical problem lying at the heart of utilizing risk assessment instruments in the criminal justice system. This is that the data gathered to compile the risk scales is aggregate data, the data of a designated population. Thus when an individual is rated on these population derived scales (predominantly based on male Caucasians in North American prisons), they are being treated in part not in and of themselves on the basis of their individual behaviors, attributes, histories and personalities but as points on a population scale compiled from the aggregate data of others. To treat people on the basis of the histories and actions of others infringes the criminal law principle of individual justice which requires that justice, both in sentencing and penalty, be tailored to the individual offender themselves and to their actions and culpability, not to them as a type, example or member of a collective. Otherwise people are being punished for the crimes of others. This fundamental objection tends to be acknowledged briefly in the literature, but then skipped over, such is the 'scientific' appeal of risk assessment. Here in this objection, risk assessment does not treat the individual in their specificity and individual humanity.

Moreover, due process and civil and legal rights are seen as obstructions within the utilitarian calculus of efficiency and certainty as risk increasingly permeates the criminal justice system. General procedural fairness requirements such as protections against discrimination and bias and the ability to comprehend and contest the decision making process all tend to be diminished where decision making is reliant on risk instruments and algorithms that are largely "opaque, inscrutable and incontestable" (McKay 2019: 13).

A second and contrary problem with risk assessment practice, even in its more open 'dynamic' and reflexive form, is that its transaction through CBT and other similar programs isolates the individual, the aim being to change the individual's thinking, their conceptions, responses and behavior at the expense of locating the individual in their wider context. This context includes their background and history, and the social, economic and political forces which have shaped their life chances and pathways. While some of these factors, especially drug and alcohol issues, are encompassed in dynamic varieties of risk assessment practice, the tendency is for engagement with the broader social structural factors to be bracketed out as too difficult, nebulous or beyond the control of change agents such as community corrections officers, or reconceived as individual deficits or non-criminogenic needs. Thus issues such as the prevalence of trauma (and the existence of intergenerational and specific community trauma), along with more mundane issues of access to housing, employment and the provision of a range of services, tend to be set aside as too difficult to address, "always there", too general, insufficiently targeted, economically inefficient or of less immediacy in a political context in which the reduction of recidivism has become the key measure of success. For it is politically preferable that measurable success bolstering claims of increased certainty and efficiency, and thus political capital, be delivered within the short-term electoral cycle.

There is another way in which an individual can be treated not in and of themselves but as a type whose possible reoffending would pose a significant risk, not just to the community but also to the corrections agency and indeed the government. This represents a form of agency or political risk, not often officially acknowledged, although clearly operating at the level of media campaigns, public interest and political legitimacy. A glimpse of political or agency risk can be seen in some risk assessment tools. The NSW CIA, for example, factors in the risk to the organizational integrity of CSNSW as an agency. In the Scoring Guide to the CIA (CSNSW 2013: 12), it is noted:

Due to the high levels of public and media interest in this category, re-offence committed by sex offenders can also represent risk to the integrity of the agency. This political risk, whilst it cannot be ignored, should not be given undue weighting.

By way of explanation, the Guide (ibid.: 22) asks in Item 12:

is the offender of significant media or political interest? … Although public interest is often inconsistent and dependent on factors unrelated to offending behaviour, the repercussions of adverse publicity can have consequences for offender management across CSNSW. (Ibid.)

This is certainly true, as illustrated by the fact that high-profile cases, involving notorious defendants or the commission of horrific rapes and homicides by people on bail or parole, such as those of Julian Knight, Craig Minogue, Adrian Bayley, Sean Price, Dimitrious Gargasoulas and Yacqub Khayre in Victoria and Man Haron Monis in NSW have led to legislative change in parole and bail (Bartels 2013; Brown and Quilter 2014; Freiberg et al. 2018; Moffa et al. 2019).

The acknowledgment by CSNSW that agency and political risk are factors in the overall risk assessment process and the numerous examples of legal changes to bail, parole and community sanctions eligibility brought about by high-profile cases of reoffending cut across portrayals of the risk assessment process as a science, a neutral, value-free, technical stand-alone exercise. That governments' and correctional agencies' own reputational risk management is incorporated in offenders' risk assessments shows how deeply risk assessment is embedded in the wider political context which suffuses and shapes the risk assessment process.

Linking Risk Assessment and Desistance Theory

Further, risk assessment needs to be connected to and integrated with developments in desistance theory and practice (McNeil 2006; McNeil et al. 2012), for the two discourses have tended to travel in tandem and require integration. Digging down into the issues raised by the community corrections agencies outlined above, it is apparent that risk assessment technologies and practices need to be (re)connected with the broader concerns evident in the recent desistance literature (Ward and Maruna 2007). Among the insights that desistance approaches bring to the table are the recognition that it is a process—an individual, social and political process—which goes well beyond the cessation of criminal behavior to issues of identity and belonging, social integration and reciprocity, and the issue, as McNeill notes, of "what people desist *into*" (2016: 153). This question ushers in concepts of "citizenship, integration and solidarity" (ibid.), notions that cannot be adequately addressed in terms of an individual trajectory or biography. As Raynor (2016: 41) remarks: "the reduction of antisocial behavior is more likely to happen in pro-social communities".

Issues like accountability and responsibility raised in the interviews cannot be located only in the individual offender but involve examining the responsibility and accountability of the state and of government agencies to the offender, in short an exercise in state 'reflexivity'. This requires acknowledging past failures in service provision and the failure to alleviate and redress criminogenic environments and histories. These include the damaging consequences of incarceration, child removal, institutional sexual assault and abuse, homelessness, police targeting and racial profiling, as well as the importance of treating people fairly and with respect as a step to building trust and reflexivity in the individual. In short, the lens must be focused not only on the individual but also on the wider social structures and, more specifically, on the processes and practices of criminal justice agencies, to ensure that the pursuit of virtue is seen as a social project involving the whole polity, and not something to be foisted on an excluded and marginalized group who are responsibilized as the sole authors of their own destiny. This is even more imperative where service provision is being cut, privatized or devolved onto inadequately funded NGOs or community groups. Otherwise, as Trotter et al. point out: "social issues such as poverty, unemployment and social disorganization are turned into individual deficits" (2016: 242).

Risk Assessment and Vulnerable Populations

Penality, more generally, and the criminal justice system and its forms of punishment, more specifically, bear disproportionately on communities of vulnerability. Community sanctions are constructed in specific ways and have different meanings and effects for people who suffer from intellectual and physical disability, certain Indigenous communities and peoples, people with disabilities, marginalized women and young people. Not only are people in these groups disproportionately likely, for a range of reasons, to become subject to the criminal justice system, but the operation of different community sanctions and their availability are experienced and lived out in very different and specific ways.

An example of the gap between the way different groups in society experience different community sanctions is financial penalties. Leading risk theorist Pat O'Malley has explored financial penalties as a form of "monetized" or "simulated" justice, a technology of freedom suited to a

consumer society (O'Malley 2009a, b, c, 2010). He characterizes financial penalties as "a form of 'simulated' governance that regulates 'flows
and circulations' or 'traces'" (O'Malley 2010: 796). Financial penalties
have "been designed … to cause as little disturbance as possible to the
circulation of valued bodies, utilities and things" (ibid.). In O'Malley's
account, it is a form of governance and "justice" which for most people
becomes just another cost, price or license, "empty of content" and largely
"stripped of moral meaning or any element of condemnation" (Quilter
and Hogg 2018: 16). O'Malley's analysis is theoretically sophisticated
but it neglects the damaging and punitive effects of monetary penalties
on specific groups who do not enjoy full access to, and the benefits of, the
consumer society, their marginality and precariousness exacerbated at a
time of increasing inequalities (Brown et al. 2017; Quilter and Hogg
2018). These consequences can include crippling debt, loss of employment and housing, incarceration and death in custody (Clarke et al.
2009; Williams and Gilbert 2011; Porter 2016).

There is an expanding literature on the way risk and need are both
racialized and gendered (Smith et al. 2009; Hannah-Moffatt 2009; Shaw
and Hannah-Moffat 2013; Van Voorhis 2012). Hannah-Moffatt (2009)
argues that "gender neutral'" assessments build male-based normative criteria into risk instruments, obscuring the gendered context of women's
offending, characterized by their economic marginalization and histories
of victimization and abuse. Similar arguments have been made in relation
to ethnicity and race, noting the tendency for "needs" and structural disadvantage to be reconceptualized as "risks" (Shepherd et al. 2014; Wilson
and Gutierrez 2014; Day et al. 2003; Crenshaw 2012). This has led in
some instances to Aboriginality, for example, being treated as a risk factor.
In NSW, The Group Risk Assessment Model (GRAM 2) identifies
"indigenous status" as one of 13 static risk factors in the prediction of
reoffending (Stavrou and Poyton 2016: 3). Citing this example, Cunneen
(2019: 11) argues that "racialized young people become defined through
their membership of a risk-defined group", so that risk assessment processes "reconfigure the experiences of discrimination, inequality and a
pro-active, interventionist justice system into high risk scores. High risk
scores foreshadow greater intervention which itself further compounds
discrimination and marginalization" (12).

Democracy, Professionalization and Social Justice

Much of the risk assessment literature concentrates on the importance of improving professional assessment and supervision techniques and practices (Trotter 2012). But without a strong democratic component, such moves can tend to further entrench professional knowledges, control and power, at the expense of client and community-centered definitions and approaches. Recruitment into activism in community organizations and social movements around criminal justice issues and post-release services arguably has demonstrable "therapeutic" effects, as "ex-offenders" and "criminals" become "citizens", engaged in political struggle over their own destinies. If the road to desistance, recovery and living a "good life" involves becoming an active subject, engaged in both a personal and a broader struggle within wider social structures, then more attention must be devoted to the ways in which "clients" are and can be further engaged in these processes, especially in defining their problems and issues rather than being simply played upon by government and professionals. In short, a political engagement in the name of social justice must address power differentials and inequality in the ability of different agents and groups to define problems and issues and to be heard and listened to in struggles over their amelioration. A step in this direction is the mentoring movement involving former prisoners, drug users, etc. in various support roles and beyond that being employed as community corrections officers or in service agencies and in running self-help groups and community organizations. Without such involvement trust issues tend to fester.

Conclusion

The widespread adoption of risk assessment instruments and practices in community sanctions has been founded in an RNR framework. Its formal objective has been to increase criminal justice efficiency and certainty, thereby answering the increased political emphasis on the need to reduce recidivism. In reality, though, it has opened up the potential revival of notions of rehabilitation and of a shift in the ethos of community corrections officers, from compliance managers to therapeutic agents. Interviews with a group of Sydney-based rehabilitation service providers threw up a number of issues such as the limits of using recidivism as the key measure of success; the artificial nature of reliance on the LSI-R offender risk profiles and the portal in determining eligibility to their programs; the rigid nature of funding limited to a 12-week cycle; the need for a longer term commitment to outreach services; the paucity of pre-release and post-release services; the centrality of trauma in the lives of released offenders; the importance of building relationships and trust; and developing responsibility and accountability that cuts both ways.

The comments of the service providers were broadened out into a set of more general themes: "systemic responsivity", the individualizing tendency of risk assessment and the inclusion of political risk as a factor; the need to link risk assessment and desistance theory; the problematic nature of risk assessment for vulnerable populations; and the social justice implications of the professionalization attendant on risk assessment practice.

If the potential reconfiguration of community sanctions in the direction of a genuinely therapeutic and rehabilitative practice is to be realized it will be necessary to grapple with these and other issues. In particular, the shift in focus away from service provision and tangible assistance in the post-release phase in favor of a concentration on individual cognitive behavioral change to attitudes and associations, conducted under the rubric of evidence-based practice, obscures the link between crime and social structure, and thereby absolves corrections agencies and governments from responsibility for some of the consequences of inadequate social provision.

The community post-release service managers interviewed for this study are grappling daily with the tension between political demands for the efficiency, certainty and security supposedly to be delivered through the use of risk instruments, and the lived experience of the social, economic and political marginality inhabited by the people they seek to assist. Despite being schooled in the benefits of the new risk technologies and enticed by the allure of the "transformative risk subject", these agencies and their workers retain a reflexive skepticism toward risk's "scientific" claims along with a residual commitment to the helping values of an older, penal welfare habitus, and to the prospect of a revival of rehabilitation beyond "criminogenic need".

Notes

1. The Rethinking Community Sanctions Project is an ARC-funded project conducted by Julie Stubbs, Eileen Baldry, David Brown, Chris Cunneen, Sophie Russell and Melanie Schwartz.
2. For a report on the workshop see: Melanie Schwartz, Sophie Russell, Eileen Baldry, David Brown, Chris Cunneen and Julie Stubbs, *Obstacles to Effective Support of People Released from Prison: Wisdom from the Field* (Rethinking Community Sanctions Project, UNSW, 2020).

References

Andrews, D. and Bonta, J. (1995) *The Level of Service Inventory – Revised*, Multi-Health Systems, Toronto.

Andrews, D. and Bonta, J. (2010) *The Psychology of Criminal Conduct* (5th ed.), Matthew Bender & Company Inc., New Providence, NJ.

Baldry, E., McDonnell, D., Maplestone, P. and Peeters, M. (2006) 'Ex-prisoners, Homelessness and the State in Australia', *Australian and New Zealand Journal of Criminology*, 39(1), 20–33.

Bartels, L. (2013) 'Parole and parole authorities in Australia: a system in crisis?' *Crim LJ*, 37, 357–376.

Brown, D. and Quilter, J. (2014) 'Speaking Too Soon: The Sabotage of Bail Reform in NSW', *International Journal for Crime, Justice and Social Democracy*, 3, 4–28.

Brown, D., Cunneen, C., Schwartz, M., Stubbs, J. and Young, C. (2016) *Justice Reinvestment: Winding Back Imprisonment*, Palgrave Macmillan, Basingstoke.

Brown, D., Cunneen, C. and Russell, S. (2017) 'It's All About the Benjamins: Infringement Notices and Young People in NSW', *Alternative Law Journal*, 42(4), 253–260.

Butts, J. A. and Schiraldi, V. (2018) 'Recidivism Reconsidered: Preserving the Community Justice Mission of Community Corrections', Harvard Kennedy School, https://www.hks.harvard.edu/sites/default/files/centers/wiener/programs/pcj/files/recidivism_reconsidered.pdf. Accessed 26 April 2019.

Carlen, P. (2008) Imaginary penalties and risk crazed governance, in P. Carlen (ed.) *Imaginary Penalties*. Willan Publishing: Cullompton, Devon.

Clarke, S., Forrell, S. and McCarron, E. (2009) *Fine but not fair: Fines and disadvantage*, Law and Justice Foundation of NSW, Sydney.

Corrective Services NSW (2006) *NSW Compendium of Offender Assessments*, 4th edn, Assessment and Case Management Support Team, NSW Department of Justice: Sydney.

Corrective Services NSW (2013) *Community Impact Assessment Scoring Guide*, Offender Assessment Unit, https://www.dropbox.com/home/community%20corrections/Risk?preview=Community+Impact+Assessment+Scoring+Guide+-+Version+1+-+March+2013.PDF. Accessed 28 April 2019.

Crenshaw, K. W. (2012) 'From Private Violence to Mass Incarceration: Thinking Intersectionally about Women, Race and Social Control', *UCLA Law Review*, 59(6), 1418–1472.

Cunneen, C. (2019) 'Youth Justice and Racialization: Comparative Reflections', *Theoretical Criminology*, 1–19. https://journals.sagepub.com/doi/pdf/10.1177/1362480619889039.

Day, A., Howells, K. and Casey, S. (2003) 'The Rehabilitation of Indigenous Prisoners: An Australian Perspective', *Journal of Ethnicity in Criminal Justice*, 1(1), 115–133.

Duff, A. (2001) *Punishment, communication and community*, New York, NY: Oxford University Press.

Duff, A. (2003) 'Probation, punishment and restorative justice: should altruism be engaged in punishment? *The Howard Journal*, 42(1), 181–197.

Feeley, M. and Simon, J. (1992) 'The New Penology: Notes on the Emerging Strategy of Corrections and its Implications', *Criminology*, 30(4), 449–474.

Freiberg, A., Bartels, L., Fitzgerald, R., and Dodd, S. (2018) 'Parole, politics and penal policy', *Queensland University of Technology Law Review*, 18(1), 1–26.

Grant, L., Martin, AM., Caruana, R., Ware, J. and Hainsworth, J. (2017) 'Enhancing the Quality of programs and Supervision to Reduce Reoffending in New South Wales', *Advancing Corrections Journal*, Edition 3, 167–182.

Hannah-Moffatt, K. (1999) 'Moral agent or actuarial subject: Risk and Canadian women's imprisonment', *Theoretical Criminology*, 3(1), 71–94.

Hannah-Moffat, K. (2005) 'Criminogenic needs and the transformative risk subject: Hybridizations of risk/need in penality', *Punishment and Society*, 7(1), 29–51.

Hannah-Moffatt, K. (2009) 'Gridlock or Mutability: Reconsidering "Gender" and Risk Assessment', *Criminology and Public Policy*, 8(1), 209–219.

Maurutto, P. and Hannah-Moffat, K. (2006) 'Assembling Risk and the Restructuring of Penal Control', *British Journal of Criminology*, 46(3), 438–454.

McKay, C. (2019) 'Predicting risk in criminal procedure: actuarial tools, algorithms, AI and judicial decision-making', *Current Issues in Criminal Justice*. https://doi.org/10.1080/10345329.2019.1658694.

McNeil, F. (2006) 'A desistance paradigm for offender management', *Criminology and Criminal Justice*, 6(1), 39–62.

McNeil, F. (2016) The Collateral Consequences of Risk, in C. Trotter, G. McIvor and F. McNeil (eds) *Beyond the Risk Paradigm in Criminal Justice*, Palgrave, London.

McNeil, F. and Farrall, S. (2015) 'A moral in the story? Virtues, values and desistance from crime', in M. Cowburn, M. Duggan, A. Robinson and P. Senior (eds) *Values in Criminology and Community Justice*, Policy Press, Bristol.

McNeil, F., Farrell, S., Lightowler, C. and Maruna, S. (2012) 'Re-examining Evidence-Based Practice in Community Corrections: Beyond "A Confined View" of What Works', *Justice Research and Policy*, 14(1), 35–60.

Moffa, M., Stratton, G., & Ruyters, M. (2019) 'Parole populism: The politicization of parole in Victoria', *Current Issues in Criminal Justice*, 31(1), 75–90.

NSW Government (2016) Press release, 'NSW Budget: New prisoner beds, record corrections funding', 16 June, https://www.justice.nsw.gov.au/Pages/media-news/media-releases/2016/NSW-Budget-New-prisoner-beds-record-corrections-funding.aspx. Accessed 26 April.

NSW Government (2018) Media Release: 'NSW among world's best in inmate programs', https://www.justice.nsw.gov.au/Documents/Media%20Releases/2018/CSNSW-amongst-worlds-best-inmate-programs.pdf. Accessed 25 April 2019.

O'Malley, P. (2009a) 'Fines, Risks and Damages: Money Sanctions and Justice in Control Societies', *Current Issues in Criminal Justice*, 21(3), 365–381.

O'Malley, P. (2009b) *The Currency of Justice: Fines and Damages in Consumer Societies,* Oxford: Routledge-Cavendish.

O'Malley, P. (2009c) 'Theorizing Fines', *Punishment and Society*, 11(1), 67–83.

O'Malley, P. (2010) 'Simulated Justice: Risk, money and telemetric policing', *British Journal of Criminology* 50, 795–807.

Porter, A. (2016) 'Reflections on the coronial inquest of Ms Dhu', *Human Rights Defender*, 25(3), 8–11.

Quilter, J. and Hogg, R. (2018) 'The Hidden Punitiveness of Fines', *International Journal for Crime, Justice and Social Democracy*, 7(3), 9–40.

Raynor, P. (2016) 'Three Narratives of Risk: Corrections, Critique and Context', in C. Trotter, G. McIvor and F. McNeill (eds) *Beyond the Risk Paradigm in Criminal Justice,* Palgrave, London.

Robinson, G. (2016) 'The Rise of the Risk Paradigm in Criminal Justice', in Trotter, G. McIvor and F. McNeill (eds) *Beyond the Risk Paradigm in Criminal Justice,* Palgrave, London.

Royal Commission into Institutional Responses to Child Sexual Abuse (2017) *Final Report*, AGPS: Canberra. https://www.childabuseroyalcommission.gov. au/final-report. Accessed 29 April 2019.

Russell, S. and Sotiri, M. (2018) 'How we can put a stop to the revolving door between homelessness and imprisonment', *The Conversation*, February 19.

Shaw, M. and Hannah-Moffat, K. (2013) How Cognitive Skills Forget About Gender and Diversity. In Mair, G. (ed) *What Matters in Probation*. Cullompton: Willan Publishing.

Shepherd, S., Walker, R., McEntyre, E. and Adams, Y. (2014) 'Violence Risk Assessment in Australian Aboriginal Offender Populations: A Review of the Literature', *Psychology Public Policy and Law*, 20(3), 281–293.

Smith, P., Cullen, F. and Latessa, E. (2009) 'Can 14,737 Women be Wrong? A Meta-Analysis of the LSI-R and Recidivism for Female Offenders', *Criminology and Public Policy*, 8(1), 183–208.

Stavrou, E. and Poyton, S. (2016) 'The Revised Group Risk Assessment Model (GRAM 2): Assessing risk of reoffending among adults given non-custodial sanctions', *Crime and Justice Bulletin*, 197. Sydney: Bureau of Crime Statistics and Research.

Taxman, F. (2014) 'Second Generation of RNR: The Importance of Systemic Responsivity in Expanding Core Principles of Responsivity', *Federal Probation*, 78(2), 32–40.

Trotter, C. (2012) Effective Community-based supervision of young offenders. *Trends & Issues in Crime & Criminal Justice*. No. 448.

Trotter, C., McIvor, G., and McNeil, F. (2016) 'Changing Risks, Risking Change', in Trotter et al. (eds) *Beyond the Risk Paradigm in Criminal Justice*, Palgrave, London.

Van Voorhis, P. (2012) 'On Behalf of Women Offenders: Women's Place in the Science of Evidence-Based Practice', *Criminology and Public Policy*, 11(2) 11–45.

Ward, T. and Maruna, S. (2007) *Rehabilitation: Beyond the Risk Paradigm*, Routledge, London.

Williams, M.S., and Gilbert, R. (2011) *Reducing the Unintended Impacts of Fines*, Indigenous Justice Clearinghouse.

Wilson, H. and Gutierrez, L. (2014) 'Does One Size Fit All? A Meta-Analysis Examining the Predictive Ability of the Level of Service Inventory (LSI) with Aboriginal Offenders', *Criminal Justice and Behavior*, 41(2), 196–219.

Character Retribution as a Brake on Risk-Driven Criminal Justice

Netanel Dagan and Hadar Dancig-Rosenberg

Introduction

This chapter explores the role of "character retribution" theory as a means of limiting the utilitarian breaches of human rights posed by risk-based sentencing. Through analyzing parole decision-making in the USA and Israel, this chapter will demonstrate how incorporating character retribution considerations into the sentencing discourse might, in fact, thwart some of the inherent dangers of allowing risk to determine criminal justice outcomes.

Recent decades have produced volatile penal theory and policy (O'Malley 1999; Simon 2005), but since the 1970s, the hegemonic

N. Dagan (✉)
Institute of Criminology, Faculty of law, The Hebrew University of Jerusalem, Jerusalem, Israel
e-mail: netanel.dagan@mail.huji.ac.il

H. Dancig-Rosenberg
Faculty of Law, Bar-Ilan University, Ramat Gan, Israel
e-mail: Hadar.Rosenberg@biu.ac.il

© The Author(s) 2020
J. Pratt, J. Anderson (eds.), *Criminal Justice, Risk and the Revolt against Uncertainty*,
Palgrave Studies in Risk, Crime and Society,
https://doi.org/10.1007/978-3-030-37948-3_4

rehabilitative penology has been replaced mainly by retributive ideology (von Hirsch 2017; Pratt 2007). Indeed, in many Western jurisdictions, sentencing policy is based on proportionality, usually as part of limiting retributivism (Tonry 2018).[1]

However, retributivism is certainly not alone in the penal field today. Scholars have argued that current sentencing practice has been based not on proportionality, but on penal excesses, ranging from "incarceration mania" (Harcourt 2009; Garland 2001) to risk prevention in the form of controls on many who have not even committed a crime. In recent years, preventive penal strategies have been part of the arsenal of many Western states such as the USA, United Kingdom, Australia, Germany, France, and Israel (Ashworth and Zedner 2014). Civil, administrative, and executive preventive orders are prevalent in many common law systems. The "culture of control" (Garland 2001), the "new penology" (Feeley and Simon 1992), and "managerial" and "actuarial justice" (Feeley and Simon 1994) are some of the conceptual tools that aim to identify significant developments in criminal justice as constituent parts of a larger phenomenon that signals the rise of the "Preventive State" (Ashworth and Zedner 2014). State security laws, preventive orders, policies, and practices are not unrelated and, in different ways, are all motivated by the same preventive impetus to minimize risks and future harms. The rise of preventive sentencing manifests itself in various ways such as extended sentences of preventive, indefinite, and whole-life sentences for dangerous offenders as well the range of ordinances and similar restrictions on much lower levels of disorder, justified on the basis that, if left alone, these will only lead on to more serious crimes (Wilson and Kelling 1982; Harcourt 2009).

Wide scholarly attention has been focused on the growing use of risk technologies at each stage of the criminal process, from profiling by police and risk assessment with respect to pretrial detention and at sentencing to risk-based decisions with respect to sentencing and parole (Zedner and Ashworth 2019).

Philosophical, legal, and criminological scholarship explores the tension between preventive justice and human rights describing the relations between the fields as conflicting (e.g., Murphy and Whitty 2007; Ashworth and Zedner 2014). Scholars often emphasize that preventive justice does raise normative concerns, such as sentencing based on a fear of what individuals might do, not as a sanction for what they have done. In addition, with respect to autonomy and free will, past sanctions consider the fact that the defendant chose to perform in a punishable manner, which eliminates the impact on their autonomy when imposing the punishment. Therefore, sanctions based on predictions dismiss the individual's autonomy and free will by determining the individual is not able to conform to society's normative expectations (Ashworth and Zedner 2014; von Hirsch 2017). Finally, imposing sanctions for future acts raises the danger of selective sentencing based on gender, race, or ethnicity. Selective sentencing worsens when considering that predicting what a person might do is based, almost by necessity, on generalizing groups and individuals. The norm that determines that when judging people on their past acts, we should not judge their status, is not in play when using predictions (Ashworth and Zedner 2014; Monahan and Skeem 2016). Those problems are especially stressed in an age of "penal populism" (Pratt 2007). The law-based, political institutions in many democratic societies are being challenged by fast-growing populist movements, parties, and leaders, while policy-makers and legislators often define crime as the biggest problem in society, and have favored extreme preventive measures. There are normative tensions between those who seek ever more governmental powers to bolster national security and defense, and those who hold that such concentrations of power undermine their rights that call for a balance between individual rights and social responsibilities (Etzioni 2018; Pratt and Miao 2018). In short, currently, the tension between human rights and the will to protect the general public is prominent.

Other tendencies which are traditionally described as normatively conflicting are the risk-based sentencing and retributive justice. Preventive justice may lead to disproportionate and unfair sentences that do not necessarily reflect the seriousness of the past offense (Ashworth and Zedner 2014; von Hirsch 2017). However, the possible interrelation of risk and retributivism has received, so far, less attention. That is especially true for "softer" and more expansive versions of retributivism—such as character retributivism, which this chapter will focus on.

A good starting point is a classic version of retributivism—just desert (von Hirsch 1976). Just desert, a dominant retributivist penal theory from the second half of the twentieth century, is based on a demand for proportionality between the seriousness of the offense and the severity of the punishment, measured by harm and culpability. It usually ignores the personal characteristics of the offender, as long as they are not directly related to the assessment of the severity of the offense. According to just desert theory, consideration of the offender's post-offense personal characteristics is perceived, usually, as irrelevant to the seriousness of the past offense. Calibrating the sentence based on risk factors that are unrelated directly to the seriousness of the past offense may harm fairness and equality, and convey a misleading social message about the real severity of the offense (von Hirsch 1976; von Hirsch and Ashworth 2005).

In contrast with just desert, character retribution theory suggests a *softer* concept of retribution (Murphy 2003). Character retribution expands the concept of the offender's culpability, thereby extending the relevant time frame for assessing the deserved punishment beyond the sentencing moment (Dancig-Rosenberg and Dagan 2018). The relations between softer versions of retribution and risk have received relatively little attention to date. Although philosophers and criminal law theorists are usually attracted to normative questions regarding proportionality in sentencing, criminologists and sociologists are interested in questions of risk (Murphy and Whitty 2007).

This chapter explores the relatively neglected intersection between risk and character retribution considerations, showing its importance both for risk-driven criminal justice and for retributive justice alike. We analyze the US and Israeli sentencing and parole case laws to demonstrate how risk, just desert, and character retribution considerations are used "in action" to support the legal decisions. As we shall show, in some cases, just desert, character retribution, and risk-based considerations complement each other, whereas in other cases they are in conflict. We hypothesize why courts need *both* risk and character retribution reasons to reach their decisions. In other words, we suggest why courts need an additional perspective of character retributivism to support their decisions beyond the "traditional" discourses of risk and just desert. We suggest that each of the traditional discourses alone, risk-based and just desert-based, suffers from weaknesses and does not fully reflect the circumstances of the offender and of the offense. Character retributive analysis provides an additional normative lens for viewing the case, helping the legal decision-maker exhaust its complexity and to advance its legitimacy in the eyes of decision-makers, crime victims, and the wider public. Finally, we discuss the normative and practical meanings of the intersection between risk assessment and character retribution and show that character retributivism might sometimes function as a brake on risk-driven criminal justice system in an era of mass incarceration.

Risk and Just Desert as Conflicting Theories

Criminal law is, among others, a blaming institution, in which criminal convictions and sanctions properly convey censure both to offender and to public (von Hirsch 2017). Expressions of blame serve to recognize the importance of the rights violated by the offense and to confirm the offender's responsibility, by treating them as a responsible moral agent, capable of differentiating between right and wrong. In such a system, the relative severity of sanctions imposed on various offenders must be closely correlated with the harm and blameworthiness of the offenders ("ordinal proportionality"), so that equally culpable offenders receive equally severe sanctions. This principle is known as the requirement of parity (Frase 1997; von Hirsch 2017).

Risk-based sentencing is based on clinical prediction or actuarial risk-assessment tools (Frase 1997; Robinson 2001; von Hirsch 2017). Risk-based sentencing and just desert are traditionally perceived as normatively conflicting because whereas the former seeks to achieve the utilitarian goal of reducing crime, thereby providing security, the latter follows a censure-based, backward-looking rationale (Roberts and Maslen 2015). The censure-based argument for proportionality assumes the existence of a sanction that connotes censure or blame (Raynor 2016; von Hirsch 2017). From a just desert perspective, risk prediction is an unacceptable basis for suspending the liberty of a person who does not otherwise deserve prison as punishment (Simon 2005). Indeed, if two equally blameworthy offenders commit the same crime but one poses a higher risk of future reoffending, then putting the low-risk offender on probation and sending the high-risk offender to prison may effectively promote public safety. From a retributive perspective, however, this produces disparate, disproportionate, and unfair sentences, and undercuts the normative value of criminal law (Frase 2013; von Hirsch 2017).

Risk and just desert, therefore, are normatively perceived as distinct criteria because "they inevitably distribute liability and punishment differently. To advance one, the system must sacrifice the other" (Robinson 2001: 1441). In other words, the drive to public protection from risk might come at the expense of the protection of individual rights. As a result, if criminal justice is defined strictly according to the tenets of just desert, taking into account post-sentence conduct as part of risk-based sentencing is unjustifiable (Slobogin 2011; von Hirsch 2017; Monahan and Skeem 2016).[2] In a similar vein, Monahan (2006: 396) argued that:

> Assessing the likelihood of future crime is jurisprudentially irrelevant to sentencing under the backward-looking principle of punishment as just deserts, but is a central task of sentencing under the forward-looking principle of crime control.

One may argue that despite their distinct normative standpoints, in practice, both just desert and risk considerations may occasionally lead to the same sentence, as, for example, in the case of a high-risk offender who intentionally committed a severe violent crime. According to both theories, the desired sentence may be a severe one: from a just desert perspective, the offender deserves a sentence proportionate to the severity of the offense and to the high blameworthiness of the offender; from a risk-based perspective, the offender should be incapacitated for a substantial period of time, to prevent him from harming others. It is important, therefore, to distinguish between the *practical consequences* of sentencing based on just desert and risk, and the *normative justifications* underlying each group of sentencing considerations. The fact that both theories may at times support the same sentence should not blur the substantial distinctions between the rationales that stand behind each of them.

What would be the case if one adopted a *softer* conception of retributivism, such as character retribution? Would the interrelations between risk prevention discourse and character retribution be the same as those between the former and just desert? We will argue that the answer to this question is complicated by the nature of character retribution.

Character Retributivism

Character retribution theory is based on a retributive rationale, but it allows taking into consideration the offender's post-offense conduct as well. Some penal theorists have made the argument that a convincing theory of criminal culpability cannot be based only on the culpability of particular acts. Instead, they suggest the need to develop a theory of blame for character revealed by the criminal act in question (Murphy 2003; Whitman 2014). The drive to punish people among us because they are fundamentally "bad" leads criminal theorists to premise punishment on underlying character. In order to do so, criminal acts are used to measure the underlying immoral character traits of the criminal offender (Yankah 2003). Character theorists have argued that we blame "bad persons" for their inner badness (Murphy 2003; Whitman 2014). According to the theory of character retributivism, retribution should be a function not merely of wrongful conduct but of the quality of the offender's underlying moral character (Murphy 2003). According to just desert theory, the concept of culpability is static and backward-looking. By contrast, character retribution proposes not to focus exclusively on the moment of weakness during the commission of the offense, but rather to examine the entire moral personality of the offender, to determine the proportionate punishment. In other words, punishment should be proportionate to the offender's inner weakness. Character retributivism, therefore, makes a broader judgment about the totality of the offender's moral being (Whitman 2014; Dancig-Rosenberg and Dagan 2018).

According to one of the foremost versions of character retribution that has been developed, punishment should take into account the character that the offender has developed over time, including positive post-offense changes in the offender's personality. For example, by taking responsibility, by showing remorse, regret, penance, or apology, by making amends, or by paying compensation to the crime victim, the offender may transform themselves into a meaningfully different person who deserves less penal censure. Such an approach expands the relevant time frame for assessing the deserved punishment, so that both offense and the offender's post-offense circumstances carried out by him are considered relevant (Whitman 2003; Smith 2016).

On one hand, character retribution shares with just desert theory the retributive rationale as a sole justification for punishment, the requirement of proportionality, and the backward-looking focus on the severity of the offense. On the other hand, character retribution shares with risk-based sentencing the possibility of also taking into account post-offense conduct, but as part of assessing the proportional punishment, rather than of focusing on utilitarian considerations (Dancig-Rosenberg and Dagan 2018). We conceptualized elsewhere character retribution as a part of a broader trend in punishment theories. This trend, which we termed *retributarianism*, suggests an individualization of punishment based on a retributive rationale (Dancig-Rosenberg and Dagan 2018).

Character retributivism raises, no doubt, theoretical, normative, and practical problems for modern, liberal criminal justice system. Some argue that punishing offenders because they are "bad" people is unjust since it ignores the critical difference between what is legitimate in personal moral judgment and in political morality. Also, focusing on criminally liable autonomous choices, the law recognizes the difficulty of truly measuring a person's character. Furthermore, it may be argued that there are difficult questions concerning the extent to which character can be thought to truly dictate action. Another critique is raised from the risk of an enquiry into the offender's character as part of a liberal and secular criminal justice system (Yankah 2003). While we cannot address these complex problems here, our aim is to explore the role of that theory "in action" by using parole as a case study which typically involves risk considerations.

Just Desert, Character Retribution, and Risk in Action: Parole as a Case Study

Despite their contradicting theoretical orientations, character retribution and risk-based discourse may, in practice, intertwine. In the sentencing and parole cases discussed below, the court expanded the analysis, beyond questions of risk and rehabilitation, to include factors that are character-oriented in nature as part of its decision whether or not to grant the prisoner an early release. Parole is an instructive case study for examining retribution-based considerations because such cases are typically judged on risk-based considerations (Medwed 2007). When an offender applies to be released on parole, often many years after the sentencing hearing, the considerations of the parole decision and the objectives of the process usually depend on two principal questions: (a) does the prisoner pose a significant risk to the community, and (b) will his conditional release promote his rehabilitation (Medwed 2007; Roberts 2009). Retributive considerations do not seem to be relevant to either of these questions. At best, the severity of the offense at the time of its commission may be used as a reason for rejecting a prisoner's application for parole (usually in serious cases, e.g., Paratore 2016). However, as we shall argue, character retributive considerations based on post-sentencing changes while the offender is serving the sentence may have a role in parole jurisprudence. In practice, therefore, character retributive arguments are also part of the parole decision-making process. Parole cases illustrate how risk-based discourse may combine character retributive terminology, despite the different philosophical rationales of risk and character retribution considerations (utilitarian versus deontological).[3]

Character retribution reasoning, as part of parole analysis, is found in the landmark case of *Graham v Florida*, 560 U.S. 48 (2010), where the US Supreme court held that sentencing a juvenile to life imprisonment without possibility of parole for crimes other than murder violates the Eighth Amendment ban on cruel and unusual punishment. The court reached the conclusion that life without parole conflicts with just desert because juveniles are less deserving of the most serious forms of punishment owing to their lesser culpability. The court held also that retribution does not justify imposing the second most severe penalty on the less culpable juvenile non-homicide offender. Although risk-based incapacitation may be a legitimate penological goal, sufficient to justify life imprisonment without parole in other circumstances, it is inadequate for justifying this punishment for juveniles who did not commit homicide. Justifying life imprisonment without parole on the assumption that the juvenile offender will forever be a danger to society requires the sentencing judge to reach the decision that the juvenile is incorrigible, whereas "incorrigibility is inconsistent with youth" (p. 2029). The court added that from Graham's previous offense, "it does not follow that he would be a risk to society for the rest of his life" (p. 2029). This decision reflects the court's willingness to challenge risk-based utilitarianism in favor of the protection of individual rights of juvenile non-homicide offenders.

The court also raised a character retributivism-based argument against life imprisonment without parole, stating that "[t]his sentence … means that good behavior and character improvement are immaterial," and explained:

> Terrance Graham's sentence guarantees he will die in prison without any meaningful opportunity to obtain release, no matter what he might do to demonstrate that the bad acts he committed as a teenager are not representative of his true character, even if he spends the next half century attempting to atone for his crimes and learn from his mistakes. The State has denied him any chance to later demonstrate that he is fit to rejoin society based solely on a nonhomicide crime that he committed while he was a child in the eyes of the law. This the Eighth Amendment does not permit. (p. 2033)

Other jurisdictions have also showed the relevance and importance of character retribution in parole cases. Parole case law in Israel provides another example. In the *Ganame* case (PPA 3340/16 *Ganame v Attorney General* (22.5.2016)), a case dealing with a prisoner who was sentenced to 30 years' imprisonment for kidnapping and murdering a child, the Israeli Supreme court addressed denial of guilt in parole decisions. The court emphasized that public protection considerations are prominent among the factors that the parole board takes into account. Justice Yitzhak Amit explained why the prisoner's denial of guilt may be taken into account when considering early release, based on *both* risk prevention considerations and character retributive grounds:

> The prisoner's denial is not mentioned in … the Israeli Parole Act. But case law has ruled that there is no exhaustive list of considerations. In principle, a prisoner's denial may be seen as relevant in parole decision for two reasons: first, as an indication of future risk due to an absence of remorse for the past conduct; and second, as an indication of absence of internal-moral change of the prisoner. Whereas the first reason is forward-looking, the second reason emphasizes a more "retributive" consideration in nature, in

the sense that it considers the offender's characteristics and not his future risk. (par. 10)

The use of character retributivism perspective *in addition* to public protection perspective offers, in practice by the court, two alternative theoretical frameworks—risk-based analysis and character retributive analysis—to assess the prisoner's post-sentencing conduct and expands the court's analysis. While in some cases both alternatives may lead to the same practical outcomes, in other cases the character retributive analysis might lead to different outcomes than those that could have been achieved by adopting a risk-based analysis.

Generally speaking, adding the "character" lens to the parole equation, in fact, opens the parole process to a new normative discourse. When discussing the prisoner's parole prospects, the court may use considerations of character in addition to "traditional" risk-assessment analysis. The court examines whether the prisoner "deserves" to be released based on character improvement, and not only on whether he still poses a risk to society or his rehabilitation prospects. At times, it considers the severity of the offense as a relevant factor for determining the question of merit. At other times, it may consider the moral change the prisoner has undergone. Either way, the character retributive discourse is integrated within the traditional risk assessment of the parole regime. That opens a whole new option for the parole decision-making process.

What, then, are the differences between the interrelations of risk considerations with just desert on one hand and with character retributivism on the other? Each group of considerations emphasizes different aspects the court may take into account: (1) risk (through risk dynamics and static risk-assessment tools), (2) just desert (through severity of the past offense), and (3) character retribution (through positive post-sentencing conduct that shows a positive moral character change, such as showing remorse, apology, and making amends to the crime victim). In some cases, all three groups of considerations point to aggravation (e.g., dangerous offender, severe past offense, and "bad" character before and after the sentence). In other cases, all three groups of considerations point to mitigation (low-risk offender, relatively minor offense, and morally improved character while in prison). In many cases, however, different groups of considerations lead to different outcomes. The dangerous prisoner, from the point of view of future crime prospects, may show a transformation by expressing remorse or making amends to the crime victim. Alternatively, a prisoner who showed no positive change may still be a low-risk one.

In the *Graham* case, the character retributive argument of the court was well integrated with the offender's low-risk assessment. Not granting the possibility of parole to *Graham*, a juvenile, convicted in non-homicide offense, was considered as unconstitutionally disproportionate.

Ganame showed that the court attributes a dual role to the admission of guilt: both as an indication of future risk and as that of a positive character change. Both risk and character retribution offered an overall holistic and individualistic assessment of the offender's (usually dynamic) factors, albeit for different theoretical reasons.

Overall moral assessment is conducted, therefore, not only for risk-assessment purposes, but also for retributive ones. The parole question is not a mere data-driven management of actuarial risk, but also, at times, an individualized, character-driven inquiry into personal redemption, moral character improvement, and the appropriate deserved censure based on post-sentencing positive change (Bierschbach 2012). As the cases discussed above show, questions of the offender's character and the proper punishment he deserves are intertwined with questions of risk. At times, the court views sincere admissions of guilt, remorse, or apology as evidence of adherence in the prisoner's rehabilitation process, and hence reduced future risk, *as well as* an indication of being more morally deserving of release. The court considers both the actor and the act, rather than taking a one-dimensional perspective, based exclusively on the severity of the crime and the blameworthiness of the offender at the time when the offense was committed. Therefore, in parole rulings, future risk assessment is combined with character retribution considerations.

In other words, bringing in character retributivism considerations might break from the rigidity and inflexibility of risk assessment. The court considers not only the empirical question of whether this type of person should be released, but also the normative question of whether this particular person *deserves* release (Ball 2011). As part of such a "mixed" assessment of the question whether the prisoner should be released, some of the factors evaluated by the parole board relate directly to future dangerousness; others concern a positive moral change in the prisoner's character; yet others reflect a capacity for rehabilitation or a potential to contribute to society; and some are merely related to the severity of the past offense (see also Roberts and Maslen 2015). When a mitigating factor is relevant to more than one purpose of the punishment, the parole board is to consider its effect on any of the purposes to which it may relate (Bierschbach 2012).

It is important to note that risk assessment can be an evaluation of one's character, which, in some sense, may be relevant to retributivism while not being bounded only to risk calculations. If we understand a person's moral character as a comprehensive set of dispositions to manifest attitudes, emotions, and behavior relevant to the assessment of the person as a moral agent, they may also be relevant to risk. A dangerous offender who is prone to violence because of his vicious, selfish, or callous disposition would reasonably be considered dangerous because of a defect in his moral character (Schopp 2010). Slobogin (2019) argued that "[c]haracter is an amalgam of choices—choices not only about whether to engage in antisocial conduct, but choices about one's friends, family life, education and work; the places one frequents; the amount of drugs or alcohol one ingests; and whether to seek treatment for emotional problems such as anger and impulsivity" (p. 6). All these are also related to risk. Indeed, a risk-based sentence can even be linked to criminal choices, specifically to choices whether or not to commit crimes in the future.

Why Do Courts Apply Dual Analysis?

Why do courts apply character retribution considerations at the risk-focused stage of parole decision-making? We hypothesize that the courts do so because the classic risk-based discourse does not fully capture the complexity of the case, nor does it properly reflect the moral agent who stands before the court. As research shows, risk assessment shapes, but does not eliminate, discretion (Douglas and Skeem 2005; Hannah-Moffat et al. 2009; Maurutto and Hannah-Moffat 2006).

In addition, there is a lack of clear evidence about the accuracy and validity of risk-assessment tools when it comes to false positive and false negative outcomes (Hanson and Morton-Bourgon 2005; Assy and Menashe 2014). This may lead courts to use character assessment as well, to bring an additional perspective in support of its decision to advance its legitimacy in the eyes of the decision-makers, crime victims, and the wider public. Character retributivism analysis, understood in this way, gives the parole board or the court an opportunity to truly individualize the sentence and promote a more just decision, possibly, even if risk prediction justifies longer period of incarceration.

Furthermore, as Crewe (2011) argued, actuarial methods of calculating risk use information generalized from populations and apply it to individuals. Such methods may signal to prisoners their lack of individuality by placing them within aggregate risk categories. Similarly, structured clinical interviewing requires prisoners to fit their life histories into the parameters of psychologically manageable categories, carving up complex identities into abstract units to meet the requirements of the "information system." These categories cannot fully capture subjective understandings, the ambiguities of identity, narrative progression, or the social context in which personhood is enacted. Feelings of dehumanization are exacerbated by the sense that one's character is set in the aspic form of static risk factors, and by the implication that the window of opportunity to change is barely open (Crewe 2011). It may be argued the character retributive perspective may be used to overcome at least some of these problems by offering a more nuance, human, and individualistic approach to the prisoner.

Finally, character retribution analysis may add yet another "constraint" to the severity of the custodial punishment in future cases. In cases of a crime committed by a prisoner who seems to show a moral change, character retribution analysis might provide an additional framework for calibrating the proportionate sentence beyond the "narrow" question of his future risk to society after release from prison. Character retributivism thus allows for reductions in imprisonment sentences in contrast to the punitive sentiments of populism that drag risk-driven criminal justice in that direction. In such cases, although usually it is the seriousness of the offense that is considered as the main limit for proportionality, character retribution may add another important limit to the length of the sentence *after* it was imposed, because just desert, as a backward-looking theory, does not have internal resources to mitigate the sentence after it was calibrated at the moment of sentencing. By contrast, character retribution ascribes importance to positive changes of the prisoners' character during post-sentencing stage, enabling the court to use it as a resource to control excessive sentences.

That said, integrating character retributivism assessment into a risk-based parole process raises theoretical and policy concerns. First, generally speaking, many argue against the validity of character retributivism theory. Liberal retributivists reject character theories, viewing them as violating the commitment of the state to neutrality in judging one's vision of the good, unless it violates the rights of others (Yankah 2015). Second, character assessment seems to be highly subjective, and undermines equality, fairness, and accuracy in sentencing. It may also be in conflict with a liberal sentencing regime that punishes acts, not character, and leaves the prisoner's morality to himself. Third, beneath the surface, the doctrine and practice of criminal law have often attested to a deep-seated desire to punish the "bad guys." This view of dark and threatening characters as permanently bad undergirds much of the US criminal punishment in the form its "three strikes" laws, "life without parole sentences," and so on (Yankah 2015). Although the cases discussed above demonstrate character arguments used for mitigation, character assessment may easily be used for aggravation as well. It also may distort the parole question from one of early release, to denying parole as a punishment for the prisoner's "bad," depraved, and immoral character, even if from a risk-based perspective he should be released. Fourth, to the extent that parole must be focused on rehabilitation and risk, character retribution discourse may blur the line between risk and retribution, and lead to obscure and vague decision-making processes. For example, is the offender's remorse considered as a sign of reduced future risk, as a sign of positive moral transformation, or both? How exactly does the parole board distinguish between dynamic risk factors and moral character? How often should the parole board assess character change? Who is the best decision-maker for assessing character, assuming that it is possible at all to assess character? And how exactly are the severity of the offense, post-sentencing positive character change, and risk to be balanced if they conflict with one another?

While we cannot fully discuss these questions here, it is enough to say that we believe that in the era of mass incarceration, where disproportionate sentencing regimes are common in common law criminal justice systems, character considerations in prison, if at all, should be saved only for mitigation, and not for aggravation in case of poor moral performance by that prisoner while in custody. Aggravating the sentence for a "bad" prisoner means that the state coerces them to change their ways—which clearly violates the fundamental concept of retributive liberal sentencing that respects the offender as a rational, autonomous, and moral agent free to ignore the penal message (von Hirsch 2017; Duff 2001). Prisoners may be forced to hear the penal message, but they should not be forced to listen to that message or be persuaded by it. In any case, the parole board cannot aggravate the sentence beyond punishment pronounced in court.

Conclusion

The chapter explored the interaction between risk, just desert, and character retribution considerations, showing its importance to contemporary trends in penal theory and policy. By analyzing American and Israeli sentencing and parole cases, we showed how, in practice risk, just desert, and character retributivism discourses are present in parole case law and may support the decision of the court in some cases. We show that character retributivism offers a new lens that cut through the traditional risk assessment/just desert binary. Character retributivism opens the parole process to a whole new field on inquiry and analysis, and might, in some cases, pose limit to risk-assessment tools. In other words, character retributivism may function as a brake on excessive punishment and bring to the parole table individualistic assessment as part of retributive sentencing framework. The rise of character retributivism may show how it is possible to challenge the theoretical claims that risk is becoming *the* driving force of contemporary criminal justice. Other rising normative forces, such as character retribution, create a brake on risk-driven criminal justice.

We also hypothesized that courts use both risk and character retribution because character retributive analysis provides an additional perspective in support of its decision, to advance its legitimacy in the eyes of the decision-makers, crime victims, and the wider public. Also, character retributivism analysis gives the parole board or the court an opportunity to truly individualize the sentence and promote a more just decision. The chapter's analysis calls for a more theoretical and empirical research regarding how risk and retributive discourses act in theory and practice.

Acknowledgments The authors are grateful to Henrique Carvalho, Bernadette McSherry, Michelle Miao, Jonathan Simon, and John Pratt for helpful comments on an early draft of this chapter. We also thank John Pratt and Jordan Anderson for organizing the symposium that encouraged us to think about the interrelations between risk and soft conceptions of just desert. The authors contributed equally to this chapter.

Notes

1. "Limiting retributivism" is the most influential hybrid theory of sentencing. According to this theory, retributive principles set upper and lower limits on the severity of the punishment. Within this range, of what he called "not undeserved" punishment, utilitarian concerns—such as the offender's likelihood of recidivism—can be taken into account to calibrate the exact sentence (Monahan and Skeem 2016; Frase 2013).
2. Past criminal behavior is the only scientifically valid risk factor for violence that implicates blameworthiness—as mark of "bad character," as culpable disobedience, or as an omission on the part of the repeat offender to prevent himself for committing another crime (Lee 2018); therefore, it is the only factor that should enter into the jurisprudential calculus in criminal sentencing (Slobogin 2011).
3. The use of character in criminal justice in American case law is not unique for parole stage. In *Deck v. Missouri* 544 U.S. 622, 633 (2005), while holding that unless the shackling pertains to a specific defendant for specific state interests, the Constitution forbids the shackling of a defendant in the sentencing phase of a trial, the court ruled that "character and propensities of the defendant are part of a 'unique, individualized judgment regarding the punishment that a particular person deserves'. And it

thereby inevitably undermines the jury's ability to weigh accurately all relevant considerations." Also, regarding the death punishment jurisprudence, while holding that it is unconstitutional to impose capital punishment for crimes committed while under the age of 18, the US Supreme court held that "[t]he reality that juveniles still struggle to define their identity means it is less supportable to conclude that even a heinous crime committed by a juvenile is evidence of irretrievably depraved character" (*Roper v. Simmons*, 543 U.S. 551, 570 2005).

References

Ashworth A & Zedner L. (2014). *Preventive Justice.* Oxford: Oxford University Press.

Assy, R., & Menashe, D. (2014). The catch-22 in Israel's parole law. *Criminal Justice and Behavior, 41*, 1422–1436.

Ball, David W. (2011). Normative elements of parole risk. *Stanford Law & Policy Review, 22*, 395–412.

Bierschbach R. A. (2012). Proportionality and Parole, *University of Pennsylvania Law Review, 160*, 1745–1788.

Crewe, B. (2011). Depth, weight, tightness: Revisiting the pains of imprisonment. *Punishment & Society, 13*, 509–529.

Dancig-Rosenberg, H. & Dagan N. (2018). Retributarianism: A new individualization of punishment, *Criminal Law and Philosophy, 13*, 1–19.

Douglas K. S. & Skeem J. L. (2005). Violence risk assessment: Getting specific about being dynamic, *Psychology, Public Policy & Law, 11*, 347–383.

Duff, R. A. (2001). *Punishment, communication, and community.* New York: Oxford University Press.

Etzioni, A. (2018). *Law and society in a populist age: Balancing individual rights and the common good.* Policy Press.

Feeley M. & Simon J. (1992). The new penology: notes on the emerging strategy of corrections and its implications. *Criminology, 30*(4): 449–474.

Feeley M & Simon J. (1994). Actuarial justice: the emerging new criminal law. In *The Futures of Criminology*, ed. D. Nelken, pp. 173–201. London: SAGE.

Frase, R. S. (1997). Sentencing principles in theory and practice. *Crime and Justice: A Review of Research, 22*, 363–433.

Frase, R. S. (2013). *Just sentencing: Principles and procedures for a workable system.* Oxford: Oxford university press.

Garland D. (2001). *The culture of control: Crime and social order in contemporary society*. Oxford: Oxford University Press.

Hannah-Moffat K., Maurutto P. & Turnbull S. (2009). Negotiated risk: Actuarial illusions and discretion in probation, *Canadian Journal of Law & Society*, *24*, 391–409.

Hanson, R. K. & Morton-Bourgon K. E. (2005). The characteristics of persistent sexual offenders: a meta-analysis of recidivism studies. *Journal of Consulting and Clinical psychology*, *73*, 1154–1163.

Harcourt, B. E. (2009). *Illusion of order: The false promise of broken windows policing*. Harvard: Harvard University Press.

von Hirsch, A. (1976). *Doing justice: The choice of punishments*. New York: Hill and Wang.

von Hirsch, A. (2017). *Deserved Criminal Sentences*. Portland, Oregon: Bloomsbury Publishing.

von Hirsch, A. & Ashworth, A. (2005). *Proportionate sentencing: Exploring the principles*. New York: Oxford University press.

Lee, Y. (2018). Multiple offenders and the question of desert, In *Sentencing multiple crimes* (eds. Ryberg J., Roberts J. V. & Keijser J.). Oxford: Hart.

Maurutto, P. & Hannah-Moffat K. (2006). Assembling risk and the restructuring of penal control. *British Journal of Criminology*, *46*, 438–454.

Medwed, D. S. (2007). The innocent prisoner's dilemma: Consequences of failing to admit guilt at parole hearings, *Iowa Law Review*, *93*, 491–558.

Monahan, J. (2006). A jurisprudence of risk assessment: Forecasting harm among prisoners, predators, and patients, *Virginia Law Review*, *92*, 391–435.

Monahan, J. & Skeem J. L. (2016). Risk assessment in criminal sentencing. *Annual Review of Clinical Psychology*, *12*, 489–513.

Murphy J. G. (2003). *Getting even: Forgiveness and its limits*. New York: Oxford University Press.

Murphy, T., & Whitty, N. (2007). Risk and human rights in UK prison governance. *British Journal of Criminology*, *47*, 798–816.

O'Malley P. (1999). Volatile and contradictory punishment. *Theoretical Criminology*, *3*, 175–196.

Paratore, L. (2016). Insight into life crimes: The rhetoric of remorse and rehabilitation in California parole precedent and practice. *Berkeley Journal of Criminal Law*, *21*, 95–125.

Pratt, J. (2007). *Penal populism*. Routledge.

Pratt, J. D., & Miao, M. (2018). From protecting individual rights to protecting the public: The changing parameters of populist-driven criminal law and penal policy. In G. Fitzi, J. Mackert, & B. S. Turner (Eds.), *Populism and the*

Crisis of Democracy. Volume 2: Politics, Social Movements and Extremism (pp. 47–63). Oxford: Routledge.

Raynor, P. (2016). Three narrative of risk: Corrections, critique and context. In *Beyond the Risk Paradigm in Criminal Justice* (Trotter C., McIvor G. & McNeill, Eds.). pp. 24–46.

Roberts, J. V. (2009). Listening to the crime victim: Evaluating victim input at sentencing and parole. *Crime and Justice: A Review of Research*, *38*, 347–412.

Roberts, J. V. & Maslen H. (2015). After the Crime: Post-Offence Conduct and Penal Censure. *Liberal Criminal Theory: Essays for Andreas von Hirsch* (Portland, Oregon, Hart Publishing): 87–110.

Robinson P. H. (2001). Punishing dangerousness: Cloaking preventive detention as criminal justice. *Harvard Law Review*, *114*, 1429–1456.

Schopp R. F. (2010). "So sick he deserves it": Desert, dangerousness, and character in the context of capital sentencing. *Action, Ethics, and Responsibility*. (Edited by Joseph Keim Campbell, Michael O'Rourke and Harry S. Silverstein). MIT Press. 259–280.

Simon, J. (2005). Reversal of fortune: The resurgence of individual risk assessment in criminal justice. *Annual Review of Law Social Science*, *1*, 397–421.

Slobogin, Christopher (2011). Prevention as the primary goal of sentencing: The modern case for indeterminate dispositions in criminal cases, *San Diego Law Review*, *48*, 1127–1172.

Slobogin C. (2018–2019). A Defense of Modern Risk-Based Sentencing, in *Risk and Retribution: The Ethics and Consequences of Predictive Sentencing* (J. de Keijser et al., eds., Oxford: Hart Publishing). 1–24.

Smith N. (2016). Dialectical retributivism: Why apologetic offenders deserve reductions in punishment even under retributive theories, *Philosophia*, *44*, 343–360.

Tonry, M. (2018). Punishment and human Dignity: Sentencing principles for twenty-first-century America. *Crime and Justice*, *47*(1), 119–157.

Whitman, J. Q. (2003). *Harsh justice: Criminal punishment and the widening divide between America and Europe*. Oxford: Oxford University Press.

Whitman, J. Q. (2014). The case for penal modernism: Beyond utility and desert. *Critical Analysis of Law*, *1*, 181–143.

Wilson, J. Q. & Kelling, G. (1982). Broken windows. *Atlantic monthly 3*: 29–38.

Yankah, E. N. (2003). Good guys and bad guys: Punishing character, equality and the irrelevance of moral character to criminal punishment. *Cardozo Law Review 25*, 1019.

Yankah E. N. (2015). Republican responsibility in criminal law. *Criminal Law & Philosophy*, *9*, 457–475.

Zedner, L, and Ashworth A. (2019). The Rise and Restraint of the Preventive State, *Annual Review of Criminology*, *2*, 429–450.

Case Law Cited

Deck v. Missouri 544 U.S. 622 (2005)

Graham v. Florida, 560 U.S. 48 (2010)

PPA (SC) 3340/16 *Ganame v. Attorney General* (22.5.2016) (Israel).

Roper v. Simmons, 543 U.S. 551 (2005).

Part II

Risk and Penal Policy

Dangerous Neighbors: Risk Control, Community Notification and Sex Offender Release

Jordan Anderson

Introduction: The Emergence of Community Notification

This chapter examines community notification as an exemplar of the type of risk-driven penal policy and practice that has emerged as part of a distinct strand of penal policy development in advanced liberal democracies. Community notification policies across these societies grew out of case-driven sex offender legislation in the US in the 1990s. Registration of sex offenders in the US came first, following the sexual murder of eleven-year-old Jacob Wetterling in 1989. After concerted campaigning by the child's mother, the federal Jacob Wetterling Crimes Against Children and Sexually Violent Offender Registration Act was passed in 1994. This Act required states to implement registration of sex offenders and perpetrators

J. Anderson (⊠)
Institute of Criminology, Victoria University of Wellington,
Wellington, New Zealand
e-mail: jordan.anderson@vuw.ac.nz

© The Author(s) 2020
J. Pratt, J. Anderson (eds.), *Criminal Justice, Risk and the Revolt against Uncertainty*,
Palgrave Studies in Risk, Crime and Society,
https://doi.org/10.1007/978-3-030-37948-3_5

of crimes against children. Registration involves the collation of identifying details, which can include full names, addresses, offenses, places of work, vehicle registration details and intent to travel. The purpose of registration as stated in the Act was to provide a tool to law enforcement for a more effective monitoring and management of sexually violent predators.

Sex offender registries, active to various degrees throughout the US, Australia, Canada, the UK and, most recently, New Zealand, are schemes designed to collate information on sex offenders to enhance public protection. When paired with an enforcement mechanism (e.g. GPS tracking, policing), they can also operate to limit the movement of registered offenders in certain types of public spaces (e.g. parks, beaches, schools, public amenities). Registration policies in these jurisdictions have often been followed in quick succession by community notification policies. Often conflated, registry and notification are distinct procedures which are consistently legislated separately. While registration involves the collation of information about sex offenders for public protection, community notification involves the 'systemic disclosure' of information about registered sex offenders residing in the community to members of the public (Whitting et al. 2014).

In the US, federal notification requirements were first introduced in 1996 as a subsection of the 1994 Act—'Megan's Law' was named after another child victim of sexual murder, seven-year-old Megan Kanka. The justification for notification was that, in addition to the service to law enforcement provided through registration, community notification would add an additional layer of public protection by enabling the public to use the information to manage their own risk. Notification is often justified by politicians as a necessary step to ensure public safety—in particular, the protection of children, who are thought to be particularly vulnerable to those who would do them 'irreparable' harm (deemed to be of a sexual nature).

However, no other western democracy goes so far as the US in providing the level of access to the public that occurs in that country, a product of the very powerful victims' movements there (Jones and Newburn 2005). Formally at least, beyond the US, notification details are kept within the respective state organizations and NGOs working in this area.

This is not to say, though, that de facto notification does not occur. This chapter will examine the operation of de facto notification in New Zealand. This, along with calls for greater transparency and more comprehensive notification practices, will be discussed within the wider context of the delegation of all kinds of risks to individuals through the restructuring of much of economic and social life from the 1980s. While some individuals have been enabled by these reforms to succeed and prosper in the conditions of 'liquid modernity' (Bauman 2000), others exist in communities left behind, as all that was familiar and certain dissolves around them. Those left behind as a consequence of this restructuring are less able to adapt to change, and to respond to the array of risks that this has brought into existence. In this chapter I will use the case of the revelation of sixteen sex offenders being housed in a boarding house in the Auckland suburb of Ōtāhuhu to illustrate the lived experience of risk and de facto notification through the prism of Bauman's *Liquid Modernity*. The Ōtāhuhu case study illustrates the ways that the state is prepared to offer levels of protection from particularly intolerable risks, and the way in which these levels of protection are provided on an unequal basis. Those communities left behind in the course of restructuring are likely to find additional risks imposed on them in this process. Those that have prospered in the course of restructuring will be left to roar ahead to more success, unburdened by such risks.

The New Zealand Case

In New Zealand, sex offender registration policy, echoing that found in the Wetterling Act, was passed into law in 2015 within the Child Protection Act. This Act mandated the registration of offenders convicted of qualifying offenses against children. In the same vein as the federal Adam Walsh Child Protection and Safety Act in the US, the legislation classed offenders into three tiers based on the level of risk, meaning that individuals would be registered for eight years, fifteen years or life, depending on the seriousness of their ongoing risk. However, the Child Sex Offender Register in this country is not accessible to the public; the New Zealand Police hold the register and employ specialist teams to manage the monitoring of registered individuals. The Child Protection Act 2015 is an example of legislation created with public protection as its main intention—more explicitly, the protection of children. Although this registration policy closely reflects its US origins, New Zealand has not gone on to legislate for community notification, and the Child Sex Offender Register remains confidential to the police. The development of registration policy in this country has occurred following the build-up of pressure over a number of years from a highly visible and vociferous law and order campaigning group in this country, the Sensible Sentencing Trust (see, e.g. Pratt 2007).

In reality, though, New Zealand communities frequently experience de facto community notification: notification practices that exist in reality, without any basis in law. Despite the absence of de jure notification policy, and the reality that many de facto notification practices are illegal, it is commonplace and occurs in a range of ways. This includes the actions of the police: giving direction to reporters, making and dropping flyers themselves,[1] giving warning to community leaders; the actions of the Department of Corrections: making public announcements, informing school principals, and employees leaking information to the media (as in the Ōtāhuhu case); the actions of the media receiving and publishing leaked information, often in sensational ways; and finally the actions of the vigilant community member posting photos, letters, articles, and information online, harnessing the power of social media to spread information about perceived risks. In New Zealand, and in similar societies, the lack of legislative mandate for a particular kind of notification has not stopped the practice from occurring.

In addition to the violations of human rights and foundational justice principles that occur as a result of de facto notification, notification has resulted in individuals who are targeted and shunned from communities, sometimes being shut out altogether. Two examples in particular illustrate the potentially explosive consequences of de facto notification. First, the 2012 release of Stewart Murray Wilson was announced well in advance by the Department of Corrections. In 1996, Wilson was sentenced to imprisonment for serious sexual and violent offending against sixteen women and girls, including rape, attempted rape and indecent assault (New Zealand Parole Board 2012). The offenses for which Wilson was sentenced spanned over twenty-two years, from 1972 to 1994, and also included charges of stupefaction and bestiality (New Zealand Parole Board 2012). During the reporting of Wilson's 1996 trial, reporter Bernadette Courteney popularized the moniker Wilson was given: 'Beast of Blenheim' (a reference to the South Island town where his crimes had occurred), and this began the construction of Wilson's image as a kind of 'frenzied sex beast'. The media sensationalism which surrounded this case was demonstrative of the way that sensational reporting on 'exceptional' cases seizes the public's imagination and promotes an 'absolute otherness' fostered by the perceived complete detachment of (particularly sexual) offenders from social norms (Greer and Jewkes 2005: 21; Jewkes 2015). Eighteen years after Wilson was convicted, in September 2012, the Department of Corrections announced his impending release to Whanganui—a small North Island town to which he had no previous connection. The reaction of the local people to this announcement was significant—well-attended community meetings were held in response, a 'community shunning' of Wilson using trespass orders was coordinated, and the local government gathered funds to sue the Department of Corrections for the 'release' of Wilson in that location. As set out in Pratt and Anderson (2016), the state acted swiftly in response, by introducing retroactive civil detention legislation as well as containment measures for some sex offenders at the end of finite prison terms to ensure that the community would be protected from any exposure to 'the Beast', despite the expiration of his finite sentence: his parole, in fact, consisted of him being moved to a house on the prison grounds, where he would face more restrictions on his liberty and be under closer surveillance than was the case while he was actually in prison.

Second is the case of *Brown v Attorney General* of New Zealand (2006), this time notification was carried out by the New Zealand Police. In 2006, Barry Grant Brown, previously convicted of sexual offenses against children, had been released on parole to an address in a Wellington suburb. Following his placement in the community, two police officers, one uniformed and one plain clothed, went to Brown's house and took photos of him, stating that they were for 'identification purposes'. The officers then returned to the police station and prepared a flyer on the New Zealand Police letterhead containing Brown's personal details and photograph, and proceeded to distribute it in nearby streets and to local businesses. Brown later sued the New Zealand Police under the tort of privacy, and for Bill of Rights Act violations, and was eventually awarded NZ$29,000 in damages by the court. In responding to the illicit behavior of the officers involved, New Zealand Police claimed these men were acting of their own volition, without instruction or permission from the police, and that the police organization would not condone or allow such behavior.

Regardless of the lack of legislative mandate for notification, what is particularly striking about these examples is the willingness of the authorities, or individual representatives of them, to overturn long-standing and important legislative and justice principles for the sake of averting risk and of preserving 'public safety'. Why should this be so?

De Facto Notification in the Context of Liquid Modernity

The weakening of the authority of the modern state since the 1980s due to neo-liberal economic and social restructuring and political reform has significantly influenced policy processes throughout the advanced liberal democracies, particularly those policies regarding the politics of risk management. Zygmunt Bauman (2000: 40) argued that the public sector consistently "fails to perform its past role" as the strategic principles of public power have frayed, and have been replaced by escape, avoidance and disengagement. Throughout these societies, the confidence of the population in the power of the central state has declined along with its inclination to intervene, and the state has withdrawn from areas of life it had previously occupied. Private interests now rule, and the state that once defended the autonomy of its citizens has begun to require defense itself, as it continues to shrink away from its past strength and status (Bauman 2000). With the loss of its "awesome and resented oppressive potency" since the reforms of the 1980s, state power has lost a significant part of its enabling capacity, and its inclination to use the traditional legal apparatus of control to provide security for its subjects has been diminished (Bauman 2000: 51).

In *Liquid Modernity*, Bauman (2000) proposed that the fluid nature of life in the modern society has brought about profound changes to all aspects of the human condition. He argued that the modern state is shifting toward a light, software-based 'advanced' modernity, and away from the hitherto solid, anchored hardware-focused modernity. The solid nature of the latter had meant that the western societies were dependable in their provision of services, security and safety. As Rose (2000) explained, from the late nineteenth century but especially in the era of the post-1945 welfare state, collective security had been maintained through universal provisions by the state on behalf of its citizens, ranging from pensions and housing, to socially funded services such as police and fire brigades. Expectations and provisions in the experience of everyday life were predictable, and the state provided its guarantees of stability and cohesion. In contrast, by its fluid nature, 'liquid modernity' means that the destination of individual, self-constructing labors is "endemically and incurably undetermined" (Bauman 2000: 7). Within this new liquid state, all norms are fragile, and therefore the fragility of all identities is magnified (Bauman 2000). In a practical sense, values such as mobility, flexibility and individuality become inevitable in the era of liquid modernity, and success is earned by those individuals who are elastic, adaptable and mobile enough to seek it for themselves. Within this social formation, the traditional importance of communitarian values and social solidarity is traded for the increased value attributed to individualism and the pursuit of personal success that this is thought to bring with it.

Bauman (2000) argued that modern society's safety nets that had previously existed in many forms—including structural features like social welfare, the dependability of the traditional nuclear family and community ties and values—quickly began to fade into obscurity as restructuring took effect. Following the particularly volatile period during the 1970s when various rights movements campaigned for significant lifestyle and social policy changes, economic restructuring from the 1980s added to the demands for greater individual freedom and marked the beginnings of the 'liquid state'.

Since the economic reforms, the preoccupation of individuals with risk, and the way that it narrows the possibility of everyday life, has had a defining impact on the conduct of everyday life and the state's oversight of this. While being exhorted to take care of themselves and plot their own way through life, in the free market society, individuals now find themselves with none of the previous supports and landmarks to guide them. One impact of this has been the ways in which 'risky individuals' are seen to pose a particularly acute threat to the wellbeing of the rest of the community, in the absence now of previous informal community controls and safeguards. Such risks of unpredictable, irreparable harms that these suspicious individuals are thought capable of inflicting have elicited significant public, media and government responses in the form of extra-penal measures of control, such as post-prison and indefinite detention for some sex offenders. Pratt and Anderson (2016) have referred to this phenomenon as 'the rise of the security sanction', whereby, rather than reacting to crime that has been committed, penal policy is created to promote public safety by preventing future crime. The preventive framework also includes comprehensive restrictions on movement through public space on offenders deemed by the state to pose risk, from vagrants and beggars, and anti-social youth, to those presumed dangerous due to previous convictions (Pratt and Anderson 2016).

These responses represent a departure from the traditionally moralistic considerations of populist punitiveness: policy is no longer all about punishing better and harder for retribution and for the defense of our moral community. Rather, the focus shifts to the prevention and removal of these particular risks from the community, with a growing range of penal sanctions and regulatory policy ready to be deployed to protect individuals from them, or to eliminate them altogether. The "varied, sporadic, and strategic" deployment of the security sanction across the advanced liberal democracies has included registration of violent and sexual offenders, as well as notification policies designed to delegate the responsibility for personal safety to the individual (Pratt and Anderson 2016: 13).

In seeking to explain responses of communities to the release of 'risky' individuals, it is important to consider this broader context of change in which communities in advanced liberal democracies have been operating over the last forty years. Bountiful opportunities have been provided by the lighter mode of living in liquid modernity. Opportunities for greater wealth, experience, travel and diversity are at the fingertips of those who can let go of the safe but pedestrian old life and embrace these new opportunities that more liquid social arrangements bring. Those communities rejecting liquefaction, or that have been left behind by it, have been doomed to an eternity of insecurity and anxiety in relation to the fluid, unrecognizable and swirling world around them. The reforms fostered anxiety and insecurity because they stripped away all the previous ties and loyalties that secured the individual's place in their community through work, community groups and family relationships (Pratt 2015). The restructuring era has seen the rise of individual contracts of employment, the demise of trade union membership and power, the rise of divorce, the decline of the church, increasing transience of the population, increasing immigration, the rise of sole-parent families in conjunction with the number of individuals living alone, the second-wave feminist movement providing new collectivities severed from previous social class ties, a growing prominence of women in the workplace, and reforms intended to restrict welfare access. In former British colonies such as New Zealand, previous racial homogeneity and social cohesion have been dissipated by immigration from Asian countries especially. Informal community controls have also dissipated. For example, the ideal of a good neighbor has been transformed with the progression of this liquefaction: from being a friend and watchful eye, the 'good' neighbor has become someone who keeps their distance and keeps to themselves (Dunkelman 2014).

Overall, the transformation of the authority of the central state in this era of economic and social restructuring has driven a reliance on punitive law and order regimes to provide a sense of security and stability. However, it is also the case that there is a newfound inability on behalf of state bodies to govern without the threat of exclusion from society using penal instruments (Bauman 2000; Pratt 2015; Garland 2001). Of all the limitations on state intervention to come out of the 1980s, diminished security of the individual and the community has had a particularly acute affect. This restructuring has meant that individuals have been expected to take much more responsibility for their own risks. In return for individuals gaining much more freedom of choice on the use of their income, and how they want the course of their lives to develop, they must also accept these responsibilities in relation to self-management of risk. Nonetheless, and in apparent contrast to their message that individuals must take their own precautions against risk, governments are reorganizing criminal law and penal policy to provide protection, especially around risk, and particularly from sex offenders. There are two reasons for this, both of which are related to the unanticipated consequences of restructuring. First, the dramatically declining numbers of young people in the population gives them a special value, and a need to be protected from risks to their wellbeing at all costs from predatory pedophiles and the like (Hacking 2003; Furedi 1997; Valentine 1996). Second, the way in which consumer-driven economics of restructuring have transformed the adult body into a prized vehicle for pleasure and self-fulfillment has led to demands for special measures of protection from those who pose risks to it (Bauman 2000). Although governments are creating penal policies to manage these otherwise intolerable risks that individuals cannot insure themselves against, the winners and losers of neo-liberalism experience the effects of such policies very differently.

Solid State Communities? A Case Study

In March 2018, a national news media network in New Zealand exposed the presence of sixteen high-risk sex offenders living in a South Auckland boarding house.[2] TVNZ revealed to an unsuspecting public that these sex offenders were on various forms of community release in Ōtāhuhu and were being managed by the Department of Corrections, whose decision it was to place them in close proximity to local schools, parks, childcare centers and churches. Initially, the reaction of the Department of Corrections to the media attention was to contest the numbers (the District Commissioner claimed that it was, in fact, eleven offenders). Meanwhile, both the community reaction and the media coverage gained traction over the subsequent days, with all national news networks picking up the story, and more details, perspectives and interviews with concerned locals being published each day. Seven days after the story broke, and on the morning of the public meeting that the local community leaders had arranged to discuss the issue, all of the offenders who had been living in the boarding house were removed from the property and relocated by the Department of Corrections. That public meeting went ahead, and spirited demands for notification and greater levels of information sharing throughout the community were shared among attendees.

The case of Ōtāhuhu presents a fraught and complex example of community notification. In this instance, community notification was apparently initiated through a leak by a Department of Corrections staff member to a journalist. The Department later claimed to have engaged in limited community notification around this case before the media picked up the story, informing select community leaders of the presence of at least some of the offenders living on this property.[3] Much to the disappointment and vocal frustration of many attendees at the public meeting, the Department refused to share any information about the new location of the individuals who had been moved out of the boarding house that morning. Demands for more information and transparency around state decision-making on the placement of offenders were voiced at the meeting. Though no representatives of the Department were in attendance, locals were asking: why their community? Several attendees voiced concerns that echoed the media coverage of the case: that South Auckland, and in this instance Ōtāhuhu, was being used by the state as a 'dumping ground' for those deemed unfit to reside in more affluent and prosperous communities. Rather than demonstrating a complete intolerance of risk, or even intolerance to the presence of sex offenders, the concerns expressed at the public meeting and in interviews centered on exasperation with the actions of the state, and frustration with being shouldered with the risks that other communities had apparently rejected as being an intolerable menace. This is the result of their experience of living in what might be termed a 'solid state' community.

There are a significant number of such communities in New Zealand, as elsewhere—those that have been left behind in the restructuring of modern society. Pratt (2016) has referred to these communities that have missed out on the benefits of liquid modernity as 'immobilised communities'—places that are motionless within a world that values lightness and mobility. Compared to their more modern neighbors, these places have narrow horizons, and have lost out on the opportunity for the global connections that mobilize individuals and foster opportunities for modern 'success' in other parts of the country. However, it is also the case that these solid-state communities are not filled with anxious individuals fractured from one another and clinging to the remnants of a dying, irrelevant value set (as Bauman had predicted). Rather the opposite, these communities are tight-knit, savvy and very familiar with the causes and effects of their social problems.

Fragmentation and Deprivation in Ōtāhuhu

The Ōtāhuhu suburb in South Auckland is part of an area that McIntosh (2004: 135) has described as being cast "as a social penitentiary whose residents are unable to break through the constraints of poverty, unemployment, and other forms of social disorganisation". It is a vibrant location, but its vitality is often overshadowed by a long series of negative social indicators. The suburb itself is very small—an isthmus between expansive and dominant neighboring suburbs. Ōtāhuhu's population is diverse, and Pākehā (New Zealand Europeans) make up a comparatively small minority. The suburb is home to an enormous Pasifika population: 60.1 percent identifying as Pacific peoples here eclipsing the national average of 7.4 percent (Statistics New Zealand 2013a). Tongan flags line the streets of the township, and many community leaders affectionately refer to the area as 'Little Nuku'alofa' (named for the capital of the Kingdom of Tonga). Historically an industrial hub due to its flat land and ease of access to waterways, Ōtāhuhu was heavily impacted by the economic restructuring of the 1980s. The decline of industry during this period, including the closure of its large employers such as railway workshops and freezing works, contributed to the particularly severe negative impact of neo-liberal restructuring on this community.

Ōtāhuhu has thus become a community left behind for Bauman's purposes, but it has also been left out in a more literal sense by successive central and local government action. For decades, Ōtāhuhu occupied a boundary zone between two local government jurisdictions, where neither Council would take full responsibility for the community. Even now with Auckland's evolution into a 'supercity' (i.e. a major conurbation with one central governing authority) in 2010, Ōtāhuhu is the supporting act to a much larger South Auckland suburb within the Council ward system. In the view of the community leaders that were interviewed as part of the doctoral research on which this chapter is based,[4] the local government—traditionally responsible for 'rats, rates, roads and rubbish'—has consistently, and to this day, failed on all four counts. For residents of Ōtāhuhu, the actions of the state in setting risk free through deregulation, privatization and corporatization during the neo-liberal reforms served to destabilize their lives and bring about an era of deprivation and fragmentation. In the face of these ongoing challenges, Ōtāhuhu has retained an unsteady grip on a form of a more traditional community—it has strong informal social controls, and, despite an overlay of transience, the base of the community is tight-knit.

The impact of neo-liberal restructuring is still felt strongly in this community today, with levels of unemployment and deprivation consistently above the national average. The suburb houses more renters and state housing tenants than average; within Ōtāhuhu's Local Board area, 41.6 percent of households are owner-occupied, comparing unfavorably with the 64.8 percent national average (Statistics New Zealand 2013b). The Deprivation Index shows that the entirety of Ōtāhuhu is categorized within most extreme of the five levels of deprivation (New Zealand Index of Deprivation 2013).[5] Within this context of deprivation, exploitative housing practices have flourished, including a boom in the number of boarding houses in this area. Boarding houses are typically concentrated in low socio-economic areas with high levels of deprivation. One notable exception is a large facility in an upmarket central Auckland suburb, which received over 100 objections from concerned residents during the consent hearing; nobody with any choice wants a boarding house in their neighborhood (Cumming 2000). A 2018 discussion document issued by the Ministry of Business, Innovation and Employment (2018: 41) acknowledged that boarding houses are conceptually built on a problematic foundation:

> Boarding house tenants might be more vulnerable to exploitation by landlords, have more limited knowledge of their rights, and be less likely to exercise their rights or lay a complaint due to a lack of alternative accommodation options. In general, it is likely to be more difficult for people in boarding houses to hold their landlords to account in the same way that tenants in the general rental market can, especially if their landlord lives on the premises.

In Ōtāhuhu, boarding houses have become symbolic of the ongoing exploitation of local residents by the state, as well as those who would seemingly profit from the misfortune of others. While conditions of liquid modernity have enabled many individuals to prosper and reach hitherto unimaginable levels of wealth, there are entire communities of people who have been left behind by the social and economic restructuring. Members of solid-state communities like Ōtāhuhu can be ill-equipped to keep up with the pace of the liquid modern world, and individuals within them can therefore be at the mercy of those possessing liquid modernity's virtues of mobility and flexible capital. It appears that in Ōtāhuhu, the state is enabling the exploitation of those most vulnerable in society by those more equipped to thrive. For years, this community has been fighting against the Council granting any more consents for boarding houses due to their predatory and exploitative practices, and this fight came to a head when it was revealed that the Department of Corrections had placed a large number of offenders in a local boarding house that had not received consent to operate.

Within the context of this case, the desire of the community for notification and transparency can be understood. This community was exposed to risk by the state in these circumstances, and they responded with demands for information to enable them to manage their own risks, given that the state did not appear to be doing this for them. The experience of discovering the existence of this risk through sensational national media stories was jarring for local residents, including community leaders who felt unable to shepherd their community through the situation. As two community leaders explained:

The unfortunate thing about finding out like that—if we all found out via [TV]3 News, that means everyone goes into shock, panic, and you're not able to get around the community and say all right, hold up everybody. Because no one actually knows where they are, and that's probably not important, but there was no kind of leader in the community that could say 'it's okay, I've been aware of it, and here's how we can manage our way through this and navigate it'. There was none of that, and all of us were caught off guard, and that's what I found unacceptable. (Interview of Ōtāhuhu community leaders, 2018) [community notification via the media] does nothing for the cultural intelligence that exists in the community as well, we could've dealt with it a whole lot better. (Ibid.)

For the people of this community, the presence of sex offenders presented a dual issue: the moral threat of having them in a community with large numbers of children and vulnerable people *and* the threat of being stepped on once again by an uncaring state. Many of the leaders that were interviewed, as well as a significant number of people at the public meeting, were primarily concerned with the failure of the state to comply with its own regulations, and to act in good faith for the protection of vulnerable members of the community. The risk of sexual harm to children was also raised. However, rather than this taking the form of a crisis reaction to this threat of irreparable harm placed on their doorstep, many of these community members understood the realities of offending and appreciated that many of these people had been around for a while without significant incident (cf Ilea 2018). Community leaders explained the intersections and the nuance of the reaction of local people to the revelation of this situation, noting the understanding that many community members had of the challenges of reintegration:

I think people were pretty horrified. I mean they were really horrified that the schools didn't know, they were horrified that so many people were living in one property. As things came out, people were also then horrified that the offenders didn't really have good living conditions ... it's not rehabilitative to shove a whole lot of people into a substandard situation without any support. As it developed, it was really interesting that there were two strands: there was real concern about safety of individuals, women and children in particular, but there was also real concern about, well, how is this doing the persons concerned any good? Sort of both strands came through, and sometimes those were voiced by the same people. (Interview of Ōtāhuhu community leaders, 2018)

I definitely felt that the older Palagi [New Zealand European] community had a stronger reaction to the moral safety issue, and they often speak louder. I often talk about the loud minority, and I think there was a loud minority that probably facilitated quite a lot of the fear ... a lot of the people struggling with transience and poverty and housing affordability, or just somewhere to stay, may not have been at that meeting. And it's those—my expectation is that a lot of them would have said oh nah I understand, we get it. (Ibid.)

The Ōtāhuhu case is demonstrative of the ad hoc and unpredictable nature of sex offender release amidst de facto notification processes. The community leaders that were interviewed in this community wanted some form of formal community notification processes put in place to enable the community to continue to manage attendant risks as appropriate to them. Many specified that they would never trust the Department of Corrections or the New Zealand Police to manage these risks effectively, or to do the right thing by the community—they could only trust their own representatives to do that now, given what has occurred. Nonetheless, the community in Ōtāhuhu did not demonstrate atomization and anxiety in the face of risk. Though the national media sensationalized the story and undoubtedly triggered the anxieties of some members of the public, conversations with local community leaders seemed to show that this was not an example of overwhelming anxiety—it was a strong and very well-networked community fortifying against a common threat and a familiar foe in the state. Ōtāhuhu has a history of uniting as a community against common threats, which often involve the authorities. After the experiences it has endured, it would appear that this community is unwilling to take on more than what they view as their fair share of the risks delegated to them by an unfriendly state.

The Role of the State

In Ōtāhuhu, the actions of the Department of Corrections in this case did not demonstrate the pursuit of a positive result for the community or for the individuals being released. The Department clearly intended to keep these released individuals apart from the community to the greatest extent possible, as evidenced by the zoning of the area of the boarding house near a school so they could not move freely, away from support services, and housed with other offenders. When they were removed a week after the media picked up the story, a number of these offenders were temporarily moved onto prison grounds (Department of Corrections 2018).

The *Accommodation Review* commissioned by the Department in the wake of this case discussed the increasingly difficult task of sourcing appropriate housing to enable offenders to reintegrate into the community. Though the Department is not set up as an accommodation provider, it is increasingly required to organize housing in order to facilitate reintegration of offenders released from prison who do not have an existing 'appropriate' address (Department of Corrections 2018). The review explains the difficulty of this task within the context of a national housing shortage, public hostility to sex offenders, and the ever-increasing pressure on the state housing system. The result of this, by the Department's own admission, has been that "a convenient and accessible alternative is accessed through boarding houses and in some instances emergency accommodation in motels" (Department of Corrections 2018: 9). Though motels are no longer used to house child sex offenders (following another high-profile media exposé),[6] their use is illustrative of the questionable options the Department has resorted to in recent times. The response of the state to these ongoing and deeply sensitive issues has been to construct facilities such as Te Korowai—an alternative accommodation option for released sex offenders, north of Wellington; on the prison grounds but outside the wire, it provides a non-punitive, 'last resort' option for these individuals. This regional facility adds eleven beds to the stock across four other post-release sex offender facilities set up across the country. In part, at least because of the way in which the media has both reported on and further generated public anxieties about the release of sex offenders from prison, their reintegration is becoming so fraught, that the only option for many of them upon their release is to remain on prison property in another correctional facility.

Conclusion

The decision of the Department of Corrections to place a large number of sex offenders in a boarding house in Ōtāhuhu in 2018 triggered a series of actions that demonstrate the salience of Bauman's theory of liquid modernity in understanding modern life. As Pratt and Anderson (2016) have established, despite the withdrawal of the state from much of public life following neo-liberal restructuring, throughout the advanced liberal democracies the state has performed 'spectacular rescues' when there has been the perception of intolerable risks of irreparable harm, posed by sex offenders especially. It would seem from this overview of de facto community notification and its consequences that the cost of protecting communities from such risks is that the human rights of those deemed to be risky become secondary to the issue of protecting communities from them. The movement of many of the offenders who had occupied the boarding house onto prison grounds, even as a temporary measure, is illustrative of this. It would also seem that these levels of protection provided by the state are not shared equally. Until it was exposed by the media, the state had been willing to expose seemingly powerless marginal solid-state communities to disproportionately high levels of risk. It had been prepared to transfer otherwise intolerable risk to those who have the least resources to manage it.

For Ōtāhuhu, responsibility for risk control and management of particularly unwanted members of society has been delegated to them in the course of the restructuring of modern society. Charged with this task, however, they have still found themselves left with insufficient information to effectively manage the risks dropped in their laps by the state. Demands for notification in this community have grown out of this state-sanctioned exposure, as residents seek to protect themselves and their children not just from the immediate risk of harm from these offenders, but from the duplicity of the state. The solid-state nature of this community has enabled its members to demonstrate a collectivity and unity uncharacteristic of liquid modernity. Though this community, along with others, has been left behind in the course of this, its inertia has enabled the retention of a cohesive collectivity in contrast with more 'successful', sought-after areas where individuals manage their own risks—through living in gated communities, for example. Collectivity and cohesion are what enabled this community to organize in opposition to the threat posed by the offenders, manifested in opposition to the Department of Corrections itself.

A combination of the delegation of responsibility to individuals and policy initiatives that take the form of spectacular rescues by the state (e.g. retrospective post-prison civil detention measures) has created an unpredictable and seemingly flexible system of regulation for sex offender control and release in New Zealand. The official avenues for notification are murky and inconsistent, and the unofficial (and often illegal) means of notification cause problems for communities and individuals on release alike. However, they have also been instrumental in the revelation of government incompetence and poor, possibly dangerous, decision-making. Notification in the context of this case is representative of the desperation of the community in the face of the operation of the liquid state. Solid-state communities are willing to tolerate (and are experienced in tolerating) risks. But, they are unwilling to accept the state's additional risk delegation. The state is no longer a source of authority nor support for these kinds of communities—notification enables the community to manage their own risk.

Notes

1. See *Brown v Attorney General* of New Zealand.
2. This number is contested: my interviewees consistently claimed that the number was sixteen, while the Department of Corrections publicly claimed the number was eleven.
3. All of the community leaders I spoke to in Ōtāhuhu disputed this claim, though some were approached by the Department after the media had picked up the story.
4. The fieldwork for my doctoral research included interviews of thirty-three community leaders across three New Zealand communities. I defined 'community leaders' as being either directly representative of a community subgroup, or as holders of a role as a spokesperson of some facet of

the community. This included school principals, elected officials, NGO employees, journalists and representatives of community interest groups.

5. The Deprivation Index is an integrated data set that draws together data on indicators including crime, education, healthcare, employment, housing and income.

6. According to the Department of Corrections (2018: 10) themselves, the practice of accommodating sex offenders in motels ceased due to public concerns following media reports of a child sex offender residing in the same motel as children and families managed by the Ministry of Social Development (in lieu of social housing).

References

Bauman, Z. (2000). *Liquid Modernity*. Cambridge, UK, Polity Press.

Brown v Attorney-General. (2006). NZAR 552 (DC) Child Protection (Child Sex Offender Government Agency Registration) Act 2016 (NZ).

Cumming, G. (2000). Boarding Houses: The Neighbour Nobody Wants. *New Zealand Herald.* Retrieved from https://www.nzherald.co.nz/nz/news/article.cfm?c_id=1&objectid=150325.

Department of Corrections. (2018). *Accommodation Review.* Released to me under the Official Information Act.

Dunkelman, M. (2014). The Vanishing Neighbor: The Transformation of American Community. New York: W. W. Norton & Company.

Furedi, F. (1997). *Culture of Fear: Risk-taking and the Morality of Low Expectations.* London: Continuum.

Garland, D. (2001). *The Culture of Control.* Oxford: UK, Oxford University Press.

Greer, C., and Jewkes, Y. (2005). Extremes of Otherness: Media Images of Social Exclusion. *Social Justice, 32*(1), pp. 20–31.

Hacking, I. (2003). Risk and Dirt. In R. V. Ericson and A. Doyle (Eds.) *Risk and Morality.* Toronto, CA: University of Toronto Press.

Ilea, A. (2018). What about the sex offenders? Addressing sexual harm from an abolitionist perspective. *Critical Criminology, 26*(8), pp. 357–372.

Jewkes, Y. (2015). Media and Crime. London: Sage Publications Ltd.

Jones, T, and Newburn, T. (2005). Comparative Criminal Justice Policy Making in the United States and the United Kingdom: The Case of Private Prisons. *British Journal of Criminology, 45*(1), pp. 58–80.

Ministry for Business, Innovation, and Employment. (2018). *Reform of the Residential Tenancies Act: Discussion Document.* Retrieved from https://info-council.aucklandcouncil.govt.nz/Open/2018/10/ENV_20181016_AGN_8219_AT_files/ENV_20181016_AGN_8219_AT_Attachment_63141_2.PDF.

McIntosh, T. (2004). Living Southside. In I. Carter, D. Craig and S. Matthewman (Eds.) *Almighty Auckland?* Palmerston North: Dunmore Press.

New Zealand Index of Deprivation. (2013). *Deprivation Index.* Retrieved from http://www.imd.ac.nz/NZIMD_Single_animation_w_logos/atlas.html.

New Zealand Parole Board. (2012). *Decisions of Public Interest: Stewart Murray Wilson.* Retrieved from http://www.paroleboard.govt.nz/decisions-statistics-and-publications/decisions-of-public-interest/WILSON_-_Stewart_Murray-_07082012.html.

Pratt, J. (2007). *Penal Populism.* Oxon, UK: Routledge.

Pratt, J. (2015). 'Immobilisation in the Age of Mobility' in Anna Eriksson (Ed.) *Punishing the Other: The Social Production of Immorality Revisited.* Oxon, UK, Routledge.

Pratt, J. (2016). Risk Control, Rights and Legitimacy in the Limited Liability State. *British Journal of Criminology.* Retrieved from https://academic.oup.com/bjc/article-lookup/doi/10.1093/bjc/azw065.

Pratt, J., and Anderson, J. (2016). "The Beast of Blenheim", Risk and the Rise of the Security Sanction. *Australian & New Zealand Journal of Criminology, 49*(4), pp. 528–545.

Rose, N. (2000). Government and Control. *British Journal of Criminology, 40*(2), pp. 321–339.

Statistics New Zealand. (2013a). *Māngere Ōtāhuhu Local Board Area Cultural Diversity.* Retrieved from http://archive.stats.govt.nz/Census/2013-census/profile-and-summary-reports/quickstats-about-a-place.aspx?request_value=13625&tabname=Culturaldiversity.

Statistics New Zealand. (2013b). *Māngere Ōtāhuhu Local Board Area Housing.* Retrieved from http://archive.stats.govt.nz/Census/2013-census/profile-and-summary-reports/quickstats-about-a-place.aspx?request_value=13625&tabname=Housing.

Valentine, G. (1996). Angels and Devils: Moral Landscapes of Childhood. *Environment and Planning D: Society and Space, 14*(1), pp. 581–599.

Whitting, L., Day, A., and Powell, M. (2014). The Impact of Community Notification on the Management of Offenders in the Community: An Australian Perspective. *Australian & New Zealand Journal of Criminology, 47*(2), pp. 240–258.

Joint Enterprise, Hostility and the Construction of Dangerous Belonging

Henrique Carvalho

Why this sudden bewilderment, this confusion?
(How serious people's faces have become.)
Why are the streets and squares emptying so rapidly,
everyone going home lost in thought?
Because night has fallen and the barbarians haven't come.
And some of our men just in from the border say
there are no barbarians any longer.
(Cavafy 2007: 17)

Introduction

The growing importance of risk in the development of criminal law in the twenty-first century has brought about significant changes not only to the scope of criminal law itself but also to rules of evidence, policing and

H. Carvalho (✉)
School of Law, University of Warwick, Coventry, UK
e-mail: H.Carvalho@warwick.ac.uk

© The Author(s) 2020
J. Pratt, J. Anderson (eds.), *Criminal Justice, Risk and the Revolt against Uncertainty*,
Palgrave Studies in Risk, Crime and Society,
https://doi.org/10.1007/978-3-030-37948-3_6

prosecutorial strategies and, more generally, to the increasing primacy given to public protection over the need to guarantee individual rights (see Ericson 2007; Pratt 2016). The most notable of these changes were broadly identified as preventive in nature, following strategies that deviate from the common paradigm of criminal liability centered around culpability and harm done, to focus instead on the need to control and restrain criminal activity to prevent harms from occurring in the first place (see Ashworth and Zedner 2014). One of the main guiding forces behind this preventive shift is a process of "dangerization", defined as "the tendency to perceive and analyse the world through categories of menace", leading "to continuous detection of threats ... to the prevalence of defensive perceptions ... and to the dominance of fear and anxiety over ambition and desire" (Lianos and Douglas 2000: 267). Consequently, preventive criminal laws tend to focus on activities, groups and individuals that are perceived as posing an unwarranted, often exceptional, danger to the public, and whose dangerousness justifies the aforementioned deviation from procedural safeguards, such as sexual violence, serious organized crime and terrorism.

However, although these new preventive strategies represent a significant shift in the framework of criminalization, they are only the most recent and, in some instances, more radical manifestation of criminal law's persistent concern with dangerousness (Carvalho 2017). It would be misleading to see preventive criminal offences as fundamentally departing from an otherwise liberal model of criminal law (Ashworth and Zedner 2008), for criminal law as a whole espouses a tension between its contradictory roles as a guarantor of individual justice on the one hand, and as an instrument of social control on the other (Carvalho 2017). Through this tension, dangerization influences the entire structure of criminal liability. This chapter will analyze one such instance where dangerization and a concern with risk influence and disrupt the paradigmatic criminal offence in English law, the law of murder. It will do so by exploring recent developments in one of the most controversial and contentious areas of criminal law and justice in England and Wales, that of joint enterprise (JE) liability.

Although a broad and imprecise term, generally used to refer to cases in which two or more (sometimes as many as sixteen) people are accused of having engaged in criminal activity together, JE has become notorious as a set of rules (often called a 'doctrine') and prosecutorial strategies used to convict people of a serious offence, usually murder, which occurs in the midst of another criminal activity. Widely criticized, JE has received considerable attention from the media, politicians, courts and scholarship for some time now, and especially in the last decade. This criticism mainly decried JE as a discriminatory form of criminalization whose wide application has tended to produce violent and exclusionary outcomes while disproportionately targeting vulnerable, marginalized and racialized populations. At the same time, JE had been repeatedly defended by criminal justice enforcers and politicians, and reaffirmed by the courts as an important and effective tool to protect the public against those thought to be dangerous and risky, especially those identified as part of gangs.

It is unsurprising, then, that when in February 2016, the UK Supreme Court ruled on the case of *R v Jogee* (2016) to formally abolish the main legal principle grounding JE liability, the decision was immediately seen as a watershed moment that seemed to break with the previous consensus. Jogee was hailed by many as the first step toward the correction of long-standing judicial injustices; it was also admonished by some as a potential threat, not least because it could lead to a significant number of appeals and releases of those who had been imprisoned by the application of this doctrine (see e.g. BBC 2016; Walton 2016; Ormerod and Laird 2016). This decision momentarily caused bewilderment, especially among criminal justice scholars in England and Wales who strived to understand its meaning and potential repercussions. There was, similar to the passage in the beginning of this chapter, confusion and a sense of loss, as a predominant doctrine on which so much debate and critique had relied appeared to be no longer there.

However, three years on, the picture around Jogee is radically different. Although the main legal principle grounding previous JE cases remains formally abolished, nearly all previous decisions were unaffected by this change, and appeals continue to be dismissed (see e.g. Traynor and Nathan 2019). Furthermore, JE cases still abound in the courts and in the media, and are being decided in essentially the same manner as before, in practice if not in principle. How can JE be formally rebuked, its main principle declared 'bad law' by a Supreme Court judgment and yet remain substantively the same?

This chapter argues that the answer to this question lies in the afore-mentioned ambivalence within criminal law, which leaves it intrinsically vulnerable to the demands of insecurity and uncertainty that drive concerns with risk. The first section discusses the context of JE as an area of criminalization; it explores the legal rules around JE together with their symbolic aspects and their concrete consequences. The second section then characterizes JE as an instance of what I call hostile criminalization, a form of criminalization that is geared at channeling hostility toward individuals and groups that are identified as dangerous others. JE achieves this construction of dangerousness around those it criminalizes primarily through the 'gang' label. The third section explores the consequences of JE's disproportionate targeting of marginalized and racialized populations, and how the hostile character of JE is controversially found to be the main source of its appeal and perceived usefulness and social necessity.

The fourth section of the chapter then focuses on the decision in Jogee and its aftermath. It explores the ambivalence around the decision, as it seeks to 'correct' JE's semblance of unfairness at the same time as it strives to preserve the shape and scope of its application. It suggests, further-more, that this ambivalence in Jogee is a reflection and manifestation of the deeper ambivalence within criminal law, which seeks to promote individual responsibility and justice at the same time as it follows a pre-ventive logic geared at managing tensions arising from conditions of structural inequality and violence in society. The chapter concludes by suggesting that forms of hostile criminalization, and the overwhelming concern with the risk of dangerousness displayed by them, cannot be eas-ily dispelled through formal efforts at legal reform. This is because hostile criminalization serves a (deeply problematic) social function, one which is increasingly relied upon, especially by populist and authoritarian dis-courses, and which needs to be seriously tackled before concrete legal change is possible.

The Problem of Joint Enterprise

As mentioned above, 'joint enterprise' is an imprecise term with a range of possible meanings. More generally, it refers to different rules and strat-egies aimed at "holding co-defendants equally responsible for offences which appeared to evince a common purpose" (Squires 2016a: 937). For instance, if three people decide to rob a store together, they can all be convicted of robbery, even if only one of them actually went into the store and pointed a gun at the cashier (i.e. committed the principal offence), while the other two contributed to the crime in other forms (i.e. primarily acted as accessories or accomplices to the principal offence), such as driving the car or looking out for the police. It is important to note that although the idea of a common purpose has traditionally been seen to underpin the notion of a JE, many scholars highlight that this term does not adequately encapsulate the broad array of situations where a JE can be established in law. For this reason, they have suggested other ways of understanding what constitutes a JE. A popular alternative is the notion of causation, where someone can be deemed to be part of a JE when they make a substantial contribution to the criminal activity, even in the absence of a common purpose (see e.g. Krebs 2010)—for instance, someone providing assistance in return for money, but otherwise having no investment in the outcome of the crime.

In this more general sense, JE is simply an instance of accomplice liability, that is, of rules that govern when someone can be held liable for assisting or encouraging a criminal offence. However, the most controversial and problematic aspects of JE relate to what has been known as the doctrine of JE 'proper', known formally as parasitic accessorial liability (PAL). This doctrine primarily governed cases in which, during the course of joint criminal activity, one or more of the participants go on to commit a further crime. By far the most common type of case covered by this doctrine involved situations in which, during the course of some criminal activity (such as a fight, a burglary or robbery, an affray), a murder occurred. In such cases, PAL stipulated that "it is sufficient to found a conviction for murder for a secondary party to have realised that in the course of the joint enterprise the primary party might kill with intent to do so or with intent to cause grievous bodily harm" (*R v Powell and English* 1997). In other words, if during the course of a joint criminal activity one of the participants went on to commit murder, then all of the participants of the joint criminal activity could also be held liable for this murder, as long as they realized that such murder might occur.

From a doctrinal perspective, the main problem with this doctrine was that it set a very low threshold of culpability to hold defendants liable for the most serious crime in English law. This created a situation in which it can be practically easier to convict several defendants than it is to convict a single defendant for murder. This is because, for someone to be convicted of murder as a principal offender, it must be proven that the defendant killed with the intent to kill or with the intent to cause grievous bodily harm—a requirement of culpability that has been made more stringent through the years. Meanwhile, if the killing happens in the course of a JE, according to PAL, it was sufficient for the prosecution to prove that any participant of the JE foresaw this intentional killing as a real possibility to convict them of murder. This doctrine exposed a curious mix between notions of individual responsibility and a process of collective dangerization, in which each participant in a JE is constituted as a threat, and this allows them to be deemed individually culpable for any harm arising from that criminal activity, even those which they did not intend or even expect to bring about.

The elasticity of culpability engendered by JE has allowed the doctrine to be widely (and quite effectively) deployed in recent years to deal with homicide cases. A report by the Bureau of Investigative Journalism (McClenaghan et al. 2014) found that, between 2005 and 2013, 4590 prosecutions for homicide involved two or more defendants (44% of all homicide prosecutions in that period), while 1853 people have been prosecuted for homicide in a charge that involved four or more people, which amounted to 17.7% of all homicide prosecutions in that period. This is particularly significant since a conviction for murder carries a mandatory life sentence, meaning that individuals were sent to prison for long periods of time, potentially their whole lives, based on loose arguments such as having "associated [themselves] with a foreseen murder" (*R v ABCD* 2010). The Bureau's report estimated that around 500 people were serving life sentences for convictions based on JE at the time of its publication in 2014. More recently, JE was the focus of a debate in the House of Commons, where it was estimated that at least 4500 people, including children, were incarcerated or detained because of the doctrine, "serving long sentences for crimes that they did not commit" (HC Deb 2018).

Although there were many attempts to rationalize the scope of criminal liability under JE, the main rationale grounding JE rules and decisions can be directly linked to its perceived usefulness and effectiveness in prosecuting and convicting those identified as dangerous criminals, even though the crimes they had actually committed did not sustain this view of them. This is evidenced by one of the main decisions laying out PAL, the often-cited *R v Powell and English* (1997). In this judgment, the then House of Lords, perhaps in a rare moment of candidness, reinstated and defended the doctrine of JE by asserting that "rules of common law are not based solely on logic but relate to practical concerns and, in relation to the crimes committed in the course of joint enterprises, to the need to give effective protection to the public against criminals operating in gangs." This is perhaps one of the clearest illustrations of how rules of criminal liability can be shaped and bent by a concern with dangerousness and risk. The perceived need to 'protect the public' from danger effectively displaces one of the main bastions of the liberal model of criminal law: the high threshold of culpability required for liability for murder. While in principle it appears that a conviction for murder requires possibly the highest degree of scrutiny and certainty in criminal law, in practice, nearly half of those prosecuted for murder may have been subjected to a much lower standard, their guilt established by association.

However, the main problems with JE are not simply linked to how it expands liability for murder; rather, they refer to how this expansion ostensibly targets specific groups and populations. This targeting is done primarily through an "application of the 'gang' discourse" as a strategy for criminalization that is deeply problematic, as it "is reliant upon a 'common-sense', racialized and stereotypical discourse that links Black, Asian and minority ethnic (BAME) men with an involvement with gangs, drugs and violence" (Williams and Clarke 2016: 16). JE both fuels and is fed by socially constructed anxieties and insecurities, contributing to the marginalization of those captured by the 'gang' label at the same time as it derives a sense of legitimacy from such marginalization, since it appears to be responding to a serious social problem. The dynamics of this relation can be examined through an analysis of the hostile character of JE.

Joint Enterprise, Hostile Criminalization and Dangerous Belonging

The criminalization and punishment of specific groups of people through JE highlights who is likely to be deemed dangerous in our society, and illustrates how the ascription of dangerousness follows a risk-based logic that reflects broader social insecurities and structural inequalities. In so doing, it also says something about 'us', the general members of society, who are placed in the position of punishers. More specifically, the construction of dangerousness through notions of identity and belonging in JE derives its strength from how it symbolically conjoins two different but related kinds of anxiety: a specific fear of violent crime, and a more generalized anxiety about socio-political fragmentation and uncertainty, linked to conditions of structural violence. In a collaborative project, Anastasia Chamberlen and I have examined how the allure of punishment in society—the feeling that it is useful and necessary—largely and primarily relates to the fact that punishment produces a sense of social solidarity through hostility (Carvalho and Chamberlen 2016, 2018; Chamberlen and Carvalho 2019a, b). Especially in times of particular stress, the urge to punish departs from the narrow parameters of criminal law and is thought of, commonsensically, as something that should be imposed on those 'associated with' other criminals or otherwise 'at risk of crime'. In a nutshell, "punishment promotes the image of an ordered society bound together by moral values and legal rules and protected by a strong and legitimate coercive apparatus" (Chamberlen and Carvalho 2019a: 106). This image possesses significant emotional appeal, particularly in moments and situations of social fragmentation and conflict, and to those people who feel alienated or neglected by the social order, but who long for a strong sense of belonging. This image of civil order (Farmer 2016; Carvalho 2017) promoted by punishment speaks directly to individuals' feelings of insecurity, so that it becomes more appealing the less it is concretely experienced by those who aspire to it.

However, the most significant and concerning aspect of the symbolic role of punishment is that it relies on the identification of dangerous others toward whom feelings of insecurity, anxiety and aggression, especially those arising from the lack of concrete social solidarity, can be channeled.

Such channeling is engendered through hostility, by pitting the community against the dangerous other(s) and in the process "producing a kind of solidarity that allows individuals to pursue emotional release together with a sense of belonging, without having to question or address why it is that they felt alienated and insecure in the first place" (Carvalho and Chamberlen 2018: 228; see also Mead 1918). This relationship explains the fundamental link between punishment and political exclusion: the civil order sustained by punishment requires groups and individuals who fall outside of it. Within any specific social setting, the most likely candidates to be made targets of such hostility are those groups and people who are already marginalized by socio-political conditions, something which is highlighted by the long-established notion that punishment, and especially incarceration, "represents a means to manage aggregate 'undesirable' groups" (Davis and Gibson-Light 2018: 17; see also Fassin 2018; Wacquant 2009; Feeley and Simon 1992).

While hostility is a predominant aspect of the affective and symbolic dimension of the role of punishment in society, punishment and criminalization are intimately linked. More specifically, for punishment to be able to effectively engender hostility, it relies on the many rituals of criminalization (Carvalho and Chamberlen 2018) performed by the law and in the many stages of the criminal justice system. Criminal laws and criminal justice agents and institutions define and reproduce images that symbolically tie factors and characteristics of deprivation together with notions of violence and criminality. Through this process of dangerization directed toward undesirable groups and individuals (not necessarily law breakers themselves), criminalization enacts one of its primary functions: that of reassuring law-abiding citizens (i.e. those who are not criminalized) of the security and legitimacy of society's civil order. It does so by channeling their insecurity, as well as the broader insecurity of social, economic and political relations in society (itself a product of its structural violence) toward the perceived threat of those identified as dangerous others (see Carvalho 2017).

The context and application of joint enterprise can be seen as a direct manifestation of such hostile deployment of the reassurance function of the criminal law. Besides being a prime example of what has been termed 'overcriminalization' (Husak 2007), since it stretches and distorts what are considered the appropriate limits of criminal liability, JE also overwhelmingly and disproportionally targets young Black, Asian and minority ethnic (BAME) males from impoverished urban communities (see Bridges 2013; Williams and Clarke 2016). In the report *Dangerous Associations: Joint enterprise, gangs and racism*, Patrick Williams and Becky Clarke (2016) have discussed how the symbolism of the gang as a paradigmatic "folk devil" (Cohen 1972) has proven to be a powerful tool through which groups of young BAME individuals can be effectively essentialized into the figure of dangerous others. By symbolically linking them to 'gang culture', traits that would otherwise expose a condition of vulnerability—a socially deprived background or context, lack of opportunities, experiences of discrimination and alienation, exposure to violence—are strategically reinterpreted as "markers of dangerousness" (Lianos 2013: 73). This process of essentialization works to estrange these individuals from the social order, thus conditioning a specific kind of response against their perceived otherness—a punitive form of criminal justice instead of a broader kind of social justice, for instance.

By conflating the threat of violent crime with an essentialized conception of gang culture, JE produces a conception of 'group threat' (Davis and Gibson-Light 2018) which concentrates feelings of hostility upon specific populations, generating a skewed picture of the problem which misidentifies it and downplays its complexity. This mechanism establishes the broad image of a group as a suspect community (Pantazis and Pemberton 2009), and so any indication of association with or belonging to that group becomes a marker of dangerousness, thus driving disproportionate criminalization. For instance, Williams and Clarke's study has shown that the 'gang' label is overwhelmingly attributed to Black men, even though a much lower proportion of Black men is involved in the kind of violence that is attributed to them: 81% of individuals identified by the police as gang members in Manchester, and 72% in London were Black, while Black individuals constituted only 6% of those involved in serious youth violence in Manchester, and 27% in London (Williams and Clarke 2016: charts 4 and 5).

JE thus reproduces a form of criminalization that can be conceptualized as hostile, since it is directly geared at identifying and constructing images of normative otherness (Lianos 2013) which impel the need for ostensive control and exclusion. It is important to note that such forms of criminalization are often grounded on what can be seen as legitimate concerns; in the case of JE, for instance, it is difficult to deny that there is a serious social problem around knife crime and youth violence in socially deprived urban environments in England and Wales. However, by conjoining these concerns with an essentialized notion of dangerous belonging that leads to the disproportionate targeting of marginalized populations, criminalization through JE is not only unfair and discriminatory, but it also fails to adequately identify and address the concrete harm in question. In so doing, it constructs a heightened sense of risk which cannot be effectively tackled by it. Instead, it seems that the main purpose of such criminalization is precisely to provide a suitable target for hostility.

The Dangerous Consequences of Hostile Criminalization

The essentialized, racialized and exclusionary definition of gang violence as the primary danger targeted by criminalization through JE not only shapes its deployment, making it disproportionately affect specific marginalized populations, but it also enables such deployment in the first place. First, it facilitates the prosecution and conviction of defendants. Besides being widely decried for unduly expanding the scope of criminalization by lowering the threshold of culpability, especially in cases involving murder, JE rules have also been criticized for being unclear, and juries have often said they found them confusing to apply (Crewe et al. 2015). The idea that, for individuals to be liable under PAL, it must be established that they had actively foreseen that a murder might be the possible consequence of another criminal activity can be quite nebulous and difficult to ascertain. This is particularly true when, as it has often been the case, the criminal activity in question involves occasions of spontaneous, and not necessarily serious, violence, and when the defendant in question has only been, at most, indirectly involved in such violence—for instance, they were present at the bar when a fight ensued, and they were acquainted with people who took part in the brawl. But when defendants are characterized as gang members (something which can often be accomplished through loose affiliations with notions of 'gang culture', sometimes as loose as living in a specific post code), it generates a presumption of dangerousness which makes it easier, almost natural, to infer that these individuals were likely to expect serious violence arising from their actions and those of their associates (see Krebs 2015). There is thus a significant forensic usefulness in this characterization, as it assigns a form of character responsibility (Lacey 2016) to defendants that sets them apart, thus making it easier to charge and prosecute them, and for juries to convict them.

Such is the symbolic power of the image of the dangerous other, and its capacity to engender hostility, that it significantly conditions assessments of culpability in areas of criminalization where it predominates, often taking precedence over material circumstances and even over procedural guarantees such as the presumption of innocence. This means, for instance, that a range of mainly circumstantial evidence, such as phone, text and social media records, or more recently the use of Rap and Drill videos posted online, can be effectively used by the police and by prosecutors to establish guilt in such cases (Pitts 2014). The often-confusing legal rules concerning foresight, when coupled with the construction of dangerous belonging that is enacted primarily around images of youth violence and gang culture, enable criminal responsibility to be mainly "presumed, legally inferred or juridically established by proximity, appearance, and implied normative association. When it looks like a gang—and especially when the police call it a gang—it *must* be a gang" (Squires 2016b).

Besides making it easier to charge, prosecute and convict the individuals and groups that it targets, the construction of dangerous belonging also enables hostile criminalization by giving it the semblance of social utility. To present defendants in JE cases not as complex, socially deprived and often vulnerable individuals, but as violent gang members, makes their criminalization seem desirable, even necessary. Under this prism, such cases are represented as manifestations of a broader conflict between an ordered, peaceful, legitimate society and those dangerous others who deliberately pose a threat to it. This allows a process of estrangement from those who are constructed as dangerous, who are dehumanized—often characterized as "wolf packs" (Green and McGourlay 2015) or "packs of hyenas" (Crewe et al. 2015) in judgments and media coverage—and essentialized by their criminalization. This, in turn, makes it acceptable—indeed, expected—for them to be treated with hatred and aggression. These affective dynamics of hostility provide a significant emotional appeal to such forms of criminalization, as they allow general social insecurities and anxieties to be 'worked through', externalized from the normative image of civil order in society and channeled toward those affected by the construction of dangerous identities (see Carvalho and Chamberlen 2018). This, in turn, feeds back into processes of criminalization in the form of a risk-based demand for efficiency and decisiveness, rather than due process.

Thus, while this affective dimension works primarily at a symbolic level (so that, in some ways, the idea of punishing dangerous criminals—or those at risk of criminality which therefore makes them dangerous—is nearly as attractive as their actual punishment—hence the importance of rituals of criminalization), it has real and significant consequences to these criminalized populations. Forms of hostile criminalization feed directly into the chaotic state in which prisons in England and Wales have found themselves in the past few decades (see Chamberlen and Carvalho 2019a). They do so firstly by contributing to prison overcrowding, by enabling instances of 'wholesale' criminalization such as that made possible by JE. And, secondly, they provide the means through which marginalized groups are disproportionately targeted and imprisoned, something which is clearly illustrated by the constitution of the prison population in England and Wales, where essentially all factors representing some form of social deprivation—such as homelessness, poverty, drug and alcohol dependency, persistent mental health issues, learning disabilities and belonging to a largely marginalized ethnic minority—are over-represented in relation to the general population (Prison Reform Trust 2018). The stigma of a dangerous identity has persistent and severely detrimental consequences; once someone is legally declared a risk to public protection, they are continuously subject to further risk control measures and scrutiny as inmates, and this continues once/if they are released from prison on a life license, possibly accompanied by additional preventive measures.

Furthermore, JE not only feeds into the constant state of crisis affecting the English and Welsh penal system but also effectively deepens it. Its ostensible targeting of young Black men from impoverished urban communities through mechanisms that effectively enhance the likelihood of them being convicted for serious crimes, often murder, exacerbates some of the worst aspects of mass incarceration. It sends a large number of marginalized individuals to prison for long sentences, often for crimes that they did not commit in any substantive sense. A series of studies by members of the Institute of Criminology at the University of Cambridge found that those convicted under JE were generally serving longer sentences than other individuals convicted of similar crimes, and that there was an even higher over-representation of BAME individuals in JE convictions than in the general prison population (Crewe et al. 2015). BAME individuals convicted under JE were also usually younger, were serving longer sentences and usually had more co-defendants during trial (Williams and Clarke 2016). In addition, a significant number of those convicted under JE felt that they were not justly treated by the criminal justice system; for this reason, they often failed to understand or accept their conviction, and frequently appealed against it (Crewe et al. 2015). This dissonance tends to undermine these individuals' capacity to adapt to the prison environment and makes them more likely to rebel against it, thus worsening the already painful and detrimental effects of the experience of incarceration (see Liebling and Maruna 2005) and hindering any of the potential benefits of rehabilitation.

Perhaps most concerning, the suggestion that JE is a form of hostile criminalization, which itself is linked to a largely pathological role performed by punishment in society, indicates that JE's problematic aspects cannot be easily dealt with, as they are part of a broader socio-political framework of structural violence, with which aspects of criminal law and justice are largely complicit. An analysis of the recent decision of Jogee and its aftermath arguably provides a clear illustration of the pervasiveness of dangerization and risk-based logics in the deep structure of the criminal law.

The Ambivalence of Jogee

After sustaining substantial criticism in recent years from legal scholars, campaigning organizations and governmental bodies, including a report by the House of Commons Justice Committee (2012), the UK Supreme Court finally addressed JE in its decision in Jogee, in a way that seemed to recognize and attempt to tackle its issues. In a detailed judgment that reviewed many previous cases, the Supreme Court stated categorically that it did "not consider that the [PAL] principle can be supported", and concluded "that the introduction of the principle was based on an incomplete, and in some respects erroneous, reading of the previous case law, coupled with generalised and questionable policy arguments" (*R v Jogee* 2016, at para 79). The formal outcome of this decision was to abolish the doctrine of parasitic accessorial liability, or JE 'proper'. From then on, cases falling within the area previously covered by this doctrine should be decided based on the general rules and principles of accessorial liability. The main consequence of this was that, to convict individuals of murder in cases involving JE, mere foresight was no longer sufficient; juries would from now on be satisfied that the defendants in question intended to assist or encourage the commission of the murder. In doctrinal terms, this is considered a significant change, as intention is supposed to represent the highest threshold of culpability, or *mens rea*, in English criminal law.

However, the transformation brought by this presumably watershed decision to this area of law was soon revealed to have changed very little in substance. In reality, the ineffectiveness of Jogee to produce concrete change should not have been surprising, as there were already indications in the judgment that its real purpose was not to revolutionize the legal treatment of defendants in JE cases. Primarily, the 'correction' of the legal rule regarding these cases is not as significant as it might seem at first sight. Rules regarding intention and culpability in criminal law are rather vague, and often counter-intuitive; for instance, in law, someone can be held to have 'intended' an outcome even if such outcome was not the aim or purpose of their actions. This is the case even in the law of murder, where the rules regarding intention have been most comprehensively debated and defined (see Norrie 2018). This vagueness is acknowledgedly the product of the fact that it is very difficult, arguably even impossible, for prosecutors to prove and juries to determine what individuals intended or not to do in any particular circumstance. For this reason, English criminal law is replete with attempts to manage this uncertainty in different areas of the law, which often lead to further disparity.

The general rules of accomplice liability are a prime example of this tendency. Although the law says that, for accomplices to be held liable, they must have intentionally assisted or encouraged the commission of the substantive offence, such 'intention' is usually established by recourse to discussions of what the defendant knew or foresaw about the substantial offence. Assessments of intention are usually heavily reliant on assessments of foresight, something that the decision in Jogee explicitly recognized, when it stated that cases in this area are still likely to depend on foresight as the main basis for culpability. "The error was to equate foresight with intent to assist, as a matter of law; the correct approach is to treat it as evidence of intent" (*R v Jogee* 2016, at para 87). Although it could be argued that to use foresight as evidence of intention is different from taking foresight as a sufficient basis for culpability, what this effectively means is that JE cases are likely to continue to rely on the same construction of dangerous identities and belonging as a pathway to criminalization. Moreover, since such construction effectively generated a presumption of dangerousness and guilt in JE cases before Jogee, it is difficult to imagine why this would change after the decision.

In addition, perhaps the main evidence that the correction brought forth by Jogee was mainly formal and aesthetic lies in how, at the same time as the judgment declared that the law in this area had been defective for at least 35 years, it also paradoxically maintained that previous convictions under the doctrine should not be overturned unless 'substantial injustice' could be demonstrated. Furthermore, the decision suggested that such findings of substantial injustice would be rather unlikely; the justification for this position is quite telling:

> The error identified, of equating foresight with intent to assist rather than treating the first as evidence of the second, *is important as a matter of legal principle, but it does not follow that it will have been important on the facts of*

the outcome of the trial or to the safety of the conviction. (R v Jogee 2016, at para 100, emphasis added)

This sentence highlights an inherent ambivalence within the decision: it strived to formally abolish an established and widely applied legal doctrine, symbolically sending a message that an injustice was being corrected, at the same time as it intended this change not to substantially affect the outcomes of cases in this area. This aim has so far been quite successful: nearly all appeals against previous convictions under JE have been dismissed (see *R v Johnson and others* 2016). Furthermore, the Court of Appeal, in a decision (*R v Anwar and others* 2016) three months after the Supreme Court's judgment in Jogee, further clarified that cases falling under joint enterprise ought to continue to be decided in much the same way, dismissing suggestions that the change in the threshold of culpability would mean that it would be harder to prosecute defendants from then on. The judgment stated that:

> [W]e find it difficult to foresee circumstances in which there might have been a case to answer under the law before Jogee but, because of the way in which the law is now articulated, there no longer is [...] [T]he same facts which would previously have been used to support the inference of mens rea before the decision in Jogee will equally be used now. What has changed is the articulation of the mens rea. (*R v Anwar and others* 2016, at para 20, 22)

Consequently, despite the promise initially ascribed to Jogee, criminalization through JE seems to have remained essentially the same. Individuals continue to be convicted in controversial JE cases involving murder (see e.g. Tobin 2018); defendants continue to be mostly young BAME people from economically deprived areas; and the police and prosecutors continue to rely on the same strategies for detecting and ascertaining guilt.[1]

Therefore, any hopes that the decision in Jogee would restrain criminal liability in this area appear to have been in vain; in fact, its effect may well be to expand the scope of criminalization in some respects. The reason for that is slightly technical; to summarize, when the UK Supreme Court abolished PAL, it also abolished something called the 'fundamental departure' test, a rule developed in *R v Powell and English* (1997) which allowed defendants to escape liability for murder if they could show that the killing arose in circumstances which were fundamentally different to the conditions as foreseen by the defendant. The most common way of relying on this rule was to show that the victim was killed by use of a lethal weapon, and that the defendant did not know that such weapon was being carried by the person who committed the substantive offence. According to the old rule, defendants in these circumstances were not liable for any offence related to the killing. Now, the judgment in Jogee determined that, in such situations, even if defendants could escape liability for murder, they could still be convicted of the lesser, but still quite serious, offence of manslaughter, effectively widening the application of this offence.

The failures of Jogee could be dismissed as a pragmatic reluctance to allow for a wave of appeals to inundate and discredit the criminal justice system; however, such a perspective downplays how this decision is exemplary of a broader and deeper dynamic within the criminal law. One of the primary functions of the criminal law is to manage a tension, between liberal values and emancipatory aspirations on the one hand and structurally violent conditions of inequality and exclusion on the other, which lies at the core of society's civil order (Carvalho 2017). This function requires the law to be inherently ambivalent, since it demands a constant effort to reconcile its image of a rational enterprise that aims to promote individual autonomy, equality and justice on the one hand, with its reality as an institution that works to preserve an inherently unequal and structurally violent social order on the other. One of the ways in which the criminal law strives to perform this function is by estranging certain individuals and groups from society's civil order through processes of dangerization. This allows for insecurity and anxiety to be symbolically removed from society and attributed to those identified as dangerous others, who are then scapegoated through hostile criminalization.

The ambivalence in Jogee is thus best understood as the manifestation of this deeper ambivalence in criminal law. The Supreme Court's formal abolition of PAL is meant to speak to the rationality of society's civil order, to symbolically adhere to its precepts of individual responsibility and to thus reassure individuals in society that the law is a fair and considerate instrument of justice. However, at the same time, the judgment was also unwilling to challenge the risk-based logic of JE that constructs those it targets as belonging to a dangerous culture and in need of control. The result is a decision that pays lip service to due process and effectively preserves a demand for efficiency grounded on hostility.

Conclusion

> And now, what will become of us without barbarians?
> Those people were some sort of a solution.
> (Cavafy 2007: 17)

The exclusionary and discriminatory character of JE, its broad and ostensive application and its persistence in lieu of significant criticism and attempts at judicial reform make this area of criminal justice a prime example of the hostile dimension of criminalization and punishment. This dimension exposes the persistent and pervasive influence of dangerization and of risk-based logics at the very heart of English criminal law. Criminalization in this area reflects broader socio-political phenomena that not only significantly condition the whole framework of criminal justice, but also go beyond it, as they relate to structural problems that are sustained by a problematic conception of social order within our social imaginary.

One of the main consequences to which the analysis in this chapter alludes is that attempts to tackle issues surrounding instances of hostile criminalization such as JE through localized legal reform are problematic, especially because they are likely to neglect the deeper structures from which these issues originate. As a result, efforts at legal reform such as the decision in Jogee not only fail to acknowledge the violence and exclusionary character of criminalization through JE, but because of this they also end up contributing to obscuring and perpetuating it.

If issues around hostile criminalization are to be properly addressed, due attention must be given to the context and the socio-political dimension of the criminal law. Such attention is particularly crucial today, as political discourse, agents and institutions are increasingly affected by a wave of far-right populism which strives to channel and exacerbate feelings and perceptions of insecurity and uncertainty, which set more and more individuals from particular backgrounds as risky to our civil order. Forms of hostile criminalization such as that of JE cannot be de-coupled from the many crises of solidarity experienced in contemporary societies. The risk-based logics of dangerousness which such criminalization deploys turn marginalized and vulnerable populations into scapegoats, upon which an anxious public learns to rely in order to deal with its insecurities. Until we can comprehensively challenge these logics, exclusionary laws like JE will continue to thrive, as our societies will, regrettably, continue to rely on their barbarians.

Note

1. Although it must be said that the Crown Prosecution Service (CPS) has now, after criticism, amended its post-Jogee guidance on accessorial liability, which had initially shown a heavy reliance on the term 'gang' as evidence of liability. See Crown Prosecution Service (2018).

References

Ashworth, A. and Zedner, L. (2008) 'Defending the criminal law: Reflections on the changing character of crime, procedure, and sanctions'. *Criminal Law and Philosophy*, 2(1), 21–51.

Ashworth, A. and Zedner, L. (2014) *Preventive Justice* (Oxford: Oxford University Press).

BBC (2016) 'Joint enterprise law wrongly interpreted for 30 years, Supreme Court rules'. *BBC* [Online]. Available at: https://www.bbc.co.uk/news/uk-35598896 (Accessed: 9 January 2019).

Bridges, L. (2013) 'The case against joint enterprise'. *Race & Class*, 54(4), 33–42.

Carvalho, H. (2017) *The Preventive Turn in Criminal Law*. Oxford: Oxford University Press.

Carvalho, H. and Chamberlen, A. (2016) 'Punishment, justice and emotions'. In: M. Tonry (ed.) *Oxford Handbooks Online in Criminology*. Oxford: Oxford University Press, 1–31.

Carvalho, H. and Chamberlen, A. (2018) 'Why Punishment Pleases: Punitive Feelings in a World of Hostile Solidarity'. *Punishment and Society*, 20(2), 217–234.

Cavafy, C. P. (2007) *The Collected Poems with parallel Greek text* (translated by Evangelos Sachperoglou). Oxford: Oxford University Press.

Chamberlen, A. and Carvalho, H. (2019a) 'The Thrill of the Chase: Punishment, Hostility and the Prison Crisis'. *Social and Legal Studies*, 28(1), 100–117.

Chamberlen, A. and Carvalho, H. (2019b) 'Punitiveness and the Emotions of Punishment: Between Solidarity and Hostility'. In M. H. Jacobsen and S. Walklate (eds.) *Emotions and Crime: Towards a Criminology of Emotions* (London: Routledge), 96–112.

Cohen, S. (1972) *Folk Devils and Moral Panics: The Creation of the Mods and Rockers*. London: MacGibbon and Kee.

Crewe, B., Liebling, A., Padfield, N. and Virgo, G. (2015) 'Joint enterprise: The implications of an unfair and unclear law'. *Criminal Law Review*, 252–269.

Crown Prosecution Service (2018) *Secondary Liability: charging decisions on principals and accessories* [Online]. Available at: https://www.cps.gov.uk/legal-guidance/secondary-liability-charging-decisions-principals-and-accessories (Accessed: 9 January 2019).

Davis, A. P. and Gibson-Light, M. (2018) 'Difference and Punishment: Ethno-political Exclusion, Colonial Institutional Legacies, and Incarceration'. *Punishment and Society* (Online First), 1–22.

Ericson, R. (2007) *Crime in an Insecure World* (London: Polity Press).

Farmer, L. (2016) *Making the Modern Criminal Law: Criminalization and Civil Order*. Oxford: Oxford University Press.

Fassin, D. (2018) *The Will to Punish*. New York: Oxford University Press.

Feeley, M. and Simon, J. (1992) 'The new penology: Notes on the emerging strategy of corrections and its implications'. *Criminology*, 30(4), 449–474.

Green, A. and McGourlay, C. (2015) 'The Wolf Packs in Our Midst and Other Products of Criminal Joint Enterprise Prosecutions'. *The Journal of Criminal Law*, 79(4), 280–297.

HC Deb (2018). 25 January 2018, vol. 635, col. 445 [Online]. Available at: https://hansard.parliament.uk/commons/2018-01-25/debates/00389B37-64AA-4AC8-BBBB-BE6B98F9C5C1/JointEnterprise (Accessed: 9 January 2019).

House of Commons Justice Committee (2012) *Joint Enterprise*. London: The Stationery Office Limited.

Husak, D. (2007) *Overcriminalization: The Limits of the Criminal Law*. Oxford: Oxford University Press.

Krebs, B. (2010) 'Joint Criminal Enterprise'. *Modern Law Review*, 73(4), 578–604.

Krebs, B. (2015) 'Mens Rea in Joint Enterprise: A Role for Endorsement?' *Cambridge Law Journal*, 74(3), 480–504.

Lacey, N. (2016) *In Search of Criminal Responsibility: Ideas, Interests, and Institutions*. Oxford: Oxford University Press.

Lianos, M. (2013) 'Normative Otherness: From 'Sovereign Subjects' to 'Collateral Damage''. In M. Lianos (ed), *Dangerous Others, Insecure Societies*. Farnham: Ashgate.

Lianos, M. and Douglas, M. (2000) 'Dangerization and the End of Deviance: The Institutional Environment'. *British Journal of Criminology*, 40, 261–278.

Liebling, A. and Maruna. S. (2005) *The Effects of Imprisonment*. Willan Publishing: London.

McClenaghan, M., McFadyean, M. and Stevenson, R. (2014) *Joint Enterprise: An investigation into the legal doctrine of joint enterprise in criminal convictions*. London: The Bureau of Investigative Journalism.

Mead, G.H. (1918) 'The psychology of punitive justice'. *American Journal of Sociology*, 23(5), 577–602.

Norrie, A. (2018) 'Legal and Social Murder: What's the Difference?', *Criminal Law Review*, 7, 531–542.

Ormerod, D. and Laird, K. (2016) 'Jogee: not the end of a legal saga but the start of one?' *Criminal Law Review*, 8, 539–552.

Pantazis, C. and Pemberton, S. (2009) 'From the 'Old' to the 'New' Suspect Community: Examining the Impacts of Recent UK Counter-Terrorist Legislation'. *British Journal of Criminology*, 49(5), 646–666.

Pitts, J. (2014) 'Who Dunnit? Gangs, Joint Enterprise, Bad Character and Duress'. *Youth and Policy*, 113, 48–59.

Pratt, J. (2016) 'Risk Control, Rights and Legitimacy in the Limited Liability State'. *British Journal of Criminology*, 57, 1322–1339.

Prison Reform Trust (2018) *Bromley Briefings Prison Factfile: Autumn 2018* [Online]. Available at: http://www.prisonreformtrust.org.uk/Portals/0/Documents/Bromley%20Briefings/Autumn%202018%20Factfile.pdf (Accessed: 9 January 2019).

R v ABCD (2010) EWCA Crim 1622. *Westlaw* [Online]. Available at: https://legalresearch.westlaw.co.uk (Accessed: 15 April 2019).

R v Anwar and others (2016) EWCA Crim 551. *Westlaw* [Online]. Available at: https://legalresearch.westlaw.co.uk (Accessed: 15 April 2019).

R v Jogee (2016) UKSC 8. *Westlaw* [Online]. Available at: https://legalresearch.westlaw.co.uk (Accessed: 15 April 2019).

R v Johnson and others (2016) EWCA Crim 1613. *Westlaw* [Online]. Available at: https://legalresearch.westlaw.co.uk (Accessed: 15 April 2019).

R v Powell and English (1997) 3 WLR 959. *Westlaw* [Online]. Available at: https://legalresearch.westlaw.co.uk (Accessed: 15 April 2019).

Squires, P. (2016a) 'Voodoo Liability: Join Enterprise Prosecution as an Aspect of Intensified Criminalisation'. *Oñati Socio-Legal Series*, 6(4), 937–956.

Squires, P. (2016b) 'Constructing the Dangerous, Black, Criminal "Other"'. *British Society of Criminology Newsletter*, 79, 1–4.

Tobin, O. (2018) 'Jermaine Goupall killer has to be held back in the dock as he lashes out after being found guilty'. *Croydon Advertiser* [Online]. Available at: https://www.croydonadvertiser.co.uk/news/croydon-news/jermaine-goupall-killer-held-back-1215673 (Accessed: 9 January 2019).

Traynor, L. and Nathan, F. (2019) "Blind" boy, 15, jailed for life over murder he 'didn't see' set to be released', *Mirror* [Online]. Available at: https://www.mirror.co.uk/news/uk-news/blind-boy-15-jailed-life-14914727 (Accessed: 10 May 2019).

Wacquant, L. (2009) Punishing the Poor. Durham, NC: Duke University Press.

Walton, G. (2016) 'Hundreds of convicted killers may seek to appeal after 'joint enterprise' law wrongly interpreted for 30 years'. *The Telegraph* [Online]. Available at: https://www.telegraph.co.uk/news/uknews/law-and-order/12162445/Supreme-Court-joint-enterprise-ruling-accessories-to-murder.html (Accessed: 9 January 2019).

Williams, P. and Clarke, B. (2016) *Dangerous associations: Joint enterprise, gangs and racism*. London: Centre for Crime and Justice Studies.

Re-examining Risk and Blame in Penal Controversies: Parole in England and Wales, 2013–2018

Harry Annison

Introduction

In January 2018, the Parole Board for England and Wales' decision to release prolific sex offender John Worboys was made public. This led to a furore with significant effects, it being regarded by many as the latest example of the criminal justice system failing the dozens of women harmed by his crimes. I use the set of inter-linked controversies for the Parole Board prompted—and intensified—by this high-profile scandal as a 'way in' to examine penal change (Annison 2018a). Specifically, I consider what insights these developments relating to parole might provide for our understanding of risk and populism, two concepts that have been central to scholarly understanding of penal politics in the late modern era.[1]

In support of this goal, I utilize Sparks' (2000b) earlier examination of risk and blame in a series of scandals facing English prisons in the

H. Annison (✉)
Southampton Law School, Southampton University, Southampton, UK
e-mail: H.Annison@soton.ac.uk

© The Author(s) 2020
J. Pratt, J. Anderson (eds.), *Criminal Justice, Risk and the Revolt against Uncertainty*,
Palgrave Studies in Risk, Crime and Society,
https://doi.org/10.1007/978-3-030-37948-3_7

139

mid-1990s as a point of comparison. Sparks argued that analysing developments that might appear to be merely 'sorry stories of organizational failings and battles for political survival' holds the potential for providing valuable conceptual insights for penal theory (Sparks 2000b: 136).[2] Sparks was considering the value and limits of the sociology of punishment literature on risk and populism for understanding specific (crucial, high-profile) developments in England and Wales in the mid-1990s. Here I pursue a similar objective, twenty years on: examining the controversies besetting the Parole Board in the mid-2010s.

Sparks examined the succession of high-profile escapes in the 1990s that placed a harsh spotlight on the political and organizational leaders responsible for criminal justice. To summarize: in September 1994, six Irish Republican prisoners briefly escaped from Whitemoor prison's Special Security Unit, resulting in the wounding of a prison officer. This was followed by a further three inmates escaping from Parkhurst dispersal prison in January 1995, who remained at large for several days, alongside the suicide of mass murderer Frederick West in his Birmingham prison cell (Sparks 2000b: 134). The ensuing enquiries (Woodcock 1994; Learmont 1995), and journalistic investigations, led to further failings emerging.

The media focused increasingly upon the question of responsibility. With the memories of the 'worst series of prison riots in the history of the British system' in spring 1990 still fresh (Woolf 1991), amidst the political battle to gain ownership of the 'law and order' mantle (Downes and Morgan 1997), there was little room for manoeuvre. Whether the escapes were a result of '"operational" failure' or 'from defects of "policy"' became of crucial importance (Sparks 2000b: 136). The survival of the Director General of the Prison Service and the Home Secretary depended on it.

While there are distinctions between these episodes—Sparks' centred upon prison controversies, while here I focus on parole—there are also notable similarities. Both saw central elements of the criminal justice system subjected to sustained media criticism and public opprobrium for their perceived inability to meet their fundamental *raison d'être*: public protection. Both controversies boiled down to a battle for survival between two protagonists. Further, in both cases, the central dynamic in play was between a government department with political responsibility for criminal justice and an independent body with responsibility for the specific organization in question.[3]

I will argue that cultural and political developments affecting understandings of victimhood and inclusion in the public arena have implications for our understanding of both risk and populism. Where accounts to date have tended generally to depict victims being used by cynical populists for electoral ends, here we see that victims were more commonly viewed as active subjects, shaping the course of penal change. This in turn has implications for risk. While debates surrounding risk rumble on in a manner that are in many regards not fundamentally distinctive to those of the mid-1990s, the 'pressing in' of publics provides ever-smaller space in which experts and elites can operate. In closing, I point to the importance for penal theory of identifying not only concerning trends, but also more positive developments that may give glimpses of ways towards a better penal policy and penal culture.

Dilemmas and Discourses Regarding Parole, 2013–2018

In recent years, the English Parole Board has faced challenges that have resulted in significant changes to its policy and practice. These include: ongoing questions regarding the independence of the Parole Board from government (or lack thereof); the pressures placed on the Parole Board by a surge in indeterminate sentences at the turn of the century; the need to tackle a considerable backlog of cases and related delays; and the growth—in number and strength—of (often competing) calls from various 'publics' for changes to parole policy or practice.

In this section, I first set out the pressures and challenges the Parole Board has faced over recent years. We see that there are competing priorities in play: at various points concerns about administrative efficiency take precedence; at others the focus is justice and fairness; further still, concerns about public protection predominate. I then discuss the decision by the Parole Board to release Worboys from an indeterminate sentence in 2018.

The Independence of the Parole Board

Issues regarding the independence of the Parole Board for England and Wales have been a recurring source of controversy (and indeed has been since its inception in 1967, as Guiney notes, 2018: 239). In the case of *Brooke*,[4] the Court of Appeal held that the Parole Board did not satisfy the requirements of art.5(4) ECHR (Padfield 2016). The then Lord Chief Justice, Lord Phillips, concluded:

> Neither the Secretary of State nor his Department has adequately addressed the need for the Parole Board to be and to be seen to be free of influence in relation to the performance of its judicial functions… The close working relationship between the Board and the unit acting as its sponsor has tended to blur the distinction between the executive role of the former and the judicial role of the latter.[5]

Following the *Brooke* judgment, sponsorship of the Parole Board was moved from the National Offender Management Service (NOMS, now HM Prison and Probation Service, or HMPPS) to the Access to Justice Directorate of the Ministry of Justice. In 2009, the government launched a consultation on the parole system, including questions regarding its appropriate legal status (Ministry of Justice 2009). However no further actions have been taken at the time of writing.

The Long Tail of an English Surge in Indeterminate Sentencing

Part 12, Chapter 5 of the Criminal Justice Act 2003 was titled 'Dangerous Offenders' and represented an important English element of the more general trend towards the 'pre-emptive turn in criminal justice' (Zedner 2009). The provisions contained therein, and most prominently the indeterminate Imprisonment for Public Protection (IPP) sentence, resulted in a dramatic increase in the numbers of indeterminately sentenced prisoners in England and Wales. While the sentence itself was relatively short-lived, its substantial effects continue to reverberate.[6]

The IPP sentence was created by the Labour government in 2003, intended to target individuals who posed a 'significant risk of serious harm' to the public but whose immediate offence did not merit a life sentence. Driven by dominant political ideologies of the time and a simplistic, favourable view of the capabilities of emerging risk assessment practices, the sentence was developed in over-broad terms and in a manner which overly constrained judicial discretion (Annison 2015).

IPP prisoners could not achieve release unless a parole panel was persuaded that their continued detention was no longer necessary for the protection of the public. By default, released IPP prisoners remain on licence for life. Having been amended in 2008, in 2012 the sentence was abolished. It was accepted by the then Justice Secretary that the sentence was fundamentally unfair in principle and unworkable in practice (Annison 2015). However, existing IPP prisoners remained: their situation was not addressed by the legislation.

The current Parole Board chief executive has publicly recognized the feelings of injustice caused for IPP prisoners and their families by this situation. He has described the legacy of this sentence as 'one of failure', leaving a 'dreadful legacy' (Jones 2019). The Parole Board has stated that it 'is clear that more can and should be done to give hope and a reason to engage in rehabilitative activity to the majority' of IPP prisoners (Parole Board 2016: 3).

In terms of substantive action, while the Parole Board estimates that its own efforts to increase the rates of release will realistically lead to a decline to approximately 1500 IPP prisoners being inside by 2020 (Parole Board 2018a: 11), they have advised government on measures required to have a more significant impact on this issue of concern (see Annison 2018b). They have also continued to argue that more needs to be done 'to find alternatives to recall', emphasizing the need to encourage probation officers 'to exercise their professional judgement to keep people in the community' (Jones 2017b).

Backlog of Cases

Longstanding concerns about the ability of the Parole Board to cope with its burgeoning caseload have been raised for some time now. This was exacerbated by the additional pressures placed on it by the indeterminate sentences discussed above, and a failure to adequately resource the Parole

Board (and indeed any relevant part of the criminal justice system (Annison 2015). This has led to considerable compensation payments to prisoners over the past decade (National Audit Office 2017).

Ongoing efforts to resolve the delays besetting the parole process were dealt another blow in the case of *Osborn*.[7] In this case, Lord Reed held that the Parole Board should hold an oral hearing 'whenever "fairness" demands it'.[8] This dramatically expanded the number of oral hearings required—as opposed to paper hearings (where release or progression is considered merely 'on the papers'). The operational pressures placed by the judgment on the Parole Board—albeit welcome in terms of prisoner rights—were compounded by the ongoing lack of funds and a concomitant shortage of board members to conduct more oral hearings. This resulted in a backlog of cases, "which hit a high of 3163 cases in early 2015" (Parole Board 2016: 3).

While by 2017/2018, the Parole Board's fiftieth year, the Board had successfully cleared the backlog of cases (Parole Board 2018b: 5), deferral rates for hearings remained high. The Parole Board leadership has recognized the potential for postponing of hearings, often at short notice, to call into question the effectiveness of the system and to exacerbate the distress of all involved, causing unnecessary and 'increased uncertainty for victims, prisoners, and their families' (Jones 2017a).

The background factors discussed above operated within, and sometimes contributed to, the competing dynamics that have marked public debate on penal policy in recent times. These include concerns about the rights of victims and how appropriately to recognize and respond to their needs (Hoyle and Zedner 2007; Burman and Gelsthorpe 2017); public and professional aversion to risks of further offending and public suspicion of non-transparent expert decision-making about such matters; and many elements of the criminal justice system being seen to be fundamentally flawed (Justice Committee 2018, 2019).

The Decision to Release Worboys

Found guilty of committing nineteen offences against twelve women, including sexual assault and rape, John Worboys (now calling himself

John Radford) was given an IPP sentence, with a minimum tariff of eight years, in 2009 (BBC News 2018). Public concern quickly began to mount as the tabloid and news media began publishing the outcome of his parole hearing. Held in November 2017 to consider his request for release, the decision was publicized in January 2018. Taking into account time spent on remand, at the time of the announcement, Worboys had spent almost ten years in custody. In accordance with Parole Board rules of the time, the conditions placed upon his licence were not made public. Some of Worboys' victims, their legal representatives, and campaign groups rightly highlighted the acute distress the decision caused.

In a statement issued in Parliament on 19 January 2018 the Secretary of State for Justice responded to public concern and announced a review of the 'Law, Policy and Procedure Relating to Parole Decisions'. Another particularly notable development was the successful efforts by a number of parties, including several victims, *The Sun* newspaper and the Mayor of London Sadiq Khan, to pursue an application for judicial review of the Parole Board's decision. The hearing, which began on 13 March 2018, was to examine the 'reasonableness' of the decision to release Worboys (in line with standard principles of English public law). Further, the parties sought to challenge the lawfulness of Rule 25 of the Parole Board Rules 2016, which prohibited publication of the reasons for release or detaining inmates.

Concerns relating to Worboys did not begin and end with the decision to release. Some have seen the Parole Board as finding itself acting as a 'lightning rod' for the earlier failings of both the police and the Crown Prosecution Service (CPS) in their investigations of allegations by victims of Worboys, and subsequent decisions regarding prosecution strategy (see Guiney and Prison Reform Trust 2018). These early failings conditioned the length of Worboys' original sentence, considered by many to be insufficient. The very imposition of an IPP sentence rather than a 'standard' life sentence flowed directly from the prosecution decisions, a fact that has caused acute concern to families campaigning for release of IPP prisoners who often had committed relatively minor offences (Annison and Condry 2019).[9] Compounding all of this was the failings of the Victim Contact Service, for whom the National Probation Service held responsibility, to inform relevant individuals about the decision to release (HM Chief Inspector of Probation 2018: 14).

In seeking to address some of these concerns, shortly after the decision to release was made, the then Parole Board chairman stated:

> I do not make decisions on individual cases, but I have observed many hearings and am struck by the careful and sensitive way panels make their decisions. Do they always get it right? No ... But I would not be honest if I pretended risk could be eliminated completely. Parole Board members need to be confident a prisoner will not reoffend—but they cannot be certain. If certainty is required that needs to be reflected in the length of the original sentence. (Hardwick 2018b)

Penal reform charities in England and Wales were notably silent, with their lack of contribution to the public debate justified on the basis that they do not comment on individual cases.

The mounting pressures facing the Parole Board reached a crescendo at the end of March 2018 when the High Court overturned the original decision to release and ordered that a fresh hearing be conducted. In light of allegations that Worboys perpetrated over 100 sexual offences against other women, which were dropped by the CPS for lack of evidence, the Court held that whilst it is not the Parole Board's role to determine whether the prisoner has committed other offences, it is not 'precluded from considering evidence of wider offending when determining the issue of risk'.[10] As a consequence, the Court determined that 'the Parole Board ought to have carried out, or have instigated the carrying out of, further inquiry'.[11]

In light of this decision, then Parole Board Chief Executive Nick Hardwick was forced to resign by the recently appointed Justice Secretary David Gauke. In an illuminating resignation letter, Hardwick accused the Justice Secretary of encroaching on the independence of the Board:

> You told me that you thought my position was untenable. I had no role in the decision of the panel in the case and believe I am capable of leading the Parole Board through the changes, many of which I have advocated, that will now be necessary ... I want to state my concern about the independence of the Board. I believe this matter raises very troubling questions

about how the Board's independence can be safeguarded. I hope Parliament will consider what structural changes are necessary to ensure this independence is protected in future. (Hardwick 2018a)

This development strengthens arguments made by scholars including Padfield (2016) and Guiney (Guiney and Prison Reform Trust 2018), who have raised concerns about the ongoing failure of government to relinquish control of this 'court-like body' component of the criminal justice system.

Conceptual Implications

Sparks rightly reminds us that administrative systems such as prisons and parole "almost only come to public notice under conditions of scandal" (Sparks 2000b: 139). And such moments hold the potential to provide insights into broader conceptions of penal trends in the sociology of punishment. In light of the recent controversies relating to parole in England and Wales, what might we learn as regards conceptual understandings of risk and populism?

Risk

In an effort to capture a vast body of literature and debates therein, one might fairly state in summary that risk has tended to be explored in two broad senses within penal theory: in terms of recourse to technology (primarily actuarial risk assessment tools), as a means of "identifying, classifying and managing groups assorted by levels of dangerousness" (Feeley and Simon 1994: 173); and as a way of thinking, a 'risk-logic' (Adams 2003; Mythen 2014).

At a general level this characterization of policy and public debate in criminal justice remains apposite when applied to these developments in parole. We have seen that the debate was centred around risk and public protection (and the Parole Board's duty to accurately assess risk and thus keep the public insulated from the 'dangerous'), just as it was in relation to prisons in the 1990s (and their duty to prevent the escapes of serious criminals). Criticisms as regards Worboys' release tended to take the form of arguing that risk was being 'done wrong' (wrong types of knowledge, Parole Board members being gullible dupes etc.)[12]; it was not that this form of logic in itself was no longer appropriate.[13]

Thus, Pratt's characterization of the conceptualization of dangerous offenders within neoliberal society remains apt:

> That group of offenders whose propensity to repeatedly commit crimes of a non-capital but otherwise serious nature puts the well-being of the rest of the community at risk. (Pratt 2000: 35)[14]

Second, the developments in parole surveyed above provides a vivid illustration of the diminishing 'space' afforded to experts in which they are able to operate. Deference to experts and evidence has declined across developed nations, and the field of criminal justice is no exception (Pratt 2007; Reiner 2007). Criminal justice workers in probation, parole and elsewhere have become increasingly aware that they are liable to face severe and sustained public attack, and scapegoating, where perceived errors of judgment occur (Burke and Collett 2014; Fitzgibbon 2011). The Worboys furore was no different. The Parole Board, and the members involved in the decision, faced sustained criticism from, and via, the tabloid media.

Drawing on the work of Mary Douglas (1992), Sparks argued that "risk comes into public focus in 'forensic moments'—i.e. when the question of accountability arises" (Sparks 2000b: 132). And indeed, notwithstanding some readings of the rise of the 'new penology' (Feeley and Simon 1992), the developments discussed above make clear that risk is never as neutral as it can sometimes appear. It is never truly technocratic, 'domesticated'. It is always tied up with "dread, danger and catastrophe" (Sparks 2000b: 132).

Indeed, some of the psychologists involved in the decision to release Worboys (writing anonymously) spoke to these dynamics when they raised concerns at

[t]he void of professional representation that might have led a measured response to the public by the British Psychological Society on behalf of its members, the lack of informed debate, and ultimately the failure to defend the professionalism and expertise of psychologists in the field of risk assessment. There has been commentary from psychologists on social media, but unfortunately, this has primarily been ill-informed, and has simply exacerbated the situation, failing to set a high standard of debate. (Anonymous 2018)

Equally, the developments discussed above provide one illustration of a 'pressing in' on penal policy and its attendant politics by groups who traditionally have found themselves excluded (Loader 2006; Ryan 2003). 'Publics' including prisoners, ex-prisoners, families of prisoners, victims and many more besides are increasingly welcomed by organizations as 'service users', 'experts by experience' and 'co-producers' (Durose and Richardson 2016).[15] Substantive examples in England and Wales included the Prison Reform Trust's nascent Prisoner Policy Network (Prison Reform Trust 2018), and the ongoing efforts of organizations including User Voice and Clinks.

While these initiatives can pose challenges, it is undoubtedly a generally positive—and likely unavoidable—development. It flows, for example, with Dzur's compelling call for the fostering of 'load bearing participation' in criminal justice (Dzur 2016) and with Loader's desire for a better politics of crime control (Loader 2010). A corollary of this within criminal justice has been the challenging of narrow, individualized conceptualizations of risk that are—or certainly are often perceived to be—relied upon by many practitioners within probation, parole and psychology (Shapland and Bottoms 2017). Where an individualized conception of 'risks' and 'needs', deficiencies requiring remedial 'treatment', had predominated from at least the 1990s (Ward and Maruna 2007; Robinson and Crow 2009), this paradigm has been challenged by scholarly works engaging with the lived reality of both criminal offending and desistance from crime (see, e.g., Maruna 2001; McNeill 2006; Sampson and Laub 1993). This latter perspective has grown significantly in influence amongst policymakers and practitioners in recent years (Moffatt 2015).

Populism and Blame

When reflecting on the developments set out above, the conceptions of penal populism that came to predominate in the mid-1990s hold little explanatory value per se. Two early conceptions of populism sighted within criminal justice scholarship comprised 'authoritarian populism' and 'populist punitiveness'. The former is a term introduced by the late sociologist Stuart Hall. Developed during the period of Thatcherism in Britain, he described Thatcher's form of populism as:

> First, forming public opinion, then, disingenuously, consulting it—the tendency to 'reach for the law' above, is complemented by a popular demand to be governed strictly from below. Thereby the drift to law and order above secures a degree of popular support and legitimacy amongst the powerless, who see no other alternative. (Hall 1978: 2)

This denotes, in short, a strategic decision by elite politicians to stir up 'public opinion' and then 'respond' to it.

The latter term was introduced by Anthony Bottoms. It captures an approach to crime and penal policy in which particular policy positions are adopted due to the belief that they will find favour with the public. It conveys "the notion of politicians tapping into, and using for their own purposes, what they believe to be the public's generally punitive stance" (Bottoms 1995: 40). Again, this denotes a cynical move taken by elites, rather than genuine engagement with the public. We can helpfully conceive of these as 'agential' definitions of populism.[16]

In the case of the parole controversies—and indeed in Sparks' examination of the earlier prison controversies—we saw not so much 'authoritarian populism' (Hall) or 'populist punitiveness' (Bottoms), but an effort by a recently arrived Justice Secretary to survive the tidal wave of political risk presented by the Worboys furore.[17] Therefore the literature on blame and crisis management is perhaps most pertinent (Boin et al. 2005; Hood 2011). When crises 'fix the spotlight on those who govern' (Boin et al. 2005: ix), the political imperative is not only to address the substantive issue, but to tame the political risks inherent in such scandals (Hood 2002).

This is not to say that the actions of relevant policymakers are irrelevant or unworthy of sustained analysis in relation to penal theory; far from it (Annison 2018a).[18] But the blame game (see Hood 2002) that took place in these English parole controversies, and the political risks that were apparent, are influenced by the broader cultural context, of which what we could term the 'structural' components of penal populism are an important component.

Pratt et al. (2005) argued that a key driver of what those authors termed the 'new punitiveness' is the destabilizations and dislocations of traditional social relations which led people "to feel more insecure and more prone to emotional outbursts in a world where security and certainty are perceived as absent" (Pratt et al. 2005: xxiv). Pratt later expanded on this initial discussion, arguing that penal populism denoted "a dramatic reconfiguration of the axis of penal power, with the strategic effect of reversing many of the previous assumptions that had hitherto informed post-war penal policy" (Pratt 2007: 35).

Ryan similarly argued in 2003 that "democracy is changing—[the] transmission of public preferences into the heart of government, demanding day by day more attention be given to them is something that all politicians have to learn to live with" (Ryan 2003: 135). This of course has been super-charged by the rise of social media (Gerbaudo 2018; Sunstein 2017).

One dynamic of particular note as regards the controversies surrounding parole, and the decision to release Worboys in particular, is that relating to the role of victims, and related perceptions of 'victimhood'. In terms of the role of victims in the sociology of punishment, Pratt has argued previously that "*penal* populism speaks to the way in which criminals and prisoners are thought to have been favoured at the expense of crime victims in particular and the law-abiding public in general" (Pratt 2007: 12). Garland has written of the growing power of the 'symbolic figure of the victim', taking 'a life of its own, and playing a key role in political and policy argument' (Garland 2001: 144). Indeed, there are many high-profile examples of victims of crime—or their close relatives—taking an active role in penal policy debates over recent decades (Pratt 2007).

But in the discussion of such developments within the sociology of punishment canon over the past three decades, the dominant driver of penal policy tends to be cast as an abstract notion of 'victim': an emotionally powerful construct that is utilized by cynical populists including media moguls and politicians (Simon 1998; Garland 2001). Victims and their families, even those doing their best to exert agency, to right the wrongs of the crime they have suffered or to try to ensure fewer future victims of crime, are cast—more or less implicitly—as passive, serving as figurative *objects* for the achievement of other individuals' political goals.[19]

But these accounts—without further careful elaboration—risk obscuring the complex dynamics in play and the heterogeneous nature of the category 'victims of crime' (Bosworth and Kaufman 2013), and responses to them (Hoyle and Zedner 2007). Walklate et al. have noted that since the 1980s the shape and form of victims' influence on policy debates have shifted "from the influence and presence of victim centred organizations to the rise of the high profile individual victim" (Walklate et al. 2019: 1). The Worboys case suggests that the landscape may be shifting once more. In this case, the victims engaged in public challenge and the ensuing legal action were—*and were widely recognized to be*—pro-active, reasoned, brave individuals. They were responding to a clear issue of public concern, and—contrary to one of the common scholarly concerns with 'victim campaigns'—actually *did* represent a large number of victims, given the apparently considerable extent of Worboys' crimes. They were overwhelmingly regarded as survivors, as active *subjects*.

I do not seek here to deliver moral judgment on the range of high-profile cases that have come to form part of accounts of penal change. Rather, I make the observation that specific cases are always affected by, and exemplary of, the interaction between specific individuals and the broader social context. For victims' stories to have moral force for both publics and policymakers, they must resonate with wider cultural understandings of the time (Walklate et al. 2019: 13). And this cultural context has shifted dramatically over the past twenty years. In recent years, campaigns on social media, such as #metoo and #yesallwomen, have been part of a new wave of efforts to challenge sexism in general, and sexual offences (and the fear of sexual assault) against women in particular (Serisier 2018).

Just as allegations against film producer Harvey Weinstein in the United States served as a concrete case around which 'ambient' concern could swell and gain a momentum of their own, similarly the offending by John Worboys—and concerns about the actions taken by the police, Crown Prosecution Service (CPS) and Parole Board—gave rise to sustained actions by women who had been sexually assaulted by Worboys, who had decided, in the terms of one prominent campaign, that 'time's up'. The actions of some of Worboys' victims, and their supporters, in challenging criminal justice decisions, including the Parole Board's decision to release—with some waiving their right to anonymity in order to speak publicly about it—speak to (and themselves contribute to) the shifting social and political context as regards the treatment of women by the criminal justice system, and concerns with misogyny and harassment more generally.

Concerns about the treatment of (female) victims of crime have, of course, a much longer history (Serisier 2018). Maintaining our focus on recent decades, we could note, for example, the increased efforts as regards the policing of domestic violence (Hoyle 1998) and the political shifts towards recognizing victims' rights through the 1990s (Rock 2004). The sentiments underlying this most recent wave of activism are perhaps captured by Serisier's statement that behind much of the related campaigning activity is a view that 'producing and disseminating a genre of personal experiential narratives can end sexual violence' (Serisier 2018: 4). What was particularly striking in this present case was the *receptivity* of organizations to recognizing the issues raised, facilitating both discussion and action. In this regard we can see connections with the efforts by criminal justice organizations, noted above, to engage with a range of publics in ways considered inappropriate until only recently.

I do not argue that the developments around the Worboys case are entirely novel, that this is the first occurrence of the (re-)framing of victims as survivors who must be heard (Rock 1998). I suggest, rather, that the broader social and cultural context had—and continues to have—important effects on the substantive development of this case. And this, in turn, has implications for our conception of the relationship between victims, blame, populism and penal change.

Conclusion: Risk, Blame and Political Culture

I have examined the highly publicized controversies prompted (and intensified) by the decision to release John Worboys on parole in 2018 as a 'way in' to examine penal change. Using Sparks' (2000b) earlier examination of risk and blame in a series of scandals facing English prisons in the mid-1990s as a useful point of comparison, I have considered how these recent, high-profile developments regarding parole might inform our understandings of the concepts of risk, populism and blame, and their place within penal politics in the late modern era.

Here, it is possible only to sketch arguments that invite more detailed exposition. Nonetheless, I have sought to suggest that we observe, in some ways, a remarkable durability and persistence of these concepts and their relevance to penal policy. What we might call 'risk talk' and underlying systems of assessment and management remain dominant. Sparks' assertion in his earlier work remains convincing and pertinent: namely, that the 'bones of contention' that tend to feature in public debate around penal policy tend to centre upon 'both the capacity of the penal system to deliver justice (however defined by the contending parties) and its capacity to contribute to the safety of an uneasy public' (Sparks 2000b: 128). But within these broad similarities across the past two decades, the dynamics of the more recent controversies I have examined indicate subtle but important change.

Mary Douglas, reflecting on the ways in which debates surrounding risk and danger, justice and blame, have taken shape in different communities at different times, has asserted that they are never fixed in abstraction, but always "rhetorical resources" that are inescapably part of a "cultural debate" (Douglas 1992: 25). And while we no longer (generally) speak of sin and taboo in the manner of 'pre-modern' communities, the same underlying impulse remains: to develop a consensus "on the kinds of solidarity that will help [us] to cope collectively with their environment of disease, accident and war" (Douglas 1992: 30). The general theme within dominant accounts of penal policy at the turn of the century was of a 'volatile and contradictory' combination of impersonal risk logics and emotive 'acting out', demonizing criminals and other out-groups as a means of building solidarity (and indeed of shoring up a crumbling political project: Sparks 2000b).

As noted above, for Pratt (2007), penal populism represented, and was driven by, general trends that reached beyond criminal justice, including a generalized sense of insecurity in the face of "disintegrating social and moral cohesion" (Pratt 2007: 37); the fragmentation of social bonds and resulting lack of trust; and a lack of deference to one's 'betters', with a related diminishing of respect and support for public servants. And as we have seen above, the predominant view within penal theory is that to speak of penal populism is by definition to point to various examples of the deleterious outcomes that flow from these structural changes in developed Western (and in particular Anglophone) nations.

A reading of the parole controversies, discussed here in light of predominant literature on the role of dangerous offenders and victims in the modern era, would likely focus on the extent to which sexual offenders (as a category: Feeley and Simon 1992) are perceived as monsters to be banished from society (Simon 1998). Within this exclusionary 'politics of vengeance' (Simon 1998), other courses of action such as those which seek (re-)incorporation of such offenders in the community are from such a perspective inherently antithetical to the proper recognition of victims' rights and needs.

Given its focus on risk and the release of some of the most 'dangerous' prisoners, parole is perhaps *the* point at which penal politics is—or is capable of being—at its most polarized, febrile and anti-political. In England and Wales, this current dynamic is indeed the 'gift' bestowed by the earlier period of 'dangerous politics' at the turn of the century and the dramatic rise in indeterminate sentences that ensued (Annison 2015). At the same time, concerns relating to the rule of law, professional ethics and the influence of longstanding organizational cultures place counter-posing demands for evidenced, expert-led decision-making that rebuts majoritarian pressures and simplistic public demands (Padfield 2016; Ashworth and Zedner 2014). Hence, and as we have seen above, the views of victims, prisoners, families, the tabloid press, politicians, practitioners, experts and publics (and others) can seem to clash fundamentally.

But there is a more positive reading of the dynamics discussed here. One where the victims of Worboys' offences and their supporters sought (and are seeking) to re-shape the criminal justice system and public debates about it, in a manner which ensures better protection both from those committing serious sexual offences, and from the related failures of the criminal justice system that were revealed by that case. These can be understood, in other words, as efforts to re-shape dominant conceptions of solidarity in a manner that is appropriate for modern times. The arguments were generally not about scapegoating whole offending groups, being cognizant of the exceptional nature of Worboys' crimes, but rather focusing on the systemic issues raised.

Further, the decline in deference in public life is clearly identifiable and presents significant challenges. However, it has also brought with it various publics' sense of agency and their right to challenge actions by the penal state (including current or former prisoners, families of prisoners and victims of crime). Particularly striking is the extent to which many organizations are increasingly receptive to such claims; a manifestation of the view, in other words, that such efforts by publics are *legitimate*, and *should be heard* (Durose and Richardson 2016). Rather than victims being represented by others—for example, 'brought in' by politicians in a manner that has tended to engender organizational resistance[20]—they are increasingly themselves 'welcomed in' to debates on penal policy, and the development of specific policies and practice. This has included service users (McCulloch 2016), prisoners (Wainwright et al. 2019); victims (Walklate et al. 2019), families affected by imprisonment (Annison and Condry 2019) and other 'experts by experience'.

Political cultures act as "filters for risk", selecting problems for attention, suggesting appropriate images of threatening people and situations, proposing diagnoses (Sparks 2000a: 138). I have suggested here that there are indications of stability, 'standard' moralized emotionally charged contestation around criminal justice, in the English developments discussed. But there are also indications of a 'welcoming in', and sometimes equally a 'pressing in', by various oft-excluded individuals and groups to debates surrounding penal policy and practice in a manner that at least holds the potential for genuinely progressive outcomes.

Any moment in penal history cannot be boiled down to one fixed analytical position—be that a particular point on a pendulum's swing (Goodman et al. 2017), or a binary situation where risk either does, or does not, predominate (O'Malley 2010: 32). The challenge, as ever for penal theory, is to capture and critique concerning trends, while remaining open to alternative "lines of flight" (Deleuze 1995: 172–3, quoted by O'Malley 2010: 82–3) that contain within them the potential for better penal culture, penal policy and penal outcomes.[21]

Notes

1. See, for example, Feeley and Simon (1992, 1994), Garland (2001), Pratt (2000, 2007), Hudson (2003) and Cunneen et al. (2013).
2. For a detailed exposition of the orientations underpinning Sparks' approach, see Loader and Sparks (2004).
3. The independence of the Parole Board is discussed below. As regards the prison service, it had at that time become an 'executive agency', intended to operate as a distinct organization (see Sparks et al. 1996).
4. *R (Brooke) v Parole Board* (2008) EWCA Civ 29.
5. Ibid., paragraph 78.
6. For detailed discussion of the IPP sentence and its lessons for penal theory, see Annison (2015). For more recent discussion of its ongoing deleterious effects, see, for example, HM Chief Inspectors of Prisons and Probation (2016) and Annison and Condry (2019).
7. *R (Osborn) v The Parole Board* (2013) UKSC 61.
8. Ibid., paragraph 71.
9. Underlining these arguments, in June 2019 Worboys pleaded guilty to four counts of further offences under the Sexual Offences Act 2003 (Siddique 2019).
10. *R. (DSD and NBV & Ors) v The Parole Board of England* and Wales & Ors and John Radford (2018) EWHC (Admin) 694, (2018) 3 W.L.R. 829, Para 154.
11. Ibid., paragraph 159.
12. See, for example, Hinsliff (2018).
13. There were, of course, other perspectives in play, not least the view that Worboys' release after nearly ten years of imprisonment did not meet the requirements of retributive justice. Nonetheless, such arguments tended to run alongside, rather than clash with, risk-based arguments (see, e.g., Townsend 2018).
14. See also O'Malley (2010: 42).

15. For an illuminating discussion of these developments, and its limited substantive influence in the context of drugs policy, see Monaghan, Wincup and Wicker (2018).
16. We should recognize, however, that Hall's argument regarding his concerns at what he elsewhere termed the 'great moving right show' of the 1970s was not only a consideration of elite political agency, but a compelling consideration of the broader dynamics in play.
17. This political risk was heightened by the Justice Secretary's widely derided decision not to challenge the Parole Board's decision himself.
18. And, of course, the more general rise of populist politicians, within broader anti-political sentiment, is of acute concern and the focal point of important scholarly work (see, e.g., Clarke et al. 2018; Mudde 2017).
19. Thanks to Louise Jackson for helping me to develop this observation.
20. See, for example, accounts of criminal justice organizations' reaction to proposals for a public notification 'Sarah's Law' in England and Wales (Kemshall and Wood 2007).
21. Thanks to Kelly Mackenzie for her exemplary research assistance. Thanks to Nina Jørgensen, Ian Loader, John Pratt and Jordan Anderson for comments on earlier drafts.

References

Adams J. (2003) Risk and Morality: Three framing devices In: Doyle A. and Ericson R. V. (eds) *Risk and Morality.* Toronto: University of Toronto Press.

Annison H. (2015) *Dangerous Politics: Risk, Political Vulnerability, and Penal Policy,* Oxford: Oxford University Press.

Annison H. (2018a) Towards an Interpretive Political Analysis of Penal Policy. *Howard Journal of Crime and Justice* 57(3): 302–320.

Annison H. (2018b) Tracing the Gordian Knot: Indeterminate-Sentenced Prisoners and the Pathologies of English Penal Politics. *The Political Quarterly* 89(2): 197–205.

Annison H. and Condry R. (2019) The pains of indeterminate imprisonment for family members. *Prison Service Journal* 241: 11–19.

Anonymous. (2018) Psychological expert evidence and the Parole Board. Available at: https://thepsychologist.bps.org.uk/volume-31/may-2018/psychological-expert-evidence-and-parole-board.

Ashworth A. and Zedner L. (2014) *Preventive Justice,* Oxford: Oxford University Press.

BBC News. (2018) John Worboys: Victims 'terrified' by prison release. *BBC News*.

Boin A., Hart P. t., Stern E. and Sundelius B. (2005) *The Politics of Crisis Management: Public leadership under pressure,* Cambridge: Cambridge University Press.

Bosworth M. and Kaufman E. (2013) Gender and Punishment. In: Simon J. and Sparks R. (eds) *Handbook of Punishment and Society.* London: SAGE.

Bottoms A. (1995) The Philosophy and Politics of Punishment and Sentencing. In: Clarkson C. and Morgan R. (eds) *The Politics of Sentencing Reform.* Oxford: Clarendon Press.

Burke L. and Collett S. (2014) *Delivering Rehabilitation,* Abingdon: Routledge.

Burman M. and Gelsthorpe L. (2017) Feminist Criminology: Inequalities, powerlessness and justice. In: Liebling A., Maruna S. and McAra L. (eds) *Oxford Handbook of Criminology.* 6th ed. Oxford: OUP.

Clarke N., Jennings W., Moss J. and Stoker G. (2018) *The Good Politician,* Cambridge: CUP.

Cunneen C., Baldry E., Brown D., Brown M., Schwartz M. and Steel A. (2013) *Penal Culture and Hyperincarceration,* Abingdon, Oxon: Routledge.

Douglas M. (1992) *Risk and Blame: Essays in cultural theory,* London: Routledge.

Deleuze G. (1995) Postscript on control societies. In: Deleuze G. (ed) *Negotiations 1972–1990.* New York: Columbia University Press.

Downes D. and Morgan R. (1997) Dumping the 'Hostages to Fortune'? The politics of law and order in post-war Britain. In: Maguire M., Morgan R. and Reiner R. (eds) *The Oxford Handbook of Criminology.* Oxford: Oxford University Press.

Durose C. and Richardson L. (2016) *Designing Public Policy for Co-Production,* Bristol: Policy Press.

Dzur A. W. (2016) Participatory Innovation in Criminal Justice: Why, how and how far? In: Farrall S., Goldson B., Loader I. and Dockley A. (eds) *Justice and Penal Reform.* Abingdon, Oxon: Routledge.

Feeley M. and Simon J. (1992) The New Penology: Notes on the Emerging Strategy of Corrections and Its Implications. *Criminology* 30: 449–474.

Feeley M. and Simon J. (1994) Actuarial Justice: The Emerging New Criminal Law. In: Nelken D. (ed) *Futures of Criminology.* London: SAGE.

Fitzgibbon W. (2011) *Probation and Social Work on Trial,* Basingstoke: Palgrave.

Garland D. (2001) *The Culture of Control: Crime and Social Order in Contemporary Society,* Oxford: Oxford University Press

Gerbaudo P. (2018) Social media and populism: an elective affinity? *Media, Culture & Society* 40: 745–753.

Goodman P., Page J. and Phelps M. (2017) *Breaking the Pendulum,* Oxford: OUP.

Guiney T. (2018) *Getting Out: Early Release in England and Wales, 1960–1995,* Oxford: Oxford University Press.

Guiney T. and Prison Reform Trust. (2018) Prison Reform Trust response to the Ministry of Justice Review of the Law, Policy and Procedure Relating to Parole Decisions. London: PRT

Hall S. (1978) *Policing the Crisis: Mugging, the State, and Law and Order,* Basingstoke Macmillan

Hardwick N. (2018a) *Letter of Resignation from Nick Hardwick to the Secretary of State for Justice.* London: Parole Board.

Hardwick N. (2018b) Professor Nick Hardwick responds to concerns about Worboys' case. Available at https://www.gov.uk/government/news/professor-nick-hardwick-responds-to-concerns-about-worboys-case

Hinsliff G. (2018) John Worboys is to Stay in Prison: But why was release ever recommended? *The Guardian.* London/Manchester: GMG.

HM Chief Inspector of Prisons. (2016) Unintended Consequences: Finding a way forward for prisoners serving sentences of imprisonment for public protection. London: HMIP.

HM Chief Inspector of Probation. (2018) Investigation into the policy and process followed by the victim contact scheme in the case of John Worboys, London: HMIP.

Hood C. (2002) The Risk Game and the Blame Game. *Government and Opposition* 37: 15–37.

Hood C. (2011) *The Blame Game: Spin, bureaucracy, and self-preservation in government,* Princeton: Princeton University Press.

Hoyle C. (1998) *Negotiating Domestic Violence: Police, criminal justice and victims,* Oxford: OUP.

Hoyle C. and Zedner L. (2007) Victims, Victimization and Criminal Justice. In: Maguire M., Morgan R. and Reiner R. (eds) *Oxford Handbook of Criminology.* 4th ed. Oxford: OUP.

Hudson B. (2003) *Justice in the Risk Society,* London: SAGE.

Jones M. (2017a) *IPPs, recalls and the future of parole.* Available at: www.russell-webster.com/martin-jones2/.

Jones M. (2017b) *The parole board faces up to new challenges.* Available at: www.russellwebster.com/parole-board-50/.

Jones M. (2019) Hope for Progress. *Inside Time.* Available at: https://insidetime.org/parole-revolution-justice-secretary-david-gaukes-landmark-reform/

Justice Committee. (2018) Transforming Rehabilitation. London: House of Commons.

Justice Committee. (2019) Prison Population 2022: Planning for the future. London: House of Commons.

Kemshall H. and Wood J. (2007) Beyond Public Protection: An examination of community protection and public health approaches to high-risk offenders. *Journal of Criminology and Criminal Justice* 7: 203–222.

Learmont J. (1995) Review of prison service security in England and Wales and the escape from Parkhurst Prison on Tuesday 3rd January 1995. London: Home Office.

Loader I. (2006) Fall of the 'Platonic Guardians': Liberalism, Criminology and Political Responses to Crime in England and Wales. *British Journal of Criminology* 46: 561–586.

Loader I. (2010) Is it NICE? The Appeal, Limits and Promise of Translating a Health Innovation into Criminal Justice. *Current Legal Problems* 63: 72–91.

Loader I. and Sparks R. (2004) For an Historical Sociology of Crime Policy in England and Wales since 1968. *Critical Review of International Social and Political Philosophy* 7: 5–32.

Maruna S. (2001) *Making Good: How Ex-Convicts Reform and Rebuild their Lives,* Washington, DC: American Psychological Association.

McCulloch T. (2016) Co-producing justice sanctions? Citizen perspectives. *Criminology & Criminal Justice* 16: 431–451.

McNeill F. (2006) A Desistance Paradigm for Offender Management. *Criminology and Criminal Justice* 6: 39–61.

Ministry of Justice. (2009) The Future of the Parole Board. London: Ministry of Justice.

Moffatt S. (2015) Prospects for a Desistance Agenda. London: Criminal Justice Alliance.

Monaghan M., Wincup E. and Wicker K. (2018) Experts, Expertise and Drug Policy-making. *Howard Journal of Crime and Justice* 57(3): 422–441.

Mudde C. (2017) *On Extremism and Democracy in Europe,* Abingdon: Routledge.

Mythen G. (2014) *Understanding the Risk Society,* Basingstoke: Palgrave Macmillan.

National Audit Office. (2017) Investigation into the Parole Board. London: NAO.

O'Malley P. (2010) *Crime and Risk,* London: SAGE.

Padfield N. (2016) Justifying Indefinite Detention - on what grounds? Criminal Law Review 11: 797–822.

Parole Board. (2016) The Parole Board Strategy 2016–2020. Parole Board.

Parole Board. (2018a) Parole Board for England and Wales Annual Reports and Accounts 2017/18. Parole Board.

Parole Board. (2018b) Parole Board for England and Wales Strategy 2018 to 2020 and 18 Month Business Plan April 2018 to September 2019. Parole Board.

Pratt J. (2000) Dangerousness and Modern Society. In: Brown M. and Pratt J. (eds) *Dangerous Offenders: Punishment and Social Order*. London: Routledge.

Pratt J. (2007) Penal Populism, London: Routledge

Pratt J., Brown D., Brown M. and Hallsworth S. (2005) *The New Punitiveness: Trends, Theories, Perspectives*, Cullompton, Devon: Willan.

Prison Reform Trust. (2018) Incentives and Earned Privileges.

Reiner R. (2007) *Law and order: an honest citizen's guide to crime and control*, Cambridge: Cambridge: Polity Press.

Robinson G. and Crow I. (2009) *Offender Rehabilitation: Theory, Research and Practice*, London: SAGE.

Rock P. E. (1998) Murderers, Victims and "Survivors": The social construction of deviance. *British Journal of Criminology* 38: 185–200.

Rock P. E. (2004) *Constructing Victims' Rights: The Home Office, New Labour, and victims*, Oxford: Oxford University Press.

Ryan M. (2003) *Penal Policy and Political Culture in England and Wales: Four essays on policy and process*, Winchester: Waterside.

Sampson R. and Laub J. (1993) *Crime in the Making: Pathways and Turning Points through the Life Course*, Cambridge, Mass.: Harvard University Press.

Serisier T. (2018) *Speaking Out: Feminism, rape and narrative politics*, Basingstoke: Palgrave.

Shapland J. and Bottoms A. (2017) Desistance from Crime and Implications for Offender Rehabilitation. In: Liebling A., Maruna S. and McAra L. (eds) *Oxford Handbook of Criminology*. 6th ed. Oxford: OUP.

Siddique H. (2019) John Worboys admits drugging four more women. *The Guardian*. 20 June 2019 ed. London/Manchester: GNM.

Simon J. (1998) Managing the Monstrous: Sex offenders and the New Penology. *Psychology, Public Policy, and Law* 4: 452–467.

Sparks R. (2000a) Perspectives on Risk and Penal Politics. In: Hope T. and Sparks R. (eds) *Crime, Risk and Insecurity*. London: Routledge

Sparks R. (2000b) Risk and Blame in Criminal Justice Controversies: British Press Coverage and Official Discourse on Prison Security (1993–6). In: Brown M. and Pratt J. (eds) *Dangerous Offenders: Punishment and Social Order*. London: Routledge

Sparks R., Bottoms A. and Hay W. (1996) *Prisons and the Problem of Order,* Oxford: OUP.

Sunstein C. (2017) *#Republic,* Oxford: Princeton University Press.

Townsend M. (2018) John Worboys: fury over release prompts parole system overhaul. *The Guardian.*

Wainwright L., Harriott P. and Saajedi S. (2019) What Do You Need to Make the Best Use of Your Time in Prison? London: Prison Reform Trust.

Walklate S., Maher J., McCulloch J., Fitz-Gibbon K. and Beavis K. (2019) Victim stories and victim policy: Is there a case for a narrative victimology? *Crime, Media, Culture* Online First.

Ward T. and Maruna S. (2007) *Rehabilitation: Beyond the Risk Paradigm,* London: Routledge.

Woodcock J. (1994) The Escape from Whitemoor Prison on Friday 9th September 1994. London: Home Office.

Woolf L. J. (1991) Prison Disturbances April 1990. London: HMSO.

Zedner L. (2009) Fixing the Future? The pre-emptive turn in criminal justice. In: McSherry B., Norrie A. W. and Bronitt S. (eds) *Regulating Deviance: the redirection of criminalisation and the futures of criminal law.* Oxford: Hart.

Part III

New Dimensions of Risk

Against the Odds? Unraveling the Paradoxes of Risk Prevention in Counter-Radicalization Strategy

Gabe Mythen

Introduction

Over the last forty years, the 'risk paradigm' has become increasingly influential across a range of areas of criminal justice and crime regulation, including policing practices, modes of probation and imprisonment, law and victims policy (see Kemshall 2003; Mythen 2014; Pratt 2017; Trotter et al. 2016). It is no coincidence that 'risk' rose to prominence as a mode of regulation in the 1980s and 1990s during a phase in which the capacity of criminal justice systems in affluent industrialized nations to manage crime problems was put under the microscope. During this time, what Garland (1990) dubbed the 'crisis of penal modernism' created something of a vacuum, which was to become filled with an admixture of punitive populism and the advancement of risk-based approaches to crime control. The turn to risk and the deployment of actuarial methods

G. Mythen (✉)
University of Liverpool, Liverpool, UK
e-mail: G.Mythen@liverpool.ac.uk

J. Pratt, J. Anderson (eds.), *Criminal Justice, Risk and the Revolt against Uncertainty*,
Palgrave Studies in Risk, Crime and Society,
https://doi.org/10.1007/978-3-030-37948-3_8

in crime prevention are typified by the extension of modes of targeted surveillance indexed to 'risk factors' and the expansion of predictive technologies of crime management. Partly in response to these trends, within criminology there have been concerted attempts to utilize socio-cultural theories of risk to analyze patterns in crime management, policing and criminal justice policy making. Following the trajectory of Ulrich Beck's (1992) risk society thesis, scholars have drawn attention to the increasing prevalence of risk as an analytical tool, deployed to inform decision making, prediction and intervention (see Mythen and Walklate 2006; Stenson and Sullivan 2002). Following Garland's (1990) lead, others in the discipline have developed Foucault's governmentality thesis to describe penological transitions and the emergence of new modes of crime control (see Ericson and Haggerty 1997; Feeley and Simon 1992; O'Malley 1992, 2009). In this *oeuvre*, followers of Foucault have directed attention toward the ways and means by which risk is used as a technique of governance. By way of example, Feeley and Simon's (1992) 'new penology' thesis suggests a palpable shift away from modes of punishment and penality which are individualized to an actuarial model based on aggregation that seeks primarily to regulate populations, rather than punish individual perpetrators. In this shift, models of risk assessment are depicted as increasingly central in the process of classifying offenders and discerning between 'safe' and 'dangerous' populations. As we shall see, the shift away from welfarism toward more individualized and privatized forms of risk management has been associated with longstanding problems associated with the deployment of techniques and technologies of risk that are ostensibly neutral, but disproportionately affect specific groups in practice (see Quarshi 2018; Robinson 2016).

In the criminal justice system in England and Wales a plethora of risk-based practices and policies have emerged across a range of areas, from legislation and sentencing to policing and probation reports (see Kemshall 2003; Raynor 2016). Furthermore, in certain areas of crime prevention and security policy, a pronounced motion toward policies informed by 'pre-crime' analytics has occurred, most notably around child sexual exploitation, counter-terrorism and violent crime (see McCulloch and Wilson 2016; Mythen and Walklate 2010). Despite the well-documented rise of risk, criminological analyses which have concentrated on the prevalence of risk have tended to offer a reduced account of the wider context in which such measures and metrics are introduced (see O'Malley 2009; Walklate and Mythen 2015). Thus, rather than being blinded by risk, it is important to consider the context in which such risk-based strategies and policies are operationalized. Here, the influence of political, economic and social contexts and the embedded power relationships which shape them is critical. In order to explore some of the problems and issues that result from the creeping influence of the risk paradigm summarized above, the remainder of the chapter will focus on a particular area in which rationalities of risk in general—and pre-emptive risk in particular—have been dominant: that of counter-radicalization policy. To this end, I wish to home in on the impacts of a nationwide strategy introduced in the UK to combat terrorism in general and radicalization in particular, namely *Prevent*.

In relation to the case of counter-radicalization, it is important to take account of the particular post 9/11 context in which the consolidation of discourses of risk oriented primarily toward the threat of Islamist extremism emerged. Since the start of the millennium, measures designed to combat radicalization in Britain have been undergirded by preventative strategies designed to promote intervention prior to criminality occurring (see Heath-Kelly 2013; Mythen et al. 2017). While the development of counter-radicalization strategy in the UK is indubitably a specific case, it nonetheless serves to both ground some of the preceding observations about the turn to risk within crime prevention and bring to the surface some of the contradictions and dilemmas that emerge when risk factors, metrics and profiles become focal tools in decision making around national security.

Risk Rationality in Action: Combatting Terrorism, Countering Radicalization

Before focusing in on the *Prevent* strategy explicitly, it is first necessary to provide a capsule account of the broader climate within which counter-terrorism and counter-radicalization policy has nested over the last two decades. In as much as counter-terrorism legislation was relatively developed in the UK in comparison with other European countries prior to the events of 9/11—partly as a consequence of measures introduced during the period of conflict over the sovereignty of Northern Ireland—successive British governments of all political persuasions have been engaged in a prolonged phase of unprecedented legislative reform of national security policy. In retrospect, it is clear that the attacks on the United States in 2001 impacted markedly in this regard, in terms of geopolitical priorities, global military interventions and the extension of (inter)national security strategies. Following the tenor of the 9/11 Commission Report (2004), the attacks on America led to detailed reflection on the robustness of intelligence protocols and left policy makers and intelligence strategists under significant pressure to determine how best to prevent terrorism in future. By way of response, a collection of scholars, intelligence analysts and media commentators provided competing accounts of the nature and causes of an apparently 'new' and dangerous form of terrorism. What came to be known as the 'new terrorism thesis' suggests that the events of 9/11 signaled a clear shift away from traditional forms of political violence enacted by groups such as the IRA and ETA, to more dangerous and impactful modes of attack. It is argued that many of the features of traditional forms of terrorism—largely involving local or regional struggles, led by organizations that were hierarchical in structure and seeking primarily to damage infrastructure and disrupt capital accumulation—are not shared by new terrorist groups. In contrast, new terrorist groups are said to seek to act internationally, maximize civilian casualties, work across a vertical structure and rely on global media to inspire individuals to perpetrate violence (see Burke 2007; Silber and Bhatt 2007). *Ergo*, the level of risk associated with new terrorist networks is commonly assumed to be much greater than that presented by traditional terrorist groups.

As critical criminologists have observed, the suggestion that 9/11 served as a break point, heralding a shift from 'old' to 'new' terrorism, elides historical continuities and downplays histories of cultural and economic imperialism imposed by Western nations (see Burnett and Whyte 2005; Mythen and Walklate 2006). Nevertheless, the clamor to 'explain' the events of 9/11 with reference to the phenomena of 'new terrorism' has been consistent and pervasive in media, political and policy circles. Such accounts stress the novelty and magnitude of the current threat. They also typically involve emphasizing the role of 'radicalization' in the preparatory ideational stages prior to individuals committing violence. Despite undoubted ubiquity, the process of radicalization—through which individuals are said to become persuaded to accept extreme violence as legitimate and inevitable—has been the subject of intense debate (see Ahmed 2017; Dudenhoefer 2018; Elshimi 2015; Kundnani 2015). Notwithstanding the controversy, the twin risk discourses of 'new terrorism' and 'radicalization' have grown in tenor—as both explanations for the changing nature of modes of attack and drivers of individual action for perpetrators of terrorism—since 9/11. Following on from the Madrid train bombings in 2004 and the 2005 attacks in London, over the last decade, serious terrorist attacks perpetrated by individuals sympathetic to the philosophy of radical Islam have followed in several countries, including Sri Lanka, France, Germany, Belgium, Holland, Indonesia, Turkey and Denmark. These attacks have heightened anxieties about the threat of 'home-grown' terrorism, with media attention being directed toward individuals who have traveled to Syria, Afghanistan and Iraq to engage in conflict and the concomitant risk that they may return to countries of citizenship to commit atrocities (see Francis 2015). More recently, the problem of violent extremism among white supremacists and the far right has been highlighted by the March 2019 Christchurch attacks in New Zealand. Arguably a general international tendency within the intelligence and security services to overlook the threat of far-right extremism is surprising, particularly given numerous pre-cursors, including the 1995 Oklahoma bombings in the United States, the 2011 attacks by Anders Behring-Brevik in Norway and the Charleston church attacks in 2015. In Britain, extant anxieties about 'radicalization'—rendered explicit after the 2005 attacks—escalated markedly after intelligence was leaked in the media about four British men—apparently calling themselves 'the Beatles'—who had been involved in exacting gruesome violence—including beheadings—during the Syrian conflict (Laughland and Dodd 2018).

In the UK, stringent legislation has been coupled with assorted preventative initiatives designed to tackle the problem of violent extremism and challenge religiously and politically motivated violence. A raft of legislation formally geared toward reducing the risk of terrorism has emerged in the last twenty years (see Choudhury and Fenwick 2011; Schmid 2013; Thomas 2012). This has included, inter alia, the Terrorism Act 2000, the Anti-terrorism, Crime and Security Act 2001, the Prevention of Terrorism Act 2005, the Terrorism Act 2006, the Counter Terrorism Act 2008, the Justice and Security Act 2013, and the Counter Terrorism and Security Act 2015. In order to improve pre-emptive detection of individuals that may be vulnerable to radicalization, these legal measures have been accompanied by various preventative initiatives, most notably the *Prevent* strategy.

Casing Risk: The *Prevent* Strategy in the UK

Having outlined the context in which discourses of 'new terrorism' have become prevalent and provided an account of the emergence of the concept of 'radicalization', I now wish to drill down to analyze the modeling of risk in counter-radicalization policy. In particular, attention will be drawn to the ways in which understandings of radicalization are constructed and the deployment of logics of risk that underpin various interventions designed to combat violent extremism. To do this, I wish to unpack one specific initiative mobilized in the UK. *Prevent* is one of four tiers of the UK government's counter-terrorism CONTEST strategy, the other strands being *Prepare*, *Protect* and *Pursue* (see Home Office 2011). *Prevent* was designed by the Labour government in 2003, but not publicly launched until after the 2005 terrorist attacks in London. Since then, the remit of *Prevent* has been modified, firstly by the coalition government in 2011, and again in 2015 under Conservative Party rule. Before raising critical objections regarding the mobilization of 'risk' in the *Prevent* strategy, it is worth briefly contemplating how radicalization is more broadly conceived in policy terms and the role attributed to it in the manifestation of politically and religiously motivated violence.

CONTEST, the UK government's overarching counter-terrorism strategy, defines radicalization as "the process whereby certain experiences and events in a person's life cause them to become radicalised, to the extent of turning to violence to resolve perceived grievances" (Home

Office 2006: 27). Such definitions are strikingly tautological. In effect, radicalization is defined as the process through which individuals become radicalized. As we shall see, in the *Prevent* strategy, radicalization is understood as an ideational process, with inculcation of extremist beliefs being a prime motivating factor which enables individuals to commit violence (see Kundnani 2015: 6). The logic of risk is highly pertinent here, with particular people, places and activities being prescribed as suggestive of potential harm. As we shall see, *Prevent* seeks to map out the 'drivers' of radicalization by identifying indicators of risk which may make individuals vulnerable to violent extremism (Home Office 2011: 17). In this regard, radicalization is conceived as a journey from a point of relative normality, to a state of being prepared to commit indiscriminate violence. Through the identification of risk factors, radicalization is theoretically constituted as a horizontally temporal process during which targeted intervention may prevent individuals from accepting ideologies that sanction violence. Radicalization is thus rendered tangible with reference to sequential descriptors such as 'pathways', 'journeys' and 'drivers'. This somewhat linear and mechanistic approach serves to open up a space in which risk-based decision making can be used to inform interventions (Mythen et al. 2017). Further, such an understanding of radicalization defines stages of risk that increase in severity as the individual moves from grievance, through radicalization and then on to being persuaded that violence is the only meaningful course of action (see Kundnani 2012; Pankhurst 2013). The 'conveyer-belt' assumption implicit in this rationale is significant beyond its theoretical underpinnings. Critically, it provides leverage for preventative interventions that permit a semblance of institutional control (see Edwards 2014; Thomas 2017).

As formulated in government policy, *Prevent* seeks to combat the threat of terrorism through the early identification of individuals that may be prone to radicalization (Home Office 2011). As such the strategy is geared toward intervening to support people at risk of affiliating with extremist groups and subsequently going on to carry out terrorist acts. At inception, the *Prevent* strategy originally comprised five overarching objectives and included ambitions to enhance community cohesion. However, the original community cohesion priorities were formally migrated out of the strategy in 2011, when a revised version—which remains current—was put in place. The three central objectives of *Prevent* are as follows:

1. To respond to the ideological challenge of terrorism and the threat posed by those who promote it
2. To prevent people from being drawn into terrorism
3. To work with sectors and institutions where there are risks of radicalization that need to be addressed (Home Office 2011: 7).

First presented as a 'hearts and minds' approach, the UK Government sought assistance in implementation of the strategy from the Muslim community, faith leaders, local organizations, educational institutions, youth groups and criminal justice professionals (see Mythen et al. 2017; Thomas 2017). While the strategy is designed to combat all forms of violent extremism, post the 7/7 attacks in London, the implementation of *Prevent* concentrated primarily on the threat presented by radical Islamism. To this end, various initiatives were rolled out to challenge forms of religious belief that promote violence and encouraging 'moderate' theological approaches (see Department for Communities and Local Government 2007; O'Toole 2015). While various internal disputes surfaced between the various government departments charged with delivering *Prevent* (see Ratcliffe 2012; Thomas 2012), more serious problems became apparent as the strategy progressed in practice, including accusations of discrimination against Muslim minority groups, damaged community relations and increasing cleavages between the police and targeted populations (see Dodd 2009; Travis 2011). In an attempt to address some of these tensions, the revised version of the strategy was introduced in 2011. At this juncture, as Heath-Kelly (2013) observes, the focus shifted away from community cohesion activities toward concentrating on risk-based pre-emptive interventions. While ostensibly geared toward safeguarding vulnerable individuals, the *Prevent* strategy functions, in effect, as a program of surveillance which invites reporting of suspicious activity. In practice, referrals to local *Prevent* bodies are made by either professionals in working contexts—for example, in schools, universities and hospitals—or concerned members of the public. Referrals to *Prevent* are subsequently passed on to designated police service leads who decide whether there is evidence that the individual identified as exhibiting problematic behavior is vulnerable to radicalization. If affirmed, cases are then referred to *Channel* panels that formally assess whether further intervention and support are required. These panels are police led, chaired by a representative of the local authority and include professional experts such as youth workers, social workers, doctors and religious leaders (see Home Office 2015). Promoted as a multi-agency initiative, the key objective of *Channel* panels is to protect vulnerable people by identifying potential harm, assessing the nature and extent of risk and developing appropriate mentorship and support plans for individuals at risk (see Home Office 2015). The logic underpinning *Channel* is thus tightly aligned with the broader *Prevent* strategy and geared toward making pre-emptive intercessions prior to an offence occurring:

> *Channel* is about ensuring that vulnerable children and adults … receive support before their vulnerabilities are exploited by those that would want them to embrace terrorism and before they become involved in criminal terrorist activity. (Home Office 2015: 5)

Individuals deemed to be vulnerable to extremism are placed in de-radicalization programs where mentoring, support and guidance are provided. I will return to raise some critical questions about the rationale for the pre-emptive dynamic underpinning *Prevent* in due course, but it is worth briefly discussing the key tool of risk assessment utilized by *Channel* panels, the *Vulnerability Assessment Framework* (VAF). The VAF is a risk assessment tool designed to gauge three key factors: *engagement* with a group cause or ideology; *capability* to cause harm and *intent*. This framework itself is underpinned by UK Government–approved *Extremism Risk Guidance,* known colloquially as ERG 22+ (see HM Prison and Probation Service 2017). *Extremism Risk Guidance* outlines twenty-two factors that should be considered in assessing vulnerability to extremism. Thirteen of these factors are associated with *engagement,* including excitement; comradeship or adventure; transitional periods; identity, meaning and belonging. Three factors are indexed to *capability,* which are individual knowledge, skills and competencies; access to networks and funding or equipment; and six factors are measured under *intent* to cause harm, including over-identification with a group, cause or ideology and 'them' and 'us' thinking. We will return to scrutinize the nature of the 'risk factors' detailed in ERG 22+ in due course, but suffice it to say at this juncture that the correlations between exhibiting such factors and expressing extremist views—never mind engaging in serious violence—are far from joined up. Before broaching this matter, it is first important to document the significant changes to the *Prevent* strategy introduced in 2015 (Home Office 2015). At this point, the reissuing of the *Prevent* Duty Guidance incorporated a statutory responsibility for public authorities to actively enforce *Prevent* policy. This safeguarding guidance was legally formalized in statute under Section 26(1) of the Counter-Terrorism and Security Act, (2015) which requires that 'a specified authority must, in the exercise of its functions, have due regard to the need to prevent people from being drawn into terrorism'. Importantly, whereas previous *Prevent* Duty Guidance required that those working in areas in which the risk of radicalization was palpable to be watchful of individuals exhibiting behaviors that may lead to 'violent extremism', the issuing of the 2015 Duty Guidance legally responsibilizes a much broader range of groups—including teachers, lecturers, nurses, dentists and child minders—to proactively report individuals at risk of both 'violent' and 'non-violent' extremism to local *Prevent* referral teams. The introduction of the revised Duty Guidance in 2015 thus raises to the fore a range of salient issues around the uses—and abuses—of risk as a mode of governance.

In relation to issues of definition, in the *Prevent* Duty Guidance (2015: 7), extremism is described as "vocal or active opposition to British values, including democracy, the rule of law, individual liberty and mutual respect and tolerance of different faiths and beliefs". Such a palpably imprecise definition does not provide a sound basis for consequential interventions to be made. The rather nebulous concept of 'British values' renders individuals who may choose to criticize government and state institutions as 'extremists', thereby criminalizing legitimate forms of ideological opposition and political dissent. Examining the practices of state institutions and challenging legislation that is perceived as unreasonable should be considered part and parcel of routine public sphere activity in healthy, functioning democracies. Here it should be remembered that several UK counter-terrorism measures introduced in haste have subsequently been declared illegal, including control orders, detention without charge and police section 44 stop and search powers (see Dodd 2009; Walklate and Mythen 2015).

Efficacy, Effectiveness and Effects: Examining the *Prevent*(ative) Logic of Risk

Having discussed some of the ways in which risk rationalities associated with terrorism and radicalization have been operationalized within *Prevent*, it is now worth reflecting on the efficacy of the strategy in reducing the threat of violent extremism and considering some of the wider consequences resulting from its implementation. It should be noted from the outset that such reflections are necessarily speculative and suppositional. In effect, it is impossible to accurately measure how much or how little the *Prevent* strategy has reduced—or indeed intensified—the risk of terrorist attacks. As there has historically been no formal and independent mechanism for reviewing the effectiveness—or otherwise—of the strategy, gains and losses are difficult to calibrate. While advocates within government, intelligence and the police service have posited that *Prevent* has been successful in preventing individuals from becoming radicalized, various community groups, observing parliamentary bodies, political activists, charities, academics and journalists have assembled a body of counter-evidence regarding the deleterious effects of *Prevent* (see Kundnani 2015; Lewis 2018; Taylor 2018). In order to glean an understanding of some of the controversies surrounding the strategy, I wish to focus now on four issues around the use of risk metrics, the referrals process, the problem of stigmatization and the production of iatrogenic impacts.

First, aside from the general understanding of the terrorist risk presented in the *Prevent* strategy, at the level of risk metrics, the specific risk factors defined by the VAF as indictors of future terroristic activity are questionable. The risk factors delineated in the *Extremism Risk Guidance* derive from a small-scale prison study conducted by two psychologists, Monica Dean and Christopher Dean. The study was commissioned by the National Offender Management Service (NOMS) and was specifically designed to assess risk and needs in convicted extremist offenders in England and Wales in the prison context (see Lloyd and Dean 2015). The original small-scale study was not intended to gauge drivers of radicalization outwith the prison context, nor was it intended to inform broader UK Government counter-terrorism strategy. This aside, the risk factors devised by Lloyd and Dean (2015) have been widely problematized (see CAGE 2017; Rights Watch UK 2016). In operational terms, the VAF framework elicits overall ratings in each of the defined areas of engagement, intent and capability, with the risks being scored as minimal, moderate or significant.

While intended as a practical assessment tool, it is questionable whether several of the factors measured are reliable indicators of risk as such. A report by Rights Watch UK (2016) into the implementation of *Prevent* in schools is instructive in this regard, detailing the problematic nature of the risk metrics advanced in the 2015 Duty Guidance. The 'indicators' of risk undergirded by the *Extremism Risk Guidance* appear less than dependable: 'a student studying engineering or chemistry, or wearing dress traditionally associated with a Muslim-majority community, or doing better/worse at school, discloses no link with any matter of extremism or terrorist ideology. Accordingly, were decision-makers to faithfully following the *Prevent* guidance on indicators of vulnerability, the potential exists for over-referral without justification' (Rights Watch UK 2016: 14). Aside from the oblique rationale for identifying risk factors—and the fact that the initial study involved only a small number of prisoners convicted of terrorist offences—what is most troubling here is the way in which frameworks that are not adequately supported by empirical evidence—nor tested before application—have been mobilized to direct interventions which have serious repercussions for those impacted by them. To cite one pertinent example, the ERG 22+ risk factors were recently referred to as evidence in a court case which involved removing a young person from parental custody into care:

> The Vulnerability Assessment Framework encourages the agencies of protection to look at whether the young person has a need for identity, meaning and belonging; a desire for status and a desire for excitement and adventure. (A Minor, Brighton and Hove Council v. Mother X, Father Y, page 2, para 7–9)

In instances such as this, what may, to some at least, appear to be common aspects of adolescent journeys from youth into adulthood become recast as ominous risk factors that may influence decision making within the criminal justice system. Drilling down to the operationalization of ERG 22+—and aside from the dubious character of some of the risk factors—the decisions of *Channel* panels are not determined by quantitative assessment. As a report by the charity CAGE (2016) observes 'items are not scored - more factors does not mean higher engagement or higher intent or higher capability. Therefore, if one factor is identified and professional judgment ascertains that the risk is significant, but the protective factors are not substantial, singular risk factors could lead to *Channel* and *Prevent* referrals'. Here there is significant scope for unconscious bias and 'groupthink' within panels, with subjective judgments potentially influencing outcomes.

Second, notwithstanding the problematic nature of the risk factors delineated in the *Extremism Risk Guidance*, what has been noticeable since the introduction of the *Prevent* Duty Guidance in 2015 has been a sharp rise in the overall number of referrals made. From April 2015 to March 2016 7631 referrals were lodged, with a slightly lower number of 6093 being reported from April 2016 to March 2017 (Home Office 2018a). These statistics from the period post the revised *Prevent* Duty Guidance can be contrasted with figures from the period directly before of 3955 in 2014–2015 and 1681 in 2013–2014 (see Halliday 2016). The obvious question to ask here is whether these statistical patterns signal an escalation in the scale of the terrorist threat or whether the sizeable rise in referrals is connected to heightened vigilance in public bodies legally responsible for alerting the authorities to individuals believed to be at risk of extremism. It is notable that the number of young people being referred to *Prevent* has also risen sharply, with over a third of referrals post the introduction of the 2015 Duty Guidance coming from schools and colleges (see Travis 2017). The responsibilization of millions of people who may not ultimately be best prepared to make accurate, granular decisions about risk in a national surveillance exercise is nothing short of astounding. Furthermore, with regard to whether those legally bound to report suspicious and/or vulnerable individuals are suitably qualified to so do, it has been pointed out that the available training is patchy with low uptake rates (see James 2018). This raises to the fore the thorny question of whether referrals are actually being made on the basis of sound evidence. Certainly there have been a series of cases—well publicized in the media—where the evidence for referral has been extremely specious (see Quinn 2016). These include reports of referrals of children as young as three years old in circumstances where there is no discernible evidence that would indicate risk of adopting extremist views (Travis 2017). The production of false positives and false negatives and a climate of over-referral not only produce micro-level effects, but also impact at the macro level on civil liberties and public safety (see Robinson 2016: 20).

The *Prevent* strategy is undoubtedly an archetypal example of risk-based regulation which occurs in a pre-criminal space, prior to any offence having taken place. Attendance at *Channel* panels—and receipt of any subsequent support to 'de-radicalize' the individual—is subject to the consent of the person referred (see Khaleeli 2015). The underpinning rationale for 'de-radicalization' programs is that patterns of thought and erroneous personal beliefs can be corrected, such that the client receiving support can learn to reject extremism and live an otherwise normal life. There is thus a tendency to see programs such as *Channel* as providing a magic ideational bullet that can correct perceptions that are erroneous and dangerous (see CAGE 2017; Kundnani 2012). Such a concentrated focus on the individual detracts from wider political and socio-structural factors that may impact upon people's propensity to commit to views that might be considered to be extremist in nature. An overriding focus on correcting misplaced ideas thus potentially negates discussion of what may be considered legitimate grievances regarding previous experiences or geo-political processes, such as institutional racism, harassment by the police or deleterious consequences for populations subjected to state-sanctioned international military force, including drone attacks.

Third, aside from issues arising from the dubious deployment of risk measures and false referrals, the implementation of *Prevent* in practice—alongside other forms of counter-terrorism policing—has impacted particularly severely on Muslims, who have been largely targeted and, as a consequence, further stigmatized. While the forms of prevention discussed above are suggestive of objective modes of risk control, the use of risk as a mode of categorization and classification can encourage pernicious modes of social sorting. As both the statistics on *Prevent* referrals and those on police stop and search powers under section 44 show, even in the event of neutrality in design, in practice, preconceptions about risky groups have led to the reproduction of suspect populations that are routinely questioned and over-surveyed (see Pantazis and Pemberton 2009; Quarshi 2018; Halliday 2016). It is worth pointing out here that *Prevent* funding was initially allocated to city councils according to the size of local Muslim population. Under the 2011 version funding allocations were described as "intelligence-led" and "proportionate to threat levels" (Home Office 2011: 11). Nevertheless, after the 2011 revision of *Prevent*, the twenty-five priority areas targeted were still selected on the basis of "Muslim demographics" (McGhee 2011: 1). While there has been a recent increase in the number of referrals related to right-wing extremism (see Home Office 2018b), the number of *Prevent* referrals related to Islamist extremism over the lifespan of *Prevent* has remained consistently high, averaging at around 70% (see Travis 2017).

Fourth, and relatedly, longstanding forms of institutional discrimination arising out of policies such as *Prevent* have the capacity to produce multiple iatrogenic effects (see Dalgaard-Nielsen 2010; Walklate and Mythen 2015). For groups that may already feel marginalized and discriminated against, being subjected to further invasive scrutiny is likely to compound feelings of inequity and social isolation. As Maina Kai (2017)—former UN Special Rapporteur on the Rights to Freedom of Peaceful Assembly—states: "it appears that *Prevent* is having the opposite of its intended effect: by dividing, stigmatizing and alienating segments of the population, *Prevent* could end up promoting extremism, rather than countering it".

Concluding Reflections: Resisting Risk?

I wish to bring the chapter to a close by speculating on what the future for the *Prevent* program looks like and making some broader observations regarding the place of risk in institutional security regimes.

Proponents of *Prevent* have long upheld its success in preventing violent extremism, arguing that having a proactive program of interventions both acts as a deterrent and is effective in steering individuals away from radicalization (see McElroy 2018). Despite the predominant international security focus being directed toward the threat of Islamist extremism, the risk of attacks by White supremacists would seem to be growing—aside from the Christchurch attacks in 2019, the Global Terrorism Database (2017) shows a fourfold increase in attacks by far-right and White supremacists from 2013 to 2017. This alone suggests that the security gaze needs broadening and the ideas and values cultivated by those attracted to violent extremism require further attention. For some, including the UK Security Minister, Ben Wallace, the possibility of attacks similar to Christchurch occurring in future signals the necessity for preventative counter-radicalization strategies such as *Prevent* (see Weaver 2019). Yet, given the problems and issues documented above, it is clear that the implementation of *Prevent* in practice has been highly problematic. While the number of individuals referred to *Channel* associated with right-wing extremism has risen in recent times, it is arguable that both the assumptions that underpin the strategy and its procedural rolling-out have not been suitably attuned to nor are receptive of the risk of radicalization among White males.

Following on from the criticisms of *Prevent* documented in the House of Commons Home Affairs Committee (2017), the UK Government eventually bowed to pressure to hold an independent review of the strategy. While the process for submitting evidence to the review is open, it is fair to say that the mood music from government is far from agnostic, regarding the relation to canvassing views about the pluses and minuses of the strategy, seemingly indicating a desire to silence opposition, rather than to listen to informed criticism and act on appropriate evidence (see Qureshi 2017). The purpose of public reviews such as this should surely be to engage in dialogue to improve policy and practice, rather than to attempt to mute, deflect and discredit. Given that the *Prevent* strategy is considered pioneering in terms of counter-radicalization strategy—having informed the formation of Preventing Violent Extremism (PVE) strategies elsewhere in Europe, North America and Australasia—the issues discussed above have resonance beyond the geographical boundaries of the UK (see Heath-Kelly 2013; Heath-Kelly et al. 2014; Lewis 2018). In the light of recent large-scale cross-continental attacks in the early months of 2019—in Kenya, New Zealand and Sri Lanka—policies designed to combat radicalization look set to become more, not less, critical in upcoming years.

So, at a broader level, and drawing on the case of counter-radicalization strategy, how can we develop our conceptual understanding of the limits to risk logics in criminal justice policy making? Which safeguards can be put in place that may improve institutional reflexivity around risk-based security strategies?

First, in relation to the need to engage with the rationale for—and monitor the efficacy of—risk-based policy making, appreciating and understanding the wider context is key. While a climate of fear around violent extremism is not absolute, it is fair to say that the threat is persistently rendered ever-present by the constant circulation of political and media discourses concerning the threat. In many respects, the recurrent (re)presentation of the threat in the public sphere arguably encourages perceptions that the risk is of greater magnitude than the probable level of danger. Despite the extreme violence involved, terrorist attacks remain rare and are highly infrequent relative to other harms that routinely cause personal injury and death. In this regard, the dangers of 'hyper-riskality' loom large, whereby the imagined representation of risk comes to take on greater significance of a driver for regulation than the actuarial risk, as best as it can be estimated on the basis of available evidence (see Mythen and Walklate 2010). This illustrates that processes and discourses of risk cannot be readily sequestered from material practices of regulation. Indeed, they provide the backdrop to—and the conditions in which—discrete forms of surveillance and intervention are rendered permissible and necessary.

Second, it is clear that high-consequence, low-probability risks such as terrorism present regulatory institutions in affluent, industrialized nations with something of a conundrum. Public demands for appropriate measures to reduce the threat of terrorist attacks are often vocal and there is an appetite—at least among some sections of the general public—for strong forms of intervention, even if these forms of intervention may infringe civil liberties. In the UK, various forms of draconian legislation imposed in the wake of the 7/7 terrorist attacks—including control orders and indefinite detention without charge—have subsequently been declared illegal. Such 'counter-laws'—which are frequently based on preemptive risk logics and underpinned by the principle of early intervention to prevent future harms—undermine habeas corpus (Zedner 2009). It is interesting to observe the areas of regulation in which asking the 'What if?' question is deemed to be a suitable basis for police and criminal justice interventions and those in which it is palpably absent, such as climate change and health and safety at work. While measures introduced on the back of worst-case-scenario thinking have historically been prevalent within counter-terrorism regulation, they are not readily apparent in other areas of legal regulation where the risk stakes are nonetheless high.

Third, in terms of future policy making around counter-radicalization, it is important for state actors to acknowledge the uncertainties involved and to be frank about the range and scope of risk prevention initiatives such as *Prevent*. The agencies involved in countering terrorism are entangled in a complex and dynamic space characterized by endemic uncertainty—for example, around the quality and veracity of intelligence and the capacity and intent of suspects. Aside from the 'knowns' there are a plethora of 'unknowns' which make intervening a tricky business. In theory, risk metrics and indicators—such as the VAF—should assist in this endeavor and provide gauges to support decisions made. The unstable nature of such frameworks underscores the importance of processually reviewing the efficacy of pre-emptive security policies and strategies. In the case of the UK, it is fair to say that the effectiveness of the *Prevent* strategy has been widely and legitimately questioned, and, further, that there has been more than an element of government dogma amid the covering of ears and rebuffing of criticism. While the general public expect the state to protect the security of citizens, as Beck (1992) pointed out, the logic of risk can sometimes be deployed to dramaturgical ends, leading to the cosmetic treatment of problems. The clear danger here is that the production of 'organized irresponsibility' on behalf of regulatory institutions and agencies feigns the performance of control, exacerbating rather than alleviating the problem (see Beck 1995; Mythen and Walklate 2016).

Fourth, and finally, it is vital that due scoping and assessment of a range of potential side effects and iatrogenic consequences are factored into strategic decision making and design of policy and that this process takes place a priori, rather than post hoc or in an ad hoc fashion. Here I have drawn attention to just some of the issues that arise when the balance between security and liberty becomes skewed by the logic of preemptive risk. The *problematiques* and paradoxes discussed above are, arguably, indicative of the need to think beyond risk-based forms of regulation, particularly those that are designed without due precaution and unfairly discriminate against particular populations.

References

9/11 Commission Report (2004) Washington: United States Government.

Ahmed, W. (2017) 'Prevent Referrals: The Story Behind the Headlines', *Huffington Post*. Available at https://www.huffingtonpost.co.uk/entry/prevent-referrals-the-story-beyond-the-headlines_uk_5a157af8e4b0f401dfa 7ec29, accessed March 11 2019.

Beck, U. (1992) *Risk Society: Towards a New Modernity*. London: Sage.

Beck, U. (1995) *Ecological Politics in an Age of Risk*. Cambridge: Polity Press.

Burke, J. (2007) *Al-Qaeda: The True Story of Radical Islam*. London: Penguin.

Burnett, J. and Whyte, D. (2005) 'Embedded Expertise and the New Terrorism', *Journal for Crime, Conflict and the Media* 1(4): 1–18.

CAGE (2016) *The Science of Pre-crime: The Secret Radicalisation Study Underpinning Prevent*. London: CAGE.

CAGE (2017) *The Prevent Strategy: A Cradle to Grave Police State*. London: CAGE.

Choudhury, T. and Fenwick, H. (2011) *The Impact of Counter-terrorism Measures on Muslim Communities*. Manchester: Equality and Human Rights Commission.

Dalgaard-Nielsen A (2010) 'Violent Radicalization in Europe: What We Know and What We Do Not Know', *Studies in Conflict and Terrorism*, 33(9): 797–814.

Department for Communities and Local Government (2007) *Preventing Violent Extremism: Winning Hearts and Minds*. London: HMSO.

Dodd, V. (2009) 'Government anti-terrorism strategy spies on innocent', *The Guardian*, October 16.

Dudenhoefer, A. (2018) 'Resisting Radicalization: A Critical Analysis of the UK Prevent Duty', *Journal for Deradicalization*, 14(1): 143–191.

Edwards, P. (2014) 'How (Not) to Create Ex-Terrorists: Prevent as Ideological Warfare', in C. Baker-Beall, C. Heath-Kelly and L. Jarvis (eds.) *Counter-Radicalization: Critical Perspectives*. London: Routledge.

Elshimi, M. (2015) 'De-Radicalization Interventions as Technologies of the Self: A Foucauldian Analysis', *Critical Studies on Terrorism*, 8:1: 110–129.

Ericson, R. and Haggerty, K. (1997) *Policing the Risk Society*. Toronto: University of Toronto Press.

Feeley, M. and Simon, J. (1992) 'The new penology: notes on the emerging strategy of corrections and its implications', *Criminology*, 30(4): 449–474.

Francis, M. (2015) 'If you really could brainwash Muslims, ISIS would have a lot more British recruits', *The Conversation*. July 7.

Garland, D. (1990) *Punishment in Modern Society: A Study in Social Theory*, Oxford: Clarendon Press.

Global Terrorism Database (2017) *Global Terrorism in 2017: Background Report*. Maryland: START.

Halliday, J. (2016) 'Almost 4,000 people referred to UK deradicalization scheme last year', *The Guardian*, March 20.

Heath-Kelly, C. (2013) 'Counter-terrorism and the counterfactual: Producing the 'radicalization' discourse and the UK PREVENT Strategy', *British Journal of Politics and International Relations*, 15(3): 394–415.

Heath-Kelly, C., Baker-Beall, C and Jarvis, L. eds. (2014) *Counter-Radicalization: Critical Perspectives*. London: Routledge.

HM Prison and Probation Service (2017) *A Process Evaluation of the Structured Risk Guidance for Extremist Offenders*. London: HMSO.

Home Office (2006) *Countering International Terrorism: The United Kingdom's Strategy*. Available at https://www.gov.uk/government/publications/the-united-kingdoms-strategy-for-countering-international-terrorism, accessed 2 April 2018.

Home Office (2011) *Prevent Strategy*. Available at https://www.gov.uk/government/publications/prevent-strategy-2011, accessed 2 April 2018.

Home Office (2015) *Channel Duty Guidance*. Available at https://www.gov.uk/government/publications/channel-guidance, accessed 17 June 2018.

Home Office (2018a) *Individuals Referred to and Supported through the Prevent Programme Statistics, April 2016 to March 2017*. Available at https://www.gov.uk/government/collections/individuals-referred-to-and-supported-through-the-prevent-programme-statistics, accessed 17 June 2018.

Home Office (2018b) *New figures show improved referrals to Prevent and a rise in far-right concerns*. HMSO: London.

House of Commons Home Affairs Committee (2017) *Radicalization: the counter-narrative and identifying the tipping point*. HMSO: London.

James, A. (2018) 'I'm a doctor, not a counter-terrorism operative: let me do my job', *The Guardian*, March 21.

Kai, M. (2017) *Report of the Special Rapporteur on the rights to freedom of peaceful assembly and of association on his follow-up mission to the United Kingdom of Great Britain and Northern Ireland.* Geneva: Human Rights Council.

Kemshall, H. (2003) *Understanding Risk in Criminal Justice.* Buckingham: OUP.

Khaleeli, H. (2015) 'You worry they could take your kids: Is the Prevent strategy demonising Muslim schoolchildren?' *The Guardian*, September 23.

Kundnani, A. (2012) 'Radicalization: The Journey of a Concept', *Race and Class*, 54, 2: 3–25.

Kundnani, A. (2015) *A Decade Lost: Rethinking Radicalization and Extremism.* London: Claystone.

Laughland, O. and Dodd, V. (2018) 'British Isis fighters known as 'the Beatles' captured in Syria', *The Guardian*. February 8. Accessible at https://www.the-guardian.com/world/2018/feb/08/british-isis-fighters-syria-defence-force, accessible April 4 2019.

Lewis, J. (2018) 'Prevent as an Intractable Policy Controversy: Implications and Solutions', *Journal for Deradicalization*, 15.

Lloyd, M. and Dean, C. (2015) 'The Development of Structured Guidelines for Assessing Risk in Extremist Offenders', *Journal of Threat Assessment and Management*, 2(1): 40–52.

McCulloch, J. and Wilson, D. (2016) *Pre-emption, precaution and the future.* London: Routledge.

McElroy, J. (2018) 'In Defence of the Prevent Programme', *Times Educational Supplement.* Available at https://www.tes.com/news/defence-prevent-pro-gramme, accessed June 17 2018.

McGhee, D. (2011) 'New Prevent: Different is not better', *Muslim Council of Britain.* Available at: http://soundings.mcb.org.uk/?p=38, accessed March 11 2018.

Mythen, G. (2014) *Understanding the Risk Society: Crime, Security and Justice.* London: Palgrave Macmillan.

Mythen, G. and Walklate, S. (2006) 'Criminology and Terrorism: Which Thesis? Risk Society or Governmentality?' *The British Journal of Criminology*, 46(3): 379–398.

Mythen, G. and Walklate, S. (2010) 'Pre-crime, Regulation, and Counter-terrorism: Interrogating Anticipatory Risk', *Criminal Justice Matters*, 81(1): 34–36.

Mythen, G. and Walklate, S. (2016) 'Not Knowing, Emancipatory Catastrophism and Metamorphosis: Embracing the Spirit of Ulrich Beck', *Security Dialogue*, 47(5): 403–419.

Mythen, G., Walklate, S. and Peatfield, E. (2017) 'Assembling and Deconstructing Radicalization: A Critique of the Logic of Drivers', *Critical Social Policy,* 37(2): 180–201.

O'Malley, P. (1992) 'Risk, power and crime prevention', *Economy and Society,* 21(3): 252–275.

O'Malley, P. (2009) *Crime and Risk.* London: Sage.

O'Toole, T. (2015) 'Prevent: from hearts and minds to muscular liberalism', *Public Spirit.* Available at http://www.publicspirit.org.uk/prevent-from-hearts-andminds- to-muscular-liberalism, accessed March 11 2019.

Pankhurst, R. (2013) 'Woolwich, Islamism and the Conveyor Belt to Terrorism Theory'. Available at: https://www.hurstpublishers.com/woolwich-islamism-and-the-conveyor-belt-to-terrorism-theory/, accessed March 11 2019.

Pantazis, C. and Pemberton, S. (2009) 'From the "old" to the "new" suspect community: Examining the impacts of recent UK counter-terrorist legislation', *British Journal of Criminology,* 49(5): 646–666.

Pratt, J. (2017) 'Risk Control, Rights and Legitimacy in the Limited Liability State', *British Journal of Criminology,* 57(6): 1322–1339.

Quarshi, F. (2018) 'The Prevent strategy and the UK 'war on terror': embedding infrastructures of surveillance in Muslim communities,' *Palgrave Communications,* 4(17).

Quinn, B. (2016) 'Nursery raised fears of radicalization over boy's cucumber drawing', The Guardian, 11 March.

Qureshi, A. (2017) 'Our Criticism of Prevent is Based on Facts, not Myths', *Al Jazeera.* Available at https://www.aljazeera.com/indepth/opinion/2017/07/criticism-prevent-based-facts-myths-170703072558455.html, accessed 8 April 2018.

Ratcliffe, P. (2012) 'Community cohesion: Reflections on a flawed paradigm', *Critical Social Policy,* 32(2): 262–281.

Raynor, P. (2016) 'Three Narratives of Risk: Corrections, Critique and Context', in C. Trotter, G. McIvor and F. McNeill (eds.) *Beyond the Risk Paradigm in Criminal Justice.* London: Palgrave Macmillan.

Rights Watch UK (2016) *Preventing Education? Human Rights and UK Counterterrorism policy in schools.* London: UK.

Robinson, G. (2016) 'The Rise of the Risk Paradigm in Criminal Justice', in C. Trotter; G. McIvor and F. McNeill (eds.) *Beyond the Risk Paradigm in Criminal Justice.* London: Palgrave Macmillan. 9–21.

Schmid, A. (2013) *Radicalization, De-radicalization, Counter-radicalization: A Conceptual Discussion and Literature Review.* The Hague: ICCT Research Paper.

Silber, M. and Bhatt, A. (2007) *Radicalization in the West: The Homegrown Threat.* New York: NYPD Intelligence Division.

Stenson, K. and Sullivan, R. (eds.) (2002) *Crime, Risk and Justice: the politics of crime control in liberal democracies.* Cullompton: Willan.

Taylor, J. (2018) 'Suspect Categories, Alienation and Counterterrorism: Critically Assessing PREVENT in the UK', *Terrorism and Political Violence*, 1–23.

Thomas, P. (2012) *Responding to the Threat of Violent Extremism: Failing to Prevent.* London: Bloomsbury Academic.

Thomas, P. (2017) 'Changing Experiences of Responsibilisation and Contestation within Counter-Terrorism Policies: the British Prevent Experience', *Policy and Politics*, 45(3): 305–321.

Travis, A. (2011) 'Schools counter terrorism project reviewed', *The Guardian*, 11 February.

Travis, A. (2017) 'Only 5% of people referred to Prevent extremism scheme get specialist help', *The Guardian*, 9 November.

Trotter, C., McIvor, G., and McNeill, F. (2016) *Beyond the Risk Paradigm in Criminal Justice.* London: Palgrave Macmillan.

Walklate, S. and Mythen, G. (2015) *Contradictions of Terrorism: Security, Risk and Resilience.* London: Routledge.

Weaver, M. (2019) 'Mass shooting of Muslims could happen in UK, says minister', *The Guardian*, March 18.

Zedner, L. (2009) *Security.* London: Routledge.

Locking-Out Uncertainty: Conflict and Risk in Sydney's Night-Time Economy

Murray Lee, Stephen Tomsen, and Phillip Wadds

Introduction

We believe in individual freedom and free enterprise and if you share this belief, then this is the Party for you [… we believe in …] the inalienable rights and freedoms of all people; we work towards a lean government that minimises interference in our daily lives and maximises individual and private-sector initiative. (NSW Liberal Party Website)

M. Lee (✉)
Law School, University of Sydney, Camperdown, NSW, Australia
e-mail: murray.lee@sydney.edu.au

S. Tomsen
Western Sydney University, Sydney, NSW, Australia
e-mail: S.Tomsen@westernsydney.edu.au

P. Wadds
Faculty of Law, University of New South Wales, Sydney, NSW, Australia
e-mail: p.wadds@unsw.edu.au

J. Pratt, J. Anderson (eds.), *Criminal Justice, Risk and the Revolt against Uncertainty*,
Palgrave Studies in Risk, Crime and Society,
https://doi.org/10.1007/978-3-030-37948-3_9

Over the past three decades, Sydney, like many large western metropolitan centers, has attempted to position itself as a global city. This has entailed a certain branding and refashioning to make the city attractive to international visitors as well as locals. In many respects, the city has succeeded in this pursuit, attracting around four million tourists annually who contribute in the order of $8.6 billion a year to the local economy (City of Sydney 2019). Sydney is a go-to city for international students, with over 35,000 studying in the city in any one year (City of Sydney 2019). Indeed, on brand appeal and image, Sydney was ranked as the third best city in the world in 2017 (GFK 2018). The positioning of Sydney on the world stage puts it in competition with similarly 'global cities' like London, New York, Tokyo, Berlin, and Vancouver. Part of this process of branding is to project Sydney as an exciting city; connected; culturally diverse and welcoming; and 'open for business'.

A vibrant and dynamic nightlife had previously signified Sydney as an exciting 24/7 modern global city and been a key marker of success in the global competition for status and desirability among tourists. Sydney was internationally renowned for its nightlife, with clubs in key nightspot areas such as Kings Cross in the city's inner east and George Street in the central business district (CBD) routinely filled with weekend revelers partying almost around the clock. Similarly, Darlinghurst, the historic heart of Sydney's LGBT communities, was buzzing with activity. However, with this night-time excitement and its attendant consumption of alcohol and illicit drugs came both real and imaginary risks. Risks, which this chapter will argue, became, for a time at least, cast as too great in the context of competing symbolic, economic, and demographic views of what the city should be.

A key symbol of the competing forces shaping Sydney nightlife can be found in Kings Cross, where a massive Coca-Cola sign marks the entrance to the once notorious nightlife strip. It was, and perhaps still is, an iconic image. Since its erection in 1974, this famous 'Coke sign' has been a symbol of freedom, excitement, transgression, and, of course, urban consumer capitalism. Kings Cross for many decades symbolized the sleazier and edgier side of Sydney, with its mix of strip clubs, drug culture, pubs, and nightclubs. It was a red-light district that had become synonymous with Sydney's nightlife scene with Friday and Saturday nights in the

'Cross' evolving as 'events' with their own complex management strategies. In recent years, however, Kings Cross has become one of three key nightlife areas targeted by Sydney's somewhat misnamed 'lockout laws', a set of regulatory measures introduced by the New South Wales (NSW) Liberal Coalition government in February 2014. Ostensibly aimed at reducing violence and disorder in Sydney's night-time economy through the imposition of a late-night curfew on revelers, the laws have succeeded in reducing overall recorded rates of non-domestic violence in the designated precincts, but with significant and ongoing impacts on the vibrancy and patronage of local nightlife (Lee 2016; Barrie 2016; Wadds 2018). For many, in the wake of the 'lockouts', the Kings Cross Coke sign has been re-cast as a symbol of repressive state regulation and an ongoing 'war against fun' in NSW.

Given this outcome, the opening quote from the NSW Liberal Party website takes on a somewhat ironic character. Indeed, they are the political party that introduced the strict regulations essentially curtailing what was a booming, and some would say exciting, night-time economy in Sydney. Opponents of this swathe of policy interventions have argued that the laws and regulations have taken away the very individual freedoms and private sector initiatives that the Liberal Party purports to support. In fact, that the laws are thought of by many as illiberal has been at the heart of claims made by the newly formed 'Keep Sydney Open' Party who campaigned on the issue in the 2019 NSW State election. The campaign, however, had little effect, with the left-leaning vote split across Keep Sydney Open and other parties such as Labor and The Greens.

Since the introduction of the lockout laws in 2014, debates over the regulation of nightlife have polarized the community in Sydney and NSW. Public debates have become a kind of localized culture war pitting those who argue for the 'right' to have licensed venues trading into the early hours of the morning, against those who believe 'alcohol-fueled violence' was previously out of control and could be safely managed only through limiting opening hours, restricting access to alcohol, and introducing punitive legal responses (Lee 2016; Wadds 2018). At a base level, both sides of the debate can be framed around questions of risk. While those seeking to restrict opening hours and regulate movement between venues do so on the basis of situational crime prevention and risk reduction, those seeking to drink, take drugs, and party late into the evening do so partly because of the excitement of risk taking associated with such practices (Harrison et al. 2011; Morrissey 2008) and losing oneself in the labyrinthine city as Elizabeth Wilson (1991) put it.

Yet to reduce the debate to an a-political notion of risk is also to downplay other issues and interests. As Ericson and Doyle (2003) noted, risk is never morally neutral. In fact, collectives choose the risks they worry about, and those choices shape experience (Hacking 2003). In the instance of Sydney nightlife and its governance, the deployment of 'risk' (and techniques of risk management) has fluctuated, often simultaneously, between something that is commodified and marketed to young people as a seductive element of the urban night-time experience and as an instrument for controlling these very same populations.

There are a range of stakeholders, institutions, and actors who have sought to influence how we understand and assign risk in Sydney's night-time economy. For example, the liquor lobby in NSW has sided heavily with the would-be late-night revelers, having a clear business interest in protecting a relative laissez-faire nightlife. Likewise, the music and entertainment industry has a financial stake in longer opening hours which facilitate live entertainment. On the other hand, property developers long keen to further exploit areas such as Kings Cross and its surrounds have quickly moved to acquire and develop the many closed and vacant venues that followed the lockout intervention—and were a supportive voice to those seeking increased regulation—essentially speeding up the pace of gentrification in Kings Cross in particular. Indeed, many locals disenfranchised by the lockout laws believe that the potential value of the Kings Cross real estate market during Sydney's housing market boom was a core driver of the 2014 policy shift.

Moreover, central to the lockout debates have been a range of moral entrepreneurs—many of whom never come to inner Sydney, let alone go out in the city at night—but who have been, and continue to be, drawn to the issue by the nature of the conservative moral stand it takes against the conspicuous use of alcohol and other drugs (see Wadds 2015; Flynn et al. 2016). Many of these voices have combined with medical professionals, public health specialists, and police in pushing for regulation in a more unified and effectively mobilized way than had previously been the case. The entire episode provides an excellent case study in risk governance and the limits of risk thinking. This chapter explores the deregulation and re-regulation of Sydney's night-time economy as a case of broader discourses where neoliberal political rationalities, criminal justice and public safety priorities, and divergent community expectations coalesce around risk—and what level of risk and perceived levels of disorder and interpersonal violence communities are willing to tolerate. We begin by placing the current regulatory regime in historical context before moving on to discuss the issues and implications of 'new' risks constructed around alcohol and violence in Sydney. Finally, we explore the multitude of risk discourses jostling for recognition in these contemporary debates.

Sydney's Night-Time Economy: Swills, Pills, and Bellyaches

Understanding recent debates about Sydney's nightlife requires them to be placed in historical context. The 2014 advent of the lockout measures and a much greater pessimism about the capacity of regulation and planning to address violence and disorder in Sydney's nightlife seemed like a sharp break with the past. This may be especially so among younger people who fondly recall a relatively liberal early 2000s period of venue expansion, and semi-controlled choice to buy and consume alcohol very late at night and into early morning. This was a relatively short period when Sydney's more expansive city nightlife was experienced and described as akin to the liminal dawn-time transition of other very late cities, and in which revelers were often

> caught between a numb sense of pleasure, exhaustion and doubts about when and how to depart from the night out, alongside always yawning and less sociable bar staff, security guards, fast food workers and insomniac taxi drivers. Also quite typically, there are a higher proportion of swaggering young males among those remaining in public ... The aggressive and less ordered atmosphere of this social sphere is even more surreal in spaces of cities dedicated to night leisure that also serve as central business districts during day-time hours. (Tomsen 2014a, p. 38)

However, the idea of an active late night-time and early morning economy in Sydney was a relatively recent construction. Furthermore, disillusion and alarm about the probable results of high levels of mass public drinking had been a key feature of the history of debates about drinking and night leisure in Sydney since colonization (see Wadds 2013, 2020). After its modest beginnings as a convict settlement Sydney emerged as an expanding, though socially divided, city notable for its class divisions and the fear of impoverished neighborhoods (Sturma 1983; Cunneen 1988; Lee and Ellis 2018; Wadds 2013, 2020). Bourgeois wariness about these areas was reflected in moral panics about public and disrespectable working-class leisure that included illicit forms of gambling, nocturnal revelry, and heavy drinking (Room 2010; Wadds 2020). Temperance advocates with a growing political influence equated urban social decay and vice with drinking as a wasteful form of relaxation (Chikritzhs 2009; Room 2010).

Furthermore, political unrest and the urgent imposition of social discipline in public space during an increasingly draining wartime engagement eventually sparked a new high point in the repression of night leisure in a volatile city nearing the one-million citizen mark. From 1916, a rigid late afternoon closure of public drinking venues was introduced and this remained in force until the 1950s (Chikritzhs 2009). Paradoxically, such early closing hours and the resulting practice of fast drinking—the '6 o'clock swill'—in licensed hotels serving alcohol to crowds of laborers, factory workers, and tradesmen guaranteed that same public intoxication that lurked behind official fears of unregulated drinking. State policy reflected a view that crime, public disorder, and violence were the almost inevitable consequence of the pursuit of mass drinking as a leading means of night leisure. Throughout much of the twentieth century, public drunkenness and related minor offences were harshly policed to regulate public space in a way that served to target the city's working class, poor, and Indigenous people.

This general restriction of Sydney's urban leisure was notably reversed in the last decades of the twentieth century against a backdrop of less moral constraint over social behavior, the contemporary neoliberal stress on free markets (Harvey 2005; Wadds 2013, 2018, 2020; Tomsen and Wadds 2016), and the emergence of social and economic trends that placed new emphasis on the value of consumption and the desire for individual choice. By the 1970s, Sydney had developed a limited, though lively, nightlife that built on progressively extended hotel hours, and the generally illicit operation of late bars and nightclubs. These were owned and managed by elements of the criminal underworld and unevenly 'regulated' by corrupt police officers and licensing detectives with interests well removed from notions of risk and the public interest. The late 1980s and the 1990s saw dramatic changes in the ways in which nightlife in Australian cities was governed. Indeed, a characteristic aspect of the post-industrial restructuring of cities including Sydney was the encouragement of urban night leisure as a new sphere of investment, spending, and employment (Hannigan 1998; Brenner and Theodore 2003; Wadds 2013, 2020; Tomsen and Wadds 2016). Business opportunities and casual work activity became more available in new leisure industries around bars, clubs, and restaurants, and an expanding late-night entertainment circuit for bands, DJs, comedians, and others.

From the 1990s, this shift was heralded as the financial and economic promise of the 'night-time economy' and the forthcoming '24-hour' city (Bianchini 1995). As the heart of contemporary urban nightlife, the operating hours of licensed venues were progressively extended across the week and further into the fabric of the city's night and early morning. The partial deregulation of licensing laws allowing many venues to open and serve alcohol into the early morning was justified as an attempt to develop a more 'civilized' or 'European' drinking culture. The initial confidence about doing this was bolstered by research claims about an ability to plan and shape the night-time economy and avert disorder and conflicts that had some echoes of the urban liberal progressivism of the previous century.

In Australian cities such as Sydney and Melbourne, this approach appropriated the ideologically loaded UK description of nightlife and mass drinking as the 'night-time economy'—which recast city nightlife in a positive economic light around consumption, as a marker of a modern global city, and in the utopian guise of a genteel inclusive space where diverse cultures came together (Tomsen 2014b). Indeed, the very forces of neoliberalism and liquid modernity (literally so in this case) merged together. In Australia, the UK, and elsewhere around the globe, officials seeking to badge locations as cosmopolitan tourist meccas planned the night-time revival of old industrial areas, and promoted previously marginal spaces of diversity including racial and ethnic or gay and lesbian enclaves and red-light entertainment zones as exciting, vibrant, and seductive sites of consumption. At this time, Sydney was the Australian city vying most strongly for 'global' cultural status (Wadds 2013, 2020). Unfettered nightlife was seen as a key element in attaining this goal in a manner that was often uncritical about the socially divisive aspects of this process.

However, with the utopian vision of deregulation came new risks: recorded crime and violence increased and the late-night economy itself gradually came to be seen as criminogenic; more public heavy drinking emerged; an increase in illicit drug use was associated with the longer operating hours. By 2010, the atmosphere in areas like Sydney's Kings Cross and George Street precincts, as well as in nearby regional cities like Newcastle and Wollongong, had come to be recast as risky and danger-ous, with paramilitary-style riot police deployed weekly to quell street violence and pacify anti-social behavior (Wadds 2013, 2015, 2018, 2020). In Kings Cross, Friday and Saturday nights had come to be treated by local authorities as 'events' requiring their own forms of risk manage-ment; street closures, mobile toilets, increased policing, and the installa-tion of more CCTV. Crowds of revelers streamed into the area creating an atmosphere that was vibrant and carnivalesque, but also dangerous and unpredictable in its general ungovernability. This relative ungovern-ability, excitement, and its attendant risks were key reasons why this nightlife was attractive to revelers. The inherently transgressive and dan-gerous nature of the swarm of consuming and desiring bodies, the almost endless possibilities of venues and subcultures, the seduction of a height-ened experience beyond the mundanity of suburban life made its very riskiness a key asset. Indeed, much has been written about the appeal of this 'carnival' of urban nightlife. The allure of nightlife which allows for the temporary subversion and reversal of social norms and roles has been discussed broadly in the academic literature (Presdee 2001; Measham and Brain 2005; Jayne et al. 2006; Wearing et al. 2013; Hackley et al. 2013). Here, 'determined' drinking and other drug consumption, raves, sexual exploration, and experimentation as well as immersion in music and other nightlife (sub)cultural events constitute a critical release from the alienating experiences of contemporary consumer capitalism for many young people. However, such risk taking is also a key element of neoliberal capitalism. Gone was the era when 'prudence prevailed where risk avoidance, harm minimization, diligent labor and the discipline of thrift and saving' were revered (O'Malley 2010:12). In the new consumer society, anyone seemingly could become a capitalist, a speculator, or an explorer. In fact, neoliberalism has made it the 'duty for all' to be risk adventurous (O'Malley 2010). Yet, discourses of alcohol-related risk taking in Sydney's night-time economy clearly tested the moral limits of government and many in the general public.

There was no compelling research evidence of an increase in levels of drinking-related homicides and other dangerous physical violence in this expanded Sydney nightlife that was out of scale for what might be expected in the night culture of a burgeoning city of five million people and tens of thousands of night-goers.[1] Yet for police and public authorities, conflict and disorder were ongoing and more vexed issues. The very alcohol-centric aspect of this much-heralded new urban night-time economy was pronounced for those who directly observed or engaged in it at late hours and were attuned to the subjective but pervasive sense of male aggression. In a national scenario of expanded nightlife, and heated debates about trading hours and access to alcohol, there were new pressures on public police and private security to ensure public safety and inhibit, rather than ignore or incite, violence in their nightly practices. Assaults were not as removed from the public consciousness as in the past and media campaigns drove home this image of the urban night as a dangerous terrain (Wadds 2015; Tomsen and Wadds 2016). Despite the general monoculture of young adult drinking, more revelers were middle class (and more often female) and their situation was more likely to invoke public and media outrage if they were threatened or victimized by typically working-class male aggressors (Tomsen 2014b).

The Recasting of Risk

The deaths of two young men in separate 'one punch' killings in Kings Cross in 2012 and early 2014 saw the 'dangerousness' of Sydney's urban nightlife catapulted into the news. The fatal attacks came on the back of ongoing reports of assaults in Sydney and other urban centers across NSW and Victoria. On 1 January 2014, 18-year-old Daniel Christie was hit by a single punch in Sydney's Kings Cross from Shaun McNeil, a 25-year-old builder. Christie's head hit the pavement, resulting in severe brain damage. The two men were not known to one another. Christie died in hospital some days later when his family made the decision to turn off his life support. Christie's killing occurred in almost the exact location where Thomas Kelly was also 'one punched' by Kieran Loveridge in July, 2012 just over a year earlier. Kelly also died as a result of his injuries. Both cases generated a widespread media coverage and were key drivers to changing discourse, policy, and politics around the governance of nightlife. Indeed, between the 7th and 19th of July, 2012, 110 articles were written in Sydney's two leading newspapers relating to Kelly's death, alongside widespread television news and current affairs coverage (Wadds 2013). The range of debate covered in these articles provided a key case study of the various political agendas surrounding Sydney nightlife and the consumption of alcohol (Wadds 2020). The immediate coverage featured discussion about the arbitrary and senseless nature of the attack that took Kelly's life and signaled an ominous warning about the inherent personal risks associated with late-night socializing in Sydney nightlife hotspots. These warnings focused on the violent and dangerous nature of Kings Cross and the drinking cultures which were seen to dominate the precinct. In an article appearing on the front page of the *Daily Telegraph* on the 11th of July, the attack was described as 'unprovoked, wild and cold-blooded' (Frost 2012). Another *Telegraph* article, titled 'Violence Is Killing Our City' (Devine 2012), conveyed a tone of inevitability relating to violence in Sydney's night-time economy. The article opened with the following claim:

> Another Saturday night, another cohort of young men bashed, stabbed, even killed, as our streets become no-go zones … where an innocent word or a sideways look can bring the wrath of the unhinged down on a young man out having a good time with his mates.

Other similarly dystopian articles followed the deaths and subsequent trials of Thomas Kelly and Daniel Christie and conveyed concern about the prevalence of alcohol-related violence in Sydney. Here, the discourse of 'one punch' assaults became central to debates around Sydney night-life, mounting immense pressure on local and state governments to enforce a variety of measures designed to tackle the 'alcohol-fueled' vio-lent 'crime wave' (Quilter 2014). It was also a catalyst for the introduc-tion of the language of 'risk' into nightlife policy with an underlying focus on regulating out elements perceived as 'problematic' from city spaces. The first instance of this new framework came in the form of the City of Sydney's (CoS) *Open: Future Directions for Sydney at Night, Strategy and Action Plan* released in 2013. Here, according to Wolifson and Drozdzewski (2017), there was an attempt to link problematic drink-ing cultures in Sydney with the presence of young people. In this docu-ment, drinking culture is not discussed as a public health concern, but rather a 'reputational' risk for Sydney as a brand:

> Sydney's current drinking culture and the associated anti-social behaviour is an issue and left unchecked will continue to exclude many from the night-time economy and present a reputational risk. Sydney's current night-time economy consumers are overwhelmingly young, with 77 per cent aged 18–29. (COS 2013)

The framing of problematic drinking culture as inherently linked to younger patrons has continued to subtly permeate some of the City of Sydney's policy, with explicit reference to 'improving drinking culture' through the encouragement of 'a healthy aging population' into the city after dark forming a central part of efforts to change the nightlife experi-ence (CoS 2013). As part of this strategy, a freeze on new nightclubs and large pubs (with their clear and longstanding links with young and working-class populations) and deliberate encouragement of 'small bars' (positioned as inherently 'civilized' alternatives) provide more evidence of the strategic deployment of risk management into city planning (Wolifson 2018).

While slower in acting, significant legislative and regulatory pushback from the NSW state government also came in an attempt to control night-time risks. The deaths of Thomas Kelly and Daniel Christie pre-cipitated strong collective community outrage and a subsequent political response that saw some reversal of what had been a deregulation of licensing laws in Sydney—as in other major cities across Australia (Flynn et al. 2016; Lee 2016). Demands from victims' groups, talk back radio hosts, and politicians for mandatory minimum sentences for such attacks grew.

This saw the introduction of specific 'one punch' laws as well as changes to licensing regulations for hotels and nightclubs, and reductions in opening hours for such venues. Legislative change in NSW placed a mandatory minimum sentence of eight years' imprisonment on anyone who fatally punches another person while under the influence of drugs and/or alcohol (Crimes Act 1900 (NSW) Pt 3, Div 1, s 25A(2)). Victoria followed by introducing a new offence into s 4A of the Crimes Act 1958 (Vic)—manslaughter by single punch or strike—which is also subject to a statutory mandatory minimum sentence of ten years' imprisonment. The 'one punch' or 'coward punch' became a legal idea.

Indeed, these 'lockout laws'[2] actually included at least seven different pieces of legislation around licensing reforms such as a freeze on new liquor licenses, restrictions on drinks sold after midnight on weekends, limiting last drinks to 3 am in Kings Cross and the Sydney CBD, prohibiting entry into bars after 1.30 am, and prohibiting serving shots after midnight (Conigrave 2016; Quilter 2014; Lee 2016). Being spatially delimited, these regulations purport to re-regulate areas of problem nightlife. However, the lockouts do not apply to the new or established casinos, which should, by any measure, fall within their ambit, creating a sense of injustice for many (Lee 2016). The sites of risk and dangerousness were not selected on objective reasoning but also around special interests and reflecting how seemingly 'objective' risk assessments are always subjective. They blend 'science and judgment with important psychological, social, cultural, and political factors' (Slovic 1999: 689). Here, people's perceptions and histories add meaning to the risk context in individual ways, making risk 'culturally specific and historically contingent' (Lupton 2013: 26).

After a long period where the neoliberal discourse of market-driven 'night-time economy' was maintained and extended through a mix of individual responsibility and situational crime prevention, the new laws reimagined the risks of Sydney's nightlife. The market had failed, risk has not been sufficiently governed through responsibilization, and attempts to regulate the risks of the night-time drinking culture were recast. As argued elsewhere (Flynn et al. 2016), the 'one-punch' incidents came to be seen as manageable through only two key strategies. The first was a populist discourse, which emphasized common and largely unquestioned beliefs about causes, perpetrators, and 'solutions' to such violence. A recurring message within this discourse was that limiting access to alcohol was critical in reducing violence and disorder. It posited almost a mechanical view of human behavior which saw violence as an inevitable outcome of readily accessible alcohol. This theme drew in public health and medical discourses but also encompassed situational crime prevention and crime science, introducing strategies to keep motivated offenders away from potential victims via the regulation of bodies in time and space. The second theme was legal—populist, featuring an elevated and exclusive focus on the mechanics of the offence and dangerousness of the offender (Pratt and Miao 2019), with little interest in the wider situational and social contexts of offenders' lives. This discourse contended that increasing penalties to deter offenders would discourage violence through deterring motivated offenders. The 'lockout laws', essentially illiberal when judged in relation to the market-based night-time economy previously fostered, were a rejection of the notion that risk could be managed through minimal governmental regulation.

Revolting Uncertainty: Designer Nights-Out and the Death of Excitement

> There's a whole Orwellian nomenclature that has been made up to deliberately keep the general public in a constant state of confusion that some terror has swept across the city: 'king hit', 'coward punch', 'alcopop', 'alcohol-related violence'. Being quite a respectable lot, we've all been guilt shamed into thinking that something in the Australian psyche is ugly and that mixed with alcohol we turn into raging brutes, or that by simply having fun somehow we've been breaking some great moral code, the eleventh commandment: thou shalt not have fun. (Barrie 2016)

As Matt Barrie (2016) notes in a scathing and widely disseminated anti-lockouts commentary, easily digestible discourses around the relationship between violence and alcohol consumption were pervasive in informing the political and public mood post intervention (also see Moore 2016). The discourse that circulated through the Australian (and in particularly Sydney's) press and broader media following the 'one punch' deaths was one of 'alcohol fueled violence' (Wadds 2015). Though not entirely clear in its meaning, the term seems to imply a causal link between alcohol consumption and violence that belies research which demonstrates this relationship is far from determined (for an overview, see Graham and Homel 2008). Whatever the case, the discourse was pervasive and influential in raising the levels of danger perceived in relation to a night out. Ironically, discourses of *alcohol-related violence* overlook the complex relationship between the two. Accepting this unproblematically renders an observer ill-equipped to unravel the cultural meanings of the relationship in Australia and similar or different societies where any such relationship is less apparent. Many of the discourses below helped maintain this simplified notion of the relationship between harm and alcohol consumption.

Putting Risk on the Map

Increasingly risk is mapped. The sophistication of crime and safety mapping using Geographic Information Systems (GIS) and crime incident report data has meant that risk is no longer just a statistical concept. Represented visually in the NSW Bureau of Crime Statistics and Research's 'hotspot' map of alcohol-related assault, risk appears as large round circles of black, pink, and red superimposed on a one-dimensional map of the city (see Fig. 1). These 'hot-spots' seep across the map like drops of blood and 'dangerize' particular areas, specific streets, and specific licensed venues. Stripped of the specific context of the harm that might have occurred, or indeed of the joy and celebration of human excitement that might take place in these locations, the map speaks only of risk as danger—of something to be reduced if not completely erased. Stubborn ink spots of red blot the otherwise clean rational map of the city (De Certeau 1984). The violence is there for all to see. In Fig. 1 we see a before and after hotspot map of the Sydney CBD in which it would appear the 'lockout laws' have reversed the blood red stains and rendered

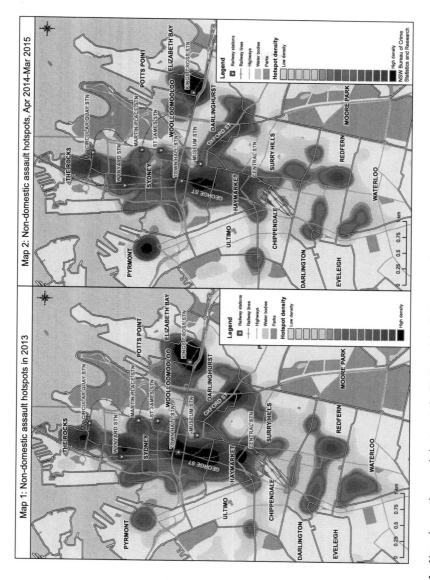

Fig. 1 Non-domestic assault hotspots in 2013 and April 2014–March 2015

them clean and blue. Such maps don't simply represent risk, they communicate it to a public unlikely to understand the contingencies and ambiguities of crime hot-spot mapping.

Risk and Public Health

Perhaps one of the strongest and most persuasive voices in favor of the lockout laws have been health professionals—particularly those working on the coalface in emergency departments at places like St Vincent's Hospital in inner Sydney. The Medical Director of the Emergency Department (ED) nearest Kings Cross, Dr. Gordian Fulde, reminds us what it was like before the laws: '[A]s time passes it's harder for people to remember just what those days were like—but those of us who work on the frontline, we remember. Quite simply, it was a war zone' (AAP 2016). The role of alcohol in maxillofacial injuries is significant with 30–60 per cent of all such trauma occurring with the influence of alcohol and alcohol being present in 55–87 per cent of assault-related maxillofacial trauma (Hutchison et al. 1998). Emergency admissions data and great numbers of injuries like orbital fractures were used to argue for the lockouts. While there has been a significant drop in admissions following the introduction of the lockout laws, this reduction is not as great as might have been expected. For example, a study in the *Medical Journal of Australia* (Fulde et al. 2015) reported the number of cases of orbital fracture relating to violence at the hospital dropped 10 per cent over two years after the controversial legislation came into effect. The cost savings are estimated to be greater than $450,000 over the period, with 27 fewer operations needed and 14 fewer patients who had their injuries managed outside the operating theater. This is a significant shift, but not necessarily in line with the massive reduction of foot traffic in the area. In other words, the gain is modest compared to large-scale deactivation that has occurred in the hospital's key catchment area.

Risk and the Economy

Neoliberal capitalist economies are—at least in relation to capital—built on risk. The ethos of 'taking a chance', 'playing the game', 'gaining a competitive edge' all speak to a market economy organized around risk taking. These risks are seen to be good risks—central to the health of late capitalism. The night-time economy fostered in Sydney can be seen as a clash of the will to expand economic profit opportunities and produce tax revenue with the state's role in reducing violence and regulating anti-social behavior (Wadds 2013, 2020). Dubbed a 'violent hypocrisy' elsewhere (see Hobbs et al. 2005), this confluence of market profits and physical and existential risk marks the night-time economy of the early twentieth century in Sydney and in many cities around the world.

Risk also creates other economic opportunities—even for 'environmental' criminologists. Such crime preventers trumpet their success in situationally reducing risk through clever design, creative activations, or 'designer nights-out'. These might include upmarket street vendors, night markets, softer outdoor lighting, street performers, and interactive games, all designed to activate sites of risk or encourage greater levels of natural surveillance in the city after dark (Dorst 2016). Of course, such interventions are, on one level, sensible. But there is a question as to whether all revelers really want 'designer nights-out' as the advertising suggests. Indeed, part of the problem is designing risky excitement out of the evening and night-time economy, since this is often a central reason why people are attracted to nightlife.

But it is certainly true that there are other solutions beyond lockouts. As Sydney Mayor Clover Moore puts it:

> [T]he big changes to our night-time economy depend on the NSW government: running public transport 24-hours; replacing lifetime liquor licenses with renewable liquor licences, as in New York and Vancouver, that encourage better behaviour from venues; and new measures to manage venue growth and concentration, including the introduction of new 'saturation zone' rules, that consider the number and type of licensed premises in a given area, along with relevant crime data and transport options.

In recent parliamentary debates around the status and regulation of Sydney nightlife, better governance and a less fragmented coalition of state and local government authorities has been suggested as a first step towards re-balancing nightlife. That all sides of politics have come together marks a rare bi-partisan recognition that the recent approaches have perhaps been too heavy-handed.

Measuring Success

There is little doubt that the number of injuries resulting from violence in Kings Cross and other areas dropped dramatically following the introduction of the 'lockout laws' (Menéndez et al. 2015; Donnelly et al. 2017). However, this is not surprising when the foot traffic in the area reduced significantly. While post-lockout pedestrian counts varied in number and quality, even conservative estimates indicate a significant and ongoing decline in foot traffic to the effect of 40–50 per cent (CoS 2011; Evershed 2016). Observers could argue the number of assaults reduced because of less access to alcohol, or due to the very notable absence of people in the area.

Yet, for all the mapping of risks, The Star Casino was exempted from the lockouts. This simply resonates as unfair and unjust—and demonstrates that the laws were not simply about a global conceptualization of risk, but about particular risks associated, in particular, with the young and reckless and particular venues. Such exceptionalism also advantages some of Australia's most wealthy and powerful people and creates the perception—accurately or not—that the government is reluctant to control risk when it comes to 'mates in high places'. To put it in perspective, if The Star Casino complex were counted in crime statistics as a single venue it would be by far the most violent venue in NSW according to assault data. As a precinct far smaller than Kings Cross, The Star records around 6.5 assaults per month or 78 assaults a year (Menéndez et al. 2015). Indeed, Kings Cross recorded 212 assaults in the 2014–2015 collection period down from 512 in 2012. The Casino and other excluded nightlife areas like Newtown and Bondi have also recorded significant increases in assaults since the lockout laws (Donnelly et al. 2016)—albeit these do not offset the reductions in areas such as Kings Cross. 'The Star' was both exempted from the lockout laws, and exempted from the 'three strikes disciplinary system' which lists and imposes increasingly onerous trading restrictions on venues with high number of violent or other offences (i.e. serving minors, intoxicated patrons, etc.) recorded against them (Liquor and Gaming NSW 2019). It appears that the extent to which risk is to be taken seriously as danger depends on the type of establishment being discussed. Perhaps in some instances, the political economy of risk does not trump a risk to state revenue.

Conclusion and Postscript

The expansion of commercial night leisure shaped around the constant use of alcohol has generated multiple layers of conflict in Sydney's night-time economy. Considerable blame shifting about disorder and violence among politicians and regulators has been a key feature of recent public and political discourse. High-profile incidents of 'alcohol-fueled' violence and disorder have further driven an ongoing media spectacle, and sustained rival lobbying of industry interests and police, health professionals, community groups, and more localized clashes between night users and local residents who have directly voiced their irritation with late-night disorder, noise, and related inconveniences. The attraction of mixed groups of people to new and established nightlife areas set off a greater level of tension over aspects of social identity shaped by concern about crime and violence (Tomsen 2014b).

As a sphere of commodified leisure, the night-time economy is a mirror of unresolved divisions and inequalities in post-industrial cities. Views of rival night-time leisure often reflect conflicting visions of what a city should offer and to whom (Hollands and Chatterton 2003). The wavering fear of physical assaults and abuse in nightlife is often overridden by a more constant and conscious aversion toward inclusive mixing with a wide range of social groups, including the young and working class (Lee 2007). As befits the uncertainties and central concern with social identity in post-industrial settings (see Bauman 2001), cultural differences are experienced as indefinite and fluid phenomena, albeit with very real demarcations grounded in material inequalities of wealth and social class. Despite the utopian promise of diversity and relaxed social mixing, and the implied general invitation to participate and spend in after-dark leisure, the night-time economy largely affirms this exclusionary urban trend (Tomsen 2014b; Wolifson and Drozdzewski 2017; Wadds 2020).

At the collective level, social inequality fosters a sense of division from other people and groups. Furthermore, it feeds mistaken attitudes toward safety when night users opposed to stricter venue regulation also espouse a view that they can personally always calculate and deal with risk as wholly self-responsible individuals (Tomsen 2014b). In contradictory state-initiated or -sanctioned campaigns and imagery to both deter and promote drinking such as the 'Think Again' (No Author 2014) campaign or the 'Drink Wise' campaign, ideal neoliberal night users are consumerist, hedonistic, and self-governing individual selves oscillating between the uncertain polarities of safe and dangerous consumption (Wadds 2013). The more recent years of crackdown and restraint reflect how removed the idealized vision of a diverse and inclusive nightlife was from the sharp reality of social division over leisure practices and access to inner-city spaces. They also indicate that a large proportion of Sydney's population were antithetical to relatively unbridled deregulation and uncertainty of the night-time economy.

On reflection, the controversial lockout laws can be seen as an attempt to reduce risk—but whose risk and by how much? Many people and interests are preoccupied with risk and its reduction in contemporary society (Beck 2019). Nevertheless, risk has both positive and negative connotations (O'Malley 2010; Mythen 2014). Risks pertain not only to negative potentialities, but to the excitement of the unknown. Many revelers head to late-night venues precisely because they want to lose themselves to and embrace the 'positive' risks of the urban night-time carnival with its apparent freedom to transgress, explore, subvert, and play. The neoliberal model of self-regulated excitement has, in Sydney at least, succumbed to a reaction against uncertainty. The extent to which this will endure is yet to be determined. However, as a postscript to this article as it goes to print, the NSW Government has announced that many of the 'lockout' regulations in the CBD will be relaxed in January 2020 noting that the laws are costing NSW 16 billion dollars a year (Foster 2019). Nonetheless, they will remain in place in Kings Cross, highlighting the stuggle over prime real estate. Conflict over nightime leasure remains unresolved, however the economic price of the lockouts appears to be becoming too much for the NSW Government.

Note

1. For a study of types of homicide related to Australian nightlife, and the location of this fatal violence across inner city, suburban, regional, and small town settings, see Tomsen (2018).
2. The 'lockout laws' are actually just one (albeit major) part of a much broader suite of regulatory controls implemented as part of the Sydney CBD Entertainment Precinct Plan of Management, which introduced 1.30 am 'lockouts' and 3:00 am cessation of service in two designated nightlife 'zones' in the city (Kings Cross and Sydney CBD); a state-wide 10 pm closing time for all bottle shops and liquor stores; a mandatory minimum eight-year gaol sentence for 'one punch' alcohol-related assaults; an increase in the maximum sentence to 25 years for the illegal supply and possession of steroids; increased police fines for offensive language, behavior, and drunk and disorderly conduct; new police powers to conduct drug and alcohol testing in cases where they suspect an offender has committed an alcohol- or drug-fueled assault; an extension of the liquor license freeze in the Sydney CBD and key urban nightlife precincts; the removal of voluntary intoxication as a mitigating factor in judicial sentencing; the introduction of drink restrictions for all venues (including no shots, no doubles, limitations on number of drinks purchased); a ban on outlaw motorcycle gang colors in the designated city precincts; the introduction of restrictions on drink promotions encouraging 'high-risk drinks'; the banning of people seen drinking in alcohol-free zones from entry into venues inside the designated precincts; and a range of other rules and policies around responsible service of alcohol guidelines, staff and recording of violent incidents inside licensed venues.

References

Bauman, Z. (2001) 'Identity in the globalizing world', *Social Anthropology*, 9, 2, pp. 121–129.

Barrie, M (2016) 'Would the last person in Sydney please turn the lights out?', *LinkedIn*, 3 Feb, 2016. https://www.linkedin.com/pulse/would-last-person-sydney-please-turn-lights-out-matt-barrie/ (accessed 20/07/2018).

Beck, U (2019) The Risk Society: Towards a New Modernity, London, Sage.

Bianchini, F (1995) 'Night Cultures, Night Economies', *Planning Practice and Research*, 10, 2, pp. 121–126.

Brenner, N., Theodore, N. (Eds.) (2003) *Spaces of neo-liberalism: urban restructuring in North America and Western Europe*, Oxford, Wiley Blackwell.

Chikritzhs, T. (2009) 'Australia', P. Hadfield (Ed.), *Nightlife and Crime: Social Order and Governance in International Perspective*, Oxford, Oxford UP.

City of Sydney (CoS) (2011) *Late Night Management Areas Research Project*, accessed 10/04/2019. https://www.cityofsydney.nsw.gov.au/__data/assets/pdf_file/0017/131741/LateNightManagementAreaResearchReport.pdf.

City of Sydney (CoS) (2013) *OPEN Future Directions for Sydney at Night, Strategy and Action Plan* (City of Sydney).

City of Sydney (2019) https://www.cityofsydney.nsw.gov.au/ accessed 10/09/2019

Conigrave, K (2016) 'Last Drinks Laws: A Health Perspective', *Current Issues in Criminal Justice*, 28 (1).

Cunneen, C. (1988) 'Policing Public Order: Some Thoughts on Culture, Space and Political Economy', in M. Findlay, R. Hogg (Eds.), *Understanding Crime and Criminal Justice*, North Ryde, Law Book Company, pp. 189–208.

De Certeau, M. (1984) *The Practice of Everyday Life*. University of California Press, Berkeley.

Devine, M. (2012) 'Violence is Killing Our City', *The Daily Telegraph,* 11 July 2012, p. 13.

Donnelly, N. Weatherburn, D. Routledge, K. Ramsey, S. and Mahoney, N. (2016) 'Did the 'lockout law' reforms increase assaults at The Star casino, Pyrmont?', *NSW Bureau of Crime Statistics and Research Bureau Brief,* Issue paper no. 114 April 2016.

Donnelly, N., Poynton, S. & Weatherburn, D. (2017). 'The effect of lockout and last drinks laws on non-domestic assaults in Sydney', *Crime and Justice Bulletin No.* 201. Sydney: NSW Bureau of Crime Statistics and Research.

Dorst, K. (2016) 'Designer nights out: good urban planning can reduce drunken violence', *The Conversation,* January 6, 2016. Accessed 10/08/2019. https://theconversation.com/designer-nights-out-good-urban-planning-can-reduce-drunken-violence-52768.

Ericson, R. and Doyle, A (2003) 'Risk and Morality', in R. Ericson and A. Doyle (eds) *Risk and Morality*, University of Toronto Press, Toronto.

Evershed, N. (2016) 'Sydney's lockout laws: five key facts about the city's alcohol debate', *The Guardian*, accessed 10/04/2019. https://www.theguardian.com/news/datablog/2016/feb/11/sydneys-lockout-laws-five-key-facts-about-the-citys-alcohol-debate.

Flynn, A. Halsey, M. and Lee, M. (2016) 'Emblematic Violence and Aetiological Cul-De-Sacs: On the Discourse of 'One Punch' (Non) Fatalities', *British Journal of Criminology*, Vol 56 (1), pp 179–185.

Foster, A. (2019) Controversial Sydney lockout laws to be rolled back in January, NEWS.com, https://www.news.com.au/national/nsw-act/news/controversial-sydney-lockout-laws-to-be-rolled-back-in-january/news-story/e2094c1337bf523dbd165adc9ecf976f accessed 10/01/2020

Frost, C. (2012) 'Young man senselessly murdered in random act of madness: Kings Cross Bashing', *The Daily Telegraph,* 11 July 2012, p. 4.

Fulde, G. W., Smith, M., & Forster, S. L. (2015) 'Presentations with alcohol-related serious injury to a major Sydney trauma hospital after 2014 changes to liquor laws', *Medical journal of Australia, 203*(9), 366–366.

Graham K., and Homel, R. (2008) *Raising the Bar: Preventing aggression in and around bars, pubs and clubs.* Devon: Willan Publishing.

Hacking, I. (2003) 'Risk and Dirt', in R. Ericson and A. Doyle (eds) *Risk and Morality*, University of Toronto Press, Toronto.

Harrison, L. Kelly, P. Lindsay, J Advocat, J. & Hickey, C. (2011) '"I don't know anyone that has two drinks a day": Young people, alcohol and the government of pleasure', *Health, Risk & Society*, 13:5, 469–486.

Hackley, C. Bengry-Howell, A. Griffin, C. Mistral, W. Szmigin, I & Hackley, R. (2013) 'Young adults and 'binge' drinking: A Bakhtinian analysis', *Journal of Marketing Management*, 29:7–8, 933–949, https://doi.org/10.1080/02672 57X.2012.729074.

Hannigan, J. (1998) *Fantasy City: Pleasure and Profit in the Postmodern Metropolis*, London, Routledge.

Harvey, D. (2005) *A Brief History of Neo-liberalism*, Oxford, Oxford UP.

Hobbs, D., Hadfield, P., Lister, S., and Winlow, S. (2005) 'Violent Hypocrisy: Governance and the Night-time Economy', *European Journal of Criminology* 2 (2). pp: 161–183.

Hollands, R., Chatterton, P. (2003) 'Producing nightlife in the new urban entertainment economy: corporatization, branding and market segmentation', *International Journal of Urban and Regional Research*, 27, pp. 361–385.

Hutchison, I. & Magennis, P. & Shepherd, J. & Brown, A. E. (1998) 'The BAOMS United Kingdom survey of facial injuries part 1: aetiology and the association with alcohol consumption. British Association of Oral and Maxillofacial Surgeons', *The British journal of oral & maxillofacial surgery*. 36. 3–13.

Jayne, M., Holloway, S. L., and Valentine, G. (2006) 'Drunk and Disorderly: alcohol, urban life and public space', *Progress in Human Geography,* 30, 4, pp. 451–468.

Quilter, J, (2014), "The Thomas Kelly case: why a 'one punch' law is not the answer" *Criminal Law Journal,* 38(1), pp: 16–37.

Lee, M. (2007) Inventing Fear of Crime: Criminology and the Politics of Anxiety, Willan, Cullompton.

Lee, M. (2016) 'Sydney's lockout laws: for and against, *Current Issues in Criminal Justice,* Vol 28 (1), pp 117–122.

Lee, M. and Ellis. J. (2018) 'Qualifying fear of crime: multi-methods approaches', in M. Lee and G. Mythen (eds) *The Routledge International Handbook on Fear of Crime,* Routledge, Oxon.

Liquor and Gaming NSW (2019) Fact Sheet FS3015, https://www.liquorand-gaming.nsw.gov.au/documents/fs/fs3015-three-strikes-disciplinary-scheme.pdf.

Lupton, D. (2013) *Risk,* 2nd Edition, Routledge, London.

Measham, F., and Brain, K. (2005) 'Binge' drinking, British alcohol policy and the new culture of intoxication', *Crime, Media, Culture,* 1(3): 262–283.

Menéndez, P. Weatherburn, D., Kypri K, and Fitzgerald, J. (2015) 'Lockouts and last drinks: The impact of the January 2014 liquor licence reforms on assaults in NSW, Australia', *NSW Bureau of Crime Statistics and Research Crime and Justice Bulletin,* Contemporary Issues in Crime and Justice Number 183.

Moore, C. (2016) Lockouts have hurt Sydney's cultural life. We have to improve our night-time economy, *The* Guardian, 23 August 2016, https://www.theguardian.com/commentisfree/2016/aug/23/lockouts-have-hurt-sydneys-cultural-life-we-have-to-improve-our-night-time-economy (accessed 29/10/2018).

Morrissey, S. (2008) 'Performing risks: catharsis, carnival and capital in the risk society', *Journal of Youth Studies,* 11:4, 413–427.

Mythen, G. (2014) Understanding the Risk Society, Red Globe Press, London.

O'Malley, P. (2010) Crime and Risk, Sage, London.

Pratt, John and Michelle Miao. (2019) Risk, Populism, and Criminal Law. *New Criminal Law Review: An International and Interdisciplinary Journal* 22(4): 391–433.

Presdee, M. (2001) *Cultural Criminology and the Carnival of Crime.* London, Routledge.

Room, R. (2010) 'The long reaction against the wowser: The prehistory of alcohol deregulation in Australia', *Health Sociological Review,* 19(2): 151–163.

Slovic, P. (1999) 'Trust, Emotion, Sex, Politics, and Science: Surveying the Risk-Assessment Battlefield', *Risk Analysis*, Vol 19(4), pp. 690.

Sturma, M. (1983) *Vice in a Vicious Society: Crime and Convicts in Mid-Nineteenth Century NSW*, St. Lucia, University of Queensland Press.

Tomsen, S. (2014a) A dangerous proximity: the night-time economy and the city's early morning. *Lo Squaderno: Explorations in Space and Society*, *32*, pp. 36–40.

Tomsen, S. (2014b) 'Identity wars. Crime, safety and conflict in Sydney's night-time economy', *Etnografia e ricerca qualitativa*, *7*(3), pp. 463–480.

Tomsen, S., & Wadds, P. (2016) Nightlife ethnography, violence, policing and security. In Stubbs, J., and Tomsen, S. (eds), *Australian Violence: Crime, Criminal Justice and Beyond*, pp. 194–209.

Tomsen, S. (2018). Homicides with direct and indirect links to the night-time economy. *Drug and Alcohol Review*, *37*(6), 794–801.

Wadds, P. (2013) *Policing nightlife: the representation and transformation of security in Sydney's night-time economy*. Unpublished Thesis, Western Sydney University.

Wadds, P. (2015) Crime, policing and (in) security: Press depictions of Sydney's night-time economy. *Current Issues in Criminal Justice*, *27*(1), 95–112.

Wadds, P. (2018) 'It's not like it used to be': Respect and nostalgia in the policing of nightlife. *Australian & New Zealand Journal of Criminology*, https://doi.org/10.1177/0004865818781204.

Wadds, P. (2020) Policing Nightlife: Security, Transgression and Urban Order. London, Routledge.

Wearing, S. McDonald, M. & Wearing, M. (2013) 'Consumer culture, the mobilisation of the narcissistic self and adolescent deviant leisure', *Leisure Studies*, 32: 4, 367–381, https://doi.org/10.1080/02614367.2012.668557.

Wilson, E. (1991) *The Sphinx in the city: Urban life, the control of disorder and women*. London: University of California Press.

Wolifson, P. (2018). '"Civilising" by Gentrifying: The Contradictions of Neoliberal Planning for Nightlife in Sydney, Australia', J. Nofre and A. Eldridge (eds.). *Exploring Nightlife: Space, Society and Governance*. Lanham: Rowman & Littlefield International, London. pp. 35–52.

Wolifson, P., & Drozdzewski, D. (2017) 'Co-opting the night: the entrepreneurial shift and economic imperative in NTE planning', *Urban policy and research*, 35(4), 486–504.

Climate Change and Migration: Managing Risks, Developing Hostilities

Elizabeth Stanley

The contemporary world is marked by constant movement. Technological shifts, entrepreneurship and economic growth have allowed modern societies to open up routes for people, trade and finance. As one indicator, international tourism (once reserved for privileged groups) has flourished since the 1980s. With one pound fares from the UK for some European flights, air travel is accessible to the masses. Well-resourced travellers have enthusiastically found pleasures in exploring more hard-to-reach landscapes and pristine environments—ultimate honeymoons on Pacific islands, seeing penguins in the Antarctic, and even the exclusive promise of space travel. Some modern elites now enjoy "global citizen" status; with unencumbered capital and movement, limited only by imaginations, they have few ties to national or civic responsibilities. Global freedoms and luxury escapism are emulated by many others, from the cruise

E. Stanley (✉)
Institute of Criminology, Victoria University of Wellington,
Wellington, New Zealand
e-mail: elizabeth.stanley@vuw.ac.nz

© The Author(s) 2020
J. Pratt, J. Anderson (eds.), *Criminal Justice, Risk and the Revolt against Uncertainty*,
Palgrave Studies in Risk, Crime and Society,
https://doi.org/10.1007/978-3-030-37948-3_10

217

ship passengers who circuit around fabulous destinations to the budget-conscious travellers who prop up the adventure tourism industry.

These global movements rely upon a "treadmill" of production (Stretesky et al. 2014) that entwines with late capitalist cultures to prioritize the new and assign status to those who consume not only products but also experiences (Ruggiero and South 2013). Within this neo-liberal setting, "agglomerated financial interests dominate" to such an extent that resources (of materials and labour) are regularly exploited to meet immediate consumer desire for products, travel or other activities (Brown 2017, 29). However, these modernization processes that provide pleasure and excitement, and the technologies that underpin them, have unleashed new hazards. Chief among them is climate change, a permanent threat that has no boundaries (Beck 1992).

Climate change is a pre-eminently modern risk. It is global in nature, and will affect everyone in some way. How, we do not yet know. The nature and consequences of manufactured environmental uncertainties are not easily calculated, predicted, controlled or repaired (ibid.). From early indications, the scale of climate risks will be far more extensive than individual governments or insurance agencies will compensate.

What is clear, however, is that the rise of populism is likely to exacerbate these risks, even though populism itself represents a revolt against the uncertainties brought about by neo-liberal economics. At a general level, populist politicians seek to protect nationhood at the expense of the international treaties and co-operation that are desperately needed if the world is to find a solution to climate change. US President Trump or Brazilian President Bolsonaro, for example, go out of their way to not only deny climate change but also to extend its effects. Trump tries to put new life into sunset industries such as coal mining while Bolsonaro wants to destroy even more of the Amazon rainforest.

This chapter considers how climate change risks have been ignored and minimized by states and corporations focused on economic growth, technological development, financial profits and institutional competitiveness. Amid removals of regulatory frameworks as well as the growth of populist anti-science narratives in some countries, emissions and warming are even cast as left-leaning conspiracies that are diminishing business opportunities. From these economic and political rationalities, climate changes are creating multiple insecurities for humans, land, oceans and whole life systems, including the potential loss of nation-states. Reflecting on how dominant carbon-producing states have responded to the "unknown unknowns" of climate change by developing increasingly secure border controls (Beck 2006, 335), this chapter exposes three principal risk-prevention techniques—hostile legalities, hostile solidarities and hostile hospitalities. Taken together, these techniques operate to blame and control those least responsible for climate change risks while polluting states and corporations fail to pursue the economic, political and technological shifts necessary to prevent climate change harms. That said, it is also clear that a significant body of resistance is gathering force, consisting primarily of young people, posing questions to governments, raising public awareness and demanding multi-lateral actions to alleviate the global insecurities of climate change.

The Realities of Climate Change

Notwithstanding the contemporary disregard of climate science by populist governments, the risks of climate change have long been known. Over a century ago, even a local newspaper in New Zealand *The Rodney and Otamatea Times, Waitemata and Kaipara Gazette* (14 August 1912, 7) included a brief "Science Note" on the matter:

> The furnaces of the world are now burning about 2,000,000,000 tons of coal a year. When this is burned, uniting with oxygen, it adds about 7,000,000,000 tons of carbon dioxide to the atmosphere yearly. This tends to make the air a more effective blanket for the earth and to raise its temperature. The effect may be considerable in a few centuries.

The author was perhaps optimistic on time frame. In 2014, the Intergovernmental Panel on Climate Change (IPCC) confirmed the unequivocal nature of climate warming. Greenhouse gas (GHG) emissions—developed through the extraction and burning of fossil fuels (such as oil, gas and coal) alongside other industrialized practices—have concentrated carbon dioxide, methane and nitrous oxide to "unprecedented" levels (IPCC 2014, 1). Since 1901, the earth's surface has warmed by about 0.7–0.9 °C, with the rate of warmth escalating from 1975 (Lindsey and Dahlman 2018). Projections affirm a rise past 2 °C by 2040, and forecast a potentially "catastrophic level of 5 °C" by the turn of the next century (White 2018, 4). In 2018, a year when global emissions increased to a record high (Figueres et al. 2018), the IPCC spelt out stark impact warnings on a rise of just 1.5 °C and reiterated the urgency for action (IPCC 2018). Still, warming is a new normal, even if emissions completely stopped today, warming would continue for another generation.

It is difficult to predict the risks—climate change exacerbates the natural variability of climate patterns, meaning that changes are erratic and uncertain. It will "amplify existing risks and create new risks" in "unevenly distributed" ways (IPCC 2014, 1). There are numerous well-established concerns. Raised ocean temperatures, melting glaciers and shrinking ice sheets are leading to sea level rises that seriously threaten coastal areas and low-lying countries. Extreme weather events—heat waves, fires, droughts, frosts, heavy rainfall, hurricanes, cyclones, tornadoes—are increasing in intensity, frequency and duration (Kramer 2020; White 2018). These effects are exacerbated through "feedback loops"—for example, as air warms, it retains more water vapour, which assists in retaining energy from the sun that warms the climate further. Melting ice sheets reduce the heat-reflective properties of the Earth, meaning that oceans absorb more heat, which increases ice-melt (Kramer 2020). Rising Arctic temperatures slow the circulation of the "jet stream" and other winds that influence the circulation of weather pressure systems—this brings slower, more intense hurricanes as well as prolonged hot weather. These synergies can create "extreme extremes" (Coumou et al. 2018, 9).

We are living, then, in an era of unprecedented global uncertainties. Every year, new records are set for global temperatures. This is having a devastating toll on the natural environment, from the acidification of coral reefs to the looming realities of significant animal and insect extinction from climate disruption and habitat loss (Kramer 2020; White 2018). Populations around the world are faced with major new harms as thousands are killed in climate "disasters", millions of people are displaced, vast swathes of land are scorched, and homes and even whole towns are destroyed from fires, storms and floods.

Extreme weather events bring other kinds of long-term problems, such as disease outbreaks, infrastructure loss, land degradation, declines in food production and increased competition and conflict over resources and territory (ibid.). The usual norms of farming and crop productivity are all affected by increased salinization of low-lying agricultural land, changes in rainfall, temperature increases and shifts in atmospheric chemistry, such as higher CO_2 or low-level ozone concentrations (Black et al. 2011). In Honduras, for example, declines in rainfall and warmer temperatures have culminated in the dramatic loss of corn, bean and coffee crops over the last decade, an issue that has triggered mass migration from rural areas (Biggs and Galiano-Rios 2019). Across the Pacific, droughts have been accompanied by coastal and marine ecosystem destruction from sea level rises. In the small island state of Tuvalu, this has led to the contamination of potable water sources, a demise in food sources (such as coconut, taro or papaya) and the decimation of fish stocks (Pratt and Melei 2018). The environmental impacts are expansive and prolonged, their cumulative effects on resources, work, health and daily lives are profound.

These global risks affect everyone, including future generations. However, they are differentially experienced, and they legitimize and exacerbate social landscapes of inequality. Enterprising individuals may mitigate their risks through finance, insurance and law as well as luck. For example, in the 2018 Californian fires, the insurers for the wealthiest—such as Kim Kardashian—engaged private fire officers to protect substantial homes (Madrigal 2018). Their experiences are substantively different to those most vulnerable to "natural" disasters. Economically disadvantaged populations (especially poor racial minorities, older people and women) are more likely to live in areas that are environmentally precarious and less likely to enjoy protections (White 2018; Wonders and Danner 2015).

Developing countries bear the brunt, as they experience the most hazardous weather events. Those in most danger from rising sea levels or storm surges, for example, reside in Pacific island states or in cities across Africa and Asia (Goldberg 2017). These countries often have the least capacity to protect populations. They have long-standing problems of food insecurity, pollution and disease epidemics, unreliable access to potable water and limited technological resources or capacity (Beck 2006; Kramer 2020). They are regularly made more vulnerable through poverty, political instability, entrenched inequalities and repression (Green 2008). Further, they hold little international power to mitigate or stop the climate risks perpetuated by more developed countries.

The systemic "organized irresponsibility" in operation is such that those who produce the risks encounter little accountability while those most affected have few chances to control decisions or practices about their futures (Beck 2015, 76). Small island nations endure the greatest vulnerability, with states such as Kiribati, Tuvalu and the Maldives being faced with the potential of absolute destruction from rising sea levels. As Maeed Mohamed Zahir, the Director of Ecocare in the Maldives, spelt out, this would not just encompass a loss of land or territory, but the loss of "nationality, an identity, a cultural history, a language, a script … everything" (cited in Brisman et al. 2018, 309). There is a colonial logic of obliteration in operation here—these nations (and their life worlds) are to make the ultimate sacrifice of dispossession for advanced global capitalism.

Displacement

The above discussions establish the conditions under which individuals or entire populations are forced to move from their homes in search of safety. The number of those displaced by global warming or climate change is unclear. The displacement of "victims" is under-reported and mostly uncounted (cf Weber and Pickering 2011)—even the recent Paris Agreement avoids terms like "refugees", "migration" or "mobility" (UNFCCC 2015). Nonetheless, the International Displacement Monitoring Centre recently estimated that "more than 19 million people from 100 countries were forced to flee their homes in 2014 because of natural disasters" (Lieberman 2015). The United Nations has also noted that 20 million people are displaced from climate change effects each year, "with more than 85 percent from poor and/or developing countries" (Brisman et al. 2018, 301). The predicted number of environmental migrants by 2050 oscillates between 25 million and a staggering one billion people, with 200 million being the most widely cited (IOM 2018). These migration flows are clearly going to intensify, and dystopian images of mass migrations are easy to imagine (Lewis 2018).

One difficulty in counting such victims relates to the complex factors—such as inequalities, income volatility, civil wars, genocide, slum lives, limited employment, political corruption, authoritarianism, disease, the search for education and so on—that can also "count" when people decide to flee climate change dangers (Black et al. 2011; Green 2008). Migration is a long-established system "of social and demographic interaction and change" (Black et al. 2011, 54); it is a normal, interconnecting feature of human life (Baldwin and Bettini 2017, 3). Further, while migration is triggered by extreme environmental events, it also emerges from environmental risks experienced over long periods of time (such as continuing crop failures or increased food prices). The "push" and "pull" motivations often interlink (Randall 2013) and they influence whether migration is temporary or permanent, and whether it entails internal displacement (to ever-densely populated urban areas) or movement across immediate borders or further afield. In short, climate change events can operate as "tipping points" amid ongoing "economic, social and political pressures" (McAdam 2015, 132). These complicated situations require state responses that are co-ordinated, agile and supportive. However, as the rest of this chapter illustrates, Western responses to the global risks of climate change, and those most affected, are largely driven by hostilities.

Minimizing the Risks of Climate Change

Powerful nations have largely resisted global attempts to avert climate change through agreements on greenhouse gas (GHG) emissions and carbon taxes. Notwithstanding the 2016 Paris Agreement, the priorities of economic expansion, corporate success, technological advancements and resource extraction continue to dominate (Bulkeley 2001). Across major polluting countries (including the United States, China, India, the United Kingdom, Canada and Australia), governments continue to support risky industries: oil and coal, fracking, deep-water drilling, extracting heavy bitumen from tar sands, mining and mass-production farming (Kramer 2020; White 2018). Even New Zealand, with its international "100% pure" reputation, makes a significant contribution to global warming through dairy herds that continually emit methane. Elsewhere, deforestation for fuel, mining, crops (such as palm oil) or pastoral ends undermines opportunities to mitigate climate-related changes. Deforestation demolishes biodiversity, and it also accounts for a fifth of all emissions—the mass logging in Indonesia and Brazil ensures that these countries are now dominant polluters (Phillips 2018; White 2018).[1]

The responsibility for emissions is increasingly complicated. In some respects, it appears that no one group can be singled out for opprobrium in modern societies as all are involved in the creation of hazards. Yet, from 1988 to 2014, 100 industrial carbon producers (of oil, gas, coal and cement) accounted for 71% of emissions, with just "25 corporate and state producing entities accounting for 51%" of emissions. Their emissions are increasing (Griffin 2017, 8) despite long-standing corporate knowledge on the harmful effects of GHG emissions. Five oil and gas companies—Chevron, BP, Exxon Mobil, Shell, Total—spent over US$1bn "in the three years following the Paris Agreement on misleading climate-related branding and lobbying" (Influence Map 2019, 2).[2] They have manufactured uncertainty, funded groups that "scientifically" cast doubt on climate science, promoted industry interests and ignored alternative energy sources (Kramer 2020; Lynch et al. 2010; Ruggiero and South 2013; White 2018).

Of course, how risks are imagined is contingent on political, economic and socio-cultural constructions (Beck 1992). Unlike other global risks (such as terrorism) that receive urgent attention and preventative resources across government agencies, climate change has encountered a more muted response. For example, the United States has failed to substantively address climate change or to accept the established science of manufactured global warming. There have been glimmers of hope—President Obama led a 2013 "Climate Action Plan" and a 2014 "Clean Power Plan" to reduce emissions, develop alternative energies and operationalize a regulatory "Environmental Protection Agency" (Kramer 2020). His administration developed an agreement with China (the second largest emitter) and signed the historic Paris Agreement (ibid.). However, the Republican Trump administration has actively rejected all the established climate change science and ridiculed expert calls for emergency action. Clearing the White House website of references to global warming, the administration has reduced funding for scientific gathering of information on climate change effects and unleashed fossil fuel industry constraints—approving pipeline projects and new mining leases, issuing executive orders to remove industry "burdens", repealing the Clean Power Plan, stopping contributions to the Green Climate Fund and withdrawing from the Paris Agreement (ibid.). Similarly, Australian Former Prime Minister Tony Abbott has remarked that climate change is "probably doing good" and that Australia should pull out of the Paris Climate Agreement (Mathiesen 2017; Yaxley 2018). Newly elected Prime Minister Scott Morrison has long supported the Australian coal industry and avoids mentioning the c-word, even while vast swathes of his country burns. The logic of capitalist expansion has not waivered in the midst of apocalyptic narratives and deadly climate experiences.

In the US, climate change science is still cast as a "hoax", a "conspiracy" and a "fantasy" by leading Republicans and across some conservative media (Brisman and South 2015, 451). In 2018, the four major television networks (FOX, NBC, CBS, ABC) contributed a total of just 142 minutes to the issue in nightly news coverage and political shows (this included a forty-six minute specialist NBC broadcast in December 2018) (Macdonald and Hymas 2019). Studies on international media reporting demonstrate that mainstream news reports have tended to frame climate change in terms of disaster, such as the human impact from specific climate-related events (Painter 2013). In this respect, climate change has often been missing from broader reporting on economy, employment, health, travel or housing. Similarly, the problem has almost been absent from "non-news" contributions. For example, recent UK research analysed the subtitles from 128,719 "non-news" programmes, across forty channels, from September 2017—September 2018. The words "climate change" (n = 3215) were mentioned far less than "cake" (n = 46,043) or "dog" (n = 105,245), while "global warming" (n = 799) was less prominent than "zombie" (n = 2488) (BAFTA 2019).

However, in 2019, these knowledge absences are being challenged on a daily basis. Youth activists have propelled significant social media and political action on a newly labelled climate "crisis" or "emergency". Mainstream news providers, such as the BBC and the New York Times, have now appointed specialist journalists to increase their coverage. In September 2019, over seventy international media organizations engaged in a week of intensive reporting as part of a commitment to increase the visibility of climate risks.

There are then, signs of substantive challenges to the silencing of climate change. But, in many ways, this is a time in which many people are in a process of remembering and forgetting on climate change. As Klein (2014, 4) recounts, "We engage in this odd form of on-again-off-again ecological amnesia". Even in states that accept climate risks, there has been relatively little action to shift practices. A common narrative has been that "the market" will find technological solutions (such as spraying sulphate into the atmosphere to dim the sun's rays, or capturing carbon dioxide with machines), so we should not stem economic growth or consumption patterns (Klein 2014; Wyatt and Brisman 2017).

Managing Climate Change "Risks"

Western state responses to climate change migration have, to a large extent, mirrored broader actions towards asylum seekers and other "noncitizens". However, they are also evolving in different ways. The "unknown unknowns" of climate change have prompted states, already driven by stringent border controls, to insist upon further security expansions (Beck 2006, 335). In Australia, for example, defence chiefs have recently warned of the "substantial security threat" to the country from climate change, noting that the military will need to increase sea patrols to intercept climate migrants (Willacy 2019).

Three principal risk-avoidance techniques are now operationalized by Western carbon-producing states. First, states exclude climate migrants from legal protections, at international levels. "Hostile legalities" mean that those fleeing climate change effects must often establish their protections through circuitous, often criminalizing, routes. Second, states are re-establishing their own security in the face of climate change risks. This entails new claims to assert food, water or territorial security, and it relies upon fortress logics that perpetuate a "hostile solidarity" (Carvalho and Chamberlen 2018). But, third, alongside these dominating security responses, states simultaneously advance humanitarian actions to "save" climate change victims. These activities can sometimes reflect an ethos of care, but they are also contingent on victims taking some responsibility (but not too much) for their own survival. This is a "hostile hospitality" (Khosravi 2009) for those who cannot adapt, who don't have the right "attitude" or who make too many demands. These techniques intersect to blame and responsibilize those least responsible for climate change risks, while taking the focus away from polluting states and corporations to address their globally threatening activities.

Hostile Legalities

The international legal framework provides no effective protection for those who need to move from environmental dangers. The 1951 UN Refugee Convention requires individuals to have a "well-founded fear" of persecution on the grounds of "race, religion, nationality, membership of a particular social group or political opinion" and to be unable or unwilling, "owing to such fear", to return to their country of nationality (art. 1A[2]). There are multiple issues that climate change migrants cannot meet. Generally, they cannot satisfy the legal concept of "persecution"—after all, vulnerable nations are engaged in multiple efforts to mitigate climate change impacts (McAdam 2015). The risks they endure are also largely indiscriminate, rather than directed to specific personal attributes. And, any "persecution" is actually undertaken by the countries to which they might seek refuge, so the usual "refugee paradigm" is "completely reverse[d]" (ibid., 34). Given these hurdles, climate change migrants are legally trapped.

Nonetheless, those from small island states have sought legal protection to escape worsening environmental conditions. Even New Zealand, with its geographic isolation from those affected by worsening environmental conditions, has found itself facing legal uncertainties around climate change. As a case in point: in 2013, Mr. Ioane Teitiota[3] argued for refugee status on the grounds of environmental degradation in Kiribati (pronounced "Kiribass"), a Micronesian country of 800 sq km, divided across thirty-two atolls and reef islands that straddle the equator, about half-way between Australia and Hawai'i. The population of Kiribati (about 100,000 people) face inundation from rising sea levels, resulting in food shortages, destruction of homes and infrastructure and land loss. These problems, together with the salinization of fresh water "caused by sea-level rise associated with climate change",[4] are creating uninhabitable conditions. The Immigration and Protection Tribunal (IPT) found that his "concerns about Kiribati and its future were justified" (§6) but that he could not be determined to be a refugee, or a "protected person" under the International Covenant on Civil and Political Rights. The Tribunal noted that Teitiota had engaged in "voluntary adaptive migration" that was not "forced".[5] His appeals to the High Court and the Court of Appeal were denied, and the Supreme Court dismissed his application, on the grounds that the government of Kiribati was taking steps to protect its citizens.[6] Teitiota, along with his wife and three New Zealand-born children, was deported back to Kiribati in September 2015. There has yet to be a successful claim for climate change protection.

At the same time, the term "refugee" is also refused by many at risk from climate change.[7] The term "refugee" is significant; it demands a requirement for "refuge" but, as often demonstrated, it is also linked to the "refusal" of protection, and for those claiming assistance to be determined to be disposable, "refuse" (Evans 2017, 71). The toxicity of debate and the degradation of law (as detailed below) are such that many climate change migrants do not want to be identified as "refugees". Conversely, if justly applied, the label "refugee" requires a determination that the person is a "victim" who has run out of options. Those suffering the worst effects of climate change contest this vision. They stress their agency and argue that climate change victimization should not be normalized or accepted (the total destruction of island states is not, after all, an inevitable outcome). Besides, the term "climate refugee" naturalizes displacement, as it infers that migration results from "natural" factors, rather than being the result of state-corporate decisions (Saldanha 2017, 156). The "chain of causality between industrialization, global warming and displacement" becomes lost in the labelling of refugees (ibid., 157).

Those who bear the greatest risks from climate change effects are subject, then, to "legal hostilities". Climate change is not yet deemed an acceptable reason to seek permanent residence across borders. Those who flee climate change effects have to establish their protection by other means, such as by entering states on tourist or temporary work visas (or no visa) and becoming "illegals" or "overstayers". For example, New Zealand Immigration estimates that there are over 10,000 overstayers in the country, with over half from Pacific states (TVNZ 2018). Anecdotal evidence indicates that climactic conditions—particularly cyclones and storms that have devastated homes and sustainable lands—are increasingly central to decisions by Pacific people to "overstay" (Scoop 2016). The consequences are significant. Notwithstanding family supports, those without visas enjoy few services and live precarious lives. Further, official institutions emphasize threats—of the "harm being caused by overstayers and the financial cost to our communities" (NZ Immigration cited in TVNZ 2018). Authorities increasingly focus on the identification and expulsion (through deportations or "voluntary departures") of non-citizens. Such hostile legalities, creating criminals to legitimize punishments and expulsions (Khosravi 2009), are dovetailed with approaches to pre-empt and minimize risks by securing territory and borders.

Hostile Solidarities

A culture of suspicion has long been established towards the unknown "aliens" who arrive at the border, and national or ethnic difference is often represented as an indicator of an inherently risky nature (Malloch and Stanley 2005). The expansive risks of climate crisis are providing new levels of anxieties in countries that endure the brunt of environmental insecurities but also within states that may receive climate migrants. Descriptors of climate change—"waves", "floods", "swell"—are commonly applied to those seeking protection (Russo 2017, 202). Fears of an uncontrollable planet combine with long-established narratives of invasion or terrorism, reflecting well-worn colonial and racially indexed stereotypes (Baldwin and Bettini 2017). With increasing regularity, Western political leaders invoke a "white civilization in terminal crisis" from the "hordes of desperate and dangerous masses" (Saldanha 2017, 156–57).

Under these "insuperable manufactured uncertainties", governments turn their attention to increased securitization (Beck 2006, 335), a point illustrated in President Trump's rhetoric of invasion, wall-building and military defence towards the 2018 caravan of migrants fleeing the impacts of climate change in Honduras and other central American countries (Timm 2018). The unbounded nature of climate change risks (including fears of "mass migrations") provides limitless scope to exclude, detain, punish and expel populations on the basis that they may pose a future threat. States engage pre-emptive rationalities to demarcate borders, per-formatively sorting between "citizens" and suspect communities (Pickering and Weber 2014, 1007). This sorting reflects individual attri-butes (such as criminal pasts, education or work skills), but it increasingly invokes group characteristics (Valverde 2010)—risks are deemed to be ubiquitous across particular nationalities, ethnicities, religious groups or those associated with them (Krasmann 2007).[8] The "finely meshed gra-dation of states according to … security risk" (Aas 2013, 29) coalesce with climate change risks to produce exclusionary practices. While responding to the caravan of migrants, for example, President Trump reiterated the narratives of Latin Americans as violent criminals and ter-rorists (Serwer 2018). Relatedly, in the UK, racist stereotypes of Afro-Caribbean populations as being violent or welfare scroungers have ensured that these populations are now almost completely excluded from settlement across the UK at a time when Commonwealth Caribbean countries endure considerable dangers from rising sea levels and hurri-canes (Sealey-Huggins 2017).[9]

Such efforts to exclude those found unpalatable serve to re-emphasize the included "us", propounding mythical sensibilities of national "social and symbolic integration" (Beck and Levy 2013, 4). The performances reassert state territoriality and reinforce socio-cultural, moral and politi-cal frontiers (Weber and Pickering 2013) and, while engaging a "sense of belonging" and a populist "emotional release" for those deemed accept-able, they advance a "hostile solidarity" towards those who do not belong

(Carvalho and Chamberlen 2018, 228). For politicians like President Trump, the backlash against perceived outsiders (as well as the liberals deemed intent on destroying corporate freedoms) has resulted in numerous hostilities. This has included the demonization and criminalization of migrants in the "caravan" heading towards the United States, and the escalation of punitive border controls such as the inhumane detention of separated young children. While re-affirming and soothing social demands for national security and enhancing a populist US sovereignty, these measures ignored the climate change realities (such as unworkable farming conditions) from which many in the "caravan" had fled (Milman et al. 2018). More broadly, the suspension of legal norms, indefinite and traumatizing detentions, deportations and death are now commonly experienced by "non-citizens" across polluting states (Farbotko and Lazrus 2012; Krasmann 2007; Malloch and Stanley 2005). These treatments and conditions produce people as "deportable" on grounds of offending but also their claims on "our" territory or resources.

Protectionist actions against "risky" others are, however, a distraction from the significant systemic and institutionalized global harms and environmental risks that we all now face. While they may propel political capital within anxious states, they function to solidify state power, labour management, economic productivity and capital accumulation (Baldwin and Bettini 2017). Under these conditions, those with economic power develop solidarities in building "walled sanctuaries" (Brisman et al. 2018). A common refrain is that, given climate change, powerful states can no longer support overseas aid, fair trade or support to less powerful countries (Klein 2014). Similarly, those with economic power assert their own ownership of and access to resources. This entails reconfigurations of state territories and control. For example, as environmental changes have created insecure access to vital commodities (like water or food), many corporations and states are pre-empting future rations by buying land or access to water in other countries (White 2018). Businesses are also increasingly involved in privatized tree plantings, reinsurance schemes, carbon credit ventures or security technologies (Klein 2014). Under "shock doctrine", corporate interests and powerful nations are attuned to exploiting risk-based crises for their own advancement (ibid.). In this respect, dominant responses to climate change re-emphasize the structures that underpin escalating environmental degradations (such as economic growth, financial profits, competitiveness and nationalist security) while depleting human security, financial protections or resource opportunities for those most affected by climate impacts.

Hostile Hospitalities

Although migrants are often excluded in increasingly vitriolic and dehumanizing ways, these are not total responses. Notions of human rights, compassion, humanitarianism and hospitality are entangled with abjection and exclusion (Aas 2013). These contradictory flows mean that Western state responses are "partly caring, partly punitive; partly endangering (deportation), partly saving … partly forced, partly empowering; partly a site of hospitality, partly a site of hostility" (Khosravi 2009, 53). After securing the borders (and often having secured colonial benefits from "appropriation and enslavement"), states also declare themselves as places of "rights and freedoms" for the "very deserving few who might be genuine refugees" (Colebrook 2017, 118). On paper, those forcibly pushed from adverse climate dangers could hold something close to "ideal" status in the hierarchy of those arriving at the border.

Yet questions of who can be welcomed or included are also linked to a sense of "shared sacrifice" within the context of neo-liberalism (Brown 2016). Those who belong—"the fully responsibilized citizen[s]" (ibid., 12)—do not seek protection from the vagaries of capitalism's failings or changing global circumstances, including environmental dangers. The risks of climate change are unevenly shared so that while developing countries bear little responsibility, they are seen to be responsible for not thriving amid the extreme changes in their conditions. In this context, migration from climate change is also determined to be a sign of limited responsibility or an abdication of risk management in dealing with environmental pressures "at home". Polluting states have rarely sought to inhibit their own advancements to provide protections from these grave risks.[10] Indeed, they have frequently positioned themselves as the superior "experts", able to scientifically mediate climate risks for others through modelling or technological solutions (Bulkeley 2001). These "reassuringly technical" responses (Bettini 2017, 84) advance "ecological neo-liberalism", as they take the "lead in knowledge and development over poorer countries" (Beck 1996, 6).

Of course, the most vulnerable states have engaged adaptations and mitigation efforts for many years (Russo 2017). Across Pacific states, for example, people have (among other things) secured their land, adapted crop techniques, preserved foods, changed building approaches, reorganized warning systems and developed clear practices for community responses to extreme weather events—adaptation "could almost be viewed as a fact of life" (Bryant-Tokalau 2018, 82). Migrants have also been "virtuous adaptation agents" by "mobilizing their human capital" (Baldwin and Bettini 2017, 11) and self-financing these adaptations through the use of remittances (Bettini 2017). They have sought to avoid opprobrium through active economic and political engagement, whatever the sacrifices.

Many states under threat are well aware of how "migration as adaptation" requires the disciplining of labour under advanced global capitalist conditions. They understand that they will be expected to be "a docile labour force" for recipient states (Baldwin and Bettini 2017, 11). In Kiribati, a central feature of the "Migration with Dignity" plan relates to training local populations to allow them to leave as "skilled migrants" (Randall 2013, 3). Raising the level of qualifications can allow Kiribati communities to increase their migration options, becoming more attractive as productive migrants, in tune with the global economy (Angell 2017; Ransan-Cooper et al. 2015). To survive well they must be regarded as fully responsibilized would-be citizens.

However, migrants' survival depends largely on the behaviours of recipient states. Those who are officially welcomed as migrants or refugees can find that they are managed in "subtle ways" (Johansen 2013, 257). States can give the appearance of humanitarianism (invoking care, respect or culturally safe relationships) whilst also pursuing a "hostile hospitality" (Khosravi 2009). Many new migrants, particularly refugees, find that they are forcefully isolated from public, social and economic life. Western government policies ensure their "limbo" status—as they deny their access to community welfare benefits or to usual pay levels, while rights to health care, education or work are regularly waived (Diken

2004). These practices are so entrenched that migrants frequently experience a "funnel of expulsion" (Johansen 2013, 258) in which they ultimately "choose" to leave as their "life situation is designed to be as deprived as (politically) possible" (ibid., 258). In this respect, migrants take the decision for their own expulsion (Khosravi 2009). But where might climate change migrants go? At present, international policies and law reiterate a (false) presumption that displaced populations can return to their place of origin, but climate change will make that impossible for some.

Conclusion: Anticipating Endangered Futures

Discredited migrants are increasingly made to disappear. This disposal includes direct harassment, violence and deportations, but it also entails getting non-citizens to choose to leave or to endure conditions in which they cannot easily live (Brown 2017). In terms of climate change, this is a profoundly counterproductive form of risk management. In the focus on "dangerous" or "irresponsible" migrants and the impetus on bolstering border controls, powerful polluters remove attention from the absolute destruction of environments and global ecosystems (Brisman and South 2015). Amid these hostilities, climate catastrophes have become somewhat normalized and anti-migration sentiments (as well as the drive for capital accumulation, territorial sovereignty and disciplined labour) are reinforced (Bettini 2017).

Meanwhile, the polluting states and corporations that derive most benefits from the global capitalist economy fail to substantively submit to necessary global shifts in economy, technologies or power. Financial and resource supports for adaptation technologies or processes remain deeply limited (Bettini 2017; Ruggiero and South 2010), and there remains no shared agreement on the global structural changes required for mitigation efforts. Those at risk of climate change impacts have relatively few options to protect themselves from environmental threats and disasters. Notwithstanding the overwhelming responsibility of powerful states and corporations for climate change risks, those least responsible are blamed and responsibilized for global insecurities.

Global insecurities are amplified under populist conditions and free-market extremism. This is most evident in the frenetic escalation of US President Trump's rhetoric and actions against climate change science (to expand fossil-fuel industries, remove corporate regulations, weaken environmental protections) while enhancing popular anxieties about "Others" (from racial fear-mongering to consolidating repressive border controls). The revolt against the uncertainties associated with neo-liberal economics that led to Trump's populist agenda in the United States has in turn escalated the long-term risks, harms and hostilities around the world. The President's support base has not waivered, as voters willingly support the erosion of rights and repression against identified threats under these "shocks" (Klein 2017). The nature of global insecurities also means that those who protest climate change are often criminalized (Goyes 2016) and can be physically attacked. Global Witness records that, on average, four "environmental defenders" are killed each week around the world. From 2015 to mid-2018, 145 people were killed in Brazil alone; most were Indigenous people challenging illegal logging in the Amazon (Ulmanu et al. 2018).

However, while populist states have resisted evidence of climate change risks with a doubling down of denial and disdain of science, other populations—and especially young people—have started to revolt against the uncertainties, and revolt against the certainty of climate change. Following the internationally acclaimed example of Swedish teenager Greta Thunberg, there have been global student and worker strikes to demand action on climate change. The international movement "Extinction Rebellion" has also disrupted many cities through peaceful acts of disobedience. In April 2019, they brought parts of London to a grinding halt. Despite over a thousand arrests and calls by a former head of counterterrorism for more "proactive", stringent action towards this "political extremism" (Hymas 2019), there has been growing public support for the actions. British broadcaster David Attenborough, long treasured for his natural history programmes, heralded the hope shown by young activists and argued that "we cannot be radical enough" in targeting climate change (Vaughan 2019).

There are now hundreds of lawsuits to compel government and corporate action against global warming (Setzer and Byrnes 2019) and, increasingly, local councils and governments are making climate "emergency" declarations, and developing new targets to reduce emissions targets. Meanwhile, initiatives (such as the Nansen Initiative and the Platform on Disaster Displacement) are developing better data and building protective actions towards cross-border displacements.[11] Ad hoc options are also evolving at national levels. For example, New Zealand announced its consideration of a "humanitarian visa category", to provide an annual 100 visas for Pacific peoples displaced by rising seas.[12] Such welcome albeit limited actions reflect thinking that our "common exposure" to climate change necessitates new interdependencies and strategies for "collective survival" (Beck and Levy 2013, 12, 23).

The requirements to adapt to new migration flows will invoke significant anxieties across societies. While the emphasis has to be on mitigation efforts, there are significant questions on how those primarily responsible for global risks will ensure that climate migrants are able to "move with dignity", having "some choice in the timing and circumstances of their movement" and supported to "become active members of their new communities" (Randall 2013, 2). The political and ethical dilemmas for Western societies can, to some extent, be imagined and pre-empted. For example, what would territorial states owe those whose territories disappear or become unliveable? Could individual states or collective blocs agree to specified levels of migration from affected areas? While keeping an emphasis on mitigation and adaptation efforts, should states like New Zealand begin a rigorous process of settlement preparation with those from Pacific islands such as Tuvalu or Kiribati? And, how might those who lose their territories retain their agency, cultural identity, self-determination or sovereignty (Russo 2017)? Could they continue to self-determine their own futures, "collectively rul[ing] themselves" beyond their sovereign space (Angell 2017, 13)?

Ultimately, global climate change risks will require nations to evolve radically different norms and imperatives across consumption patterns, law, economics, politics, travel, work, science and social structures (Beck and Levy 2013). Ulrich Beck argued that this could well be an "emancipatory catastrophe" that triggers new technologies alongside urgent institutional and social reforms (Beck 2015, 79). For him, the unwanted side-effects of climate change will propel a new cosmopolitanization, as the "antagonisms of the world ... collide" in such a way that it requires "new ways of being, looking, hearing and acting in the world" (Beck 2015, 85, 83). At the very least, there is a need for "interactive relationship[s]" to address generational climate problems across borders (Beck and Levy 2013, 6). Any politics of climate justice will require global solidarities invoking co-operation, reciprocity and interdependence (Klein 2014), all of which fundamentally challenge the hostilities currently sustained by advanced global capitalism and its proponents.

Notes

1. Almost half of Brazil's GHG emissions is linked to deforestation—from August 2017 to July 2018, an area almost equivalent to a million football pitches was lost (Phillips 2018).
2. In 2019, just 3% of their $115bn capital investments was directed to low carbon projects.
3. Teitiota had moved with his wife to New Zealand in 2007, where they had three children. In 2010, their visas expired. After coming to official attention, he applied for refugee status.
4. AF (Kiribati) [2013] NZIPT 800413 (25 June 2013), at 2.
5. AF (Kiribati) [2013] NZIPT 800413 (25 June 2013), at 39.
6. Supreme Court—SC 7/2015, [2015] NZSC 107. Judgment, 20 July 2015. The Court noted, however, that the decision "did not mean the environmental degradation resulting from climate change or other natural disasters could never create a pathway into the Refugee Convention or protected person jurisdiction" (at 13).
7. There is no agreed term—labels include "climate-induced (involuntary) migration", "forced displacement due to climate change", "environmental refugees", "ecological migrants" and "survival migrants" (Kraemer et al. 2017).
8. High risk scores also become self-reinforcing—targeted policing leads to more discoveries of "risks", further punishments, and higher risk scores for affected populations (Valverde 2010).
9. An issue sadly underlined by the "Windrush" scandal in the UK.
10. A situation that is at odds with other risks (e.g. terrorism or sex offences), to which governments engage in extensive pre-emptive actions. Neo-

liberal states have "set a much higher bar when it comes to the risk or threat" of climate crimes (Brisman 2017: 317).

11. See: https://www.nanseninitiative.org/secretariat/ and https://disaster-displacement.org/.

12. This was dismissed by Pacific leaders who argued for a collective solution rather than an individualised visa that removed rights to be members of their own nation-state.

References

Aas, Katja F. 2013. "The Ordered and the Bordered Society: Migration Control, Citizenship, and the Northern Penal State." In *The Borders of Punishment*, edited by Katja F. Aas and Mary Bosworth, 21–39. Oxford: Oxford University Press.

Angell, Kim. 2017. "New Territorial Rights for Sinking Island States." *European Journal of Political Theory* (November 2017). https://doi.org/10.1177/1474885117741748.

BAFTA, British Academy of Film and Television Arts. 2019. *Subtitles to Save the World*. May 2019. https://www.planetplacement.co.uk/subtitles-to-save-the-world/.

Baldwin, Andrew, and Giovanni Bettini. 2017. "Introduction: Life Adrift." In *Life Adrift*, edited by Andrew Baldwin and Giovanni Bettini, 1–21. London: Rowman and Littlefield.

Beck, Ulrich. 1992. *Risk Society: Towards a New Modernity*. Translated by Mark Ritter. London: Sage.

Beck, Ulrich. 1996. "World Risk Society as Cosmopolitan Society?" *Theory, Culture and Society* 13 (4): 1–32.

Beck, Ulrich. 2006. "Living in the World Risk Society." *Economy and Society* 35 (3): 329–345.

Beck, Ulrich. 2015. "Emancipatory Catastrophism: What Does It Mean to Climate Change and Risk Society?" *Current Sociology* 63 (1): 75–88.

Beck, Ulrich, and Daniel Levy. 2013. "Cosmopolitanized Nations: Re-imagining Collectivity in World Risk Society." *Theory, Culture and Society* 30 (2): 3–31.

Bettini, Giovanni. 2017. "Unsettling Futures: Climate Change, Migration and the Obscene Biopolitics of Resilience." In *Life Adrift*, edited by Andrew Baldwin and Giovanni Bettini, 79–95. London: Rowman and Littlefield.

Biggs, Marcia. and Julia Galiano-Rios. 2019. "Climate Change is Killing Crops in Honduras – and Driving Farmers North." *PBS News Hour*, April 2, 2019. https://www.pbs.org/newshour/show/climate-change-is-killing-crops-in-honduras-and-driving-farmers-north.

Black, Richard, W. Neil Adger, Nigel Arnell, Stefan Dercon, Andrew Geddes, and David Thomas. 2011. "The Effect of Environmental Change on Human Migration." *Global Environmental Change* 21 (1): s3–s11.

Brisman, Avi. 2017. "Tensions for Green Criminology." *Critical Criminology* 25 (2): 311–323.

Brisman, Avi, and Nigel South. 2015. "New 'Folk Devils', Denials and Climate Change: Applying the Work of Stanley Cohen to Green Criminology and Environmental Harm." *Critical Criminology*, 23 (4): 449–460.

Brisman, Avi, Nigel South, and Reece Walters. 2018. "Climate Apartheid and Environmental Refugees." In *The Palgrave Handbook of Criminology and the Global South*, edited by Kerry Carrington, Russell Hogg, John Scott and Máximo Sozzo, 301–321. Cham: Palgrave Macmillan.

Brown, Wendy. 2016. "Sacrificial Citizenship: Neoliberalism, Human Capital, and Austerity Politics." *Constellations* 23 (1): 3–14.

Brown, Wendy. 2017. "Climate Change, Democracy and Crises of Humanism." In *Life Adrift*, edited by Andrew Baldwin and Giovanni Bettini, 25–40. London: Rowman and Littlefield.

Bryant-Tokalau, Jenny. 2018. *Indigenous Pacific Approaches to Climate Change: Pacific Island Countries*. Cham: Palgrave Macmillan.

Bulkeley, Harriet. 2001. "Governing Climate Change: The Politics of Risk Society?" *Transactions of the Institute of British Geographers* 24 (4): 430–447.

Carvalho, Henrique and Anastasia Chamberlen. 2018. "Why Punishment Pleases: Punitive Feelings in a World of Hostile Solidarity." *Punishment and Society* 20 (2): 217–234.

Colebrook, Claire. 2017. "Transcendental Migration: Taking Refuge from Climate Change." In *Life Adrift*, edited by Andrew Baldwin and Giovanni Bettini, 115–130. London: Rowman and Littlefield.

Coumou, Dim, Giorgia Di Capua, Steve Vavrus, Lei Wang, and Simon Wang. 2018. "The Influence of Arctic Amplification on Mid-Latitude Summer Circulation." *Nature Communications* 9: 1–12. https://www.nature.com/articles/s41467-018-05256-8.

Diken, Bülent. 2004. "From Refugee Camps to Gated Communities: Biopolitics and the End of the City." *Citizenship Studies* 8 (1): 83–106.

Evans, Brad. 2017. "Dead in the Waters." In *Life Adrift*, edited by Andrew Baldwin and Giovanni Bettini, 59–78. London: Rowman and Littlefield.

Farbotko, Carol, and Heather Lazrus. 2012. "The First Climate Refugees? Contesting Global Narratives of Climate Change in Tuvalu." *Global Environmental Change* 22 (2): 382–390.

Figueres, Christiana, Corinne Le Quéré, Anand Mahindra, Oliver Bäte, Gail Whiteman, Glen Peters, and Dabo Guan. 2018. "Emissions are Still Rising: Ramp Up the Cuts." *Nature* 564 (December): 27–30.

Goldberg, David. 2017. "Parting Waters: Seas of Movement." In *Life Adrift*, edited by Andrew Baldwin and Giovanni Bettini, 99–114. London: Rowman and Littlefield.

Goyes, David R. 2016. "Green Activist Criminology and the Epistemologies of the South." *Critical Criminology* 24 (4): 503–518.

Green, Penny. 2008. "Women and Natural Disasters: State Crime and Discourses in Vulnerability." In *Women, Crime and Social Harm: Towards a Criminology for the Global Age*, edited by Maureen Cain and Adrian Howe, 161–178. Portland: Hart Publishing.

Griffin, Paul. 2017. *The Carbon Majors Database: CDP Carbon Majors Report 2017*. London: CDP/Climate Accountability Institute.

Hymas, Charles. 2019. "Treat Extinction Rebellion as an Extremist Anarchist Group, Former Anti-Terror Chief Tells Police." *The Telegraph*, July 16, 2019. https://www.telegraph.co.uk/politics/2019/07/16/treat-extinction-rebellion-extremist-anarchist-group-former/.

Influence Map. 2019. *Big Oil's Real Agenda on Climate Change*. March 2019. https://influencemap.org/report/How-Big-Oil-Continues-to-Oppose-the-Paris-Agreement-38212275958aa21196dae3b76220bddc.

IOM, International Organization for Migration. 2018. *Migration, Climate Change and the Environment*. September 3, 2018. https://www.iom.int/complex-nexus#estimates.

IPCC, Intergovernmental Panel on Climate Change. 2014. *Climate Change 2014: Synthesis Report*. Geneva: IPCC.

IPCC, Intergovernmental Panel on Climate Change. 2018. *Special Report: Global Warming of 1.5 °C*. Geneva: IPCC.

Johansen, Nicolay. B. 2013. "Governing the Funnel of Expulsion: Agamben, the Dynamics of Force, and Minimalist Biopolitics." In *The Borders of Punishment: Migration, Citizenship, and Social Exclusion*, edited by Katja F. Aas and Mary Bosworth, 257–272. Oxford: Oxford University Press.

Khosravi, Shahram. 2009. "Sweden: Detention and Deportation of Asylum Seekers." *Race and Class* 50 (4): 38–56.

Klein, Naomi. 2014. *This Changes Everything: Capitalism vs. the Climate*. London: Allen Lane.

Klein, Naomi. 2017. *No is Not Enough*. London: Penguin Books.

Kraemer, R. Andreas, Shingirirai Mutanga, Nedson Pophiwa, Shiloh Fetzek, Katriona McGlade, Benjamin Schraven, Cristina Cattaneo, Rajat Kathuria, Aarsi Sagar, Patrick Toussaint, Syed Khasru, Lloyd Axworthy, Scott Vaughan, Emily Wilkinson, and Romy Chevallier. 2017. *Building Global Governance for 'Climate Refugees'*. G20 Insights. March 18, 2017. http://www.g20-insights.org/policy_briefs/building-global-governance-climate-refugees/.

Kramer, Ronald C. 2020. *Carbon Criminals, Climate Crimes*. New Brunswick: Rutgers University Press. https://doi.org/978-1-9788-0558-3.

Krasmann, Susanne. 2007. "The Enemy on the Border: Critique of a Programme in Favour of a Preventive State." *Punishment and Society* 9 (3): 301–318.

Lewis, Simon. 2018. "Don't Despair – Climate Change Catastrophe Can Still be Averted." *The Guardian*. August 7, 2018. https://www.theguardian.com/commentisfree/2018/aug/07/climate-change-catastrophe-political-will-grassroots-engagement.

Lieberman, Amy. 2015. "Where Will the Climate Refugees Go?" *Al Jazeera*. December 23, 2015. http://www.aljazeera.com/indepth/features/2015/11/climate-refugees-151125093146088.html.

Lindsey, Rebecca, and LuAnn Dahlman. 2018. *Climate Change: Global Temperature*. 1 August 2018. National Ocean and Atmospheric Administration. https://www.climate.gov/news-features/understanding-climate/climate-change-global-temperature.

Lynch, Michael, Ronald Burns, and Paul Stretesky. 2010. "Global Warming and State-Corporate Crime." *Crime, Law and Social Change* 54 (3/4): 213–239.

Macdonald, Ted, and Lisa Hymas. 2019. "How Broadcast TV Networks Covered Climate Change in 2018." *Media Matters*. March 11, 2019. https://www.mediamatters.org/donald-trump/how-broadcast-tv-networks-covered-climate-change-2018?redirect_source=/research/2019/03/11/How-broadcast-TV-networks-covered-climate-change-in-2018/223076.

Madrigal, Alexis C. 2018. "Kim Kardashian's Private Firefighters Expose America's Fault Lines." *The Atlantic*, 14 November 14, 2018. https://www.theatlantic.com/technology/archive/2018/11/kim-kardashian-kanye-west-history-private-firefighting/575887/.

Malloch, Margaret. and Elizabeth Stanley. 2005. "The Detention of Asylum Seekers in the UK." *Punishment & Society* 7 (1): 53–71.

Mathiesen, Karl. 2017. "Tony Abbott says Climate Change is 'Probably Doing Good'." *The Guardian*, October 9, 2017. https://www.theguardian.com/australia-news/2017/oct/10/tony-abbott-says-climate-change-is-probably-doing-good.

McAdam, Jane. 2015. "The Emerging New Zealand Jurisprudence on Climate Change, Disasters and Displacement." *Migration Studies* 3 (1): 131–142.

Milman, Oliver, Emily Holden, and David Agren. 2018. "The Unseen Driver Behind the Migrant Caravan: Climate Change." *The Guardian*, October 30, 2018. https://www.theguardian.com/world/2018/oct/30/migrant-caravan-causes-climate-change-central-america.

Painter, J. (2013). *Climate Change in the Media*. London: I B Tauris and Co.

Phillips, Dom. 2018. "Brazil Records Worst Annual Deforestation for a Decade." *The Guardian*, November 24, 2018. https://www.theguardian.com/environment/2018/nov/24/brazil-records-worst-annual-deforestation-for-a-decade.

Pickering, Sharon, and Leanne Weber. 2014. "New Deterrence Scripts in Australia's Rejuvenated Offshore Detention Regime for Asylum Seekers." *Law and Social Inquiry* 39 (4): 1006–1026.

Pratt, John, and Timi Melei. 2018. "One of the Smallest Prison Populations in the World Under Threat: The Case of Tuvalu." In *The Palgrave Handbook of Criminology and the Global South*, edited by Kerry Carrington, Russell Hogg, John Scott and Máximo Sozzo, 729–750. Cham: Palgrave Macmillan.

Randall, Alex. 2013. "Climate Refugees? Where's the Dignity in that?" *The Guardian*. May 17, 2013. https://www.theguardian.com/environment/2013/may/17/climate-change-refugees-dignity-migration.

Ransan-Cooper, Hedda, Carol Farbotko, Karen E. McNamara, Fanny Thornton, and Emilie Chevalier. 2015. "Being(s) Framed: The Means and Ends of Framing Environmental Migrants." *Global Environmental Change*, 35: 106–115.

Rodney and Otamatea Times, Waitemata and Kaipara Gazette, Rodney and Otamatea Times, Waitemata and Kaipara Gazette. 1912. "Coal Consumption Affecting Climate." August 14, 1912. https://paperspast.natlib.govt.nz/newspapers/ROTWKG19120814.2.56.5.

Ruggiero, Vincenzo, and Nigel South. 2013. "Green Criminology and Crimes of the Economy." *Critical Criminology* 21 (3): 359–373.

Russo, Katherine. 2017. "Floating Signifiers, Transnational Affect Flows: Climate-induced Migrants in Australian News Discourse." In *Life Adrift*, edited by Andrew Baldwin and Giovanni Bettini, 195–209. London: Rowman and Littlefield.

Saldanha, Arun. 2017. "Globalization as a Crisis of Mobility: A Critique of Apherology." In *Life Adrift*, edited by Andrew Baldwin and Giovanni Bettini, 151–173. London: Rowman and Littlefield.

Scoop. 2016. "Samoa, China and India Top NZ's Overstayers List." *Scoop News*. April 13, 2016. http://www.scoop.co.nz/stories/PO1604/S00170/samoa-china-and-india-top-nzs-overstayers-list.htm.

Sealey-Huggins, Leon. 2017. "'1.5°C to Stay Alive': Climate Change, Imperialism and Justice for the Caribbean." *Third World Quarterly* 38 (11): 2444–2463.

Serwer, Adam. 2018. "Trump's Caravan Hysteria Led to This." *The Atlantic*. October 28, 2018. https://www.theatlantic.com/ideas/archive/2018/10/caravan-lie-sparked-massacre-american-jews/574213/.

Setzer, Joana, and Rebecca Byrnes. 2019. *Global Trends in Climate Change Litigation: 2019 Snapshot*. London: Grantham Research Institute/LSE.

Stretesky, Paul, Michael Long, and Michael Lynch 2014. *The Treadmill of Crime: Political Economy and Green Criminology*. London: Routledge.

Timm, Jane C. 2018. "Trump Says 'Caravans' of Immigrants are Headed for the U.S." NBC News. April 3, 2018. https://www.nbcnews.com/politics/politics-news/trump-says-caravans-immigrants-are-headed-u-s-what-s-n862136.

TVNZ. 2018. "Over 10,000 Overstayers in NZ." *One News*, March 25, 2018. https://www.tvnz.co.nz/one-news/new-zealand/most-read-story-over-10-000-overstayers-in-nz-immigration-not-actively-looking.

Ulmanu, Monica, Alan Evans and Georgia Brown. 2018. "The Defenders." *The Guardian*. July 17, 2018. https://www.theguardian.com/environment/ng-interactive/2018/feb/27/the-defenders-recording-the-deaths-of-environmental-defenders-around-the-world.

UNFCCC, United Nations Framework Convention on Climate Change. 2015. *Adoption of the Paris Agreement*, Twenty-first Session, FCCC/CP/2015/L.9/Rev.1, December 12, 2015.

Valverde, Mariana. 2010. "Questions of Security: A Framework for Research." *Theoretical Criminology*, 15 (1): 3–22.

Vaughan, Adam. 2019. "David Attenborough on Climate Change: 'We Cannot be Radical Enough'." *New Scientist*, July 9, 2019. https://www.newscientist.com/article/2209126-david-attenborough-on-climate-change-we-cannot-be-radical-enough/.

Weber, Leanne, and Sharon Pickering. 2011. *Globalization and Borders: Death at the Global Frontier*. Basingstoke: Palgrave Macmillan.

Weber, Leanne, and Sharon Pickering. 2013. "Exporting Risk, Deporting Non-Citizens." In *Globalisation and the Challenge to Criminology*, edited by Francis Pakes, 110–128. London: Routledge.

White, Rob. 2018. *Climate Change Criminology*. Bristol: Bristol University Press.

Willacy, Mark. 2019. "Defence Lacks 'Overarching Strategy' to Deal with Climate Change Conflict, Internal Notes Warn." *ABC News*. July 15, 2019. https://www.abc.net.au/news/81-07-15/defence-lacks-overarching-strategy-for-climate-change-conflict/11304954.

Wonders, Nancy, and Mona Danner. 2015. "Gendering Climate Change: A Feminist Criminological Perspective." *Critical Criminology* 23 (4): 401–416.

Wyatt, Tanya, and Avi Brisman. 2017. "The Role of Denial in the 'Theft of Nature'." *Critical Criminology* 25 (3): 325–341.

Yaxley, Louise. 2018. "Tony Abbott wants Australia to pull out of the Paris Climate Deal." *ABC News*, July 4, 2018. http://www.abc.net.au/news/2018-07-04/tony-abbott-says-pull-out-of-paris-climate-agreement/9937972.

Crime, Pre-crime and Sub-crime: Deportation of 'Risky Non-citizens' as 'Enemy Crimmigration'

Leanne Weber and Rebecca Powell

Introduction

While there are increasing demands from some sectors within neoliberal democracies for governments to reaffirm their responsibility for the well-being of their populations, the situation of non-citizens in many countries is becoming ever more precarious. This is evident in policies that are making pathways to citizenship increasingly complex and contingent (Bosworth et al. 2017; Zedner 2016), blocking access to goods and services for certain groups of temporary residents (Weber 2019; Bowling and Westenra 2018) and increasing opportunities to deport non-citizens, particularly those involved in crime (Weber 2014; Bowling and Westenra 2018; Bosworth et al. 2017). The cumulative effect is to create large populations of insecure and marginalized 'imminent outsiders' (McNevin 2011).

L. Weber (✉) • R. Powell
School of Social Sciences, Monash University, Melbourne, VIC, Australia
e-mail: leanne.weber@monash.edu; rebecca.powell@monash.edu

© The Author(s) 2020
J. Pratt, J. Anderson (eds.), *Criminal Justice, Risk and the Revolt against Uncertainty*, Palgrave Studies in Risk, Crime and Society,
https://doi.org/10.1007/978-3-030-37948-3_11

At the same time, a focus on risk and the production of security within neoliberal societies has fostered governmental strategies of surveillance and exclusion which Bigo has called the 'ban-opticon' (2005). While the ban-opticon may impact many social categories, the insecure immigration status of 'imminent outsiders' opens up unique avenues that are not available in relation to citizens: notably literal banishment through deportation. Moreover, because of their 'deportability' (De Genova 2002) and lack of political power, it is generally more difficult for non-citizens to claim legal protections against these measures than it is for citizens who cannot easily be physically expelled.[1]

In this chapter we use the example of deportation from Australia on character grounds to address a question at the heart of this collection— is the reign of 'risk society' and its impact on criminal law and penal policy coming to an end. Combining empirical data from several research projects,[2] we demonstrate that risk reduction paradigms still predominate in dealings with non-citizens accused of wrongdoing, while due process protections are diminishing. In fact, we argue that risk-based regimes of exclusion in relation to certain categories of non-citizen have evolved to encompass 'pre-crime' (McCulloch and Wilson 2016), and what we call 'sub-crime', as legal bases for deportation. In order to demonstrate the full range of these developments, we include case material from two categories of deportees: New Zealand citizens living long term as 'temporary' residents in Australia, and asylum seekers residing in the Australian community pending resolution of their applications for refugee status.

To maximize the explanatory power of our analysis, we combine insights from two theoretical frameworks: one that has been formulated specifically in the context of immigration control, namely the 'crimmigration' thesis of US legal scholar Juliet Stumpf (2006); the other arising from the broader field of criminal law and security, namely the 'enemy penology' thesis published in German by legal theorist Günther Jakobs (1985, 2000), to create a hybrid theoretical framework we call 'enemy crimmigration'.

Enemy Penology Within a Crimmigration Context

Deportation following a criminal conviction is an obvious example of the merging of administrative and criminal paradigms. In her crimmigration thesis, Stumpf (2006) argues that these previously distinct legal domains are becoming linked through a shared rationale of selective exclusion, and are both mechanisms for the expression of sovereignty. For individuals judged to fall outside the parameters of the social contract, whether due to criminal offending, legal non-membership, or both, incarceration and/or deportation serve to reinforce the boundaries of membership. The crimmigration process includes the transfer of both substance and procedure from the criminal to the immigration sphere, as with the criminalization of immigration violations, and from the immigration to the criminal domain, for example, where the threshold for deportation is lowered following conviction for even minor crimes. Stumpf claims that the powers of immigration and criminal law enforcement agencies in the United States have become almost indistinguishable, noting that there has been no commensurate transfer of due process protections from the criminal to the immigration sphere, signaling an expansion of executive power. While scholars have debated their exact nature and extent, broadly similar trends have been observed in other countries (see, e.g. Guia et al. 2013).

In Australia, by combining the power to condemn under criminal law with the power to physically exclude using immigration law, deportation on character grounds is offering governments a unique risk reduction strategy aimed at 'exporting risk' (Weber and Pickering 2012). However, new trends are emerging in deportation on character grounds that cannot be fully explained using the crimmigration framework, notably the possibility of pre-emptive deportation without the need for a criminal conviction and the targeting of these measures, directly or indirectly, toward specific populations. In order to capture these dimensions of Australian policy, we extend our analytical framework to include the theory of 'Feindstrafrecht' developed by Günther Jakobs (1985, 2000)—translated variously as 'enemy criminal law' (Diez 2008; Golser 2016; Ohana 2010) or 'enemy penology' (Krasmann 2007).[3]

Jakobs has controversially proposed that 'social enemies' who pose unique threats to the community should be subjected to a system of harsh and pre-emptive criminal sanctions that is separate from the system reserved for other citizens. In his view, citizenship rights, including the due process rights normally applied within the criminal justice system, are earned by fulfilling fundamental duties, and those who fail to do so may be justifiably denied them and treated as enemies. As Ohana (2010: 721) explains, the 'substantive and procedural due process guarantees that apply as a rule within the criminal law could be relinquished within this framework for the sake of defending society against citizens whose conduct suggests they no longer consider themselves bound by its norms'. This reasoning is consistent with a risk-based paradigm, as Pratt (2017: 1334) explains: 'the government is ready—the message seems to be—to intervene against those thought to pose the most tangible and gravest risks to its citizens, nor will it be troubled by principles and conventions that had previously prohibited or limited their ability to do so'.

In Jakobs' formulation, criminal sanctions do not merely protect against individual victimization, or even guarantee a general right to security, but are tasked with preserving a broader social order and collective identity. Jakobs (2004: 495) argues that the infringement of societal norms entailed in certain types of offending amounts to a 'protest against the validity of the norm, against the configuration of society'. While we concede that terrorism offenses reflect some degree of rejection of the dominant system of law and societal norms, Jakobs also considers an individual involved in large-scale organized crime, a 'pedophile' or other habitual offender, to fall within the category of social enemy because he or she 'exhibits through his [sic] behaviour—not just in passing—that it is likely that he has durably deviated from the path of the law and that he can no longer minimally guarantee that he will conduct himself as a loyal citizen' (Ohana 2010: 726).

While enemy penology has proven to be an accurate description of certain trends in German law and of legal systems elsewhere, Jakobs' advocacy of this approach has been widely condemned, sometimes on the basis of technical legal argument, but often on the grounds of legitimacy and socio-legal implications (e.g. Diez 2008). Appealing to the concept of loyalty shifts the ground away from more conventional interpretations of criminal law toward the realm of national security. Rather than being punished, social enemies are to be 'combated, excluded if not extinguished' since they are 'non-persons' for whom a 'comprehensive legal regulation is impossible' (Krasmann 2007: 302).

Once identified as an enemy, there is no need to wait for prohibited actions to actually take place, since enemies have already placed themselves beyond the normal constraints of law. Therefore, Jakobs advocates the infliction of punishment *prior* to the commission of an offense. Rather than 'proclaim[ing] authoritatively which courses of conduct are prohibited', criminal sanctions are instead imposed 'with the stated aim to wage war against designated categories of offenders' (Ohana 2010: 727). Krasmann (2007: 304) argues that this commitment to 'inner warfare' creates a 'quasi-legal space' beyond risk that brings about a transformation, not only of law but also of democracy, heralding the creation of a 'preventive state, at least as regards those who come under Jakobs' classification of 'enemies'.

Jakobs' account makes no explicit reference to foreign-born enemies. However, it is apparent that the loyalty of those who have not yet attained formal recognition as citizens is particularly open to question. For example, Campesi and Fabini (2019) have observed that administrative detention of irregular migrants has been transformed in parts of Italy into an instrument of 'social defense', justified on the grounds of 'dangerousness'. Bowling and Westenra (2018: 1) also claim that 'criminalized immigrants' have become a 'globally recognized 'folk devil''. But as Yuval-Davis (2004: 220) explains, non-citizens may be considered social enemies even in the absence of offending: "A cultural 'other', the immigrant or a member of another community who does not share the same myth of common origin, is constructed as an alien and consequently as a potential 'enemy' who threatens 'our' national and cultural integrity and uniqueness".

Applying the preventive aspect of Jakobs' thesis within a crimmigration setting allows us to analyze developments in Australian deportation policy in terms of 'pre-crimmigration' (Weber and McCulloch

2018), charting a temporal shift from crime toward pre-crime as the basis for deportation. Jakobs' conception of crime as a rejection of societal norms helps to illuminate the expansion of justifications for deportation in Australia to include new forms of character assessments we describe here as sub-crime. An enemy crimmigration framing also highlights the selective targeting of these policies toward particular groups of non-citizens.

In the remainder of this chapter we discuss Australian deportation practices affecting two groups of social enemies, defined by their nationality and mode of arrival. The first group is New Zealand citizens who are allowed to remain in Australia indefinitely on Special Category Visas (SCVs) without meeting the strict points-based system that governs more formal migration processes. The second group are asylum seekers who are stigmatized as 'Illegal Maritime Arrivals' (IMAs), having arrived by sea without prior authorization.[4] What these two, otherwise disparate, groups have in common is that they both, through their mode of arrival or entry, undermine the 'security myth' expounded by successive Australian governments, of exerting absolute sovereign control over the nation's borders.

From Crime to Pre-crime: New Zealand Citizens on 'Special Category Visas'

New Zealanders have had an historically 'uneasy' settlement experience in Australia and have felt a degree of unwelcome for a considerable time (Mares 2014). Free movement between Australia and New Zealand was formalized in 1973 under the Trans-Tasman Travel Arrangement (TTA). This agreement remains in place today. However, it has not been balanced in terms of reciprocal residential rights and benefits. Since the TTA, New Zealanders traveling to Australia have been labeled as 'Bondi bludgers' (Mares 2014) and, for Pasifika and Asian migrants with New Zealand citizenship, as 'backdoor entrants to Australia' (Mares 2014). New Zealanders have been perceived to be arriving in Australia in 'in record numbers, taking jobs and seeking welfare benefits to boot' (Mares 2014).

New Zealanders, including Pasifika nationals with New Zealand citizenship, can enter and reside in Australia indefinitely as SCV holders. However, their migration status remains precarious, which has a particular impact for longer-term residents who have established lives in Australia. No matter how long SCV holders have lived in Australia, without citizenship they lack certain rights and benefits, and are susceptible to visa cancellation and removal under s501 and s116 of the Migration Act. They are technically 'temporary' in their migration status which is reinforced by their need to renew their SCV each time they leave and re-enter Australia, and their restricted access to certain benefits and rights afforded to citizens, such as the lack of a right to vote and limitations on access to welfare support (Weber et al. 2013).

Further, pathways toward citizenship are difficult and rely on skilled worker, family entry programs or other entry schemes such as tertiary study, but these options remain limited and are not available to all SCV holders. Changes to SCVs after 2001 have restricted pathways to permanence and enhanced temporariness even for longer-term New Zealander residents affecting just under a third of the 600,000 or so New Zealand citizens resident in Australia (Mares 2014; McMillan 2017; Hamer 2014). As a result, even for longer-term New Zealander residents in Australia, their migration status can be characterized as 'permanent-temporariness' or 'denizenship' (Weber et al. 2013), where their 'unfettered capacity to enter and remain in Australia is not matched by the entitlements associated with PR (permanent residence) or the protection against expulsion provided by citizenship' (Weber et al. 2013: 60–61).

In parallel, visa cancellation policy developments on character grounds and state-based anti-association laws (explained later) have inordinately impacted New Zealander residents of Australia, making them vulnerable to visa cancellation and removal on the basis of non-citizen and criminal status. Sections 501 and 116 of the Migration Act have both been applied disproportionately against New Zealanders living in Australia regardless of whether a criminal offense has been committed. All of these developments have constructed New Zealander residents of Australia as precarious and vulnerable members of the community. For New Zealander offenders in particular, recent developments of deportation on character grounds policy and practice play on this vulnerability, indirectly targeting New

Zealanders and other convicted non-citizens as social enemies with limited regard for their personal circumstances, seriousness of offending and length of residence.

S501: Disproportionate Visa Cancellation and Deportation on Character Grounds

Recent federal and state policy developments concerning visa cancellation and deportation against convicted non-citizens reveal a growing exclusionary, risk-based response to collective public safety and national security in the areas of crime prevention and immigration control. This presents cause for labeling convicted non-citizens who have their visa canceled as 'crimmigrants' (Aas 2011). Convicted non-citizens are routinely constructed as an unreasonable risk to the Australia community on the basis of their criminal and non-citizen status, even in cases of less serious offending. This often comes at a cost to individual human rights considerations and protections which carry less decisional weight in the visa cancellation decision-making process, including rights to family life, rehabilitation and, at times, due process, following successive changes to Ministerial guidance.[5]

Amendments made in December 2014 to section 501 of the Migration Act—refusal or cancellation of a visa on character grounds—resulted in an expansion of executive power in visa cancellation decision-making against convicted non-citizens, and powers to cancel without convictions (i.e. pre-crime). Consequently, there has not only been a steep rise in the number of s501 visa cancellations and deportations overall, but a particular increase in visa cancellations, detention and deportations of New Zealand citizens (Fig. 1). Stanley (2018: 519) has characterized these phenomena that have impacted on New Zealanders and other convicted non-citizens as 'new forms of crimmigration' that have 'expanded to include pre-emption—'non-citizens' are targeted not just on account of their criminal behaviors but also their perceived associations, 'risky' behaviors or suspicious associations'. This consequently creates multiple punishments for 'non-citizens' that far surpass the nature of their offending or their 'risk' to society.

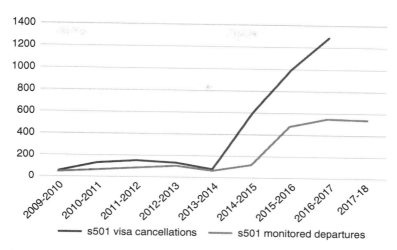

Fig. 1 Total s501 visa cancellations and removals from 2009/2010–May 2018. (Source: Department of Home Affairs n.d.)

The amendments to s501 were targeted at identified criminal groups including bikie gang members (many of whom are New Zealand citizens) and terrorists as a means to strengthen national security against the risk presented by these two groups (Bucci and Mills 2015). The reality has been though, that a far wider group of non-citizens have been left vulnerable to visa cancellation and removal (Hilkemeijer 2017) with a remarkable repercussion against New Zealanders, particularly long-term, permanent residents. This is linked in part to the size of the New Zealander population in Australia. As at June 2018, New Zealanders are the second largest group of migrants granted a temporary visa with a reported 1,856,614 New Zealander SCVs issued in the 2017–2018 reporting period (Department of Home Affairs 2018). Before the 2014 amendments, 'Australia was deporting about 65 New Zealanders a year … [A]s a result of the change, we quickly went to the figure of one a day, effectively' (New Zealand High Commission 2018: 59). Ultimately, we have seen the emergence of New Zealanders constructed as social enemies of Australia in visa cancellation and deportation decision-making on the basis of their criminal status and in the interest of protecting the Australian community from harm.

Visa cancellation and deportation policy developments from 1983 to the present reflect a long-term shift in the Australian government's perception of, and response to, convicted non-citizens as a risk to the Australian community. The policy period from 1983 to 1998 featured the introduction of the '10-year rule', protecting convicted non-citizens who had lived in Australia for 10 years or more from visa cancellation and deportation. In this period, non-citizens who committed similar serious offenses to Australian citizens were generally not deported, since more consideration was given to due process rights and mitigating factors such as length of residence and ties to the Australian community. It can be characterized as Australia's most humane policy response to convicted non-citizens, creating greater fairness within the deportation system.

Section 501 of the Australian Migration Act 1958 was introduced in 1999 following the abolition of the '10-year rule', formalizing the character test. The character test contained within s501 provided the new criteria for visa cancellation against a person with a substantial criminal record which included a prison sentence of 12 months or more as a result of their offense/s or multiple sentences that total two years or more (Hoang and Reich 2017). As Grewcock (2014) argues, from this point, visa cancellation on character grounds became the normal way of deporting convicted non-citizens from Australia.

The character test under s501 remained in place without change from 1999 until amendments were proposed in December 2014. Commenting on these amendments, then Immigration Minister, Scott Morrison MP, stated that the proposed amendments would work:

> to ensure that non-citizens who commit crimes in Australia, pose a risk to the Australian community *or represent an integrity concern* are appropriately considered for visa refusal or cancellation. (Scott Morrison, quoted in Second Reading, The Migration Amendment (Character and General Visa Cancellation) Bill 2014, see Parliament of Australia 2014, emphasis added)

These amendments reflect a hardening risk reduction approach to non-citizen offenders, with elements of 'pre-crimmigration' (Weber and McCulloch 2018) in targeting those suspected of engaging in criminal activity or falling below some 'expected' level of integrity, as espoused by Jakobs in his enemy penology thesis.

In line with the crimmigration thesis, the expansion of executive power in visa cancellation decision-making has been a hallmark of the recent s501 amendments. First, mandatory visa cancellation provisions were introduced which removed discretion from departmental decision-makers.[6] Second, expansion of the Minister's discretionary power over visa cancellation occurred through the insertion of additional grounds on which a person would not pass the character test. Visas can now be canceled on suspicion of criminal activity and/or association with a group, organization or person that has been or is involved in criminal conduct. Powers for the Immigration Minister to personally cancel visas were introduced that allow for greater efficiency in the removal of persons from the Australian community who are considered to pose a risk (The Parliament of the Commonwealth of Australia 2013–2014). Individual rights have been impacted, including the right to due process and the right to rehabilitation, for example. For those who have their visa canceled personally by the Immigration Minister, access to the appeals process is restricted.

Consequently, visa cancellations and deportations under s501 have shown a distinct upward trend for New Zealand citizens from 2014 to 2017 (as illustrated in Fig. 2). New Zealanders comprise the largest nationality group who have had their visa canceled and who have been deported from Australia under s501. They have been consistently recorded

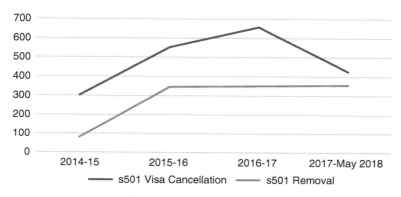

Fig. 2 New Zealander s501 visa cancellations and removals from 2014/2015–May 2018. (Source: Department of Home Affairs n.d.)

as the largest or second largest nationality group in Australia's onshore immigration detention network from August 2015 (Home Affairs Immigration Detention Statistics). Many of them are long-term residents of Australia, residing for a period of 10 years or more with established lives, families and strong ties to the Australian community.[7]

In October 2018, the Minister for Immigration, Citizenship and Multicultural Affairs introduced the Migration Amendment (Strengthening the Character Test) Bill 2018 to Federal parliament for inquiry to further strengthen his powers to cancel and refuse visas on character grounds under section 501. While this Bill was subsequently shelved pending a Federal election in May 2019, the inquiry was reintroduced in July–August this year. The proposed amendments seem to have arisen off the back of a Federal Government Inquiry from 2017 on Migrant Settlement Outcomes. That Inquiry was mandated to,

> ...give particular consideration to social engagement of youth migrants, including involvement of youth migrants in anti-social behaviour such as gang activity, and the adequacy of the Migration Act 1958 character test provisions as a means to address issues arising from this behaviour. (Parliament of Australia, December 2017)

The 2018 inquiry was announced shortly after a series of reputedly 'gang-related' events in Melbourne in which the involvement of young people from African and Pasifika backgrounds was widely reported. Australian Border Force and Victoria Police moved to cancel visas and deport those associated with these crimes, including persons under the age of 18.

The latter and first-time offenders who might ordinarily be given a non-custodial or lower level sentence are now more likely to be caught up in these expanded visa cancellation powers. The explanatory memorandum accompanying the Bill contains a clause with specific grounds for not differentiating between adults and persons under the age of 18 in the application of s501. The Bill allows visa cancellation for non-citizens convicted of 'designated offences' that are associated with serious, violent and sexual assault crime resulting in convictions which are punishable by two years in prison, regardless of mitigating circumstances, any magistrate or judicial sentencing discretion and the actual sentence imposed. This essentially replaces an 'objective' criterion based on sentencing decisions with a generic attribution of 'dangerousness'.

At state level, status offense laws have been introduced over the last few years in Queensland, Victoria and South Australia, and include bikie gang laws, affray and criminal association laws. All of these laws pave the way for s501 visa cancellation merely on suspicion of criminal activity and criminal association, without a crime having been committed. The Victorian government, for example, has implemented new laws that give police expanded powers to prevent people as young as 14 from associating with those convicted of serious offenses[8]: a risk-based response to the events in Melbourne that sparked the Migrant Settlement Outcomes Inquiry in 2017.

S116: Widening the Scope of Visa Cancellation Against 'Enemy Groups'

Section 116 is the general visa cancellation section of the Migration Act that is far broader and more expansive in its application than s501. It is also being more liberally applied against non-citizen enemy groups, resulting in far greater numbers of visa cancellations, used mainly against convicted New Zealanders. Section 116 has increasingly been used since 2013/2014 to cancel the visas of non-citizens on the basis of alleged criminal offending but before a criminal trial has commenced and, at times, without the commission of a criminal offense at all. Visas have also reportedly been canceled under s116 *on suspicion* of criminal activity or criminal association.

S116 was originally implemented to primarily target temporary visa holders who had been in Australia for shorter periods of time and to particularly target those involved in organized criminal groups. It has also been applied against those in immigration detention and the community who have breached their visa conditions. While it is not a new section of the Migration Act and predates amendments made to s501 that incorporated visa cancellation on suspicion of criminal activity or association, s116 allows the Immigration Minister to administer broad and expansive powers of discretion in visa cancellation. No distinction is made between serious and less serious offending. The cancellation power is open to wide interpretation and is directed largely in response to risk. As s116(1)(e)(i) states, the Minister may cancel a visa if they are:

> satisfied that the presence of the visa holder in Australia is or may be, or would or might be, a risk to the health, safety or good order of the Australian community or a segment of the Australian community.

It is not clear why there has been an increase in the Minister's use of s116, but what is known is that it allows for greater efficiency in visa cancellation. Figure 3 illustrates the much higher number of s116 visa cancellations in comparison to s501 because of its discretionary efficiency and broad and expansive application against non-citizens (peaking at 10,375 visa cancellations in 2016–2017 with 8432 recorded cancellations in the 2017–2018 reporting period).

Again, New Zealander long-term residents of Australia are impacted. While nationality figures for s116 visa cancellation and deportation are not publicly available, the New Zealand High Commission to Australia

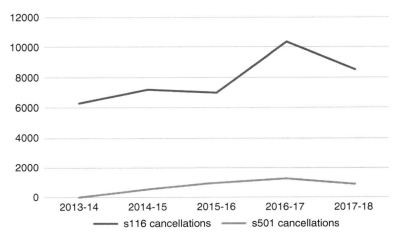

Fig. 3 Visa cancellations s501 and s116. (Source: Department of Home Affairs n.d.)

has reported that there has been an increasing number of New Zealander deportees under Section 116 of the Migration Act (Commonwealth of Australia, 12 September 2018).

The issue with s116 is that the threshold for visa cancellations is much lower than s501 and the immediate consequences much more severe, with the potential to compromise an individual's ability to access due process as a result of visa cancellation. As the New Zealand High Commissioner to Australia recently argued in opposition to the application of s116 against New Zealanders, 'this is also one of our concerns with s116, people who haven't been through a judicial process, they are just returned' (Commonwealth of Australia, 12 September 2018: 7).

Although none of the successive changes in deportation policy discussed here target New Zealand citizens explicitly, the impact on this group has been significant. Special Category Visas do apply solely to New Zealand citizens and create unique vulnerabilities due to long-term residence without access to citizenship and many essential services. The increasing use of visa cancellation on the basis of criminal convictions and pre-crime for this group of social enemies can be understood as a means of regaining control and mitigating perceived risks associated with a visa type that is otherwise loosely regulated by the strict standards of Australian immigration control. As one community worker from a Pasifika background told one of the authors[9]: 'The government is trying to get rid of as many of us as they can'.

'Illegal Maritime Arrivals', Social Enemies and the Invention of Sub-crime

Asylum seekers who attempt to travel to Australia by boat without a visa are another group of non-citizens who have been identified as social enemies. They have been the subject of extraordinarily punitive border control policies. Although arriving without a visa to seek asylum is consistent with international law, their supposedly illicit mode of arrival has been interpreted in terms of disregard for Australian law. Their physical exclusion from Australian society has been effected, in the first instance, through indefinite offshore detention pending resolution of their asylum applications. Since 2011 the possibility of release into the community on a Bridging Visa E (BVE) has been available. At the time of writing approximately 19,500 formerly detained asylum seekers are living in the Australian community on these visas (Vogl 2019). This relative freedom has come at the cost of being forced to subsist in conditions of extreme marginalization and impoverishment (Weber 2019; Aliverti et al. 2019).

The Status Resolution Support Service (SRSS) was introduced in 2015, ostensibly to provide a separate system of welfare support for BVE holders to support them while they await an 'immigration outcome'. It is marked by complexity, delays and arbitrariness, leaving recipients in a state of extreme precarity. The provision of a bespoke, and essentially punitive, system of welfare support, separate from the system provided for Australian citizens, reinforces their designation as social enemies. A lawyer interviewed by one of the authors asserted that the system 'works basically to manage risk for the department' with minimal welfare provisions intended merely to ensure that 'people under that system do not kill themselves' (NGO Interview 9). Recent budget announcements have signaled the intention to reduce levels of support still further (ASRC 2019).

The SRSS scheme is widely understood to double as a system of surveillance intended to generate both 'voluntary' and involuntary departures. Contracted non-government agencies administer the system under strict requirements to report a range of 'adverse incidents' to the Department of Home Affairs (DHA). Incidents as varied as major health events, unaccompanied minors missing school, or SRSS recipients being a victim, perpetrator or witness to a crime, can trigger a duty to report to the DHA.

Policing Social Norms Through the Code of Behaviour

In addition to the already stringent visa conditions associated with BVEs, an enforceable Code of Behaviour was introduced in 2013. Some of the main conditions within the Code are paraphrased in Table 1. The Code

Table 1 Key requirements of Code of Behaviour for asylum seekers on Bridging Visa E

BVE holders must not:
Disobey laws or instructions
Make sexual contact without consent or underage
Commit crime or lie to government official
Harass intimidate or be disrespectful to anyone
Refuse to comply with health undertaking
BVE holders must:
Cooperate with DHA over resolution of status

was introduced without parliamentary debate via Regulation,[10] reflecting the trend in immigration enforcement toward the exercise of executive power. The preamble to the Explanatory Statement reads: 'The Government has become increasingly concerned about non-citizens who engage in conduct that is not in line with the expectations of the Australian community'.[11] This indicates that the introduction of the Code was aimed at publicly reinforcing the symbolic boundary between those who adhere to 'Australian values' and those who do not. This thinking aligns with Jakobs' preoccupation with distinguishing loyal from untrustworthy members of the population, in order to preserve the integrity of established norms.

Asylum seekers are required to sign the Code of Behaviour to be eligible for a bridging visa. Breaches can result in cancellation or refusal to renew BVEs, which would lead automatically to re-detention and possible removal. The Code can be understood as introducing a regime of both pre-crime and *sub-crime* that is uniquely applied to this group. One asylum advocate noted: 'People say sometimes they've been re-detained on the smallest, stupidest little things. You'd have to detain half the country if these things were criminal offences' (NGO Interview 10).

Vogl and Methven (2015: 175) concluded that the code was introduced primarily 'as a rhetorical tool, aimed at positioning asylum seekers arriving by boat outside the imagined borders of the 'Australian community"—in other words, as social enemies. The superfluous assertion that BVE holders must obey Australian laws conveys a message that this group is particularly risky, and inherently inclined to criminality. The remaining requirements relate to vaguely defined standards of inappropriate behavior that fall well below the threshold of harm that would warrant criminal sanctions. Other broadly defined behaviors such as 'sexual contact', harassment and intimidation could potentially refer to recognized criminal offenses, but their inclusion here signals a desire to free them from the usual strictures of criminal law.

In line with the general air of secrecy surrounding immigration enforcement, the Australian government does not make official data on the operation of this system readily available. The Commonwealth Ombudsman reported that '[t]he department's data around this cohort appears not to allow for easy extraction and statistical analysis which can explain its inability to provide some of the information requested' (Commonwealth Ombudsman 2016). However, some information has been obtained through a Freedom of Information application about reported breaches of the Code during the period 2014–2016.[12] Table 2 summarizes the types of behavior that were reported to immigration authorities as alleged breaches of the Code during this period.

The largest overall category by far was driving offenses. While much lower in number, sub-crimes employing the language of the Code do appear, including alleged harassment, intimidation, causing a nuisance, sexual contact and being uncooperative. Although not specified, it is likely that the 'victims' of many of these alleged incivilities may be immigration officers or SRSS caseworkers. With the remaining criminal offenses, it is difficult to discern whether allegations were, in fact, ever

Table 2 Reason for alleged breach of Code of Behaviour 2014–2016

Sexual contact under 18	17	Harass/intimidate	36
Sexual contact	23	Nuisance disturbance	19
Sexual assault	3	Driving offenses	139
Family violence	63	Dob-in allegation	28
Assault	70	Criminal association	2
Self-harm	3	Uncooperative	1
Robbery	2	Bigamy	1
Fraud/dishonesty	12	Arson	1
Break&Enter/trespass	8	OS criminal history	1
Theft/shoplifting	19	Several offenses	17
Property damage	2	Not recorded	5
Drug offenses	27	Total	499

Data source: Freedom of Information Request to DHA

prosecuted or proven, which would assist in classifying them as instances of either crime or pre-crime.

The Code of Behaviour for BVE holders, and its associated system of welfare policing, provides a clear example of crimmigration. As Vogl and Methven (2015) have argued, the outcomes of the breaches are punitive in ways that extend beyond the criminal law, including loss of financial support, visa cancellation and return to immigration detention. This merging of criminal and immigration domains operates in both directions, as explained by (Vogl 2019): 'Criminal law is used against Bridging Visa Class E (BVE) holders to punish, to enforce racialized immigration controls and to make asylum seekers deportable, just as immigration detention and deportation are justified as crime reduction strategies'. Moreover, the Code itself stretches criminal law by referring to ill-defined 'values important to Australian society' and creating vague public order breaches concerning bullying and harassment that operate as a 'proxy for criminal law' (Vogl 2019). This distortion of the criminal law, as it applies to citizens, identifies the Code, not merely as an example of crimmigration, but also an instance of enemy crimmigration.

A wide range of actors, including the general public, share in the policing of the Code. Figure 4 shows that 68% of reports (including the 'Incident reporting' category) originate from SRSS providers.

Just as welfare providers have been turned into crimmigration police through the SRSS system, the Code of Behaviour creates informal pre-crimmigration 'courts' within the DHA, since reported breaches are assessed in-house by immigration officials. As Vogl and Methven (2015: 177) observe, this raises serious questions about due process, since 'breaches will be adjudicated in a manner at variance with the processes of the criminal justice system; and it is unclear what effect an asylum seeker's breach of the Code will have in any related criminal proceedings'. Among numerous legal principles at stake, the fundamental presumption of innocence presents itself as the greatest casualty, a significant departure from legal norms that is said to be 'proportionate to achieving [the Code's] stated purpose' which is 'to protect the public' (Vogl and Methven 2015: 178).

It is notable that the expansion of s116 powers in 2013 was justified by the former Labor government with reference to 'Illegal Maritime Arrivals',

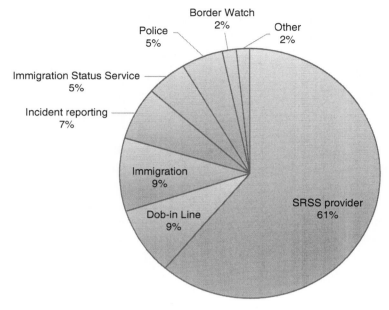

Fig. 4 Source of reported breach. (Data source: Freedom of Information request to DHA)

since the government had 'become increasingly concerned about unauthorized arrivals who engage in criminal conduct after being released into the community on BVEs' (Vogl 2019). The outcome of reported Code violations remains unclear, particularly in relation to the way in which quasi-judicial proceedings within the DHA intersect with criminal prosecutions (Commonwealth Ombudsman 2016). On the basis of the available data, Vogl (2019) concluded that 'the Code is being used to facilitate surveillance, policing and reporting, but that criminality grounds are then being used to cancel the relevant visa rather than the Code itself'. In response to a further Freedom of Information request from that author, the DHA stated that 'less than five' BVEs had been canceled under s116 of the Migration Act between 1 June 2014 and 30 August 2016 due to breaches of the Code of Behaviour alone.[13] An immigration official interviewed in 2015 by one of the authors confirmed that there had only been 'one or two' BVE cancellations at that time under the

Code itself, and even then 'some of those didn't survive merits review at the relevant tribunal' (Government Interview 1). According to that official, the majority of cancellations on criminal grounds had been made, as Vogl (2019) also found, using the broad criminal cancellation powers contained within s116 of the Migration Act.

This analysis shows how 'Irregular Maritime Arrivals' have been identified as an exceptional threat, not just to the physical security of Australian citizens, but also to some imagined conception of 'Australian values'. This marks them as 'cultural enemies' (Yuval-Davis 2004: 220) who, according to Jakobs' theory of enemy penology, threaten the very 'configuration of society' (Jakobs 2004: 495). Current efforts to lower the bar still further to incorporate what we have called sub-crimes do not seem, as yet, to have produced large numbers of additional visa cancellations. However, representatives from agencies supporting asylum seekers considered these measures to be 'hugely heavy handed' (NGO Interview 2), creating a 'terrible fear' among members of this highly vulnerable group (NGO Interview 1).

Conclusion

We began this discussion with reference to a fundamental question at the heart of this collection—is the reign of 'risk society' and its impact on criminal law and penal policy coming to an end. In relation to the two groups of non-citizens discussed in this chapter, it is clear that the answer to this question is a resounding 'no'. We have demonstrated that measures to deport non-citizens who are believed to present an unacceptable risk to the Australian public are intensifying and taking on some characteristics of enemy penology within a crimmigration context, a process we describe as enemy crimmigration. Risk-based paradigms are continuing to evolve, venturing further into 'quasi-legal spaces' in which established legal norms and procedures do not apply.

We have shown how the deployment of sections 501 and 116 of the Migration Act to cancel Special Category Visas held by New Zealand citizens, and the introduction of a Code of Behaviour that applies uniquely to asylum seekers who have arrived in Australia by boat, targets these groups for harsh measures and identifies them as social enemies. We have traced a shift from crime to pre-crime as the trigger for visa cancellation in relation to SCV holders, and a further lowering of the threshold to include sub-crime in the case of 'Illegal Maritime Arrivals'. This sustained trend toward the incorporation of ever more minor offenses as grounds for visa cancellation, although publicly justified on the basis of public safety, is consistent with the idea that the risks these non-citizens are considered to pose are, in reality, often economic (in the case of 'dole-bludging' SCV holders), or cultural (in the case of 'illegal' maritime arrivals).

At times these policies appear to be driven by fear of foreignness itself—sometimes labeled 'xeno-racism' (Fekete 2001)—and the challenge to established norms and values that the mere presence of certain groups of outsiders is thought to pose. As Vogl and Methven (2015: 175) have noted, the Code of Behaviour for BVE holders 'construct[s] asylum seekers as pre-criminal, racialized 'others', who must assimilate and adopt imagined standards of Australian civility'. In relation to both groups, we have argued that the conditions attached to these visa categories are inherently criminogenic, being deliberately designed to create precarity. As Carvalho (2017) has noted, casting risky individuals as public enemies ignores the social, economic and political circumstances that have created the threat they are deemed to pose.

The erosion of legal protections in these immigration procedures is an indicator of fundamental shifts in the Australian mode of governance, as foreseen in Jakobs' vision for a 'preventive state' (Krasmann 2007). If equal protection under the law is taken to be a central tenet of liberal democracy, there are reasons to believe that the practices reported here have a broader significance for Australian democracy beyond their impact on targeted groups. As Diez (2008: 562) concluded in his appraisal of Jakobs' theory: 'the State annihilates itself when it betrays its own rules by introducing legislation that contradicts its very essence'. And as Bosworth et al. (2017: 47) have noted: 'Hollowing out and destabilizing the notion of citizenship affects everyone. Thus, as prisons and detention centres hold increasing numbers of foreign citizens for deportation, they make clear the contingency of rights and belonging for us all'. The rise of executive power, adoption of pre-crime and sub-crime paradigms at the nexus

of immigration and crime control, and the growing disregard for rehabilitation objectives and legal protections that characterize Australia's system of deportation on character grounds signal the deepening of the
securitization agenda in relation to non-citizens and take us all along a
distinctly undemocratic path.

Notes

1. At the time of writing the Australian Parliament is debating the Counter-
   Terrorism (Temporary Exclusion Orders) Bill 2019 that would prevent
   certain dual nationality 'foreign fighters' from returning to Australia.
2. The Australian Deportation Project funded by Australian Research
   Council DP110102453, Globalisation and the Policing of Borders
   funded by Australian Research Council FT140101044, and the PhD
   project 'I still call Australia home: Balancing risk and human rights in
   the deportation of convicted non-citizens from Australia to New
   Zealand'. All quotes from interviews refer to the Globalisation and the
   Policing of Internal Borders project.
3. Since Krasmann's critique is the only English language critique published specifically for a criminological readership, we adopt her
   terminology.
4. While the official legal term is 'Unlawful Maritime Arrival', departmental and political rhetoric has popularized the more condemnatory term
   'Illegal Maritime Arrival'.
5. See s501 visa cancellation decision-making guidance, Ministerial
   Direction No. 65 (recently superseded by Ministerial Direction No. 79,
   not publicly available, but with similar decision making guidance).
   https://archive.homeaffairs.gov.au/visas/Documents/ministerial-direc-
   tion-65.pdf.
6. s501(3A) for those sentenced to a period of 12 months prison or more,
   including for multiple offenses adding up to a total of 12 months or
   more and retrospectively applied to those sentenced to a period of
   12 months or more, but who have served their time and are now back in
   the Australian community.
7. While it is difficult to find exact numbers and statistics of the number of
   long-term New Zealander residents of Australia who have their visa cancelled under s501, analysis of all publicly available New Zealander s501

appeal cases at the Administrative Appeals Tribunal show that since 2014 (2015–2018), the number of long-term residents is at 70% or above of all New Zealander appeals cases. Note that not all AAT cases are publicly available.

8. Victorian Premier Website, 'Strengthening laws to disrupt criminal gangs' 24 July 2018. Available at https://www.premier.vic.gov.au/strengthening-laws-to-disrupt-criminal-gangs/ [Accessed 14 April 2019].

9. Fieldnotes from Globalisation and the Policing of Internal Borders project.

10. Migration Amendment (Bridging Visas—Code of Behaviour) Regulation 2013.

11. Australian Government. *Migration Amendment (Bridging Visas—Code of Behaviour) Regulation 2013* Explanatory Statement available from https://www.legislation.gov.au/Details/F2013L02102/Explanatory%20Statement/Text.

12. Our thanks to Anthea Vogl and Elyse Methven for obtaining this valuable data and providing it to us. The tabulations of the data are our own. See also https://arts.monash.edu/__data/assets/pdf_file/0004/1863823/BOb-Research-Brief-15-Code-of-Behaviour-Research-Brief-FINAL.pdf.

13. Personal correspondence from Department of Home Affairs to Anthea Vogl, Freedom of Information (FOI) Internal Review Request FA 18/03/00501-R1, undated.

References

Aas, Katja F. 2011. "'Crimmigrant' bodies and bona fide travellers: Surveillance, citizenship and global governance." *Theoretical Criminology*, 15 (3): 331–346.

Aliverti, A., Milivojevic, S. & Weber, L. (2019). 'Tracing imprints of the border in the territorial, justice and welfare domains: A multi-site ethnography'. *The Howard Journal of Crime and Justice*, 58(2): 240–259.

ASRC. 2019. "*Cutting the Safety Net: The impact of cuts to Status Resolution Support Services.*" Melbourne: Asylum Seeker Resource Centre.

Bigo, Didier. 2005. "Global (in)security: The field of the professionals of unease management and the ban-opticon." *Traces: A Multilingual Series of Cultural Theory*, 4: 34–87.

Bosworth, Mary, Franko, Katja F. & Pickering, Sharon. 2017. "Punishment, globalization and migration control: 'Get them the hell out of here'." *Punishment & Society*, 20: 34–53.

Bowling, Ben, & Westenra, Sophie. 2018. "'A really hostile environment': Adiaphorization, global policing and the crimmigration control system." *Theoretical Criminology*.

Bucci Nino, and Mills, Tammy. 2015. "Mafia figures, bikies and sex fiends to be kicked out of Victoria under visa cancellation laws." *The Age*. 2 June 2015. https://www.theage.com.au/national/victoria/mafia-figures-bikies-and-sex-fiends-to-be-kicked-out-of-victoria-under-visa-cancellation-laws-20150602-ghf1dd.html.

Campesi, Giuseppe. and Fabini, Giulia. 2019. "Immigration detention as social defence: Policing 'dangerous mobility' in Italy." *Theoretical Criminology*. https://doi.org/10.1177/1362480619859350.

Carvalho, Henrique. 2017. *The Preventive Turn in Criminal Law*, Oxford, Oxford University Press.

Commonwealth of Australia 2018. "Official Committee Hansard. Joint Standing Committee on Migration. Review process associated with visa cancellations made on criminal grounds." Wednesday, September 12, 2018. https://parlinfo.aph.gov.au/parlInfo/download/committees/commjnt/8c7b3453-4332-47ae-9fad-2ce0c6e1efdd/toc_pdf/Joint%20Standing%20Committee%20on%20Migration_2018_09_12_6560_Official.pdf;fileType=application%2Fpdf#search=%22committees/commjnt/8c7b3453-4332-47ae-9fad-2ce0c6e1efdd/0001%22.

Commonwealth Ombudsman 2016. "Department of Immigration and Border Protection: The administration of people who have had their bridging visa cancelled due to criminal charges or convictions, and are held in immigration detention." Canberra: Commonwealth Ombudsman.

De Genova, Nicholas P. 2002. "Migrant 'Illegality' and Deportability in Everyday Life." *Annual Review of Anthropology*, 31: 419–447.

Department of Home Affairs. n.d. "Immigration Detention Statistics." https://www.homeaffairs.gov.au/research-and-statistics/statistics/visa-statistics/live/immigration-detention.

Department of Home Affairs. 2018. "Annual report 2017–2018." June 2018. https://www.homeaffairs.gov.au/reports-and-pubs/Annualreports/2017-18/01-annual-report-2017-18.pdf.

Diez, Carlos G.J. 2008. "Enemy Combatants Versus Enemy Criminal Law: An introduction to the European debate regarding enemy criminal law and it relevance to the Anglo-American discussion on the legal status of unlawful enemy combatants." *New Criminal Law Review*, 11(4): 529–262.

Fekete, L. (2001). "The emergence of xeno-racism." *Race & Class*, 43(2): 23–40.

Golser, Felix. 2016. "The concept of a special criminal law as a weapon against 'enemies' of the society." *Studia Iuridica*, 67: 65–77.

Grewcock, Michael. 2014. "Reinventing 'the stain'—bad character and criminal deportation in contemporary Australia." In *Routledge Handbook on Crime and International Migration* edited by Sharon Pickering and Julie Ham, 121–138. Routledge: Abingdon.

Guia, Maria J., Van der Woude, Maartje, and Van der Leun, Joanne (eds). 2013. *Social Control and Justice: Crimmigration in the Age of Fear*. The Hague: Eleven International Publishing.

Hamer, Paul. 2014. "'Unsophisticated and unsuited': Australian barriers to Pacific Islander immigration from New Zealand." *Political Science*, 66(2): 93–118.

Hilkemeijer, Anja. 2017. "Arbitrary ministerial power under the Migration Act: Permanent residents beware!" *Alternative Law Journal*, 42(3): 221–226.

Hoang, Khanh. & Reich, Sudrishti. 2017. "Managing crime through migration law in Australia and the United States: a comparative analysis." *Comparative Migration Studies*, 5(1): 1–24.

Jakobs, Gunther. 1985. "Kriminalisierung im Vorfeld einer Rechtsgutsverletzung." *Zeitschrift für die Gesamte Strafrechtswissdenschaft*, 97(4): 751–85.

Jakobs, Gunther. 2000. "Das Selbstverständnis der Strafrechtswissenschaft vor den Herausforderungen der Gegenwart." In *Die Deutsche Strafrechtswissenschaft vor der Jahrausendwende: Rückbesinnung und Ausblick*, edited by Albin Eser, Winfried Hasserner, Bjorn Burkhardt, 47–56. München: Beck.

Jakobs, Gunther. 2004. "Imputation in Criminal Law and the Conditions for Norm Validity." *Buffalo Criminal Law Review*, 7(2): 491–511.

Krasmann, Susanne. 2007. "The enemy on the border: critique of a programme in favour of a preventive state." *Punishment and Society*, 9: 301–318.

Mares, Peter. 2014. "New Zealand's 'Bondi-bludger' and other Australian myths." *The Conversation*, 11 February 2014. https://theconversation.com/new-zealands-bondi-bludger-and-other-australian-myths-22391.

McCulloch, Jude & Wilson, Dean. 2016. *Pre-crime: Pre-emption, precaution and the future*. Abingdon: Routledge.

McMillan, Kate. 2017. "Affective integration and access to the rights of permanent residency: New Zealanders resident in Australia post-2001." *Ethnicities*, 17(1): 103–127.

McNevin, Anne. 2011. *Contesting Citizenship: Irregular Migrants and New Frontiers of the Political*, New York: Columbia University Press.

New Zealand High Commission. 2018, September. "Presentation: Joint Standing Committee on Migration inquiry into review processes associated with visa cancellations made on criminal grounds." https://www.aph.gov.au/Parliamentary_Business/Committees/Joint/Migration/Visacancellationprocess/Submissions.

Ohana, Daniel. 2010. "Trust, Distrust and Reassurance: Diversion and Preventive Orders Through the Prism of Feindstrafrecht." *The Modern Law Review*, 73(5): 721–751.

Parliament of Australia. 2014. "Migration Amendment (Character and General Visa Cancellation) Bill 2014, Second Reading." https://parlinfo.aph.gov.au/parlInfo/search/display/display.w3p;query=Id%3A%22chamber%2Fhansardr%2F7a89c07c-522e-4e24-9643-d3209145b417%2F0017%22.

Parliament of Australia. December 2017. "No one teaches you to become Australian." Commonwealth of Australia. https://www.aph.gov.au/Parliamentary_Business/Committees/Joint/Migration/settlementoutcomes/Report.

Pratt, John. 2017. "Risk control, rights and legitimacy in the limited liability state." *British Journal of Criminology*, 57 (6): 1322–1339.

Stanley, Elizabeth. 2018. "Expanding crimmigration: The detention and deportation of New Zealanders from Australia." *Australian and New Zealand Journal of Criminology*, 51(4): 519–536.

Stumpf, Juliet P. 2006. "The Crimmigration Crisis: Immigrants, Crime, & Sovereign Power." *American University Law Review*, 56: 356–420.

The Parliament of the Commonwealth of Australia. 2013–2014. "Migration amendment (Character and general visa cancellation) Bill 2014." House of Representatives. Explanatory Memorandum. https://www.aph.gov.au/Parliamentary_Business/Bills_LEGislation/Bills_Search_Results/Result?bId=r5345.

Vogl, Anthea. 2019. "Crimmigration and Refugees: Bridging visas, criminal cancellations and 'living in the community' as punishment and deterrence." In *Crimmigration in Australia*, edited by Peter Billings. Springer.

Vogl, Anthea & Methven, Elyse. 2015. "We will decide who comes to this country, and how they behave." *Alternative Law Journal*, 40: 175–179.

Weber, Leanne. 2014. "Deciphering deportation practices across the Global North." In *Handbook on Crime and International Migration*, edited by Sharon Pickering, & Julie Ham, 155–178. Abingdon: Routledge.

Weber, Leanne. 2019. "From state-centric to transversal borders: Resisting the 'structurally embedded border in Australia'." *Theoretical Criminology*, 23: 228–246.

Weber, Leanne, McKernan, Helen, and Gibbon, Helen. 2013. "Trans-Tasman denizens: human rights and human (in)security among New Zealand citizens of Samoan origin in Australia." *Australian Journal of Human Rights*, 19: 51–77.

Weber, Leanne & McCulloch, Jude. 2018. "Penal Power and Border Control: Which Thesis? Sovereignty, Governmentality, or the Preemptive State?" *Punishment & Society*.

Weber, Leanne & Pickering, Sharon. 2012. "Exporting Risk, Deporting Non-Citizens." In *Globalisation and the Challenge to Criminology* edited by Francis Pakes. London: Routledge.

Yuval-Davis, Nira. 2004. "Borders, Boundaries and the Politics of Belonging." In *Ethnicity, Nationalism and Minority Rights* edited by Stephen May, Tariq Madood & Judith Squires. Cambridge: Cambridge University Press.

Zedner, Lucia. 2016. "Citizenship Deprivation, Security and Human Rights." *European Journal of Migration and Law*, 18: 222–242.

Part IV

Living with Risk

When Risk and Populism Collide

John Pratt

What happens when risk and populism collide? The hegemonic era of neo-liberal governance that has gripped many Western societies from the early 1980s seems to be coming to an end. It is in collision with an ascendant populism that promises to reverse its main characteristics. Instead of globalization, there should be protectionism; instead of free movement of labor, there should be reinforced border controls. While neo-liberalism exhorted individual entrepreneurs to take risks and shape the future, populism promises to recreate a mythical serene past—Trump's slogan in the 2016 US election "Make America Great Again" has become one of the clearest symbols of this. While neo-liberalism saw market forces as the neutral arbiter of economic development and the distributor of its rewards and losses, populism has emerged out of a revolt against all such uncertainty—most trenchantly felt and expressed by former manufacturing communities left behind because of their inability to reinvent themselves

J. Pratt (✉)
Institute of Criminology, Victoria University of Wellington,
Wellington, New Zealand
e-mail: john.pratt@vuw.ac.nz

© The Author(s) 2020   **275**
J. Pratt, J. Anderson (eds.), *Criminal Justice, Risk and the Revolt against Uncertainty*,
Palgrave Studies in Risk, Crime and Society,
https://doi.org/10.1007/978-3-030-37948-3_12

to suit neo-liberalism's new demands for service, tourism and finance industries, and by all those individuals who, after this restructuring, find themselves marooned in modern society's bargain basement. Meanwhile the winners in the casino economy that this has led to glide ever upward on its escalator of success, enjoying new wealth and fame at each floor they arrive at.

What, though, of another characteristic of neo-liberal governance—the growing use of preventive criminal law? From the early 1980s, in the main Anglo-American jurisdictions (i.e., the United States of America, the United Kingdom, Australia, New Zealand and Canada) on which this chapter is based, a range of preventive measures have been placed on the movement and conduct of individuals in public space, not as a punishment for new crimes that have been committed but because they were thought to put the well-being of the public at risk. The targets of these controls range from beggars, to gang members, to sex offenders released from prison, to potential terrorists. A second dimension of these measures involves an extension of the grasp of imprisonment on offenders or suspects who are judged to pose an ongoing risk to public safety. At the entrance to the prison, bail laws have been rewritten for these purposes, while the exit door has become more difficult to open because of risk-averse parole procedures and/or indefinite additions to existing finite sentences.

As a consequence, risk-driven criminal law has moved from being a kind of emergency, rarely used power into something that is much more central to the imposition of state control. In the course of this, the way in which human rights are understood in criminal justice has been rewritten: from protecting the rights of individuals from excesses of state power to protecting the rights of the public from those who put their safety and well-being at risk—and by deploying powers that, it used to be thought, should have only the most limited existence in these democracies.

The chapter begins with an explanation of how preventive criminal law and its umbrella of protection became so closely allied with neo-liberal governance, despite the regular exhortations from its political masters that individuals must take responsibility for their own forms of risk management. It argues that, irrespective of ideology to the contrary, this was because some measures of risk protection provided by the state became a political necessity because of the damaging effects on the social fabric by the restructuring that was being pursued. Preventive criminal law became a way of maintaining legitimacy for neo-liberal programs of government by soaking up the ensuing anxieties and insecurities that this generated. Thereafter, it has begun to play a similar but more expansive role for populism. Populism itself, despite its claims to the contrary, brings chaos rather than order, thereby making still more extensive demands on punishment and penal control to further bolster social cohesion and order. In the course of this, the very different understandings of human rights that began to be written in the neo-liberal era will be still more firmly cemented into political and public discourse. Indeed, this is inevitable. The utilitarian priorities in controlling risk mean that "efficiency in loss reduction [becomes its] moral imperative" (Ericson and Haggerty 1997, 124): at the expense of due process, high levels of proof, and other accoutrements of the rule of law, as and when necessary to ensure its effectivity.

Neo-liberalism's Need for Preventive Criminal Law

There is nothing new about criminal law being used for preventive purposes. Around the beginning of the twentieth century, most of these societies had, or were on the point of having, indefinite prison sentences for those who had not only committed crime but were also thought to be "dangerous" in terms of their propensity to commit future crime. The point is, though, that these measures were only rarely used and, throughout their existence up to the 1970s, were viewed with distaste and concern by criminal justice establishments concerned for human rights and due process, as McSherry (2020) shows in this volume. Indeed, up to the mid-twentieth century, it may also have been that the general public viewed preventive criminal law with great suspicion. The English *Report of the Departmental Committee on Sexual Offences Against Young Persons* (Home Office 1925, 61) observed that "we consider that special action is called for in cases of reported sexual offences [against children] … [but]

we are aware that the public mind is distrustful of any kind of indeterminate sentence."

Post 1945, preventive criminal law was seen as complicit in providing justification for Nazi atrocities and further fell from favor. In a bid to prevent such manifest abuses of state power ever occurring again, the 1950 UN Convention for the Protection of Human Rights and Fundamental Freedoms stipulated, inter alia, that there should be no retrospective legislation; very high burdens of proof were necessary to establish guilt; there should be no punishment unless a crime had been committed and therefore there should be no double punishments for the same crime, in effect outlawing stratagems that had previously been associated with the implementation of preventive measures in criminal law. These general principles were then largely put into practice across the Anglo-American societies. The US sexual psychopath laws, for example, introduced in the 1930s and providing as they did for a fixed term of imprisonment for the original crime after those so diagnosed were first "cured" in a mental institution, were periodically struck down as unconstitutional—they amounted to a double punishment for the same crime—or were allowed to fall into disuse as wholly discredited (Tappan 1957). A further moral objection to prevention was that it was thought there was no possibility of accurately predicting through clinical assessment, as was the method then, of whether an individual would actually commit more crime in the future (*Baxstrom v. Herold* 1966). Overall, Howard and Morris (1964, 174) acknowledged that this was a time when the concept of social defense, or preventive criminal law, "finds little acceptance in English, [US] or British Commonwealth criminology." Indeed, in New Zealand, the *Report of the Penal Policy Review Committee* (1981) recommended the abolition of the sentence of preventive detention altogether on these grounds. At this juncture, and at the beginnings of neo-liberal rule, it appeared that preventive criminal law had slipped into a terminal coma.

What was it, then, that led to its resuscitation during the era of neo-liberal governance? On the face of it, these two forces seem to be completely at odds with each other. The writings of neo-liberalism's leading philosopher, Friedrich Hayek (and later political acolytes such as Margaret Thatcher), gave great importance to "the Rule of Law." This concept, it was claimed, would provide vital guarantees whereby individuals could go about their lives and businesses free from any further interference from the state—as long as they kept to the rules that it had set in advance for them: "within the known rules of the game the individual is free to pursue his personal ends and desires, certain that the powers of government will not be used deliberately to frustrate his efforts". This also meant that law must be known and certain, and the convention of the separation of powers must be respected to preserve law's neutrality and impartiality, as opposed, for example, to any ad hominem legislation: "this prevents governments from stultifying individual efforts by ad hoc action ...; rules must not be made with particular cases in mind" (ibid.). Instead, law should take the form of fundamental, unchanging rules. As Samuel Brittan (1973, 92), evoking Hayekian scholarship, wrote: "essential to the whole idea that laws cannot be changed at a moment's notice whenever a particular effect displeases some ruler ... The more fundamental the laws, the more difficult they should be to change." Furthermore, "while the chief means of coercion at the disposal of government is punishment, the principle *'nullum crimen, nulla poena sine lege'* must be respected" (Hayek 1960, 206). That is, there could be no punishment by the state without a crime being committed and legally affirmed. Essentially then, he understood law to be a neutral mechanism intended to protect individual rights from those who would trespass on this—in his view, state officials acting on the basis of administrative fiat.

Why, then, did neo-liberal governments, following in the footsteps of Hayek, come to be associated with risk-based preventive initiatives that undermine many of these expectations and assumptions? At one level, this shift was probably inevitable. Technological advancement from the 1980s seemed to make risk much more predictable and was thereby better placed to offset the ethical dilemmas that had limited previous prediction models (Feeley and Simon 1992). Ideological purity would not be allowed to stand in the way of more certain predictions of crime. However, the enlargement of criminal law's preventive capacity can also be understood as a kind of political trade-off resulting from the consequences of neo-liberal restructuring (Pratt and Anderson 2016). One of the consequences of setting risk free from economic restraints in the course of this has been the new ability of consumers to "buy a cornucopia of products from across the world at often astoundingly cheap prices. Consumer spending soared. Electronic goods, children's toys, clothing and a plethora of other commodities flowed from countries in East Asia undergoing unprecedented high rates of economic growth" (Kershaw 2018, 459–60). Restructuring and its attendant programs of globalization and deregulation made new opportunities available for wealth creation, consumption and pleasure, at least to all who were prepared to embrace neo-liberal demands for initiative and enterprise. As regards holidays, for example: visits abroad increased by the UK citizens from 11.6 million in 1980 to 38.5 million in 2014; in 2006, 600,000 owned a holiday home, up sixty-five percent in two years; in 2012, 1.6 million of the population of England and Wales owned a second home, sixty percent of which were outside the United Kingdom. In the United States, while eight million people went overseas in 1980, this had increased to 15.7 million by 2014; in 1954, Americans flew, on average, once every four years; by 2005 this had increased to 2.5 times per year. In Australia, 706,000 went overseas in 1980, compared to 8.2 million in 2015; 270,000 New Zealanders to one million over the same period. Canadians made a record number of 28.7 million overseas visits in 2010, an increase of 9.4 percent on the previous year.

In such ways, it was as if freeing risk from economic controls had somehow led to a much greater democratization of society—at least in terms of the aspirations that its members were now able to have: enjoying luxuries, pleasures and the ability to live life to the full were no longer the prerogative of the rich and famous. All sections of society would be able to indulge themselves—from greater choice in the supermarket to purchase of exotic holidays and so on: even if, for most, their share of these enticements would represent only a tiny fragment of what those who had reached the top of the escalator of success enjoyed. Nonetheless, the pursuit of success did come at a cost, but one that at the time seemed worth paying. It was thought that its rewards would be more forthcoming if individuals were free from previous ties and bonds—family life, civic duties and responsibilities, loyalty to employers and so on—that in the past would have held them back. Rather than being norms to be respected and lived up to as had previously been the case, these former pillars of stability, support and assurance now came to be seen as unnecessary and restrictive encumbrances. Capturing the ethos of this time, Bauman (2002, 62) wrote that "individuals who are untied to place, who can travel light and move fast, win all the competitions that matter and count." For the most successful entrepreneurs such as Richard Branson (2017, 7), "a risky life is a successful life … [taking risks] didn't put me off at all. [My business ventures] had all been fun to get stuck into, and we'd learned a lot of important lessons." Without taking risks, there could be no journey along this route to success. Even when failure occurred, this was understood as only a temporary setback (for risk evangelicals at least). The lessons learned from these events would still lead to eventual triumph: "entrepreneurs, the successful ones, have on average nine failures for every success … getting it wrong is part of getting it right. Change is now more chancy, but also more exciting if we want to see it that way" (Handy 1989, 55).

But, of course, there has been another side to setting risk free from economic controls. For many others, risk-taking—and its failures—led only to disaster, with no real likelihood of recovery. From the 1980s, the number of personal bankruptcies has increased dramatically across these societies. In Australia, these increased from 7534 in financial year 1986/1987 to 17,163 in 2014/2015. In Canada, from 21,025 in 1980 to 92,694 in 2010; in England and Wales from 3986 in 1980 to 58,801 in 2010; in New Zealand, from 608 in 1980 to 6426 in 2009/2010; in the United States, from 241,431 in 1980 to 1,536,799 in 2010. This is just one symbol, though, of the way in which dreams of the wealth promised under neo-liberalism have come crashing down, shattered and broken. Indeed, for many, life in the risk society of neo-liberalism brings with it a pervading sense of isolation and precariousness (Standing 2014), notwithstanding the new opportunities for pleasure and excitement it also makes available.

In terms of economic security, public sector employment, for example, which used to be a safe haven offering annual pay rises and a healthy pension on retirement, was greatly scaled down, limiting such opportunities. From the beginning of restructuring in the 1980s, it fell from 25.9 percent of the workforce in New Zealand to 17.1 in 2013; and from 27.4 percent in the United Kingdom in 1980 to 17.2 in 2015. In

Australia, it fell from 27.6 percent to 16.5 percent over the same period.[1] Instead, (often temporary) employment now awaits most in the much more unpredictable private sector. While some, with dazzling stories of initiative and success, may be welcomed here with "golden hellos" when joining an organization, many others find that they are reduced to the uncertainties of zero-hour contracts, or life in the gig economy, neither of which provide any guarantees of a regular and certain income.

In terms of family life, the decline of marriage and growth of cohabitation and de facto relationships led Beck and Beck-Gernsheim (2001, 204) to pose the question: "Ask yourself what actually is a family nowadays? What does it mean? Of course, there are children, my children, our children. But even parenthood, the core of family life, is beginning to disintegrate under conditions of divorce. Grandmothers and grandfathers get included and excluded without any means of participating in the decisions of their sons and daughters." And in terms of community ties, civic duties and responsibilities, it has been reported in *The Guardian* that "nearly half of Britons socialise with family and friends only once a month or less ... the lack of human interaction is causing the nation's sense of wellbeing to dwindle" (Press Association 2019).

These everyday anxieties are compounded when individuals are confronted on a regular basis by many of neo-liberalism's unwanted human by-products. These include the high visibility and potential menace of all kinds of street people—the homeless, the mentally ill, beggars, "squeegee merchants," gang members and so on—for whom public space has become a necessary place of residence and/or business. The numbers of this cohort have grown exponentially over this era—the product of welfare cuts, employment uncertainty and urban regeneration. While the latter revitalizes inner city areas through the provision of luxurious accommodation and the lifestyle to go with this—rewards for all those who are flourishing from successful risk-taking—it breaks up previous community norms and disperses those who lose out in this way across the social field. This increases their prominence and visibility. Their presence seems to put quality of life at risk at a time when this has come to be an increasingly valued concept. References to quality of life can indicate the presence of a safe haven "for sailors lost in a turbulent sea of constant, unpredictable and confusing change" (Bauman 2001, 171), the embodiment of peace, cohesion, good neighborliness when a corroding social fabric largely dissolves the possibilities of this occurring organically.

Then, to add to these anxieties, there is the lurking presence of monsters such as pedophiles and sexual predators and terrorists. They all had virtually no existence in public discourse before the 1980s, but now seem to randomly roam through public space—their shadowy existence brought much more to public attention by a deregulated, hi-tech media that provides 24/7 news programs/online newspapers. Despite the reality of declining crime statistics from the early 1990s, reports of crime, disorder and destruction remain some of the most likely ways to sell these products, turning these matters into imminent threats in an era already beset by a surfeit of ontological insecurity (Giddens 1991). It is not just quality of life thought to be at risk in this decaying, uncontrolled social fabric. So too are children—so much scarcer (and thereby irreplaceable) commodities now as a result of changing demographic patters and the more general dissolution of conventional family life. So too is the human body itself, particularly the bodies of women, given both their new public prominence in everyday life and at the same time given that improving, perfecting, maximizing the potential of the human body has become a central feature of the opportunities provided during the neo-liberal program of governance. However rare in reality, each child abduction, each sexual attack, each terrorist outrage becomes a terrible reminder of the harm that can be inflicted on the innocent and unsuspecting; harm against all that has come to be valued most but against which individuals are largely unable to protect themselves.

To sustain its mode of governance and bear the inequalities and tensions that this has brought into existence, neo-liberalism had to loosen its insistence on the sanctimony of the rule of law and allow for a range of preventive controls to reduce such risks. Longstanding conventions, norms and protocols to the contrary have then been proven to be flimsy defenses against this kind of determined subterfuge. Retrospective legislation, for example, a concept described by American jurist Lon Fuller (1964) as a "monstrosity" objectionable both in terms of its morality and efficacy, has been deployed for these purposes; as has hybrid legislation—providing criminal penalties for those breaking civil law restrictions on their conduct, notwithstanding that this constitutes a subversion of criminal law: "using a non-criminal procedure and supposedly non-penal restrictions to deal with conduct that, if it does constitute a public wrong, should instead be dealt with through the criminal law; and a perversion of criminal law, in that they impose criminal conviction and punishment on those who break the supposedly non-criminal orders that are imposed" (Duff 2010, 101). Burdens of proof have been reversed or lowered if these are thought to get in the way of preventing risk (Pratt 2016).

There are also provisions that amount, in reality, if not in juridical explanation, to double punishments for the same crime. For example, sexually violent predator laws in the United States and public protection orders in Australia and New Zealand allow for indefinite detention at the end of a finite sentence because of ongoing risk to the public. The US Supreme Court in *Kansas v. Hendricks* (1997) set an important precedent when determining that "civil commitment" under that state's sexual predator law was not punitive and therefore did not violate the constitution. Similarly, assurances were given in the New Zealand Parliament that its public protection orders legislation did not signal any departure from expectations of justice in democratic societies: "it is really important that we have got pathways for these detainees—pathways so they can work towards being released at some stage, if that is an option for them. Each individual will have a management plan that identifies goals that could contribute to their eventual release. An annual review will be performed on each of these public protection orders. The High Court will look at each case every five years" (NZ Parliamentary Debates 2013, 13,484). On the contrary, some of the most vulnerable members of the community would be protected from particularly grave risks to them—a central expectation of government in democratic society—while these measures at the same time offered a pathway back to free society (however long and uncertain this might be) for those who became subject to such an order. And anyway, the numbers so detained would be very small. How then could such a measure be construed as any broader assault on human rights? More generally, it was claimed that the rights of those such powers were directed at needed to be "rebalanced" against the rights of the public to protection from them. As Tony Blair explained to the British Parliament, "the civil liberties of individuals who might be suspected of terrorism is important … but we have to balance that against the civil liberties of all the citizens of this country who also have a right in a democracy to expect to live their lives free from the fear and possibility of harm by people who act in that way" (UK Parliamentary Debates 2003, col. 954).

Legislation such as this brought governments a number of benefits. First, they won political capital, by being prepared to jettison the advice of their own experts and advisers against such measures (who were likely to maintain, e.g., that breaches of human rights protocols could not simply be brushed aside) and in so doing firmly placed themselves on the side of "the people." They allied themselves with citizens' groups, law and order organizations and others who claim to speak for crime victims in particular and the public in general. Second, these measures were, in effect, messages that the government was still in control of events, still steering the ship of state, notwithstanding the fragmentation of the social fabric. There was no need to run to the lifeboats. The government would still step in and protect their citizens from those who posed the gravest risks to them, by using innovative forms of preventive criminal law— public protection orders, anti-social behavior orders, control orders, public space protection orders and so on. Third, these initiatives became a means of shoring up social cohesion, allowed to otherwise fragment because of the insistence on individual success at the expense of broader social obligations and responsibilities. In this way, preventive criminal law was able to act as a kind of dam in which a toxic mix of uncertainties and anxieties could be stored and attended to while the existing program of neo-liberal governance roared ahead, creating still more winners and losers in its progression, extending social divisions and attendant uncertainties and anxieties.

The Dam Bursts

All the time that this was happening, however, neo-liberalism was undermining its own foundations. The dam that it had constructed to store all its waste products began to overflow and spill its toxic contents right across the social body. Preventive criminal law on its own was no longer sufficient to prop up social cohesion and allow neo-liberal restructuring to continue unchecked. Instead, the overflow has fueled a populist politics that has become rampant, amid wild promises of putting fractured societies back together. The overflow was caused by two international events.

The Aftershocks of the 2008 Global Financial Crisis

The near collapse of the international banking system in 2008 brought the frenzy of lending and borrowing, whatever the risks involved in the ability of borrowers to repay, to an end. It also brought an end to the expectations of ever-increasing prosperity and an end to the jackpots being paid out in neo-liberalism's casino economies (Reiner et al. 2001). Claims by governments that they were still steering the ship of state now seemed worthless. It was drifting out of control, whatever they claimed to the contrary, with countless individuals caught up in the collapse, left to try and find their own place in the very limited number of lifeboats made available for the rescue (it was as if places of safety had already been reserved for those most directly responsible for the crash—irresponsible bankers, disinterested politicians, international corporations and so on). The result was that "ills seep into everyday lives … spawning confusion and denial, avarice and anxiety, stoicism and black humour. For some it has meant putting off retirement or long-planned moves. For others, it meant moving their money out of stocks and bonds into foreclosed homes, gold, livestock, or even just having a good time" (Levitiz et al. 2008).

Many faced ruin. They faced ruin not because of their own profligacy but because they had been following investment advice from organizations they had put their trust in and had obeyed instructions from the politicians they had been prepared to follow—for example, Thatcher's exhortations to buy up shares in newly privatized public services as an illustration of "popular capitalism" at work. Those who had acted responsibly and saved and invested in these ways were likely to be among those who were hurt the most: "shareholders—often, ordinary people with pensions—have little control over fund managers. Fund managers have little control over Chief Executives. And [they] have had little control over trading desks, because they just didn't understand the complexities of mortgage derivatives. So traders were free to gamble with other people's money. They got multimillion bonuses if they did well, but faced almost no meaningful sanction if they failed … the result was excessive risk taking" (Dillow 2008, 32).

Of course, before the 2008 crash, there had also been a succession of financial crises, particularly the stock market crash of 1987, but this was only to be expected in societies driven by risk, where there was no such thing as certainty any more. The resulting casualties from these could simply be stepped over or ignored, with the race for wealth accumulation and riches continuing apace. In 2008, however, it was not just the size of the crash but the speed and extent of its spread—making its consequences more uncertain and dramatic, making governments seem even more helpless in its wake: "the roulette wheel is spinning too fast … as names such as Halifax, Merrill Lynch and Lehman spin into oblivion and the City shrinks, British job prospects and pension values are stakes in a game that is moving at internet speed" (Cavendish 2008, 33).

The volume of casualties it left littering the streets signaled that no one was safe. While there are still those who continue to make advances up the escalator of success, those trapped in the bargain basement not only have no way out of it but now *they know* they no longer have any exit available to them, even as the humble foundations of this edifice crumble beneath their feet. Meanwhile, governments (in the United Kingdom most especially) further intensified the extent of the casualties from the crash and their ability to recover by insisting that it was not caused by overzealous risk-taking but by governments' overspending and welfare dependency. While welfare benefits were then cut and restricted, a further squeeze on public sector employment (at a seventy-year low in the United Kingdom in 2017, and involving only 16.9 percent of the workforce, see Asthana 2017) both reduced opportunities for those trying to find work and reduced living standards for those able to hang on to their jobs.

The crash has thus sharpened existing social divisions. There are the contrasting sights now available in these societies of, on the one hand, growing numbers of gated communities where secure living can be purchased, and, on the other, increasing numbers living their lives on the street. In the former, those who wish to insulate themselves from the growing human detritus constituted by the latter see this as a shrewd investment, an opportunity to buy into community living now that organic community life is vanishing. In the latter, there are vast townships that have been formed, particularly in some American cities, made of cardboard and canvas. Hundreds, thousands, live this way. Probably even more can be found living under highway bridges in that country, or by roundabouts or in no-man's-land where the borders of one district and its neighbor meet—just a few miles away from the elegant cafes, high brand shopping malls, luxurious restaurants and so on that remain the haunts of the casino society's winners.

Anxieties About Mass Immigration

For many in the Anglo-American democracies, this phenomenon—the mass movement of peoples around the globe, usually from South to North and from East to West—threatens their own identity—all they seem to have left in many cases in the midst of all the uncertainties and insecurities around them. They envisage governments giving assistance to all such unwelcome newcomers while they themselves are left further behind. As such, mass immigration (legitimate or illegitimate), sometimes the product of climate change, sometimes the product of conflict as in the Middle East, sometimes the product of desperate individuals hoping to escape from the poverty of their own country, creates a new kind of victimization in the countries they arrive at—even if their own victimization has brought them along this nomadic path. It is as if the norms and values of the nation state have been put at risk by these vast flows of people toward its borders. Stripped of its identifying characteristics in this way, it becomes unrecognizable as a unique social formation.

This new kind of victimhood thus represents something more than individuals becoming a crime victim or fear of becoming one. These ongoing concerns have been joined by fears of what are thought to be the corrosive effects of immigration. Jobs that locals should have are thought to go to "foreigners"; wages are driven lower because these foreigners accept cheaper pay rates; and they bring their own alien cultures with them: white women are unsafe and parts of the country are turned into "no go" areas for the white (and by implication the only legitimate) population. These fears have in themselves become conflated with fears of difference, fears of otherness—qualities variously demonstrated by strangers, asylum seekers, refugees, people overheard speaking a foreign language, the LGBT community and so on (Gillespie, 2016). In the United Kingdom, these concerns were prompted primarily by the arrival of Central European migrants—Poles especially (from 58,000 migrants in 2001 to 676,000 in 2011), then Bulgarians and Romanians, also allowed to settle there without restriction since these countries joined the EU in 2004. All such legal immigrants in the United Kingdom are seen as coming from "the East" (rather than Central Europe, a more accurate geographical depiction of their countries of origin), the antipathy of the West and the highly romanticized memories of the civilized life that used to be lived there. In the United States, it has become fear of Mexican "rapists and murderers" crossing the border in the south and Muslim (which for many Americans is synonymous with terrorism) immigration in general.

In Australia, Canada and New Zealand, there was fear of Asian immigrants from the 1980s, then followed by fear of Muslims. In the words of controversial Australian One Nation MP, Pauline Hanson, "Asians have their own culture and religion, form ghettos and do not assimilate ... a truly multicultural country can never be strong or united" (AUS Parliamentary Debates 1996, 3862). Thereafter, she claimed that "Islam cannot have a significant presence in Australia if we are to live in an open, secular and cohesive society. Never before in Australia's history have we seen civil unrest and terror associated with a so-called religion, or from followers of that faith. We have seen the destruction that it is causing around the world" (AUS Parliamentary Debates 2016, 938). It has been claimed by Winston Peters, from New Zealand First and (in 2019) Deputy Prime Minister of that country, that "we are being dragged into the status of an Asian colony and it is time that New Zealanders were placed first in their own country" (NZPA 2004). And that "New Zealand has always been a nation of immigrants [but] ... New Zealand has never been a nation of Islamic immigrants" (Peters 2005). In Canada it has been claimed by prominent politicians that "the Oriental people, they're slowly taking over" (CBC News 2008); and that "Islamicism poses the greatest threat to Canada's national security" (CBC News 2011). Fears and suspicions such as these are periodically fueled by terrorist outrages that give further justification to such concerns and the horrendous dangers that these outsiders might be capable of, while reminding potential victims of their helplessness in their own countries on such occasions.

There is a great deal of political capital to be made by amplifying these concerns while simultaneously promising common-sensical solutions based around greater limits on immigration and protecting the rights of "authentic" citizens. This populist politics began to take root in the Western democracies in the 1990s[2] but its key ingredients of fear and intolerance of foreigners and immigrants found full expression in 2016—in the United Kingdom with the Brexit campaign ("Take Back Control") and the United States with the election of Donald Trump as president ("Make America Great Again"), who has since proclaimed that the United States is already "full." The anger generated by the flow of unwanted people was also directed at those thought responsible for allowing this weakening of national fiber and identity—in particular, government "elites," the "Establishment" and non-accountable supranational organizations. One of the themes of the anti-Brexit campaign was that the EU would allow Turkey to join (there was no substance at all to this claim). A "Vote Leave" poster in the referendum campaign thus featured a British passport depicted as an open door with a trail of footprints passing through it, with the slogan "Turkey [population 76 million] is joining the EU. Vote Leave, Take Back Control." As one of the leaders of the Leave campaign, Boris Johnson explained the implications of this (increasingly remote) possibility: "I certainly can't imagine a situation in which 77 million [sic] Turks and those of Turkish origin can come here without any checks at all. That is really mad" (Perring 2016).

Establishment elites are also seen as weakening the nation state by imposing foreign, alien, unwanted values and practices on it. For anti-EU populists in the United Kingdom, the European Court of Human Rights has become one of the most prominent signifiers of the imposition of unwanted European difference on British values and understandings. It seemingly has the power to insist that Britain should be "Europeanized" as it sees fit, with its intervention in criminal justice matters symbolizing such dangerous intrusion. Notably, the Court's declaration that the British "blanket ban" on all convicted prisoners' voting rights, regardless of the gravity and circumstances of their offenses, violates Article 3 of the European Convention on Human Rights (*Hirst v. United Kingdom* 2005). Similarly with regard to "whole life sentences" (*Vinter and Others v. United Kingdom* 2013), a decision that reflected, it was claimed, a European "rights madness," as opposed to British common sense (Hastings 2013). The response of the bestselling *Daily Mail* to the Court of Appeal judges who ruled that the vote to leave the EU following the 2016 referendum had to be ratified by parliament was to label them "Enemies of the People" and "out of touch judges" who "had declared war on democracy" (Slack 2016). Meanwhile, Trump breaches all rules regarding the separation of powers, complaining about "so called judges" in Federal court decisions against his immigration policies or about a judge of Mexican heritage who had the temerity to rule against him when former students won a class action against Trump University [sic] for defrauding them: "I have a judge in the Trump University civil case, who is very unfair. An Obama pick. Totally biased—hates Trump" (Trump 2016).

What is thus needed, populists claim, are magical solutions that will restore order, cohesion and solidarity and protect the purity of the nation. Take the British EU referendum. "Leave" campaigners used the logo "Take Back Control," as if by voting to leave, it would be possible to retrieve all that had been lost or stolen—presumably as a result of EU membership; it would be possible to restore national identity and rid the country of corrupting and "un-British" foreign influence; and it would be a gesture of defiance against the EU—favoring British Establishment. Take Trump's slogan, "Make America Great Again." Here too, the theme conveys the sense of loss and betrayal. Hence the need to "drain the swamp" of career politicians, supposed corruption in central government, conspiratorial international financiers, and wicked individuals such as "Crooked Hillary Clinton," all thought variously responsible for globalization, deregulation and their attendant economic ills. Replace them instead with "anti-politicians," such as Trump. Hence the need, as well, to "build a wall" as protection from unwanted immigrants, to "send them back," to protect the borders so they cannot come in; speed up deportation processes once they are caught, call out the National Guard to defend the border against a "caravan" of these foreign hordes—and bypass legal channels and human rights concerns if these get in the way. This kind of purification process is necessary if the glorious past is to be recreated.

These disruptive populist messages, intended to tear apart the existing social order and replace it with one of largely unspecified perfection, often defined as much by what it will not be rather than what it will, have been able to capture public discourse and ownership of the framework of knowledge through which these matters are addressed. From the 1980s, the ability of Establishment forces to construct public discourse has been greatly undermined. It was not simply that governments disregarded or ignored expert knowledge in their development of preventive criminal law. Nor has it simply been the deregulation and technological advances of mainstream media responsible for this. Instead, the rise of social media (in particular Facebook from 2004 and Twitter from 2008) has accelerated these trends toward the dominance of populist common sense in political discourse and the declining influence of the Establishment and its experts. On social media, individuals can not only create and fabricate their own news but also publish it before vast audiences (Donald Trump, e.g., currently has over sixty-three million followers on Twitter), which is avidly read by those for whom the world is made up of conspiracies—by the Establishment, by corrupt civil servants, by the mainstream media itself and by Jews and other ethnic minorities who are thought to lie behind the usually basement level existence of their conspiracy victims. They can create their own reality and deny the existence of what they do not want to see. Trump is an expert at this: the crowds in Washington to witness his presidential inauguration were thus the biggest ever in 2016, despite them being significantly smaller than for his predecessor Obama; while the crowds—hundreds of thousands—in London to protest against his state visit in 2019 did not exist: anyone claiming the contrary to either of these "Trumpisms" was simply propagating "fake news."

These developments have meant that news making and reporting have broken out of the paradigm of reason, rationality and truth in which it had been expected to operate in the democratic world, however elasticated this concept might previously have been. It now has no limits, no ethical standards and no set direction to constrain it or that it has to follow. Demands that truth be told, as some journalists tried to insist during the 2016 US election, were dismissed with rejoinders by the Trump campaign that this was simply evidence of "bias" against them. Indeed, for Trump himself, the journalists at CNN and the *New York Times*, who stood by truth, were "the lowest form of humanity" (Burns and Corasaniti 2016). Whatever the ability of government and the Establishment to control the terms of political and public discourse on crime and punishment that there once was, this has now dissipated amid outraged claims about "Mexican rapists," Central European "benefit fraud," wealthy beggars, refugees from the Middle East who will turn to terrorism if any leniency at the border is shown to them and so on.

Out of Uncertainty, into Chaos

This "revolt against uncertainty" is running through many democratic societies, with demands for the restoration of a more familiar and cohesive social order, bolstered as necessary by laws that have public protection from any further risks to it as their priority. In the United States, the constant replay of populist tropes during his campaign led to the presidential election of Donald Trump. In the United Kingdom, it was anti-Establishment populism that led to both demands for a referendum on Britain's membership of the EU in the first instance and the subsequent successful "Leave" vote. Elsewhere, electoral support for populists, if not putting them in government, has changed political dynamics and encouraged mainstream political parties to try and embrace at least some of their demands. Controlling immigration is one of the most straightforward mechanisms to deploy when there is a need to demonstrate affiliation with populist messages. In New Zealand, the Labour Party (n.d.), in a coalition government with New Zealand First, explains that:

> We have always welcomed migrants to our country, and will continue to do so. But in recent years our population has been growing rapidly as record numbers of migrants arrive here. This has happened without the Government planning for the impact immigration is having on our country … This has contributed to the housing crisis, put pressure on hospitals

and schools, and added to the congestion on roads. Labour will invest in housing, infrastructure, public services, and in training New Zealanders to fill skills shortages. At the same time, we will take a breather on immigration … In total, these changes are estimated to reduce net migration by 20,000–30,000. Without these changes there would be up to 10,000 more houses needed and up to 20,000 more vehicles on our roads annually.

It is as if controlling immigration especially brings about a reassertion of authority and nationhood and guarantees of a brighter future, usually of a society rebuilt around dominant white men, where jobs that used to exist before globalization made them redundant would somehow reappear. This includes breathing new life into sunset industries such as coal mining. Dangerous foreigners will be kept out and individuals will be given back what they think has been taken from them: familiarity, certainty, security. However, promises based on fundamentally flawed attempts to recreate a mythical past can never materialize. In reality, rather than bringing an end to uncertainty, the Anglo-American variant of populism only brings chaos, by tearing up existing norms, values and conventions and loyalties, further eroding the security of the individual and the nation state itself. Jenkins (2019), in fact, argues that what lies behind populist rhetoric in the United Kingdom is the belief that "occasional bouts of chaos are [thought to be] necessary. As during wars, recessions and Thatcherism, Britain needs a therapeutic shock to jolt it into a new karma, a new inner greatness." Out of chaos, something better will emerge: the time when that country was "great," or the time perhaps when much of the world map was colored red to denote the British Empire, or in yet another version of this siren song, some sort of Singaporean tax-free haven will come into existence. In reality, no one knows.

This also means that there are likely to be extra demands on punishment to provide certainty and security. Populism needs enemies (real or imaginary) to thrive and to direct all its anger toward, and it has to have victims (real or imaginary) it can sanctimoniously pledge to defend—whatever the cost, to the ends of the earth if necessary. It will build walls to keep out the unwanted; it will walk away from treaty obligations and duties. Whatever the cost, this is worth paying to be rid of EU "enslavement" and "vasseldom," as Brexit supporters maintain. Without such causes and grievances, populism itself is nothing. Furthermore, under these new demands for control and security, punishment is being asked to play a role that it was never designed for: other social mechanisms—extensive welfare and education programs, forms of central and local government infrastructure, and more permanent social relations between individuals—had previously been expected to provide cohesion, solidarity and certainty. However, when risk and populism collide, the fundamental expectations of and limits to punishment in democratic society are likely to crumble still further—in the name of a security and sense of well-being and safety that becomes ever more elusive and distant. New forms of penal control, even where no crime has been committed, have to help provide this. And for populist governments prepared to tear up international treaty obligations, pushing aside criminal justice norms and conventions to hunt down more enemies it has identified is of little consequence.

Ways can be found around any such barriers, as in the neo-liberal era. Artful play with words can be sufficient to offset any liability: just as a double punishment was not really a double punishment, so the reality of the conditions in which illegal immigrants are being on the US side of the border with Mexico border can be denied. They are being held in "family residential centres"; children separated from their parents have merely been taken to "summer camps." Journalist Adam Serwer (2019) describes the very different conditions that he found: "the children at a facility in … Texas were sleeping on concrete floors and being denied soap and toothpaste … A visiting doctor called the detention centres "torture facilities" … at a processing center in El Paso, 900 migrants were 'being held at a facility designed for 125. In some cases, cells designed for 35 people were holding 135." In the same way the preventive controls were a continuation of democratic governance rather than a departure from it, response, Trump claimed in a televised interview that "I inherited separation from President Obama. President Obama built, they call them jail cells" (NBC News 2019)—so it was not Trump's fault: he was merely following in the footsteps of his predecessor.

And anyway, such is populism's contempt for rule of law trappings, such is its contempt for the criminal justice Establishment who look to this to provide a sanctuary against the tyranny and bluster of demagogues, that it can simply try to barge its way past these flimsy barriers if it chooses to do so. As to criticisms of the denial of medical treatment in the centers, Trump (2019a) tweeted that "our Border Patrol people are not hospital workers, doctors or nurses … [even so] many of these illegal aliens are living far better now than where they [were]." And ultimately, "if illegal immigrants are unhappy with the conditions in the quickly built or refitted detention centers, just tell them not to come. All problems solved!" (Trump 2019b). Furthermore, it was in the neo-liberal era that expert knowledge, when found to be inconvenient, was disregarded in favor of popular common sense on crime control policy. Populism, too, has no interest in recruiting any such expertise to its cause, preferring instead simple but magical remedies, put forward when the opportunity arises (usually in response to a murder or mass shooting): more police, more police powers, longer sentences, arm schoolteachers (in the United States) and so on. But by the same token, it feels free to ignore science—on climate change, economic forecasts and so on—wherever this gets in the way of its promised return to its fantasy world of certainty and security: "the British people have had enough of experts," proclaimed one of the leading campaigners for Brexit in 2016 (Deacon 2016).

It had become necessary to use extensive forms of risk-driven preventive criminal law to maintain stability and social order in the course of neo-liberal restructuring. For a while, these measures broadly worked: the public largely acquiesced in this, as long as there was a realistic prospect of rewards while those who put their well-being at risk could at the same time be brought under control. But to do so, governments had to disengage themselves from their own experts, and maneuver their way around the conventions and barriers in the way of such initiatives. Ultimately, though, and with the prospect, for many, of rewards rapidly vanishing, this was not enough to hold back the wave of anger and resentment that its mode of governance had set in motion. This now gives rise to a virulent populism. To help maintain its own legitimacy, this populism builds on, extends and redevelops the preventive platform already constructed by neo-liberalism. Conventions that it was thought could withstand such attacks have been shown to have little substance in the face of these onslaughts. To what extent it will be possible to rebuild them along with all the assumptions about human rights that have been rewritten and punishment returned to what used to be its much less dominant role in democratic society remains to be seen.

Notes

1. No corresponding data for Canada and the United States.
2. For example, the ascendancy of the anti-immigration but pro-welfare state Danish People's Party in the 1990s.

References

Asthana, Anushka. 2017. "Public Sector Employment is at 70-Year Low, Says GMB Report." *The Guardian*, September 17, 2017. https://www.theguardian.com/society/2017/sep/17/public-sector-employment-70-year-low-gmb-union-report.

Australia. AUS Parliamentary Debates. House of Representatives. Vol. 208. 10 September 1996.

Australia. AUS Parliamentary Debates. Senate. 14 September 2016.

Bauman, Zygmunt. 2001. *Liquid Modernity*. Cambridge: Polity Press.

Bauman, Zygmunt. 2002. "Violence in the Age of Uncertainty." In *Crime and Insecurity*, edited by Adam Crawford, 52–74. London: Routledge.

Baxstrom v. Herold, 383 U.S. 107 (1966).

Beck, Ulrich, and Elisabeth Beck-Gernsheim. 2001. *Individualization: Institutionalized Individualism and Its Social and Political Consequences*. Translated by Patrick Camiller. London: Sage.

Branson, Richard. 2017. *Finding My Virginity: The New Autobiography*. London: Penguin.

Brittan, Samuel. 1973. *Capitalism and the Permissive Society*. London: Macmillan.

Burns, Alexander, and Nick Corasaniti. 2016. "Donald Trump's Other Campaign Foe: The 'Lowest Form of Life' News Media." *New York Times*, August 12, 2016. https://www.nytimes.com/2016/08/13/us/politics/donald-trump-obama-isis.html.

Cavendish, Camilla. 2008. "The Roulette Wheel is Spinning Far Too Fast." *The Times*, September 19, 2008.

CBC News. 2008. "Toronto Councillor Apologizes for 'Orientals' Comment." March 31, 2008. https://www.cbc.ca/news/canada/toronto/toronto-councillor-apologizes-for-orientals-comment-1.755506.

CBC News. 2011. "Harper says 'Islamicism' Biggest Threat to Canada." September 6, 2011. https://www.cbc.ca/news/politics/harper-says-islamicism-biggest-threat-to-canada-1.1048280.

Deacon, Michael. 2016. "Michael Gove's Guide to Britain's Greatest Enemy … The Experts." *The Telegraph*, June 10, 2016. https://www.telegraph.co.uk/news/2016/06/10/michael-goves-guide-to-britains-greatest-enemy-the-experts/.

Dillow, Chris. 2008. "Why aren't Hedge Funds Failing as Fast as Banks?" *The Times*, September 17, 2008.

Duff, R. Antony. 2010. "Perversions and Subversions of Criminal Law." In *The Boundaries of Criminal Law*, edited by R. Antony Duff, Lindsay Farmer, Sandra Marshall, Massimo Renzo, and Victor Tadros, 88–112. Oxford: Oxford University Press.

Ericson, Richard, and Kevin Haggerty. 1997. *Policing the Risk Society*. Oxford: Clarendon Press.

Feeley, Malcolm, and Jonathan Simon. 1992. "The New Penology: Notes on the Emerging Strategy of Corrections and its Implications." *Criminology* 30 (4): 449–474.

Fuller, Lon. 1964. *The Morality of Law*. New Haven: Yale University Press.

Giddens, Anthony. 1991. *Modernity and Self-Identity: Self and Society in the Late Modern Age*. Cambridge: Polity Press.

Gillespie, Tom. 2016. "Beggars Belief—'Disabled Limping Migrant' Who Uses a Crutch While Begging in London is Exposed as a Fraud When He Is Seen Strolling off to Buy a Takeaway." *The Sun*, September 16, 2016. https://www.thesun.co.uk/news/1764495/beggars-belief-disabled-limping-migrant-who-uses-a-crutch-while-begging-in-london-is-exposed-as-a-fraud-when-he-is-seen-strolling-off-to-buy-a-takeway/.

Handy, Charles. 1989. *The Age of Unreason*. London: Arrow Books.

Hastings, Max. 2013. "The Danger is we've Become Immune to Human Rights Lunacy. It's Vital we Stay Angry, says Max Hastings." *Daily Mail*, July 10, 2013. http://www.dailymail.co.uk/debate/article-2359048/The-danger-weve-immune-Human-Rights-lunacy-Its-vital-stay-angry-says-MAX-HASTINGS.html.

Hayek, Friedrich. 1960. *The Constitution of Liberty*. Chicago: University of Chicago Press.

Hirst v. United Kingdom, [No 2] [2005] E.C.H.R. 681.

Home Office. 1925. *Report of the Departmental Committee on Sexual Offences Against Young Persons. Cmd. 2561.* London: HMSO.

Howard, Colin, and Norval Morris. 1964. *Studies in Criminal Law.* London: Oxford University Press.

Jenkins, Simon. 2019. "Trump Created a Storm over Kim Darroch. Boris Johnson will bring a Hurricane." *The Guardian*, July 11, 2019. https://www.theguardian.com/commentisfree/2019/jul/11/boris-johnson-chaos-no-deal-brexit-britain.

Kansas v. Hendricks, 521 U.S. 346 (1997).

Kershaw, Ian. 2018. *Roller-Coaster: Europe, 1950–2017.* London: Penguin Books.

Labour Party. n.d. "Making Immigration Work for New Zealand." Accessed August 23, 2019. https://www.labour.org.nz/immigration.

Levitz, Jennifer, Ilan Brat, and Nicholas Casey. 2008. "Wall Street's Ills Seep into Everyday Lives." *Wall Street Journal*, September 19, 2008.

McSherry, Bernadette. 2020. "Predictive Algorithms, Risk and Preventive Justice." In *Criminal Justice, Risk and the Revolt Against Uncertainty*, edited by John Pratt and Jordan Anderson. London: Palgrave Macmillan.

NBC News. 2019. "Donald Trump, interviewed by Chuck Todd." *Meet the Press with Chuck Todd*, June 23, 2019. https://www.nbcnews.com/meet-the-press/meet-press-6-23-n1020766.

New Zealand. *NZ Parliamentary Debates.* Vol. 693. 18 September 2013.

NZPA (New Zealand Press Association). 2004. "Peters Warns of 'Immigrant Invasion'." July 6, 2004. Factiva: NZPA000020040706e0760003n.

Perring, Rebecca. 2016. "EU Loophole could see 77 Million Turks Head to Britain, Warn Farage and Johnson." *Daily Express*, April 18, 2016. https://www.express.co.uk/news/uk/661387/Migrant-crisis-Nigel-Farage-Turkey-EU-visa-free-travel.

Peters, Winston. 2005. "Address by Winston Peters to Members of Far North Grey Power." Far North Community Centre, Kaitaia, NZ. July 28, 2005.

Pratt, John. 2016. "Risk Control, Rights and Legitimacy in the Limited Liability State." *British Journal of Criminology* 57 (6): 1322–1339.

Pratt, John and Jordan Anderson. 2016. "'The Beast of Blenheim', Risk and the Rise of the Security Sanction." *Australian and New Zealand Journal of Criminology* 49 (4): 528–545.

Press Association. 2019. "Half of Britons Socialise with Family and Friends at Most Once a Month." *The Guardian*, June 17, 2019. https://www.theguardian.com/world/2019/jun/17/half-of-britons-socialise-with-family-and-friends-at-most-once-a-month.

Reiner, Robert, Sonia Livingstone, and Jessica Allen. 2001. "Casino Culture: Crime and Media in a Winner-Loser Society." In *Crime, Risk and Justice: The Politics of Crime Control in Liberal Democracies*, edited by Kevin Stenson and Richard Sullivan, 174–194. Cullompton: Willan Publishing.

Report of the Penal Policy Review Committee. 1981. Wellington: Government Printer.

Serwer, Adam. 2019. A Crime by Any Name. *The Atlantic*, July 3, 2019. https://www.theatlantic.com/ideas/archive/2019/07/border-facilities/593239/.

Slack, James. 2016. "Enemies of the People: Fury Over 'Out of Touch' Judges Who Have 'Declared War on Democracy' By Defying 17.4m Brexit Voters and Who Could Trigger Constitutional Crisis." *Daily Mail*, November 4, 2016. http://www.dailymail.co.uk/news/article-3903436/Enemies-people-Fury-touch-judges-defied-17-4m-Brexit-voters-trigger-constitutional-crisis.html.

Standing, Guy. 2014. The Precariat. *The New Dangerous Class*. London: Bloomsbury.

Tappan, P. 1957. "Sexual Offences and the Treatment of Sexual Offenders in the United States." In *Sexual Offences. A Report of the Cambridge Department of Criminal Science*, edited by Leon Radzinowicz, 500–516. London: Macmillan.

Trump, Donald (@realDonaldTrump). 2016. "I have a judge…" Twitter, May 30, 2016, 9:54 AM. https://twitter.com/realDonaldTrump/status/737399475509985280.

Trump, Donald (@realDonaldTrump). 2019a. "Our border patrol people …" Twitter, July 3, 2019, 12:31 PM. https://twitter.com/realdonaldtrump/status/1146501820593967104.

Trump, Donald (@realDonaldTrump). 2019b. "If illegal immigrants are …" Twitter, July 3, 2019, 1:22 PM. https://twitter.com/realdonaldtrump/status/1146514575048790019.

United Kingdom (UK). Parliamentary Debates. House of Commons. Vol. 405. 20 May 2003.

Vinter (and Others) v. United Kingdom [2013] ECHR 786.

Thinking About Risk: Responding to Threat and Disintegration in a Fraught World

Elliott Currie

I want to share with you some recent musings on how we think about risk nowadays. Let me start with a few illustrations of the way we live now in the United States:

I am talking with a good friend about her daughter's plans for the evening. It's a weekend, and her daughter, who is in her 20s, has been invited to go out to movie with friends. But she declines, her mother says: "She doesn't want to go out because of all the shootings"—meaning the mass shootings that have sharply escalated in the United States in the past few years. According to one of the more restrictive definitions—which confines the term "mass shooting" to events that are "indiscriminate," that occur in public spaces, and that result in at least three fatalities not including the shooter—there were 50 such incidents in the United States in the decade from 2008 to 2017, more than the estimated number in the previous two decades combined. And there have been another 16 since

E. Currie (✉)
Criminology, Law and Society, University of California Irvine,
Irvine, CA, USA
e-mail: ecurrie@uci.edu

© The Author(s) 2020
J. Pratt, J. Anderson (eds.), *Criminal Justice, Risk and the Revolt against Uncertainty*,
Palgrave Studies in Risk, Crime and Society,
https://doi.org/10.1007/978-3-030-37948-3_13

301

(Follman et al. 2019). My friend says she wishes that her daughter didn't have to feel that way—that she simply wouldn't be able to enjoy the movie because of the looming fear of what might happen. But she completely understands why she would.

Another illustration, also involving shootings. In August 2018 I took a trip to Chicago, the city where I mostly grew up. During the weekend that I was there, the city endured one of the most violent weekends in recent memory. Between Friday afternoon and early Monday morning that weekend 71 people were shot, 12 of whom died. The deaths and injuries, as always in Chicago, were concentrated in a handful of neighborhoods on the city's south and west signs, which were, also not for the first time, routinely described as "war zones" or "urban battlegrounds" in the media. Notably, as often in the past, police and city officials rushed to assure Chicagoans that these events were the work of a "small element" and unrelated to anything fundamental about the state of the city itself.

The third illustration, of a different kind. During the fall of 2018, like many Californians, I couldn't get away from the fires. In the San Francisco Bay Area, where I mostly live now, we spent several days with the unfortunate distinction of having to breathe what was described as the most toxic air of any urban area in the world, surpassing places like Delhi and Beijing—the result of smoke from a massive fire well over 100 miles away, which has now been ranked as the most destructive and deadly in California's already stunning history of wildfires. We lived within a surreal and eerie scene of dark yellowish skies and people hurrying through the streets hidden behind face masks, if they went outdoors at all.

I escaped that apocalyptic scene by heading down to Southern California, where I work. But on the day before the Thanksgiving holiday, I found myself driving up the Pacific Coast Highway north of Los Angeles—past the site of the *second* worst fire in the state in years. And the scene could only be described as apocalyptic—in some places, mile upon mile of utter devastation, hillsides turned black and totally denuded as far as the eye could see. And on this route, I also passed within a few miles of the site of the state's most recent mass shooting, when a lone gunman opened fire at a bar and country music venue in the usually quiet suburb of Thousand Oaks, killing 13 people.

It's fair to say that everyday life in many parts of the United States lately seems permeated by risk—risks of several kinds, some of which have not only clearly intensified in recent years but have also sometimes appeared in unexpected places. There are of course many more that I could add to the list, but that I didn't personally experience: including the hurricanes, one after the other, that have devastated large areas from Texas to the Carolinas to Florida to Puerto Rico: or the floods that have inundated large parts of the agricultural Midwest, on a scale that no one has seen for generations, which have wiped out the livelihoods of great numbers of farmers who have made their living in this region for as long as anyone can remember. Or the perils of a relentlessly crumbling physical infrastructure that has given us deadly gas pipeline explosions in a quiet Bay Area neighborhood and famously toxic water supplies in Michigan.

And the sense that we have to learn to adapt to a "new normal" in what seems like quite abnormal ways is also pervasive: from my friend's daughter's decision to avoid going to movies to our scramble in California to be sure that we stock up on the proper kind of face masks that will reliably filter out the especially toxic fine particulate matter produced by the massive and increasingly routine fires around us (a friend of mine told me with great excitement that he had just ordered several on Amazon.com so he wouldn't be caught short the next time). Unsurprisingly, many of us feel that something has changed in our core, existential sense of security. I'll grant at the outset that this sense of being saturated by risks—of being increasingly surrounded by threats that are quite real even if we would prefer not to confront them or think about them too much—may be especially prevalent in my own country in comparison to the rest of the advanced industrial world—a point I'll return to shortly. But it is by no means unique to the United States, and in some parts of the world, it is even more pervasive and even more consequential.

I bring up this sense of the *saturation* and resulting normalization of accelerating risk because I think it fits uneasily with some variants of our current discourse about risk, both in criminology and other social sciences and in the news media and public discussion generally. I can't help thinking that there is a striking disconnect between this reality of pervasive risk, at least in some places, and the tendency in some quarters to look at the very idea of risk with a fundamentally skeptical eye—to look at risk through a social constructionist lens where the default stance is to expose the ways in which risks are routinely exaggerated: either through a viscerally anxious response on the part of a misguided public, or, worse, a deliberate manipulation of that anxiety by State actors, in the service of ends that range from the merely self-serving to the truly sinister. That unjustified ramping-up of risk is often taken as involving the "othering" or even demonizing of selected people that we define as being especially risky—whether it's street criminals, or immigrants from the global South, or sex offenders, or deranged shooters.

So the underlying theoretical lens operating, explicitly or otherwise, in this strand of thinking about risk is a version of a societal reaction approach. The focus is mostly on the state's, or the public's, *reaction* to the problem rather than on the nature and origins of the problem itself. More recently, the problem has often been cast as the "populist" threat—the dangers of a mobilized public that is both irrationally fearful and fundamentally misinformed—often deliberately misinformed by unscrupulous but persuasive leaders who play on and amplify their fears. In the United States, as in some other places (see Winlow et al. 2017), that volatile and easily misled public is often identified with parts of the traditional white working class—who are seen as irrationally angry because they cannot adapt to the realities of a more diverse and more demanding social and economic order.

And there is often a specific historical dimension to this view. It's frequently argued that modern history has been, in part, the history of efforts to control or even abolish risk—in effect, to pacify society and suppress real or imagined threats of disorder and insecurity. We often point to a growing historical intolerance of risk, which predictably generates new or elaborated forms of coercive and intrusive control. We sometimes see that intolerance of risk as an essentially irrational longing for a "golden age" when things were more predictable, more stable (our conference subtitle—"The revolt against uncertainty"—reflects that historical sense).

And this has consequences for the way we think about how we should respond—for how we think about *remedies*. If the most important part of the problem is that risks are routinely exaggerated and that most proposed remedies may do more harm than good, then our best response probably involves ramping down overheated rhetoric, challenging the purveyors of overblown fear-mongering with clear-eyed analysis, and, in general, working to get an increasingly intrusive state and its agencies of social control off of peoples' backs.

Now, I hasten to add that this is something of an oversimplification of this strand of thinking about risk, which in practice is often much more nuanced. And at its most thoughtful, this perspective can be both accurate and illuminating. It has taught us a lot—perhaps especially when it comes to the handling of particularly fraught issues like crime and immigration, which are certainly frequently deployed with great insincerity but substantial effect by people who are indeed unscrupulous (in the United States today, of course, that is glaringly apparent in the narratives routinely put out by the Trump administration). But at the same time, there are themes here that make me uneasy in the context of how we live now—uneasy on both the intellectual and political levels.

What makes me uneasy is that—as is true of constructionist approaches to social issues generally—if this perspective is taken too far, it begins to leave very important things out of the picture. What's most often left out, or at least strikingly downplayed, is the underlying phenomenon itself—in this case, the tangible, inescapable reality of risk, and not just the specific risks at issue but the larger, unexpected precariousness and danger of everyday life for many people in many parts of the world.

I say "unexpected" precariousness because it really wasn't supposed to be this way. The reduction of insecurity and danger—other than that which we create on purpose for our own adrenaline—fueled enjoyment, as John Pratt points out—was supposed to have more or less steadily advanced along with technological and material progress. I remember this well as a pervasive and fundamentally unquestioned cultural expectation when I was growing up in the post-World War II United States. But it hasn't turned out that way. Instead, the level of risk that we experience in contemporary industrial societies—again, perhaps more in the United States than in most other countries of the global North—has in a way blindsided us. It is safe to say that in the 1950s the idea that in the country's booming and productive industrial heartland the availability of the absolute essentials of modern life—like safe drinking water—would be fundamentally in question would have seemed farfetched. And the issue is not, for the most part, about changes in our *perception* of the dangers: it is that one of the defining realities of our time is that in many places we face actual levels of danger and threat that are in a very real sense *inappropriate* to an advanced industrial society—"out of sync" with our potential.

This, by the way, isn't the same as saying that risk is an inevitable aspect of something called "modernity," but actually the opposite: the idea that the extremes of risk we face are products of specific decisions made by political actors—and that those decisions are part of larger agendas and underpinned by distinctive ideologies. In our time—and especially in the societies that manifest the greatest degree of this kind of "inappropriate" risk—these operate within a distinctly heedless and predatory social context. Failing to make that connection has very significant consequences—both intellectual and, perhaps even more importantly, social and political. It diminishes our ability to get to the root of some very real problems that beset us, and it fosters a distorted political discourse in which those forces most responsible for the high level of "excess" risk in American are able, all too frequently, to pass themselves off as the guardians of public security.

Let me just briefly illustrate how this plays out with two of the examples I began with—the risk posed by "everyday" inner-city violence and the risk posed by mass shootings.

The downplaying of the risk of inner-city violence in the United States has been a prominent theme in American social science and American mainstream media for a long time, and it represents a startling example of social constructionism gone haywire. It is a classic example of what we might call "risk denial." Like climate change denial, it is remarkably pervasive and resilient. And it presents itself in what are by now generally familiar forms.

Here is a recent example of this kind of denial in action. In the fall of 2018 the liberal American economist Paul Krugman wrote an opinion column in the *New York Times* in which, among other things, he argued that saying that inner-city violence was still a problem in America was basically a ploy by the Republican Party to stir up fear among the public and get their political base excited. Talking about violence, Krugman argued, may have been justified back in the bad old days when we actually *had* a lot of crime in our inner cities. But since then, he said, inner-city violence has "plunged" (in the language of risk denial, violent crime rarely just "declines" or "falls": it "plunges," or it "plummets"). So what's a fear-monger to do, Krugman asks, when there is no longer any reason for fear? And his answer is—they lie. They lie about the continued existence of the problem when in fact it has virtually disappeared as an issue—as a risk—of serious concern in American cities (Krugman 2018).

Something like this view is shared not only by a significant part of the liberal intelligentsia in the United States, by also but a fair number of people in the business of criminology (though not so often by people who have actually *studied* inner-city violence). But it is also a shining example of the triumph of a kind of ideological denial—a kind of denial that, in this case, has troubling overtones of what I would call "racialized complacency." Eleven of the twelve people who lost their lives in that weekend of gun violence in Chicago in 2018 were African-American. In the year leading up to the shootings, African-Americans, roughly 1/3 of the city's population, were about 80% of its homicide victims. Across the country, violence takes more years of life from Black men in the United States today than cancer, stroke, and diabetes combined.

I've recently been looking at a ranking of the 50 most deadly large cities in the world, as measured by their most recent homicide death rates. Most of those cities are in Latin America and the Caribbean—a few in Africa. Only four are in the global North, and all of those four are in the United States. The city of St. Louis, Missouri, ranked number 19 on this list of the world's major cities with the highest rates of violent death in 2016. Above it were eight cities in Brazil, nine in Mexico and Central America, and two in South Africa. All four of the American cities on the list—which also included Baltimore, Detroit, and New Orleans—racked up higher homicide rates than the city of Kingston, Jamaica, the most violent place in one of the most perennially violent countries in the world.

Here is a perfect opportunity to raise forcefully the obvious question: why does this one advanced industrial country make it onto this list? What is it about the social and economic structure of the United States that puts people in some of its cities at a degree of risk that is shared by no one else in the developed world? Why is it that we look more like Brazil or Honduras or Mexico in this respect than we do France or Sweden or Japan?

Again, I think it takes an almost unfathomable degree of complacency about Black lives to argue with a straight face that inner-city violence is no longer a problem that we need to care about or that anyone who says so is really trying to stir up needless fear and paranoia among an anxious and uninformed political base (we used to see the same sort of complacency in our attitudes about drug abuse in the United States until white people began dying from opiate overdoses in droves in recent years: Donnermeyer 2019).

And again, this racialized denial has consequences. There is a vast research literature by now on the structural sources of the shocking racial disparities in the risk of violent death and injury in the United States. But the denial of those risks obviously turns our attention away from those structural forces—and, therefore, away from thinking about structural *remedies*. Meanwhile, people continue to die in our cities at rates seen nowhere else outside of the most violence-torn parts of the global South. It is hard not to feel that the denial is deeply implicated in those "excess" deaths and injuries. But the consequences are also political: in the absence of an articulate and forceful progressive response to urban violence, others will step up—and have stepped up—to offer their own, typically regressive, ones, whether in the United States or, as we've recently seen, Brazil. There is no structural element in these responses: there is only the insistence on doing whatever it takes to stamp that risk out of existence. The Trump administration's chief response to violent crime has been to blame the problem on immigrants from Mexico and Central America, and to call for diverting public resources to building a border wall to keep them out. The promise of a forceful response to violent crime was an important feature of Jair Bolsonaro's campaign for Brazil's presidency, and since his election he has followed through in ways that will surely worsen the country's problem of violence, not improve it: lessening restrictions on gun ownership in the name of allowing "ordinary" Brazilians to better defend themselves: reducing punishments for police who commit manslaughter on duty; widening the already great impunity for the extrajudicial killing of street criminals in a country where, in the State of Rio de Janeiro alone, more than 1400 people were killed by police during the first three quarters of 2018 (Merkel and Pittari 2019).

The response to the recent wave of mass shootings in United States and elsewhere shares some of the same features, though typically in more complex ways. Unlike the persistence of "everyday" urban violence (Currie 2019), the threat posed by mass shootings is less often denied altogether. But it is frequently minimized in the public discourse. One common theme is that the risk posed by mass shootings is wildly over-blown, because the number of people who have actually been killed in these shootings in schools and other public places is minuscule, com-pared to ... you name it: car accidents, childhood diseases, and so on. That rhetorical strategy is pervasive in risk denial generally: you down-play the issue and its destructive impact on peoples' well-being and sense of security by pointing out that *other* risks are worse—which may simul-taneously be both technically true and humanly irrelevant (it may also, as we'll see in a moment, be false).

Let me give you a couple of examples of how this reasoning works in practice. In a 2012 article aimed at an audience of college and university administrators, two writers described as the directors of a company pro-viding security services for higher education seek to expose the "myth" that "college campuses are unsafe." (Healy and Margolis, 2012). They fret that in the face of recent tragedies on college and university campuses, we see headlines "questioning the security of those institutions." But "many data contradict the perception these splashy soundbites engender." The "many data" these writers offer to explode the myth of campus insecurity consist of a single set of figures looking at the trend in school violence for the years 2006–2010, which reveal "no significant change in the violent crime rates reported by the nation's universities." The authors begin, in other words, by challenging the belief that recent mass shootings tell us much about safety on college campuses, but then deploy a *general* mea-sure of violent crime to rebut it. And their measure tells us nothing about the seriousness of the campus violence problem—only that it hasn't *changed* much, at least within those few years, a time span which is chosen for no obvious reason. Indeed, since they offer no definition of what level of violence would count as "insecurity," or any approach to determining what constitutes an "unsafe" campus, we have no way of contextualizing the issue of campus safety, no way to place the numbers in any kind of evaluative framework. Strictly speaking, the argument is a non sequitur—but it is a kind of fallacy that is routinely found in risk denial.

The writers of this piece blame the "misperception" about campus violence that they claim to have exposed on the tendency of the media to sensationalize violence, citing the old journalistic adage "if it bleeds, it leads." And a gullible public is sucked in, since they usually don't "have access to the level of detail revealed in the analysis cited here." The public, moreover, according to these authors, routinely suffers from "cognitive biases" that lead them to regularly "underestimate common risks such as driving or cardiac disease" but "overestimate the risks of less common but more frightening possibilities such as a plane crash or cancer." And that tendency, the authors tell us, helps explain why people are susceptible to worrying overly about campus gun violence. Aside from the curious apparent assertion that car crashes cause more deaths than cancer, what's striking in this presentation is the absence of empathy—the way in which the presentation of sheer quantitative facts sidesteps the human meaning of these incidents.

The strategy of pointing to the relatively small numbers affected by mass violence as opposed to other risks overlooks an obvious point: that numbers alone tell us only a very limited part of the story when it comes to the human impact of certain kinds of risk, especially those that in a very real sense undermine peoples' sense of certainty that there are places of safety in the world. What makes the spate of shootings on school and university campuses so humanly disturbing is precisely that, with some exceptions, these used to be places where safety was rarely in question. What these incidents convey is the sense that safety is to be reliably found *nowhere*—that the unpredictable violence of the larger society and culture has worked its way into every corner of our social and personal lives, and that it can strike just about anyone at any time, anywhere. That the likelihood that it will is statistically small doesn't diminish the deeper reality—either its psychological impact or its genuinely disturbing illumination of a certain essential fragility of the surrounding social order.

Likewise, you are highly unlikely to meet a violent death in a house of worship, and far more likely to die by violence on a street corner, or in your home: and still more likely to die of cardiac arrest. But I think that applying that quantitative logic to downplay the social and psychological significance of the recent mass killings in Catholic churches in Sri Lanka, synagogues in Pittsburg and suburban San Diego, or two mosques in New Zealand would obviously miss something of enormous importance—or, more accurately, two things. First, the statistical rarity of these deaths doesn't convey the existential reality that these have traditionally been places that are experienced as havens—as sacred spaces in which even the most serious outside violence has usually been kept at bay, and thus represented a line that would not be crossed. These recent attacks, and others before them, instead generate the sense that even these places can provide no real sanctuary—that something culturally foundational has been breached. At the same time, the purely quantitative lens obscures the deeper social implications of extreme acts like these. The number of Jewish worshippers shot by a white nationalist gunman in Pittsburg (and more recently in Southern California) was small relative to the number who attend temple services, and small relative to the number who will ultimately die of cardiovascular disease: but virulent antisemitism, in the United States and the world, is not a small problem. Even the larger tally of those killed in the mosques in Christchurch is very small relative to the number who attend Muslim services regularly: but anti-Muslim extremism is not a small concern. These rare events, in short, reflect deeper social threats whose trajectory is unpredictable. And the eruption of those threats into overt acts of violence is also unpredictable and therefore difficult to defend against.

Minimizing the significance of threats is often a key element in a larger argument in support of political inaction and quiescence, and, in the United States especially, one that is frequently grounded in a deeper libertarian or conservative distaste for government. In the aftermath of one of America's worst mass school shootings—the 2007 massacre carried out by a lone student gunman at Virginia Tech University—the well-known news commentator and pundit John Stossel provided a commentary on ABC News that heaped scorn on those experts and public officials who, he believed, were over-reacting to the incident. These included California Senator Dianne Feinstein, who had convened hearings in Washington on the issue and hoped that the tragedy would "re-ignite the dormant effort to pass common-sense gun regulations in this nation." In response, Stossel wrote:

Please. That's a lot of reaction for something that almost never happens.

It is a myth, Stossel insisted, that "schools are violent." His evidence for this was that violent crime in schools "dropped by half" from 1990 to 2002—a point thoroughly irrelevant to his argument, which was neither about schools in general nor violent crime in general, but about the meaning and impact of mass shootings on college campuses. And again, there is that common rhetorical deployment of flat or declining trends as if they were evidence that the magnitude of the problem is insignificant: even truly horrific levels of school violence, by this logic, would be dismissed if they were lower than even worse levels in the past.

Like others in the mode of risk denial, Stossel also attempts to undercut the significance of school shootings by pointing out that more young people are attacked outside of schools than within them: "Statistics show that kids are twice as likely to be victims of violence away from school than they are in school." But again, Stossel has conflated general data on youth violence with the specific question of mass school shootings: and more importantly, the mere fact that the risk is even worse *out* of school cannot tell us, by itself, that it is negligible *in* school. The reality is that young Americans are vastly more likely to be victims of deadly violence, especially gun violence, than their counterparts in other advanced industrial societies (Grynshteyn and Hemenway 2016): the fact that they suffer more of that deadly violence on the street is hardly a case for the safety of America's youth, but that is precisely what Stossel makes of it.

The "actual truth," he told his audience, is that "America is safer than almost any country in human history." That "actual truth," of course, is an actual fabrication: again, the defining fact about American violence is, and has been for some time, that the level of violent death in this country far outstrips that in every other advanced industrial society on the planet. Stossel ends by quoting approvingly a psychologist who warns against the "ultimate misperception" that "America is in terrible straits and our schools are a mess and they're violent" (Stossel 2007). As this suggests, risk denial in the American context often reflects a deeply ideological slant, one that is sometimes based, as in Stossel's case, on a familiar anti-government conservatism, but is also sometimes rooted in a quintessentially

American form of liberalism that has similarly deep roots in our historic distaste for "government."

This is complicated in the case of mass shootings because there has also been a strong response among liberals that sees these incidents as an argument for more, rather than less, intervention by government. But risk denial often appears here too, since this response tends to selectively favor some explanations, and some remedies, while ignoring—or refusing to confront—others. Among some liberal commentators in the United States, there has been an almost visceral discounting of the potential role of mental illness in helping to account for these mass shootings: it is virtually sacrilegious to suggest that anything other than our lax gun control policies has anything to do with the plague of public mass violence we've recently experienced. Invoking the idea that many of the shooters are really very disturbed people is seen as either misguided, or a ploy on the part of the political right to deflect our attention from the crying need for more stringent gun regulations—and/or as an egregious form of "othering" of the mentally ill, the demonization of people most of whom will never engage in serious violence of any kind.

In the wake of the high school shooting in Parkland, Florida, in 2018—notable, as we'll see, for catalyzing a nationwide student-led movement against gun violence—one mental health advocate wrote that "the linkage between mass violence and mental illness is a red herring—misleading and grossly distorted" (Moutier 2018). The predictable spurious quantification is brought to bear: "less than 5%" of violent acts in the United States are "attributable to mental illness": much violence, indeed, is actually domestic violence in the home, which is a "much more common form of violence than mass public shootings." The latter point is certainly true, but, again, cannot by itself serve to diminish the unique impacts of school shootings. The writer goes on deploy the common trope that since not everyone who is mentally ill commits acts of violence, there is no credible connection between violence and mental illness: "most people" who suffer from an array of diagnosable mental disorders "do not exhibit violent behavior." Again, of course, the logic is spurious: it is also true that most people who smoke will not die of lung cancer, but it would be hard to find serious medical researchers who would deny the connection. Moreover, this kind of blanket dismissal obscures the reality that some kinds of mental illness are more likely to be related to mass shootings than others: one recent study, for example, estimates that while anxiety disorders are less prevalent among shooters than in the general population, the prevalence of "schizophrenia spectrum" disorders is nearly 10 times as high (Meszaros 2017).

The writer goes on to point out that the mentally ill are more likely than the general population to be *victims* of violence, and more likely to be victims than perpetrators of violent acts. But while that is surely important to know, it cannot alone invalidate the role of mental disturbance in the mass shootings that have wracked the United States in the twenty-first century. The writer's desire to counter the stigma that burdens the mentally ill is understandable: "Debunking the myth that links violence to mental illness is just one critical way we will make progress toward diminishing stigma, allowing community members to have accurate perceptions and practice more compassionate approaches to people with mental illness." All of those are worthy aims. That the mentally ill in the United States, as elsewhere, are often stereotyped and lumped together as uniformly dangerous is certainly true. But if the point is pushed too far, it once again flies in the face of everything we know about the nature of these shootings—many of which involve people who were reported again and again to official mental health agencies, without anything substantive ever happening to deflect what had often been perceived for years as a tragedy waiting to happen. All seven of the perpetrators of recorded mass shootings in America during 2012—which included the horrific slaughter of 20 small children and 6 adults at Sandy Hook Elementary School in Newtown, Connecticut—had demonstrated "prior signs of mental health issues" (Follman et al. 2019).

We *could* use these tragedies as teachable moments to illuminate the reality that our mental health system is broken and grossly underresourced in our present age of increasingly heedless austerity, and that many people are hurt as a result: most of all the mentally ill themselves, but also those harmed by people who needed real help that they did not get. Yet making this connection is often explicitly rejected by the purveyors of risk denial. A recent opinion piece in the *Washington Post* by a Yale medical historian urges us to "stop focusing on the mental health of mass shooters," and on the corollary need to "mend" a "broken mental health system." After all, "decades of research have shown that mental illness accounts for only a small proportion of violent crimes:" by linking mass shooting to "debates about mental health," we are "perpetuating the stereotype of the mentally ill as violent and the stigma that this already vulnerable group must contend with on a daily basis" (Doroshow 2019). Again, the strategic non sequitur is apparent: the role of mental illness in violent crimes generally may be relatively small, but when it comes to mass, indiscriminate shootings—the issue on the table—it is demonstrably not.

Denying that connection shifts our gaze from one of the most striking examples of preventable social neglect and governmental failure in the United States today. Just as structural pressures have escalated the levels of trauma, insecurity, and desperation that we know can exacerbate some kinds of mental illness, we have been busily hollowing out the institutions that might do something about it. In much of the country, there has been a steady retreat from investment in publicly accessible mental health care, and especially preventive care, which has meant that the criminal justice system has become the default provider of the minimal and mostly reactive care that does exist. In California, as a recent editorial in the *Los Angeles Times* (2019) notes, "For most people there is simply no entryway into care, treatment or recovery except through the criminal justice system." This is an invitation to tragedy and needless misery, and an example of a kind of systemic failure that appears again and again in the institutions of deregulated late capitalist societies. We should be putting this failure on the table as an important political issue. Too often, we don't. Framing the issue as mental illness versus guns, moreover, obscures what should be obvious: far from being mutually exclusive explanations of the tragedy of mass shootings, both unaddressed mental illness *and* lax gun regulation are part of the problem—and both reflect the larger failure of a neglectful and irresponsible social order to deliver elementary security.

There is much more to be said, but let me just conclude with some propositions that I think are important in thinking about risk going forward:

First, we need to step away from the regrettable tendency to discount the reality of some kinds of risk in contemporary society and to disparage those people who are angry and fearful in the face of the pervasive insecurity that surrounds them. That certainly doesn't mean that we shouldn't point out exaggerations of risk when they occur. But we need to replace the default response with a more careful, respectful, and empathic effort to meet people's sense of anxiety "where they are," and to offer a response and an analysis that both takes those fears seriously and provides well-articulated, credible, and progressive remedies.

We also need to rethink the view that what we're witnessing in contemporary advanced societies is an increasing effort—and an essentially utopian one—to "eliminate" risk in our social life. I think that, in important ways, this view has it backward. We are actually living in an era in which, more and more, we are being asked to accept as normal risks that in fact are neither normal nor necessary—dangers that we actually have the material resources and technological capacity to remedy, or at least to substantially reduce, and that therefore could be characterized as "excess" or "surplus" risks. The level of risk that we are asked to believe is normal in the United States today, for example—whether we are talking about interpersonal violence or so-called natural disasters or the deadly consequences of crumbling or exploding infrastructure, or the outsized risks of maternal mortality or homelessness—those "excess" levels of risk are collectively a hallmark of the increasingly heedless and predatory version of capitalism that we live under in America, a signal of profound and all too predictable social failure.

I believe that this failure—that wide disparity between our human, material, and technological potential to build a safer and more secure society and the reality of continuing, and sometimes increasing, danger and insecurity—is one of the defining social issues of our time. And it offers an opening for fundamental social action—if we are willing to seize it. That disparity creates a real possibility of uniting people around the idea that they can live with far less insecurity, far less fear, far less anxiety for themselves and their children than they now suffer—and that they *deserve* to. The failure to seize that opportunity, however, and to respond empathically and thoughtfully to the real anxieties of ordinary people in a needlessly insecure world, cedes the terrain to people whose language may suggest concern but whose policies systematically undercut the fundamental structures on which real security depends. In Donald Trump's America and in many other places around the world, responses to those anxieties marked by repression, exclusion, and neglect flourish in the absence of a clear, forcefully articulated, and broadly disseminated progressive structural analysis of where those risks come from (cf. Winlow et al. 2017).

We are beginning to see some instances of grassroots action against needless insecurity, sometimes coming from unexpected places—places where we hadn't seen it before. One of the most inspiring examples is the mobilization of young people, high school students and others, across the United States to challenge the inevitability of school shootings—and more broadly, to challenge the idea that our absence of rudimentary gun regulation is a fact of life, a reflection of hard political realities that we are powerless to change. That youthful movement is a work in progress, to be sure. But it stands as an intriguing example of a revolt against "excess" insecurity from below—one that puts squarely on the table the insistence that the threat of being attacked by a gunman in your high school is not inevitable, and not accidental—that it is not something that young people should have to live with, and that it is the product of human decisions (or the lack of them) on the part of people who are in a position of power and who, whatever their protestations to the contrary, could use that power in ways that would save lives, bodies, and minds. It is a movement that insists that the school should not be automatically assumed, in a modern society, to be a place of fear and existential uncertainty, and that it is possible to take action to reduce those threats—a movement that, in its own words, "calls bullshit" on politicians who say that nothing of substance can be done. And it has probably done more to begin to move the needle on our country's shameful gun policies than anything else in recent memory.

When we deny the reality or the seriousness of this kind of system-generated risk, on the other hand, we let a fundamentally toxic social order "off the hook": we tacitly remove the system's accountability for some of its most destructive consequences, and we miss the chance to call others to look harder and more critically at its fundamental principles of operation. Most importantly, perhaps, we lose an opportunity to instigate a vibrant dialogue about the potential alternatives—miss the opportunity of a "teachable moment." Risk denial, in short, cheats us out of the chance to shape a better and more secure future.

References

Currie, E (2019). "Getting crime right: framing everyday violence in the age of Trump." In Walter S. DeKeseredy and Elliott Currie, eds., *Progressive justice in an age of repression: strategies for challenging the rise of the right*. London and New York: Routledge, pp. 61–72.

Donnermeyer, J (2019). "Social change and drugs: rural American and the rise of Donald Trump." In Walter S. DeKeseredy and Elliott Currie, eds., *Progressive justice in an age of repression: strategies for challenging the rise of the right*. London and New York: Routledge, pp. 42–60.

Doroshow, D (2019). "We need to stop focusing on the mental health of mass shooters." *Washington Post*, May 20.

Follman, M, Aronsen G, and Pan D (2019). "U.S. mass shootings, 1982–2019: data from Mother Jones' investigation." *Mother Jones Magazine*. Retrieved from https://www.motherjones.com/politics/2012/12/mass-shootongs-mother-jones-full-data/, June 27.

Grynshteyn, E, and Hemenway D (2016). "Violent death rates: the U.S. compared with other high-income OECD countries." *American Journal of Medicine*, 129 (3), 266–273.

Healy, S, and Margolis, G (2012). "Myth: college campuses are unsafe." *The Presidency*, American Council on Education, Spring. Retrieved from www.acenet.edu, April 2019.

Krugman, P (2018). "A party defined by its lies." *New York Times*, November 1.

Los Angeles Times. (2019). "No retreat on mental health." *Editorial*, June 11.

Merkel, I, and Pittari, M (2019). Guns, crime, and corruption: Bolsonaro's first month in office." *NACLA Newsletter*, February 7.

Meszaros, J (2017). "Falling through the cracks: the decline of mental health care and firearm violence." *Journal of Mental Health*, 26 (4), 359–365.

Moutier, C (2018). "Debunking the myth of violence and mental illness." *American Foundation for Suicide Prevention*, March 7. Retrieved from https://afsp.org.

Stossel, J (2007). "The school violence myth." *ABC News*, April 18. Retrieved from abcnews.go.com.

Winlow, S, Hall, S, and Treadwell, T (2017) *The rise of the right: English nationalism and the transformation of working-class politics*. Bristol, UK: Policy Press.

Millennials and the New Penology: Will Generational Change in the U.S. Facilitate the Triumph of Risk Rationality in Criminal Justice

Jonathan Simon

Introduction: Did the New Penology Skip a Generation?

A number of social scientists observing changes in U.S. criminal justice practices from the 1970s through the late 1980s saw a new penal mentality focused on the rational assessment of risk emerging as a possible framework for criminal justice policy (Cohen 1985; Reichman 1986; Feeley and Simon 1992, 1994). The high cost of prison population growth seemed likely to push governments to look for ways to diminish jail and prison sentences and utilize risk assessment tools, drawing on social science methods that seemed a promising way to reframe the tough on crime politics that had dominated the 1980s (Greenwood and Abrahamse 1982). By the late 1990s, however, it was pretty clear that US

J. Simon (✉)
Lance Robbins Professor of Criminal Justice Law, UC Berkeley,
Berkeley, CA, USA
e-mail: jssimon@berkeley.edu

© The Author(s) 2020
J. Pratt, J. Anderson (eds.), *Criminal Justice, Risk and the Revolt against Uncertainty*,
Palgrave Studies in Risk, Crime and Society,
https://doi.org/10.1007/978-3-030-37948-3_14

penal policies were not following the logics of rational risk management but those of penal populism and zero tolerance toward crime, or even disorder (e.g., Wilson and Kelling 1982). Prison and jail populations continued to grow through the turn of the twenty-first century. Only the Great Recession of 2008 capped growth, with a modest reduction in the incarcerated population since 2011. Forced (unlike the federal system) to balance their budgets annually, and facing a multi-year gap of major proportions, political leaders had little choice but to undertake cuts in criminal justice expenses despite the possible political retaliation by the voters (Aviram 2015).

In recent years however, and even with the return of fiscal health to most states, risk management approaches to crime seem to finally be catching on. From policing, to bail reform, to sentencing, risk instruments—now anchored in algorithms and machine learning—are being championed as ways to reduce reliance on incarceration and aggressive policing. While it may yet again be premature to pronounce a "new penology" at hand, the change in receptivity toward a risk-based rationality for governing crime and away from penal populism (and governing through crime) itself raises an important question of penal and social change. What makes today's public more open to risk rationales in crime control than the publics of the 1980s and 1990s? This chapter considers one factor that could be important in explaining what seems to be a major shift in crime policies: "cohort" or "generational" effects on the politics of crime.

Students of fear of crime have recognized that "cohort," along with "period" and "age" effects, can help explain changes in fear of and attitudes toward crime (Cohen 2011; Gray et al. 2018; Simon 2017). As people age, their sense of vulnerability to crime changes, with the young being generally less afraid and the old more (despite the opposite risk distribution of victimization). Periods when crime is low, e.g., England and Wales after World War I (Knepper 2015) and the United States since the mid-1990s (Zimring 2006), may be expected to lead to less fear of crime for people of all ages and cohorts.

Cohort may be thought of as a hybrid of age and period. Sociologists have long argued that generations create important dividing lines in social experience and political imagination (Mannheim 1927; Milkman

2018). As "people travel through life with some of the political anxieties and beliefs that they were exposed to in their formative years … [t]heir formative experiences shape both their own response to pressing social issues (such as crime) and the practical and police responses they pursue" (Gray et al. 2018, 456). These effects may endure across the life course, overcoming period and aging effects that come in later adulthood (although one might expect some influence of these latter periods). The general thesis that I wish to explore here is that cohort effects may be especially significant in trying to explain broad changes in penal sensibilities and policies, such as the delayed rise of rational risk logic for criminal justice. As the authors of a recent empirical article showing evidence for a rise in utilitarian reasoning associated with Millennials (also relevant to our argument) bluntly put it: "Most cultural change is driven by cohort effects that withstand substantial variability over periods … [H]istorical change in moral attitudes and values, in particular, stems from processes of cohort replacement more than conversion" (Hannikainen et al. 2018). I offer a historical-cultural hypothesis for why Boomers rejected rational risk logics when it came to crime and why Millennials appear to be more open to it.

Looking at "period effects" on generational imaginaries reveals striking differences in the political landscape in which crime was experienced by Baby Boomers, (those born in 1946–1964), compared to Millennials, (those born in 1981–1996) (PEW 2019), these distinct cohorts as they entered young adulthood. Boomers entered adulthood from the late 1960s through the late 1980s, as violent crime in America reached and remained at historic highs and became a privileged focus of governance (Simon 2007). Millennials, in contrast, have entered adulthood over the past twenty years during the historic crime decline, when the politics of "tough on crime" have been challenged, if not replaced, by the politics of criminal justice reform.

Specifically, I believe that the major signal crimes, that is, repetitive routine crimes, or highly publicized major crimes—that criminologists have argued carry disproportionate weight in shaping public attitudes toward crime policies (Innes 2014)—of the two generations may have created quite distinctive penal sensibilities. Perhaps most importantly, the key signal crimes of the Millennial transition to adulthood have loosened the linkage between crime and two contexts that have historically driven punitive sensibilities in the United States: Black communities and central areas of large cities. I suggest that these differences help explain why Boomers were more amenable to penal populism (Pratt 2007) while Millennials are more open to risk as a penal logic.

Crime and Generations

Sociologists have argued that generations are not simply demographic patterns, but historical ones (Mannheim 1927; Grasso et al. 2019). A generation is forged by proximity between people at the same stage of life within the same history. Important events associated with social ruptures can constitute a generation with enduring fears and sensibilities. Once, perhaps, when societies were more stable, generational differences were subtle or non-existent and identity more consistently shaped by the rituals of the life course itself. But in the volatile course of modernity, there are few periods not marked by a major war, a global economic crisis, or disease threat. Different societies can be expected to generate distinct meanings associated with their cohorts. The analysis offered here applies specifically to the United States.

Generation or cohort effect can offer a promising way to think about one of the recurring puzzles of punishment and society research: why major shifts in punitiveness occur in the same society over time. Durkheim (2014/1893 original) assumed that penal sensibilities were among the slowest to change since they reflected the deepest and most settled social values.[1] Generational cleavages in the social landscape in which those values are experienced, however, can lead established sensibilities about penal sanctions to be up-ended (Garland 2001) as institutional and political power passes to a new generation. A generation's early adult experiences and awareness of crimes, along with social reactions to crime and political socialization about crime, create a distinctive generational sensibility that can endure even as crime and penal politics change. Normally this should lead to subtle changes in crime policies given all the other likely influences, but when the generations are particularly outsized, and the experiences of crime and state violence provide strong signals, those changes can be significant over a short period of time (Garland 2001).

From this perspective, Boomers and Millennials in the US offer promising differences in their crime socialization.[2] Boomers became adults in the 1970s and 1980s as crime rose and stayed high. Highly alarming "signal crimes" (Innes 2014) received significant attention from the media and took place against a background of urban crisis and racialized violence while politicians made "law and order" into a national consensus. Millennials, in contrast, have come into adulthood during a sustained crime decline in the United States that has brought crime in most places to the lowest levels for more than half a century. In this chapter I offer the hypothesis that Millennial signal crimes, set against a period of urban resurgence and a reduction in the aggressive war on drugs against Black communities, point toward very different penal behaviors and sensibilities, both at the personal and political levels. While I can only offer cultural evidence for this at the present, it may be possible to empirically test this hypothesis using surveys or experiments.

Signal Crimes

There is little doubt that American Millennials have entered adulthood after a historic crime decline, and surveys suggest that fear of crime overall has diminished since the early 1990s (although generational breakdowns are unavailable in publicly available reports). This could lead Millennials to assign less importance to crime in their view of problems overall (in fact, crime has rarely broken into the top shelf of American problems in national surveys) and to be more open to the kinds of trade-offs in crime policies facilitated by risk rationalities. But perhaps just as importantly, those crimes that do receive extensive publicity and can operate to shape how people think and feel about crime and how they change their behavior with more specificity, what criminologists have called "signal crimes" (Innes 2014), seem to be quite different between the Boomer and Millennial generations.

Criminologists have argued that "fear of crime" is too monolithic a conception of the way perceptions of crime shape peoples' lives and national sensibilities, and that different crimes in different conditions can generate different reactions, both social and individual (Innes 2014). Of particular significance to policy shifts are what Martin Innes (2014) has called "signal crimes"; certain kinds of crime or disorder operate as signals, both in the sense that they establish a level of awareness or attention that can and does fade with time, and in the way that they can help condense a substantive message about places, even nations. They become signals for what people should worry about, how they should feel about themselves and their communities, and how they should live. Signal crimes can include many different offenses and contexts, but they often involve victims that are particularly unambiguous in their victim-hood and particularly sympathetic, and acts of violence that have an element of spectacle to them.

Signal crimes can operate at the very micro- or local level, where particular crimes carry a strong message to people in the vicinity or social network, triggering shifts in perception and behavior that become embedded through repetition and are influential in shaping perceptions of the place. Signal crimes can also operate on a more macro-level, especially when highly publicized by mass media (and today, social media), where they can help shape not just crime policies but the broader political imaginary (Innes 2014; Simon 2007).

Recent empirical research by Gray et al. (2018) on the British Crime Survey has provided some evidence for just such nationally publicized and politicized signal crime effects at the cohort level. Using multiple years of the British Crime Survey, and controlling for age and period effects as well as a host of variables shown to raise crime fear for particular offenses, the researchers showed that generation, or cohort, mattered independently and in directions consistent with what they describe as "political socialization." Compared to a reference group of those who came of age before World War II, all other generations had higher levels of concern about crimes particularly associated with the rise in crime rates beginning in the late 1960s and including burglary, mugging/robbery, and car theft (447). Those who became adults in the 1960s and 1970s (which they call, following the British Prime Minister of the time, the "Wilson/Callaghan" generation), and those who did so in the 1980s and 1990s (the "Thatcher/Major" generation) showed the highest levels of worry about domestic burglary, "which is salient, given the fact that the Thatcher generation 'came of age' during the dramatic rise in property crime during the 1980s and the attendant focus on 'law and order' by politicians" (447). Those from the 1970s, the Wilson/Callaghan generation (the one most closely aligned with Baby Boomers as defined by PEW for the US), expressed the highest level of worry about robbery/muggings which, as the authors note, are the very crimes that Stuart Hall and his colleagues (1978/2013) documented as the subjects of a sustained and highly racialized political and media response contributing to the emergence of the Thatcher era. The "New Labour" generation, who came of age during 1997–2007 (which spans Generation X and Millennials for the U.S.), showed the highest levels of concern about "antisocial behavior," a focus of politicians and the media from the late Major years, which greatly expanded under Tony Blair's New Labour governments (2018, 449).

Similar research has yet to be done for the United States, but I offer a qualitative review of the most publicized and politicized U.S. crimes of Boomers and Millennials. In particular, the signal crimes relate very differently to two contexts that have historically been triggers or amplifiers of punitive responses to crime: Black communities and central cities. My argument here is that these signal crimes, if they indeed prove to be as salient for the Millennial generation, are consistent with the prediction that Millennials are generally more receptive to and accepting of a risk rational approach to crime policy.

Boomer Signals

Much has already been written on the signal crimes of mid- to late-twentieth century and the "culture of a high crime society" they created in the U.S. and elsewhere (Garland 2001; Simon 2014; Miller 2016). The signal crimes of the Boomers were not only alarming (which signal crimes always are) but also carried strong messages in terms of what (or who) to fear, what to feel, and how to behave, which shaped both the life-world of the urban poor and also the newly fortified urban and suburban landscape (Davis 1990/2006; Low 2004; Simon 2007). Importantly, they were seen against the backdrop of rapid deindustrialization and middle-class flight to segregated suburbs, which situated violent crime in a context of racialized urban crisis.

The focus on Black crime in the 1960s had a far longer genealogy, dating back to the eugenics movement in the early twentieth century, which deeply influenced criminology and criminal justice policy in its premise of race-based criminality (Muhammad 2011) and even earlier, fears of slave rebellions. What was distinctive about Black crime as a signal crime for Baby Boomers was its connection to an urban crisis largely generated by federal policies, and a national commitment to battle crime on a war-like footing that began in the late 1960s and targeted Black urban communities (Simon 2007; Hinton 2016). Boomers did not necessarily lead this war on crime (although from Clinton on, they would), as they were far from power at the time it began, but they were the generation most shaped by it.

Signal crimes point in cognitive, affective, and behavioral directions. For Boomers the key signal crimes were shocking acts of violence that directed fear at Black men and at liberal crime policies (e.g., those that permitted prison furloughs and allowed prisoners to seek rights). They directed feelings toward "dog whistle" racism and heated populist penal expressions. They directed behavior toward precautionary residential and consumption choices (including gated suburbs and shopping malls) and aggressive, punitive crime control strategies.

The single best-known figure may have been Willy Horton, the Massachusetts prisoner whose "furlough turned crime spree" became a center piece of Vice President George H. W. Bush's campaign for President in 1988, just as the youngest Baby Boomers began their transition to adulthood (Hinton 2016). Years earlier Horton absconded during a furlough from a prison sentence for murder. Horton went on a crime spree, ultimately kidnapping a White couple in their home and raping the woman. Neither was killed, but the crime had all the elements of the strongest signal crimes for Americans (vulnerable White victims, an attack in the home, and a violent Black criminal). Although the attack may have been a signal crime at the local or state level, it wasn't until its elevation by Bush's campaign manager, and the focus of intense media attention, that Horton's crime became a textbook signal crime for the late 1980s. The policy debate in the campaign almost instantly shifted from the Reagan era difficulties in the economy (with its emerging inequalities), to the question of each candidate's readiness to protect ordinary (White) citizens against crime and a focus on the death penalty and tougher prison sentences. Democratic nominee Michael Dukakis, whose reliance on statistical arguments about the death penalty's deterrence effects to explain his opposition to it, epitomized a risk rational approach to crime. Bush's response, a full-throated embrace of harsh punishment, gave penal populism its biggest national stage. Bush's substantial victory was in large part credited to differences on crime, and across the country, the national embrace of capital punishment and mandatory prison sentences for crimes associated with Black communities reached its zenith.

Millennial Signals

The Millennials began to enter adulthood with the new millennium (thus their generational tag), a period noted to have one of the historically lowest levels of all crime, including violent crime. But low levels of crime, even violent, still leaves plenty of potential for signal crimes (although it may influence how their signal is interpreted). At the national level, the US has had many well-publicized signal crimes from the turn of the century, but these crimes and their signals seem remarkably different from those of the Boomers. The message they carry about how to behave and think about crime, and government more generally, are also strikingly different.

Perhaps the defining signal crime of the era occurred on September 11, 2001, just as the first Millennials were entering their twenties. The terrorist attacks of that day took place on civil airliners and culminated in mass casualties of both passengers and people on the ground in New York City, in Washington, D.C., and the location in rural Pennsylvania where the third aircraft crashed due to the resistance of its passengers. Few crimes can match this as a national signal leading to changes in both behavior and meaning, and nearly two decades later, it has not altogether faded.

No one who enters an airport needs reminding how much our routines of behavior have changed, and a global war on terror has produced perhaps an irreversible change in the level of governmental surveillance, both global and domestic. Yet the signal of 9/11 suggests very different messages than the major signal crimes of the late twentieth century.

Although two of the three sites of mass death were in central urban areas (iconic ones), no one then or since interpreted these as "urban crimes." The major response of the security state has included foreign wars and global digital surveillance, not a major increase in the policing of Black or Brown urban neighborhoods or the incarceration of their residents.[3] It is true that the "war on terror" has in its own right racialized others, especially people of the Muslim faith (from everywhere) and people from the Middle or Near East. The recent "Muslim ban" imposed by the Trump administration shows that this signal retains its racializing power, but such exclusionary tactics have thus far shown little capacity to generate culture-wide fear or resulting behavioral changes comparable to the racialized fear of violence in the 1970s.[4]

Another type of crime that has arguably become a major signal crime for the Millennial period is those that involve mass shootings, particularly in schools or campuses. These occurred in the twentieth century as well, but, beginning with the shootings at Columbine High School in Colorado in 1999, these events have captured the national attention. Like those of September 11, these events show clear significance as signal crimes, shaping behavior and focusing fears, but in very different directions than the signal crimes of the Boomer coming-of-age era. While armed violence is a consistency, mass shootings have typically involved powerful semi-automatic weapons, not the handguns that characterized most urban signal crimes of the late twentieth century. Perhaps most importantly, the hands holding these weapons have typically been White (almost never Black), and not strangers, but often former or current students at the very schools. The typical site has been suburban rather than urban, and middle class rather than associated with poverty (where school shootings are often a very real risk but draw little national attention). Interestingly, much of the policy debate generated by these events, led by Millennials and even younger citizens, has emphasized gun control rather than punitive criminal sanctions (the killers have frequently died at their own hands during the crime).

Let us highlight one final signal crime in the U.S. during the early twenty-first century—the illegal distribution (or repurposing) of opiate drugs and the alarmingly high resultant levels of opiate overdose deaths in recent years. Although empirical studies are yet few, media assessment has been that the opiate crisis has drawn a decidedly less punitive, and even less criminal, response than the alarming rise in violence associated with "crack" cocaine of the 1980s and heroin in the 1960s (Boomer signal crimes as well). There have been some prosecutions for homicide against people who simply sold or provided the lethal drugs to victims. Other efforts have focused on prosecuting doctors and pharmacists for profiting from distribution crimes. But few, if any, new laws have been passed to enhance sentences for opiate crimes, and the police have not been aggressively deployed against opiate sellers. Instead, the goal of saving lives by fighting overdoses, treating survivors, and encouraging harm reduction for users has gained far more ground than ever before in the U.S. If opiate abuse is a Millennial signal crime, it's one that seems to signal almost the opposite of Boomer directions: trust in government and concern for strangers.

Some observers have seen this as a function of the racialization of these drug crises. Crack was associated with Black neighborhoods and especially high poverty areas. Opiate deaths have been associated with White areas, often small towns or rural areas, experiencing their own sort of economic marginalization. This seems likely and important to the meaning of opiates as a crime problem. But just because the opiate crisis is not a "moral panic" leading to a hostile and moralizing punitiveness does not mean it is not functioning as a signal crime, one that influences both behavior and meanings associated with crime (Innes 2014). If it proves to be a signal crime for Millennials, the opiate crisis may signal a deeper turn back toward penal welfarism than might have otherwise been predicted without taking generation into account.

Overall, the Millennial signal crimes point in contrasting directions to those of the Boomers. They point away from Black communities and toward alienated White people or foreign terrorists. They point away from large cities, which are enjoying a rebound, particularly in their central areas, and toward suburbs or rural areas. If they carry behavioral lessons, they're controversial, involving gun control, drug treatment, and prevention of radicalization.

Part of what shapes the meaning of a signal crime is the more or less independent developments in other prominent social contexts that are tightly connected to them (Hall 1978/2013). The signal crimes of the Boomers, ones that helped trigger penal populism and rejection of risk rational approaches to crime policy, were widely interpreted against the background of two related "crises," racialized violence and the rapid decline of certain neighborhoods in the biggest American cities. In the following sections, I consider evidence which shows how Millennial signal crimes are positioned in terms of these previously influential intervening variables.

Racial Signals

The signal crimes of the Boomer coming-of-age period were situated against a background of civil rights activism and episodes of violence with racial meanings. In contrast, Millennials have come of age at a time when signal crimes point away from Black neighborhoods and when state violence against Blacks has been its own sort of signal crime. The fact that the Millennials themselves are considerably more diverse than Boomers[5] may be a contributing factor. In this chapter, I focus on how the signal crimes of the two generations vary in the lessons they seem to provide about race, and in particular, the link between Black people and other minorities, and the threat of crime.

As discussed above, the signal crimes of the Boomer coming-of-age carried a strong focus on Black crime. While this was not new, it was set against a historic shift in civil rights and urban stratification. One set of key signal crime events was uprisings in the Black neighborhoods of Los Angeles, Detroit, Newark, and other large cities in the 1960s (Hinton 2016). These mostly died out in the 1970s, although there were sequels: 1980 in Miami, 1991 in Los Angeles. These episodes, sparked by police harassment, released anger over decades of semi-legal discrimination in housing and employment, as well as previous episodes of White vigilante violence backed up by racially directed policing. As media spectacles, however (some of the first, along with Moon shots and Presidential assassinations), they emphasized armed Black communities burning and looting White businesses and fighting with police and military forces. The studious riot commission reports that followed paid significant attention to the underlying social justice issues, but the policy response was a war on crime (Hinton 2016).

Prison uprisings, particularly the Attica prison uprising of 1971, seem to have been a second layer of racially charged signal crime events that shaped sensibilities in the 1970s. Historian Heather Thompson (2017) argues persuasively that Attica focused the nation on prisoners, re-characterizing them as mostly minorities and falsely stigmatized them as brutally violent and irrationally aggressive (which turned out to be true not of the inmates, but of the response of state actors).

The racialized threat messages of these events as publicized combined with the general rise in violent deaths (Miller 2016) to turn Boomers as a generation toward penal populism and away from concern with racial injustice in American governmental institutions. In a careful effort to examine both cohort and age effects using multiple waves of the General Social Survey, Sociologist Ruth Milkman (2017) compared the political values of Boomers and Millennials. When posed with the statement: "Government has a special obligation to help Blacks," Boomers were modestly more positive in their response than Millennials are when they were equivalent ages (27.6 percent agreeing among Boomers in the 1970s, compared to 20.1 percent among Millennials in 2017). But aging and/or period effects moved Boomers to less than half that level (13.6 percent) by 2014, making contemporary Millennials more concerned about racial justice, or "woke," to use the contemporary colloquialism intended to express almost precisely that sentiment (Milkman 2018). PEW data shows a similar gap, with thirty-six percent of Boomers today agreeing that "discrimination is the main barrier to Blacks' progress," compared to fifty-two percent of Millennials. The key question, unanswerable now, is whether Millennial signal crimes that point away from Black communities as the locus of threat will forestall, or at least mitigate, a shift away from racial justice concerns, or whether Millennials will follow Boomers in an aging effect toward racial justice conservatism.

The Boomers' turn away from racial justice, and their rejection of risk rationality as it places limits on punitive sentences and policing, may be part of a common reaction to the major signal crimes of the late twentieth century which framed Black violence as a distinctive threat to White middle-class security, and made the issue of crime in Black communities central to public debates about sentencing, prisons, the death penalty, and policing. The long history of racialization of crime and criminalization of race in the United States, particularly for Black people, has forged a link so strongly between "Black" as a social category and crime that cognitive psychologists now describe Blackness as a prototype for crime. Studies have documented "bidirectional" priming, showing that thinking about Black people raises the salience of crime and thinking about crime raises the salience of Black people (Eberhardt et al. 2004). Boomer signal crimes magnified this historical threat by locating it in the context of a broader urban crisis. The response, a national commitment to governing through crime, resulted in a massive increase in the already marked concentration of the penal state on Black communities.

Crime in the City

It is impossible to separate crime and race during the key Boomer coming-of-age period from a widespread perception of urban crisis. After peaking in population and industrial production during the Korean War in the early 1950s, most large cities in the Northeast and the Midwest, including icons like New York, Boston, Detroit, and Chicago, began losing population and well-paying industrial jobs to their suburban fringes and ultimately to both the lower labor cost "sunbelt" (the South and Southwest) and overseas outsourcing (Sugrue 2014). The result, evident from the late 1950s on in America's largest cities, included large blighted sections and a growing mismatch between working class jobs and the working class, especially Black working class, neighborhoods. The effects were particularly hard on Black people who had been segregated into the least desirable, most deteriorated inner-city neighborhoods during the mid-twentieth century, which were once at least proximate to industrial jobs but were now especially isolated from the new location of job growth in the suburbs.

At the same time, federal housing policy was reconstructing the urban landscape, with new, segregated suburbs of single-family homes drawing middle class White residents (and taxpayers) out of cities, and concentrating high-rise public housing for Black people in the now hollowing cores of the large cities (Rothstein 2017). This criminogenic and racialized landscape was further destabilized by "urban renewal" projects and freeway construction projects that destroyed traditionally Black neighborhoods and created a fragmented environment hostile to pedestrians and commercial development. By the late 1970s, cities had become synonymous with crime. The idea of the central city for many Boomers amounted to this: moving to the suburbs to escape from it or, if they never lived in the city, seeing it from a car on the way to and from an occasional trip to a museum or concert.[6]

Signal crimes pointed Boomers to central cities, and their streets, as places of extreme danger. While real crime in traditional downtown business districts was not unreasonably high, the image of the central city as a zone of danger dramatically undercut their once dominant role in local retailing. Many central business districts fought back, creating pedestrian malls and increasing police presence (Davis 1990/2006). But the commercial hub of the late twentieth century, before the internet, became the suburban mall, which could guarantee a controlled and largely segregated environment.

Since the turn of the century, large cities, especially their downtowns, have been enjoying a revival, with some enjoying heady population growth and most experiencing commercial reinvestment in their central districts. Millennials are recognizably a big part of this movement back to the cities (Myers 2016). A big part of this is the "sense of security" (Knepper 2015) that now exists in many central business districts after decades of falling crime and, in many cases, significant new commercial and residential development. Demographers continue to debate when or if Millennials will move to the suburbs, a transition historically associated with family formation and children (also delayed for Millennials compared to earlier generations). If they do, perhaps forced by housing prices in central cities, it is unlikely to be with the sense of fleeing a zone of intolerable danger or with an inclination to invest further in security as reflected in the gated communities of the 1990s that many of them grew up in (Low 2004).[7]

Home ownership is a closely related dimension. Boomers experienced the extraordinary run up of home prices and were for the most part able to take better advantage of it than previous or subsequent generations. The close proximity of urban crime and real estate losses was also a generational lesson as those left holding once prime, central city real estate suffered, and those investing on the fringe prospered. The harsh prison and policing policies of the late twentieth century reflect the preferences of Boomer homeowners living in the outer suburbs who wanted to minimize the crime risk, and even the appearance of risk, in their neighborhoods by incarcerating inner-city residents (Simon 2010).

While young people have historically been more attracted to cities and less drawn to suburbs than they have been when older with families, Millennials have been exceptionally crucial to the urban revival that has been occurring since the end of the last century, and seem to be remaining city-oriented, having yet to have families or move to suburbs at the rates expected by demographers (Myers 2016). With many of them coming of age during the housing market-based financial crisis of 2008, American Millennials are notably behind their predecessors in home ownership and many expect to remain renters (thus the recent political revival of rent control).

Cities, especially high-density rental neighborhoods, are natural places for risk rational policies around crime to find support. Harsh, zero tolerance policies can appeal to people in a gated suburb who view themselves as needing only the exclusion of others, but for those who depend on collective infrastructures, a rational approach to crime less dependent on incarceration or aggressive policing is attractive. Risk assessment tools appear likely to play a big role in legitimizing the remaining use of these methods from the perspective of urban Millennials, who are helping to elect a new vanguard of progressive big city prosecutors who rely heavily on the discourse of risk (Simon 2017).

From Fear to Dread

Many Millennials in the United States entered the adult labor market during the worst economic recession in decades. As young adults they saw those somewhat ahead of them in age losing their homes to mortgage foreclosures, and found getting a start on their own careers very difficult. As Milkman notes:

> Unlike Boomers, who came of age in a period of relatively abundant career opportunities, Millennials face a stagnant labor market with far more limited options. (2018, 9)

As a result of their own experience of precariousness, Millennials are considerably to the left of other adults on a range of social issues and the most politically active generation for their age in decades. They materialized electorally in 2008 behind Barack Obama, and their famous support for Bernie Sanders almost carried his long shot leftwing insurgent candidacy for the Democratic party's nomination to victory in 2016 (Milkman 2018).

It is not the economy alone that threatens Millennials. Climate change and the related likelihood of mass migrations and weather-related catastrophes pose an unprecedented kind of threat, especially to Millennials who will live out their adult lives as the crisis deepens. Political change in the form of ideological extremity in at least one of the two major political parties has led to a period of relative policy stagnation, while unprecedented economic inequality, abetted by Supreme Court decisions eliminating meaningful campaign finance restrictions, has created at least the appearance of a plutocracy at the top of government (grotesquely confirmed by President Trump's cabinet).

Boomers of course had existential threats of their own. During the Cold War between the United States and the then Soviet Union, the possibility of a nuclear exchange did threaten human survival. The Vietnam War also placed some older Boomers directly at risk of death and trauma while opposition to that war put other Boomers at risk of state violence. Environmental pollution was highly visible (and sometimes toxic) and the Boomers were one of the first generations to mobilize on behalf of the environment (seeking the youth vote, Richard Nixon declared the first Earth Day in 1971).

But the military threats to routine life were mitigated by the thawing of the Cold War in the 1970s. Early environmental laws (along with deindustrialization) seemed to improve the worst of the nation's pollution and more systemic environmental threats like climate change remained largely hidden to the public. In terms of social and economic prospects, the Boomers enjoyed perhaps the most propitious entry into adulthood of any generation of Americans before or since, and as a result, some Boomers are extremely wealthy or own homes worth far more than they ever expected to save. Fear of crime loomed as one of the few dark spots in this promising future. It probably pushed Boomers to the right on racial justice and toward behaviors and policies antagonistic to central cities. Concentrated as a culture of fear, anticipation of crime arguably became one of the dominant themes in Boomer America's political imaginary (Simon 2007).

If philosophically (not clinically) speaking, fear is the awareness that one may lose something dear to one in the world, and dread (or anxiety) is an awareness that one might lose the world[8] itself (Heidegger 1927), it seems plausible that Millennials are more sensitive to the latter. It would be overstating things to speak of a "culture of fear" giving way to a "culture of anxiety." Boomers have their own anxiety about the sustainability of their world (for some, channeled into xenophobia about immigrants). Millennials have their own fear of crime, but decoupled from its Boomer nexus with demonization of Black communities and central cities, it simply does not cast the same kind of shadow. More importantly, Millennials are concerned with whether the political "systems" necessary to sustainably manage the economy and protect the planet's climate can be salvaged. Crime is far less defining of the political meaning of the moment and the generation than it was for Boomers.

This balance of dread and fear makes Millennials a particularly receptive audience for a governmental rationality around crime based on risk rational approaches and methods. Perhaps this pragmatic spirit is what lies behind an interesting experimental finding from a unique double-wave experiment that examined attitudes toward utilitarian sacrifice hypotheticals (that explore the ethics of sacrificing a few to save many in situations like unavoidable motor collisions) almost ten years apart, allowing age and cohort effects to be distinguished (Hannikainen et al. 2018). The second wave showed somewhat higher acceptance of utilitarian sacrifice (with more calling it permissible across all birth cohorts) but especially for those born after 1990, later Millennials, who move from permissible toward obligatory in their moral analysis.

I lack the methods and data to test this hypothesis but I have an example from popular culture that can at least illustrate it—changes in the meaning-scape of the perennial box-office success in the United States (and I suspect globally): the zombie movie (Ozog 2013). Popular culture has long provided an important window into the fear landscapes and political imaginations of different generations. Hollywood, films, television, and now online streaming platforms profit by modeling contemporary fears in contexts that make their mastery enjoyable to large numbers of citizens—in that sense they are inherently sociological (Kracauer 1949/1959).

The zombie has operated as a very successful carrier of social fears since near the beginning of Hollywood's domination of mass entertainment (Ozog 2013). Its origins lie in perhaps the deepest racialized fear in the architecture of American insecurity, fear of slave rebellion, a fate epitomized for Americans of the nineteenth century by the Haitian revolution. Zombies were originally a signifier for Haiti, and served as a grotesque echo of slavery itself. Hollywood's first zombie movie was titled *White Zombie* (with Bela Legosi, the Jewish immigrant film star who became globally famous in the title role of Dracula). Then it was the Great Depression that provided the real social fear landscape for zombies as frightening entertainment.

But George Romero remade the zombie almost completely for Boomers in his iconic independently produced horror movie, *Night of the Living Dead* (1968). The background fears the film invokes are precisely the Boomer signal crimes: homicides, riots, racialized violence.[9] In *Night of the Living Dead* the dead rise and begin murdering the living, in assaults that look like slow motion riots, temporarily overwhelming civil authorities and leaving scrappy humans to find a way to survive together or alone. The zombie, a human-like creature but one with an insatiable and unreasonable hunger for violence, perfectly expressed the signal content of the Boomer signal crimes: the secure life of the American middle class can be turned upside down overnight by lawless individuals or groups who can overwhelm civil authority. Romero was interested in selling the temporary mastery of that fear (and playfully subverting some of its racial themes). But others would have policy answers to sell, a massive militarized buildout of the penal state.

This terrifying scenario was recreated by Romero and others through a number of successful late twentieth century sequels and imitations. In her fascinating master's thesis, sociologist Cassandra Ozog points to new trends in the enduring zombie entertainment space (which now includes a long running television series *The Walking Dead*). A good example of the Millennial turn in the genre is the 2009 film, *Zombieland*. Like many newer zombie stories, it is largely a comedy (which already suggests a significant shift in meaning). The movie tracks a "family" thrown together by necessity as they journey through a post-zombie-apocalypse America. The Millennial zombie stories share core features with the murderous walking dead of the Boomer category, but they differ in some illuminating features consistent with the claims I have made about Millennial fear of crime. First, the zombies are, generally speaking, a permanent problem in most contemporary zombie stories. The Boomers' zombie nightmare had an imaginable end, when civil authorities would come back and eliminate the remaining hordes of undead. In the Millennial version, the zombies are here to stay. In the meantime, civil society is largely broken down and still has to be reestablished through creating larger units of social trust. In the latter respect, many of the new zombie stories have a background hint of optimism in the ability of small groups of people to create solidarity, forge new family units, and rebuild society. The zombies themselves are still scary, but now they often have a backstory that allows us to see them more sympathetically, and points toward systemic threats like unregulated capitalism or technology rather than the monsters themselves, who can perhaps be made less dangerous.

If zombies are a metaphor for the fear of crime and violence in the cities of the late twentieth century, the new zombie movies suggest that Millennials are ready to live in those cities, perhaps not without fear but with a kind of pragmatic prudence, combining "terror and curiosity," as Ozog nicely puts it. That culture is exactly the *wrong* base for penal populism to thrive in, and, I would argue, fertile ground for risk-based penal logics.

Conclusion

A new penology, a way of rationalizing or governing crime based on risk, appears to be emerging in the United States a generation after it was predicted in the late twentieth century (Rothschild-Elyassi et al. 2019). This chapter offers a cohort or generational effect argument to explain that delay (Mannheim 1927; Milkman 2018). In brief, the new penology in the late twentieth century was ineffective at diverting a Boomer-led surge toward penal populism and mass incarceration. The greater success of risk rationalities for crime policy today, and promise for the future, lies in the rising political significance of the Millennial generation whose coming-of-age experiences with crime fear are quite different. The "signal crimes" (2014) of the Millennials, from terrorism and school shootings to opiate abuse and overdoses, are strikingly different from the signal crimes of the Boomers: urban and prison riots, robberies and homicides, all with their racialized overtones of urban crises. The effort to mount a new penology of risk rational policies aimed at reducing high levels of crime that were experienced in the United States during those decades, while limiting the cost, ran into penal populism: a generational shift in behavior and meaning that favored extreme measures in the name of "zero risk." While Millennials clearly care about crime, and have shown great activism on certain crimes, like sexual assault, this analysis of signal crimes suggests that they are less likely to see crime as defining of their time, but rather one among many threats in a complex political landscape of systemic threats like climate change, wealth inequality, and political paralysis.

These generational or cohort effects, if in fact valid, are part of a more complete picture that includes period effects as well. Today, the overextended penal state is facing a legitimacy crisis that was unanticipated in the 1990s. If risk rationality is now being promoted, it is in part because the penal state needs new anchors for its legitimacy, including science and technology. Prosecutors and police previously had little need to limit their own discretion by appealing to objective instruments. Today, faced with increasing skepticism and even hostility from the public over aggressive and racially marked practices of stops, arrests, and selective prosecution, the penal state and its leaders look to risk as a "smart on crime" basis for their choices. The response in 2014 to the killing of unarmed Black teenager Michael Brown by a White police officer led to nationwide protests, mostly by young people, and the emergence of a new civil rights movement under the slogan #BlackLivesMatter. While there has been some backlash since led by police unions and their political allies, the possibility of a shift in tolerance against police shootings is clear.

Where the two effects, a period of legitimacy deficit for the penal state and a generational shift in penal sensibilities, combine we will find penal policy changing fastest. It is, I would argue, no accident that so far the shift toward risk-based criminal justice is happening first and fastest in the large cities where Millennials are most disproportionately active. Still, if generational conversion is what it takes to replace penal populism with risk rational crime policies, change will be slow. Even after the 2016 election, which saw a record number of Millennials elected to Congress, PEW calculated that they now make up six percent of that federal law-making body, while Boomers are down to 53.7 percent. We can expect the decades ahead to be a mix of leftover Boomer policies (especially around violent crime) and new Millennial policies emphasizing a lighter penal hand guided by risk rationalities.

Notes

1. Durkheim seems to have come to see this as problematic and returned to the topic in his "Two Laws of Penal Evolution," where he offers some sources of shorter term changes in penal sensibilities (Durkheim 1903/1973).
2. PEW Research has cataloged considerable data on generational differences on their website. PEW defines Boomers as those born in 1946–1964, and Millennials as those born in 1981–1996. Their data also identifies the "Silent Generation" born in 1928–1945, and "Generation X" born in 1965–1980 and very recently, "Generation Z" born after 1997. I focus on Boomers and Millennials for reasons discussed but the PEW data suggests considerable continuity between Boomers and Generation X. https://www.pewresearch.org/topics/generations-and-age/.

3. Though anti-terrorism has become a major new theme in the policing of large cities (and especially places with symbolic or major tourism), it appears quite distinct from the aggressive style of crime suppression policing that began in the late twentieth century and has in many cases continued in the present although with increasing political controversy.

4. Of course the active armed parts of the war, in Iraq, Syria, and Afghanistan, involve very serious violence against Muslim civilians caught between US backed forces and militias fighting them.

5. Twice as likely to be non-White. https://www.pewsocialtrends.org/2018/11/15/early-benchmarks-show-post-millennials-on-track-to-be-most-diverse-best-educated-generation-yet/.

6. This may in fact be changing for some Boomers who are retiring back to the center attracted to lower crime rates, urban amenities, and access to reliable public transportation.

7. It will be interesting as affluent retiring Boomers return to central cities, often bidding up the price of neighborhoods beyond the reach of Millennials, with their late twentieth century security sensibilities. There could be a curious mutation as cities become even more securitized to satisfy their aging and affluent residents while the suburbs de-gate and attempt to urbanize to satisfy their Millennial residents.

8. By world here I'm following Martin Heidegger's usage in Being and Time to mean a comprehensive network of interconnecting practices, values, equipment, and physical infrastructures in which people can predictably live their lives.

9. Romero understood these racial meanings and cast a Black actor as the film's hero. Spoiler alert! He is killed at the end after surviving the apparently one-night zombie onslaught by a crew of White police officers who mistake him for a zombie and shoot him through the window of the house he has successfully sought refuge in.

References

Aviram, Hadar. 2015. *Cheap on Crime: Recession-Era Politics and the Transformation of American Punishment.* University of California Press.

Cohen, Stanley. 2011. *Folk devils and moral panics.* Routledge.

Cohen, Stanley. 1985. *Visions of social control: Crime, punishment and classification.* Cambridge: Polity Press.

Davis, Mike. 1990/2006. *City of Quartz: Excavating the Future in Los Angeles* (New Edition). Verso Books.

Durkheim, Emile. 1893/2014. *The division of labor in society.* Simon and Schuster.

Durkheim, Emile. "Two laws of penal evolution." *Economy and Society* 2.3 (1903/1973): 285–308.

Eberhardt, Jennifer L. et al. 2004. "Seeing black: race, crime, and visual processing." *Journal of personality and social psychology* 87.6: 876.

Feeley, Malcolm M., and Jonathan Simon. "The new penology: Notes on the emerging strategy of corrections and its implications." *Criminology* 30.4 (1992): 449–474.

Feeley, Malcolm, and Jonathan Simon. "Actuarial justice: The emerging new criminal law." *The Futures of Criminology* 173 (1994): 174.

Garland, David. 2001. *The Culture of Control: Crime and Social Order in Contemporary Society.* Chicago, IL: University of Chicago Press (2001)

Grasso, M., Farrall, S., Gray, E., Hay, C., & Jennings, W. (2019). Thatcher's Children, Blair's Babies, Political Socialization and Trickle-down Value Change: An Age, Period and Cohort Analysis. *British Journal of Political Science*, 49(1), 17–36. https://doi.org/10.1017/S0007123416000375

Gray, Emily, et al. "Political Socialization, Worry about Crime and Antisocial Behaviour: An Analysis of Age, Period and Cohort Effects." *The British Journal of Criminology* 59.2 (2018): 435–460.

Greenwood, Peter W., and Allan F. Abrahamse. *Selective incapacitation.* Santa Monica, CA: Rand, 1982.

Hall, S., Critcher, C., Jefferson, T., Clarke, J., and Roberts, B. 1978/2013. *Policing the crisis: Mugging, the state and law and order.* Macmillan International Higher Education.

Hannikainen, Ivar R., Edouard Machery, and Fiery A. Cushman. "Is utilitarian sacrifice becoming more morally permissible?" *Cognition* 170 (2018): 95–101.

Heidegger, Martin. 1927. *Being and Time.* Trans. John Macquarrie and Edward Robinson. New York: Harper (1962).

Hinton, Elizabeth. 2016. *From the War on Poverty to the War on Crime: The Making of Mass Incarceration.* Harvard University Press.

Innes, Martin. 2014. *Signal crimes: Social reactions to crime, disorder and control.* Oxford University Press.

Koehler, Johann A., Gil Rothschild-Elyassi, and Jonathan Simon. 2018. "The New Penology." In Heubner, Beth M. (ed.) *Oxford Bibliographies in Criminology.* Oxford University Press. Oxford, U.K.

Knepper, P. (2015). *Writing the History of Crime.* London: Bloomsbury.

Kracauer, Siegfried. 1949/1959. *From Caligari to Hitler: A psychological history of the German film*. Princeton University Press.

Low, Setha. *Behind the gates: Life, security, and the pursuit of happiness in fortress America*. Routledge, 2004.

Mannheim, Karl. 1927. "The Problem of Generations." In *Essays on the Sociology of Knowledge*. London, UK: Routledge & Kegan Paul.

Milkman, Ruth. 2017. A new political generation: Millennials and the post-2008 wave of protest. *American Sociological Review*, 82(1), 1–31.

Milkman, R. (2018). The Senior Precariat. *New Labor Forum*, 27(1), 44–52.

Miller, Lisa Lynn. 2016. *The Myth of Mob Rule: Violent Crime and Democratic Politics*. Oxford University Press.

Muhammad, Khalil Gibran. 2011. *The condemnation of blackness*. Harvard University Press.

Myers, Dowell. "Peak millennials: Three reinforcing cycles that amplify the rise and fall of urban concentration by millennials." *Housing Policy Debate* 26.6 (2016): 928–947.

Ozog, Cassandra Anne. 2013. *Fear rises from the dead: A sociological analysis of contemporary zombie films as mirrors of social fears*. Diss. Faculty of Graduate Studies and Research, University of Regina.

PEW Research Center. 2018. "Younger generations making up increasing share of US House," https://www.pewresearch.org/fact-tank/2018/11/21/millennials-gen-x-increase-their-ranks-in-the-house-especially-among-democrats/ft_18-11-16_congressgenerations_1/.

PEW Research Center. 2019. Defining Generations: Where Millennials End and Generation Z Begins, https://www.pewresearch.org/fact-tank/2019/01/17/where-millennials-end-and-generation-z-begins/.

Pratt, John. 2007. *Penal populism*. Routledge.

Reichman, Nancy. Managing crime risks: Toward an insurance based model of social control. *Research in Law, Deviance and Social Control* 8 (1986): 151–172.

Rothschild-Elyassi, Gil, Johann A. Koehler, and Jonathan Simon. 2019. "Actuarial Justice," in Deflem, Matthieu and Charles F. Wellford (eds.) *Handbook of Social Control. Wiley Handbooks in Criminology and Criminal Justice*. Wiley-Blackwell, Hoboken, NJ, pp. 194–206.

Rothstein, Richard. 2017. *The color of law: A forgotten history of how our government segregated America*. Liveright Publishing.

Simon, Jonathan. 2007. *Governing through crime: How the war on crime transformed American democracy and created a culture of fear*. Oxford University Press.

Simon, Jonathan. 2010. "Consuming obsessions: Housing, homicide, and mass incarceration since 1950." *University of Chicago Legal Forum*, Vol. 2010: 165.

Simon, Jonathan. 2014. *Mass incarceration on trial: A remarkable court decision and the future of prisons in America*. New Press.

Simon, Jonathan. 2017. "Beyond tough on crime: Towards a better politics of prosecution." *Prosecutors and Democracy: A Cross-National Study* 250–275.

Sugrue, Thomas J. 2014. *The Origins of the Urban Crisis: Race and Inequality in Postwar Detroit-Updated Edition*. Vol. 6. Princeton University Press.

Thompson, Heather Ann. 2017. *Blood in the water: The Attica prison uprising of 1971 and its legacy*. Vintage.

Wilson, James Q., and George L. Kelling. 1982. "Broken windows." *Atlantic Monthly* 249.3: 29–38.

Zimring, Franklin E. 2006. *The great American crime decline*. Oxford University Press, USA.

Epilogue

What then, do we learn from this exposition of criminal justice, risk and the geo-political context in which it operates? We learn that risk assessment technology has become an inextricable aspect of criminal justice administration in advanced democracies. While there might be opportunities to contest it in the courtroom and at parole hearings, it has become an indelible feature of the modern criminal justice system. It puts risk prediction on a quasi-scientific basis and holds out the promise of providing much greater certainty regarding future criminality. For these reasons alone it will continue to have a presence, notwithstanding that it provides justice by computer so to speak, and that it is part of an erosion of the way in which individual rights were (formally at least) protected in these settings. The promise of what risk predictions using actuarial techniques may now deliver—the apparent certainty of who is likely to commit future crime—is too valuable a prize for corrections managers and government ministers to ever relinquish. This apparent certainty and the public protection that it offers outweighs familiar criticisms about the injustice this does to individual rights and so on.

© The Author(s) 2020
J. Pratt, J. Anderson (eds.), *Criminal Justice, Risk and the Revolt against Uncertainty*,
Palgrave Studies in Risk, Crime and Society,
https://doi.org/10.1007/978-3-030-37948-3

This is so, despite the vacuity of these risk predictions when the structural inequalities underpinning the concepts on which risk is based are left untouched. It remains that the political utility of these calculations is likely to be significantly more than their social utility in pointing to areas of an individual's life that threatens their own well-being and that of others. And it will continue to have a presence, notwithstanding the way in which its categories of risk bear little relation to the difficulties those subject to such classifications are likely to have in trying to reduce their own 'riskiness.'

But risk control is also becoming more deeply entangled with the criminal justice system and, in so doing, is bringing about a large-scale reappraisal of the nature and function of criminal law and the extent to which penal controls can be used for preventive purposes in these societies. That this is occurring is also a reflection of the political context in which risk prediction and its assessment methods operate. The fact that its sphere of operation has expanded so far beyond parole adjudications is indicative of both the promise that governance through risk rather than crime offers for policy makers *and* the pressure placed on the penal system to provide certainty and security at a time when these characteristics of modern society have been crumbling and dissolving in so many other aspects of everyday life. While much of this destruction has been brought about by neo-liberal restructuring, it has also been caused by broader and extraneous geo-political events, as with climate change or the climate crisis as it is increasingly known as—and unwanted mass immigration. As this fragmentation of the social fabric of modernity has occurred, new divisions have opened up (age for example) and old hostilities (such as religion) rekindled. Indeed, the extent of this disintegrating social fabric in the era of neo-liberal governance is reflected in the way in which governments (regularly assisted by the courts) were prepared to breach norms, principles and conventions that had largely made prevention in this area taboo. Making use of criminal law and penal controls against obvious and convenient scapegoats in this way meant that for some time they were able to maintain a semblance of social cohesion. But ultimately, use of these measures has not proved sufficient.

Rather than being assuaged, so much of the uncertainty, anger and insecurity generated in the course of the neo-liberal era has only been growing and has made possible a particularly aggressive form of populism. This in turn has no doubt been aided by media innovations such as talkback radio and, more recently, what remains a largely uncontrolled social media where the most virulent messages of hate and the most deceitful conspiracy theories can be posted to further enflame it and bolster the beliefs of its adherents. At its heart, this populism wants to reverse much of the framework of neo-liberal governance in favor of some fabled time when all aspects of life were supposed to have been certain and secure. If there is any indication as to the nature of such an ideal society from populist discourse, it was one governed by authoritarian white men, and one where today's sunset industries were still thriving.

Even so, the production of such sepia-toned imagery is not sufficient on its own for populism to thrive. Obstacles to its forward march cannot be allowed to stand in its way: the Establishment, anxious to cling to the status quo that gave it its authority must be attacked, pummeled, ridiculed and the individuals this edifice houses shorn of their prestige—even marked out as 'traitors' if needs be. Treaties, obligations, norms and conventions, the rule of law must be torn up when these get in the way of its drive to power. Scientific knowledge can be disregarded or dismissed when it becomes inconvenient. As regards the Trump presidency, for example, Gebelhoff (2019) writes that 'the administration has suppressed, blocked or ignored scientific research on the environmental effects of mining in national forests, the dangers of asbestos, the status of endangered species, the effect a citizenship question would have on the US Census, the safety of children's products and countless other issues.' For this reason, the scientific credentials of risk prediction in criminal justice are only likely to be tossed aside if they do not confirm the common-sense assumptions harbored by populist governments about crime. In this context, the scientific basis of prediction gives it no automatic validity.

This epilogue is being written at a time when, in just the last two weeks, the Amazon rainforests have been allowed to burn wildly, with studied indifference from Brazilian president Jair Bolsanarro—it was only international pressure (although none from President Trump) and threat of a trade embargo that prompted action from him, although the damage already done and the additional risks to the planet are likely to be irreversible. Meanwhile, the British parliament has been prorogued by Prime Minister Johnson for the longest period since 1945, to ensure that parliamentary opposition will not be allowed to stand in the way of his Brexit plans and those of the cabal of ministers and advisers who surround him: irrespective of the risks to the social and economic well-being of that country that may also prove to be irreversible. And Trump himself deemed this time to be 'the Age of Trump,' a large part of which, he claims, relates to 'the exposing of massive dishonesty in the Fake News [i.e. any news that in any way contradicts his own unique and distorted understanding], (Mazza 2019). If this reflects his own utter pettiness and pitiful narcissism, it also reflects the way in which populism subverts truth and reason when its own magical projections fail to materialize. Here, as a result of his presidency, trust in government and the democratic process may have suffered damage that will take generations to repair: if the democratic process, tested like never before does actually survive him. If it does not, then his success will create a blueprint for his admirers to follow in similar societies. Where trust in the institutions of government becomes so corroded, as with the actions of Trump and the litany of lying and deceit associated with him, this is likely to generate a new range of risks detrimental to economic and social well-being, as Francis Fukuyama (1995) intimated—greater social divisions, economic hardship, greater suspicion and intolerance of difference, more hate and speech conduct in the absence of a belief that the government can be trusted to look after its citizens, more disorder and so on.

That we feel compelled to note such events demonstrates the extraordinary political times we are now living through. And, as this book has suggested, one of the few certainties that populism offers is that out of uncertainty, it will bring chaos. The world is becoming a much riskier place, despite the availability of risk technology to make it more certain and secure. And, in addition to the particularities of risk that individuals face in their localities such as mass shootings in the US, risks that are global in nature such as climate change still have dramatic local consequences. Some of the most immediate of these include refugees fleeing from submerged lands or lands that have otherwise become uninhabitable. They will continue to challenge the legal and physical barriers that Western democracies have put in the way of their advance in far greater numbers. In other words, then, the categories of those judged to constitute a risk or who are considered dangerous are only likely to further expand.

Furthermore, even if populism succeeds in bringing an end to the risk society of neo-liberalism and all the uncertainty associated with this, it is only likely to bring into scrutiny even large populations thought to pose risks to the social formation that it is able to put in place. Populism itself needs these dangerous others who, it claims, threaten the 'normal' sections of society to justify its own existence. Unlike mainstream political organizations, it claims that it 'drains the swamp' and then parades these otherwise hidden enemies for all to see. And yet there is also popular resistance to populism. Anger and insecurity have also fueled social movements that both oppose the Establishment whom they hold responsible for the unequal distribution of risks but which are also opposed to the chaos populism brings as a supposed remedy.

Since the Global Financial Crisis of 2008, there have been a number of such movements, some of them with greater longevity and more widespread appeal than others: some of them addressing national and local risks, some of them international; some of them born out of old, unaddressed divisions, some of them embracing new ones that have only recently emerged: for example, the Occupy Movement, Black Lives Matter, #metoo, Enough! National School Walkout 2018—against the lack of gun control in the US, and the Extinction Rebellion Movement. It is the latter that seems to have gained particular traction, with rolling strikes across the world. One such event occurred in 1664 cities in May 2019, with approximately 1.63 million students striking. While social media has been a boon to populism, it can also be used to organize against it, as the successes of these movements demonstrate.

Discussion of a movement dominated by young people provides a fitting end to this book. Many of the risks faced by this generation are the creation of the generation or two before them. Those generations happily stripped bare much of the world's landscape—advances in technology of all kinds made it possible for them to do this at a faster rate than ever before—while pricing out the Millennial generation from the opportunities they had in abundance to find security and comfort (such as employment longevity and affordable housing). And it is these Millennials, probably more than any other demographic group, who have been placed in the way of immediate and particularly dangerous risks; such as mass shootings in the US (to the astonishment of outsiders, the US government can only offer 'thoughts and prayers' to the victims and families of the 250 such incidents that occurred there by August in the year 2019) and the climate crisis. This is the first generation that will be compelled to come to grips with the consequences of the latter.

By and large, though, and as we have variously seen throughout this book, and to paraphrase Jonathan Simon here, this generation is better educated than its predecessors, more global in outlook, more likely to be of mixed race, more tolerant of strangers, less fearful of downtown urban life which promises risk, and excitement alongside possibilities of being victimized by crime, as they make their way in a world where living with and negotiating risk have all become a routine feature of everyday life. For these reasons, they are the ones best placed to redraw our understanding of risk, how to make sense of its threats, what might be the gravest of them, and how these might be challenged and controlled. This involves not being seduced by populism and its magicians promising to bring back certainty, but by addressing instead, the certainty of the dangers that populism blithely ignores.

References

Fukuyama, Francis. 1995. *Trust: The Social Virtues and the Creation of Prosperity.* New York: Free Press.

Gebelhoff, Robert. 2019. Who Does President Trump Treat Worse Than Anyone Else? Scientists. *The Washington Post*, August 22. https://www.washingtonpost.com/opinions/2019/08/22/who-does-president-trump-treat-worse-than-anyone-else-scientists/.

Mazza, Ed. 2019. Trump Declares This 'The Age of Trump.' Twitter Users Offer Some Other Names. *HuffPost*, August 29. https://www.huffpost.com/entry/age-of-trump_n_5d674e47e4b022fbceb5fede.

Index[1]

[1] Note: Page numbers followed by 'n' refer to notes.

© The Author(s) 2020
J. Pratt, J. Anderson (eds.), *Criminal Justice, Risk and the Revolt against Uncertainty*,
Palgrave Studies in Risk, Crime and Society,
https://doi.org/10.1007/978-3-030-37948-3